A Practitioner's Guide to Rational Emotive Behavior Therapy

A Practitioner's Guide to Rational Emotive Behavior Therapy

THIRD EDITION ■

RAYMOND A. DIGIUSEPPE

KRISTENE A. DOYLE

WINDY DRYDEN

WOUTER BACKX

OXFORD
UNIVERSITY PRESS

OXFORD
UNIVERSITY PRESS

Oxford University Press is a department of the University of Oxford.
It furthers the University's objective of excellence in research, scholarship,
and education by publishing worldwide.

Oxford   New York
Auckland   Cape Town   Dar es Salaam   Hong Kong   Karachi
Kuala Lumpur   Madrid   Melbourne   Mexico City   Nairobi
New Delhi   Shanghai   Taipei   Toronto

With offices in
Argentina   Austria   Brazil   Chile   Czech Republic   France   Greece
Guatemala   Hungary   Italy   Japan   Poland   Portugal   Singapore
South Korea   Switzerland   Thailand   Turkey   Ukraine   Vietnam

Oxford is a registered trademark of Oxford University Press in the UK and certain
other countries.

Published in the United States of America by
Oxford University Press
198 Madison Avenue, New York, NY 10016

Library of Congress Cataloging-in-Publication Data
    DiGiuseppe, Raymond.
    A practitioner's guide to rational-emotive behavior therapy / Raymond A. DiGiuseppe, Kristene A.
Doyle, Windy Dryden, Wouter Backx. — Third edition.
        pages cm
    Includes bibliographical references and index.
    ISBN 978–0–19–974304–9 (pbk.)
    1. Rational emotive behavior therapy.   I. Title.
    RC489.R3W34 2014
    616.89'142—dc23
    2013017563

To our teacher and mentor, Albert Ellis

CONTENTS

PART FIVE The Therapeutic Whole

FOREWORD TO THE SECOND EDITION

BY

ALBERT ELLIS

When *A Practitioner's Guide to Rational-Emotive Therapy* was first published in 1980, it was a pioneering training manual for RET practitioners, especially for neophytes. Since that time, it has served beautifully to introduce thousands of trainees to RET and has been a core text for the Primary Certificate Program and the more advanced training programs of the Institute for Rational-Emotive Therapy in the United States, Canada, Mexico, and a number of other countries in Europe, the Middle East, Asia, and Australia. When I have been a speaker and a supervisor in a large number of these programs, I have been repeatedly startled to see that some of the participants conduct amazingly good therapy sessions right from the start because they have assiduously studied and followed the exceptionally clear formulations in the first edition of this excellent book.

This second edition includes all the virtues of the 1980 presentation and brings the theory and practice of RET quite up-to-date. When I created this form of therapy in 1955, I heavily stressed its cognitive and philosophic elements, because the therapies of the 1950s, especially psychoanalysis and person-centered therapy, sadly neglected those aspects of helping clients to become less emotionally disturbed. But even early rational-emotive therapy was highly emotive and behavioral, because a good many years before I started my training as a clinical psychologist in 1942, I had used in vivo desensitization (which I borrowed from John B. Watson) and shame-attacking exercises (which I largely created myself) to overcome my own social shyness and enormous fear of public speaking. I was also an active-directive sex therapist from 1943 to 1947, when I unfortunately sidetracked myself (until 1953) by getting trained in and practicing psychoanalysis. So after I became disillusioned with analysis and created RET in 1955, 1 returned to active-directive methods and incorporated a number of emotive and behavioral techniques in my early use of RET. Why? Because a combination of thinking, feeling, and behavioral methods, I soon found, worked better than did a one-sided emphasis on cognitive restructuring.

Just as theory leads to practice, so is the reverse often true. The more I practiced RET in the 1950s in a fashion that Arnold Lazarus later nicely called "multimodal therapy," the more I developed its present emotive-evocative theory. I saw that my clients had what I called Irrational Beliefs (Ellis, 1958, 1962) and thereby disturbed themselves emotionally and behaviorally. I also discovered that their central schémas or core philosophies were Jehovian, absolutist musts and commands; that they often held these musts very *strongly* and *powerfully;* that they compellingly *felt* them and incorporated them into their psychosomatic responses; that they clearly habituated themselves to *acting* on their dysfunctional convictions; and that they holistically *integrated* their (conscious and unconscious) demands, commands, imperatives, and insistencies into almost everything they thought, felt, and did.

I also realized, by the early 1960s, that children, adolescents, and adults learn much of their goals, desires, and values from their parents and their culture, because they are born gullible, teachable, and impressionable. Therefore, their "normal" personality is—as Sampson (1989) and other social psychologists have noted—intrinsically enmeshed with their sociality. They are consequently both unique individuals *and* highly social creatures. However, as Kelly (1955) saw a half-century ago, and as many social thinkers recently have seen again (Mahoney, 1991), humans actively *construct* and *reconstruct* their ideas and behaviors, and do not *merely* and blindly accept them from their families and their societies.

Although RET has been wrongly accused by Guidano (1988), Mahoney (1991), and others of being sensationalistic and rationalistic, it is actually more constructivist than most of the other cognitive and noncognitive therapies. Let me briefly mention some, though hardly all, of its constructivist theories and practices.

1. RET holds that almost all humans have a strong, largely innate predisposition to learn or adopt familial and cultural standards and preferences and then to *create* and *construct* rigid musts and demands *about* these preferences. Thus, they dogmatically often convince themselves, "Because I greatly *like* success and approval, I *absolutely must* have them almost all the time, under nearly all conditions" (Ellis and Harper, 1975).

2. People's basic self-disturbing musts and demands are not merely superficially or consciously held, but are often tacit, implicit, and unconscious and are strongly clung to in the "deep" structures of their minds and bodies.

3. Children are usually born, as Bowlby (1980) showed, extremely attachable to their parents and significant others; but they often also *create* a dire "necessity" for being loved and seriously disturb themselves (not *get* disturbed) when their affectional preferences are not fully met.

4. RET holds that children (and adults) are largely *taught* to evaluate their behaviors as "good" and "bad," but that they mainly construct (rather than merely learn to rate) their *self or personhood* or *being.* If they act "well," they naturally tend to "deify" and if they act "badly" they easily tend to "devil-ify" or damn their entire *self,* and not merely their *behaviors.*

5. RET theorizes that virtually all humans, however reared, have two somewhat opposing creative tendencies: (a) to damn and deify themselves and others (as noted above), and thereby *make themselves* disturbed; and (b) to change and actualize themselves, and thereby *make themselves* healthy and less disturbed. RET tries to teach people how to use their self-actualizing capacity to reduce their self-disturbing tendencies, and thus to *construct* a more enjoyable life.

6. RET is opposed to rigidity, "musturbation," one-sidedness, and stasis, and strongly favors openness, alternative-seeking, non-dogmatism, and flexibility. It upholds a scientific, non-dogmatic outlook and theorizes that when people fairly consistently adopt that kind of philosophy, they are considerably less disturbed than when they are devoutly antiscientific.

7. RET tries to help people achieve what it calls "a profound philosophic or attitudinal change" and not merely to modify their unrealistic attributions and inferences, as some of the other cognitive-behavior therapies emphasize doing.

8. Mahoney (1991) states that cognitive constructivists hold that acting, feeling, and knowing are inseparable experiences of adaptation and development. RET agrees. However, as I noted in my first paper on RET that I presented to the American Psychological Association Convention in Chicago in 1956, and as I restated in *Reason and Emotion in Psychotherapy* (Ellis, 1962, p. 38), "The theoretical foundations of RET are based on the assumption that human thinking and emotion are *not* two disparate processes, but that they significantly overlap and are in some respects, for all practical purposes, essentially the same thing. Like the other two basic life processes, sensing and moving, they are integrally interrelated and never can be seen wholly apart from each other. "

9. Guidano and Mahoney, along with Freud (1965) and Rogers (1951), stress the importance of the therapeutic relationship for personality change. But, as the present book by Walen, DiGiuseppe, and Dryden clearly indicates, RET stresses collaboration between the therapist and the client; in particular, that therapists had better always give clients unconditional acceptance, and not merely *tell* but *show* their clients that they are accepted by the therapist, *whether or not* they perform adequately and *whether or not* they are nice and lovable. But in addition to *showing* and *modeling* unconditional acceptance, RET practitioners *teach* clients how to accept themselves philosophically, not because of but also independently of their therapist's acceptance (Ellis, 1973a, 1977a, 1988; Ellis & Harper, 1975). This double-barreled approach uniquely emphasizes people's ability to *choose* and *construct* their own self-acceptance and is therefore more constructivist than most other cognitive-behavioral and noncognitive approaches.

RET, then, is unusually constructivist and integrative (Ellis, 1987c). What I like immensely about this revised edition of *A Practitioner's Guide to Rational-Emotive Therapy* is that it goes beyond the first edition and emphasizes RET's integrative, constructivist, emotive, and behavioral aspects. Its discussion of RET's cognitive disputing of irrational beliefs is so good that it can easily be called superb. But it also shows that the "complete" rational-emotive practitioner disputes his and her clients' dysfunctional inferences, attributions, and core philosophies actively *and* collaboratively, precisely *and* emotively, intellectually *and* behaviorally. Specific or preferential RET, as this book shows, has its unique flavors, and significantly differs from the therapies of Beck (1976), Maultsby (1975), Meichenbaum (1985), and other cognitive behaviorists. In general, however, RET decidedly overlaps with the other major cognitive therapies and adapts and uses many of their methods.

RET also has considerable humanistic and existential elements (Ellis, 1990b, 1991c) and is probably more emotive than any of the other popular cognitive-behavior schools. Its holistic, integrative, and emotive emphases are clearly presented in this book, and whoever wants to understand the flavor and context of rational-emotive therapy in the 1990s can find them beautifully presented herewith.

Institute for   Albert Ellis, Ph.D., President
Rational-Emotive Therapy
New York City

PREFACE

It has been thirty-two years since the first edition of *A Practitioner's Guide to RET* appeared, and twenty years since the publication of the second edition. After all these years, the purpose of this book remains the same. Our goal is to provide a text that teaches therapists new to the REBT model how to put the elegant theory provided by Albert Ellis into practice. The book is aimed at practitioners new to REBT. However, because REBT is a broad cognitive-learning therapy, we assume that the reader has some knowledge of basic psychological principles, psycho-pathology, behavior modification and behavior therapy, general counseling interviewing skills, and knowledge and skills in forming a therapeutic alliance. Without this foundation, the new REBT therapist runs the risk of conducting therapy mechanically. We also anticipated that those who will read this book will have read other basic books on the theory of REBT such as *Reason and Emotion in Psychotherapy* (Ellis, 1994); *Overcoming Resistance* (Ellis, 2002); *Rational Emotive Behavior Therapy with Difficult Clients* (Ellis, 2002); *The Practice of Rational Emotive Behavior Therapy* (Ellis & Dryden, 1997); or *Rational Emotive Behavior Therapy: A Therapist's Guide* (Ellis & Maclaren, 2005).

Understanding the basic principles of REBT is not difficult. The format is simple and the concepts, as explained by Dr. Ellis, are catchy (e.g., "*Mus*turbation leads to self-abuse"). After reading *A New Guide to Rational Living* (Ellis and Harper, 1975), one can easily give an engaging lecture on the topic. In fact, many clients can give the lecture, although they may not yet be able to apply the principles con-sistently to their own problems. Leading a client successfully through the applica-tion of REBT to help resolve their own problems is more difficult. Over the years that we have trained therapists, we have found that many practitioners claim to be skilled in REBT. However, listening to recordings of the sessions indicated that they knew the theory but could not implement it.

In preparing the first edition of this book, we recorded supervision sessions at the Albert Ellis Institute, extracted the advice given, and organized the advice into categories that later became the structure for the book. In updating the book, we have kept the same structure and added the advice we have given train-ees over the years as the theory has expanded and our knowledge has (hopefully) increased.

Since the second edition, Albert Ellis has died and the world no longer has the energetic, dedicated, tireless advocate of rational thinking to help counter the human tendency for emotional disturbance. He was a wonderfully gifted theorist, therapist, and teacher. We feel an obligation to do our part to represent and extend his work by teaching therapists all over the world to implement his theoretical ideas and clinical wisdom. We hope this volume accomplishes these goals and provides part of the legacy of this great thinker and healer.

Also since the second edition, a number of changes have occurred in REBT and we have tried to reflect these in this edition. First, Ellis changed the name of the therapy from Rational-Emotive Therapy to Rational Emotive Behavior Therapy to reflect the use of behavioral interventions and homework assignments that were always part of this psychotherapy. We have tried to stress that cognitive and philosophical change is the means by which REBT tries to help clients, but rehearsal of the new ideas and the implementation of behavior change are the most important aspects of REBT or any therapy.

Furthermore, when the first edition of this book appeared the theory identified thirteen different irrational beliefs and each was considered to independently have an effect on emotional disturbance. Some irrational beliefs were considered evaluations. Distortions of reality were not considered irrational beliefs and less important for change than evaluative irrational beliefs. The line between cognitive distortions of reality and irrational beliefs was not so clear. The second edition of this book continued to identify most irrational beliefs as evaluative beliefs. Ellis changed his theory in *Reason and Emotion in Psychotherapy* (1994). He placed demandingness (i.e., shoulds, musts, and oughts) at the core of emotional disturbance, and postulated that other irrational beliefs and cognitive distortions were generated by demands on reality. Since then, many readers of the second edition could have been confused because of the discrepancy between how the second edition handled irrational beliefs and what Ellis had discussed in other more recent texts. In this edition, we have consistently presented the more modern version of Ellis' theory. Although research has lagged behind the theory, we have encouraged therapists to assess and intervene at the level of the demands and to gauge the influence of other irrational beliefs and target them when appropriate.

Over the years, many therapists received training in REBT. Even in the brief but intensive primary practicum offered by the Albert Ellis Institute and its Affiliated Training Centers, significant progress in therapist behavior occurs as participants make practice therapy recordings and receive supervision. In this supervision, one hears a strong oral tradition of REBT. Supervisors give their students (who, in turn, may become supervisors) a wealth of helpful hints for doing REBT. As is common in oral traditions, the original source of a hint may be lost but the useful information continues to circulate. Much of the clinical wisdom and advice in the present edition come from a legacy left by many of the outstanding therapists who have worked at the Albert Ellis Institute or have been a part of the REBT community. We wish to acknowledge our debt to those who have added to this legacy. This includes previous Directors or Board members of the Institute, such as Bill Knaus, Ed Garcia, Jon Geis, Janet Wolfe, Richard Wessler, Dom DiMattia, Michael Broder, Catharine MacLaren, Ann Vernon, and Jim McMahon. It also includes many fine scholars who have advanced our knowledge in REBT, such as Emmet Velten (deceased), Michael Bernard, Daniel David, Aurora Szentagotai, Howard Kassinove, Michael Neenan, Michlor Bishop, Don Beal, Len Rorer (deceased), and Mark Terjesen. There are also many outstanding supervisors, both in New York and among our international affiliates, such as Paul Hauck, Robert Moore, Virginia Waters, Rose Oliver (deceased), John Viterito, Monica O'Kelly, Ruth Malkinson, Julio Obst Camerini, Theo IJzermans (deceased), Didier Pleux, Cesare DeSilvestri (deceased), Stephen Palmer, Chrysoula Kostogiannis, Steve Nielson, Hank Robb, Mike Abrams, A. G. Ahmed and a host of others.

Since the appearance of the first edition, the field of cognitive-behavior therapy (CBT) has emerged from a small band of outcasts to the major theoretical orientation in the field. This success has become a blessing and a curse. Many therapists say they practice CBT, but cannot tell you which thoughts they target in their treatments. In addition, some therapists easily confuse negative distorted thoughts, attributions, irrational derivatives, and demanding irrational beliefs and cannot differentiate among the concepts. Thoughts about the existence of negative life events are thoughts. However, in Ellis' A-B-C model, they were part of the A – and not part of the B or irrational beliefs. To resolve this problem, we have introduced an expanded A-B-C model to discriminate between thoughts that are considered part of the A in REBT and irrational beliefs. We have also tried to identify the distinctive features of REBT, and how REBT differs from generic CBT, and when therapists can integrate other CBT interventions with the unique features of REBT.

In the last decade, considerable research has appeared on the common or non-specific features of REBT. We know much more now about the role of the therapeutic alliance and how the client-therapist relationship influences psychotherapy outcomes. We have expanded our coverage of these areas and explain how REBT therapists can behave in an active directive style, yet still keep a good alliance, and display unconditional acceptance for their clients.

REBT has expanded tremendously in the last two decades and training programs now exist on every continent and in many countries. All four of us have offered REBT training courses in numerous countries, and each year the training programs at the Albert Ellis Institute in New York City attract half of their participants from outside of the United States. REBT has become more of a global therapy. We have learned much from the application of REBT in various cultures. We realize that people all over the world will use this book to guide their therapy in their home cultures. The world has become a village, and we have tried to incorporate a multicultural awareness into this text. We have purposely used case studies shared with us while supervising therapists from all over the world. We hope we have accomplished this goal.

The second edition included chapters on getting training and a recommended list of self-help books. The growth of the Internet and the expansion of REBT have made these chapters irrelevant. The reader can go to the Albert Ellis Institute's web page to find the latest information on these topics (www.albertellis.org).

New York City, USA	R. A. D.
New York City, USA	K. A. D.
London, UK	W. D.
Haarlem, NL	W. B.
April 2013	

ABOUT THE AUTHORS

Raymond A. DiGiuseppe, a native of Philadelphia, Pennsylvania, received his B.A. in Psychology from Villanova University in 1971 and his Ph.D. from Hofstra University in 1975. He then completed a postdoctoral fellowship with Dr. Albert Ellis at the Albert Ellis Institute, where he has remained on the Institute's professional training faculty. He has published more than 120 articles and six books. Ray has studied anger as a clinical problem and has promoted the recognition of anger as a form psychopathology. He has developed standards for identifying anger diagnostic disorders. He has published two psychological tests assessing dysfunctional anger: the Anger Disorders Scale (ADS) for adults and the Anger Regulation and Expression Scale (ARES) for children and adolescents. He has also published on the development of the theory, practice, and empirical research support of Rational Emotive Behavior Therapy and Cognitive Behavior Therapies and their application to children, adolescents, and families. He has also been interested in the development of the therapeutic alliance in child and adolescent psychotherapy. He is Professor and Chair of the Psychology Department at St. John's University in New York City. He was president of the Association for Behavioral and Cognitive Therapies in 2006–2007. He is President-Elect of the Division of Psychotherapy (29) of the American Psychological Association.

Kristene A. Doyle is the Director of the Albert Ellis Institute (AEI). A native of New York City, Kristene received her B.A. in Psychology from McGill University in 1994, and her Ph.D. from Hofstra University in 1999. During her fourteen-year tenure at AEI, Kristene has held various leadership roles including Associate Executive Director, Training and Development Coordinator, and Director of Child and Family Services. She is also a Diplomate in Rational Emotive & Cognitive-Behavior Therapy (RE&CBT) and serves on the Diplomate Board. In addition to training and supervising AEI's fellows and staff therapists, Kristene has conducted numerous workshops and professional trainings throughout the world. She has trained mental health professionals in RE&CBT in Argentina, Canada, China, Denmark, the Dominican Republic, Greece, Honduras, the Netherlands, Mexico, Turkey, Panama, Paraguay, Peru, Russia, South Africa, and throughout the United States. Kristene's clinical and research interests include Eating

Disorders & Weight Management, RE&CBT treatment of children and adolescents, and Cognitive-Behavioral Therapeutic Process, Outcome & Dissemination. Kristene is an Adjunct Professor of Psychology at St. John's University where she teaches Group Psychotherapy and supervises clinical practicum students. She has served as the Coordinator of Membership Issues for the Association for Behavioral and Cognitive Therapies. She is also the external examiner for the M.Sc. in Rational Emotive Behaviour Therapy at Goldsmiths, University of London.

Windy Dryden is Professor of Psychotherapeutic Studies at Goldsmiths University of London, and is a Fellow of the British Psychological Society and of the British Association for Counseling and Psychotherapy. He has authored or edited more than 195 books, including the second edition of *Counseling in a Nutshell* (Sage, 2011) and *Rational Emotive Behaviour Therapy: Distinctive Features* (Routledge, 2009). In addition, he edits twenty book series in the area of counseling and psychotherapy, including the *Distinctive Features in CBT* series (Routledge) and the *Counseling in a Nutshell* series (Sage). His major interests are in Rational Emotive Behavior Therapy and Cognitive Behavior Therapy; the interface between counseling and coaching; pluralism in counseling and psychotherapy; and writing short, accessible self-help books for the public.

Wouter Backx (1947) studied clinical and theoretical psychology at Leiden University (the Netherlands). While working and living at the Albert Ellis Institute in New York City, he specialized in REBT, and became a Fellow and certified supervisor of the AEI. He is also an editorial board member of the *Journal of Rational-Emotive and Cognitive-Behavior Therapy.*

Back home in the Netherlands, he founded the Dutch Institute for REBT in Haarlem, an affiliate-training center of the AEI. He leads both and is active as a therapist and a trainer. He teaches REBT to novice psychologists at his Dutch Institute and at several other affiliated training centers in many countries. Teaching family physicians to use REBT in their consultations is a special interest of his. During his career, Wouter has contributed many new ideas and applications to the body of knowledge of REBT. This book utilizes and explains Wouter's tools to clarify certain phenomena of REBT for clients and practitioners.

A Practitioner's Guide to Rational

Emotive Behavior Therapy

PART ONE

A Basic Introduction to REBT

Albert Ellis and the Philosophy of REBT

WHO WAS ALBERT ELLIS? AND WHAT DID HE DO FOR PSYCHOTHERAPY?

Albert Ellis was a charismatic clinician and the consummate New Yorker. He lived for decades on the top floor of a brownstone on the upper east side of New York, overtop his Institute that trained hundreds of psychotherapists and treated tens of thousands of clients. Ellis published numerous books and articles regarding psychotherapy and in his time was one of the most famous and recognizable psychologists in the world. He was outspoken, irreverent, and inclined to say things that shocked the more genteel and somewhat stodgy psychotherapy community of the 1950s. His insights grew from his interests in philosophy and his clinical practice, and he grew restless with the orthodoxy of the day. Never one to blindly do as he was told, Ellis rebelled against the slow pace of therapy and struck off in new directions because it helped his clients. Ellis advocated for but did not do research. He did not work at a university and instead chose to focus on clinical work, teaching, and writing. He authored many theoretical works, clinical materials, and self-help books. Ellis's choice had negative implications for his approach, which he termed Rational Emotive Behavior Therapy (REBT), as we have entered the era of evidence-based practice that relies on randomized clinical trials (RCTs). However, Ellis's REBT became one of the most widely practiced therapies in the second half of the twentieth century and the early twenty-first century.

Albert Ellis is considered the grandfather of Cognitive Behavior Therapy (CBT) because of his development of REBT, probably the first formal system in that genre (Hollon and DiGiuseppe, 2010). Ellis was instrumental in transforming psychotherapy to the point where CBT represented a major paradigm for behavioral change. A 1982 survey of US and Canadian psychologists ranked Ellis as the second most influential psychotherapist in history (Carl Rogers ranked first in the survey; Sigmund Freud was ranked third; Smith, 1982). In addition, in that year, an analysis of psychology journals published in the United States found that Ellis was the second most cited author after Rogers. More recently, in a survey of more than 2,500 psychotherapists (Cook, Biyanova, and Coyne, 2009), Ellis ranked as the sixth most influential psychotherapist. Psychotherapists rated CBT as the most popular theoretical orientation. Carl Rogers remained the most influential psychotherapist; Aaron Beck came in second. At his death at age ninety-three (July 24, 2007), Ellis had authored and co-authored more than eighty books and more than 800 articles in peer-reviewed journals (see www.albertellisinstitute. org/ellisbibliography for a complete bibliography).

Ellis was born in Pittsburgh, Pennsylvania in 1913, the eldest of three children. Shortly thereafter, his family moved to the Bronx in New York City. In his youth, Albert Ellis suffered numerous health problems. At age five, Ellis was hospitalized for an extended period for a kidney ailment. He required eight hospitalizations between the ages of five and seven, one of which lasted almost a year. Ellis's literary interests nurtured his psychotherapy writings. Many of his psychotherapy principles first appeared in an unpublished autobiographical novel (Ellis, 1933) that recounted his attempts to overcome his shyness, anxiety, and shame concerning his family's poverty. During his youth, Ellis became interested in romantic and sexual relationships and read voraciously on the topic. In 1941, he founded the nonprofit LAMP (Love and Marriage Problems) Institute to disperse advice on such topics, mostly to friends and relatives. On the advice of his lawyer, he sought a professional degree to provide him with professional recognition of his expertise. He enrolled in the doctoral program in clinical psychology at Columbia University's Teachers College at the age of forty.

After completing graduate school, Ellis started psychoanalytic training and simultaneously started his practice. He quickly evolved two separate practices. One group of clients received traditional psychoanalysis on the couch, while a second group of clients with marital and sex problems received a more active set of interventions sitting face-to-face with Ellis. Ellis became discouraged with the effectiveness of psychoanalysis in the early 1950s. He discovered that he helped clients in his sex and marital therapy practice more quickly than those he treated with psychoanalysis. Initially, Ellis thought that he needed to dig deeper into his clients' pasts before they would relinquish their disturbance. Yet, after they gained insight, they still failed to improve. Ellis concluded that insight alone led to change in only a small percentage of individuals.

Ellis recognized that he behaved differently with clients in his marital and sex therapy practice. He actively taught these clients to change their attitudes. Ellis's earlier interest in philosophy had led him to read the works of the great Asian and Greek thinkers including Confucius, Lao Tze, Marcus Aurelius, and Epictetus. When freed from the constraining psychoanalytic role, he provided advice to his clients based on these philosophical works. Ellis contemplated the stoic philosophers' notion that people could choose whether to become disturbed; or in the words of Epictetus (90 B.C./1996), "Men are not disturbed by things, but by the view which they take of them" (from the Enchiridion). Ellis utilized philosophy as the foundation for his new therapy and always credited classical and modern philosophers as the source of his ideas. In 1955, he formulated his theory in a paper delivered at the annual convention of the American Psychological Association.

Despite Ellis's critical attitude toward psychoanalysis, he clearly built on some psychoanalytic skills and principles. Ellis astutely focused on his clients' emotions during the therapy sessions. As a trainee (RD), I was amazed to watch the small shifts in clients' vocal intonation and gestures that Ellis perceived, and how he then used this information to redirect therapy. Although Ellis rejected the passive stance of the psychoanalyst, he was aware of the relationship between him and his clients. He was dedicated to clients and displayed tremendous powers of concentration during the sessions. It is often surprising to those who only saw him on the lecture and workshop circuit, where he was brash and flamboyant, to imagine that Ellis could build a therapeutic alliance. Having co-led a therapy group with Ellis for two years, each of us observed his clients' attitude toward him. In the clinical context he behaved in a manner inconsistent with his stage personality, and his clients perceived him as attentive, empathic, and dedicated to helping them.

Ellis's psychoanalytic training may have influenced his theory, especially the centrality of demandingness. REBT postulates that people become disturbed when they make a want or desire into an absolute demand on the universe. When people are disturbed, they think that what they want must be, and they fail to distinguish between what they *desire* and what *is*. Emotional adjustment involves recognizing the distinction between what one *wants* and the fact that the *universe has no obligation to provide it*. Ellis once noted that demanding reflects the psychoanalytic construct of primary process thinking. Adjustment involves the distinction between desires and reality, which Freud called secondary process thinking. REBT, Ellis maintained, differs from psychoanalysis in that REBT focuses like a laser on the primary process thinking, and actively tries to change it, while traditional therapies rely on more subtle change processes.

Ellis was among the first psychotherapists to advocate actively changing clients' beliefs to induce emotional or behavioral change. Ellis was also among the first psychotherapists to use between-session homework assignments, including in vivo behavioral exposure. Ellis provided workshops, lectures, books, and written assignments to identify, challenge, and replace irrational ideas (primary process) and to reinforce the rational ideas (secondary process) that he covered in therapy. Ellis was among the first psychotherapy integrationists. Although REBT obviously had a strong cognitive component, from the onset of his practice and writings, Ellis (1955) advocated using many types of therapy methods to help people change. He encouraged the use of imagery, hypnosis, group sessions, family sessions, humor, psycho-educational readings, interpersonal support, writing assignments, singing, behavioral rehearsal, exposure assignments, action assignments, metaphors, parables, and cathartic experiences. According to Ellis (1957a), psychotherapy should include any activity that could convince the client to change. REBT may have been the first integrative psychotherapy.

When Ellis entered the profession in the late 1940s and began to publish on psychotherapy in the 1950s, two major theoretical orientations dominated psychotherapy—psychoanalysis and client-centered therapy. Psychotherapy research was in a rudimentary stage. Both of the major theoretical orientations prescribed a passive, nondirective role for the therapist. Ellis was instrumental in changing much of that. Ellis's (1957b) first study of the effectiveness of what he then called Rational Therapy (RT) came between Eysenck's (1952) classic evaluation of the poor outcomes of psychoanalytic treatments and Wolpe's (1961) pioneering report on the outcomes of behavior therapy.

It was not until 1961 that Ellis wrote his most influential self-help book (with Robert Harper), *A Guide to Rational Living.* Now in its third edition, it has sold more than two million copies. The following year, Ellis (1962) published his first professional book, *Reason and Emotion in Psychotherapy.* Ellis published dozens of self-help and professional books advancing REBT until his death in 2007 (*New York Times,* 2007).

In 1965, Ellis founded the nonprofit Institute for Advanced Study in Rational Psychotherapy for professional training, which served as his professional home for the rest of his life. It survives today as the Albert Ellis Institute. Affiliated training centers that train mental health professionals exist in several states throughout the United States, as well as in Argentina, Australia, Bosnia, Canada, Columbia, England, France, Germany, Greece, Japan, Israel, Italy, Mexico, Netherlands, Peru, Romania, Serbia, and Taiwan.

Ellis originally named his treatment **Rational Therapy** because of his focus on cognitions. He later realized that he had underemphasized the role of emotions in the title and renamed it **Rational-Emotive Therapy.** He finally changed the name to **Rational Emotive Behavior Therapy** (Ellis, 1994) at the urging of his longtime friend Ray Corsini. Corsini was revising his classic psychotherapy textbook (Corsini, 1994) when he recognized that Ellis usually used behavioral methods in therapy. He suggested that Ellis rename his approach to reflect what he practiced.

During the early days, the profession considered CBT to be on the lunatic fringe of psychotherapy. Psychoanalysts ridiculed cognitive theories as superficial and shallow, and they portrayed the active directiveness of the therapy as caustic, brutish, and harmful. Behavior therapists mocked the focus on cognition as foolish. They relegated thoughts to unimportant epiphenomenon.

ELLIS THE PERSON AND THE THEORY

A journal reviewer once remarked that REBT was whatever Albert Ellis said it was. His personality became synonymous with the theory. Although his contribution to REBT cannot be overestimated, others contributed fundamentally (Maultsby, Dryden, DiGiuseppe, Backx, Wessler, Wolfe). No history of cognitive psychotherapies would be complete without mentioning the personality of Albert Ellis. Ellis was a tireless promoter of his theory and therapy. His life consisted almost exclusively of doing therapy, writing about therapy, or teaching about therapy. He started seeing clients each day at 9:30 a.m. and continued until 11:00 p.m., with a half hour off each for lunch and dinner. He traveled extensively to give workshops and presentations. He once said, "I wouldn't go to the Taj Mahal unless I could give a workshop."

Each presentation included a live demonstration of therapy. Ellis sought volunteers from the audience to come on stage and present a personal problem with which he would demonstrate the application of REBT. These demonstrations also occurred each week at his famous Friday night workshops. At a time when the activities of psychotherapists remained shrouded in secrecy, Ellis fostered transparency. He was willing to demonstrate what he did for anyone who was interested. These demonstrations attracted large crowds for more than forty years and exposed many people to the advantages of REBT. Such demonstrations persist to this day at the Albert Ellis Institute.

All of us spent a great deal of time watching Al perform therapy and supervision. We recognized that many of his clinical interventions were not clearly reflected in his theory and writings. We have attempted to incorporate many of our observations of Al's behaviors in therapy as well as what he said he did.

Ellis was renowned for his colorful foul language and his directness. He championed sexually libertarian ideas when people considered such views scandalous. He was a devout atheist and could be described as irreverent. He enjoyed jousting with conventional wisdom. Many people would laugh at his off-color remarks, while others would walk out of his presentation when he spoke in such a fashion. Whether Ellis's personal style helped or hurt the dissemination of REBT is uncertain. He clearly was a person of renown, and his appearance at national conferences drew standing-room-only crowds.

Ellis's private personality, however, contrasted markedly with his public personality. He was a generous and accepting mentor. He encouraged dissent and debate among his staff. He was accepting of them professionally and personally. Ellis remained nonjudgmental (Johnson, DiGiuseppe, and Ulven, 1999). We would like to acknowledge our debt to our mentor without whose leadership and mentoring we could never have produced this book.

A Constructivist, Cognitive, Evolutionary Theory of Human Adaption

Ellis claimed that he based REBT on George Kelly's Personal Construct Therapy (PCT) (1955). Kelly recognized that humans evolved and survived because of their ability to impose order on a chaotic world. Understanding our world provides the first steps in developing coping and survival strategies. Kelly (1955) based PCT on understanding the constructs individuals design regarding their personal world; PCT helps clients become flexible in relinquishing constructs that fail to explain the world adequately and that lead to maladaptive behavior. PCT involves assessing and understanding clients' systems of constructs, and helping them evaluate whether their constructs help them to maneuver in the world effectively.

Kelly's theory led to the development of treatment methods based on scientific reasoning and correcting maladjustment (Mahoney, 1979). It also laid the foundation for constructivist methods that conceptualize therapy as a task of understanding a person's epistemology or philosophy of understanding the world (e.g., Mahoney, 1991; Mahoney and Lyddon, 1988; Neimeyer, 1993). A meta-analysis reviewed the outcomes studies on PCT (Metcalfe et al., 2007). The results concluded that PCT was modestly effective compared to no treatment controls and other alternative methods. Clients receiving PCT improved more than clients receiving no active treatment but not differently from clients who received other treatment methods.

Kelly's PCT served as a basis for other cognitive therapies. Ellis and Beck stated that irrational beliefs, automatic thoughts, and dysfunctional attitudes emerge from the schemas people develop to understand major life events (Beck, 2005; Ellis, 1962; 1994). Changing explanatory schema has become the primary focus of a form of CBT (Young, Klosko, and Weishaar, 2003). Thus irrational beliefs and demands in particular can be construed as maladaptive schemas or constructs of the world. They are maladaptive because the client bases the schema of the world on what they want or desire rather than what they experience the world to be.

Another influence on CBT from the perspective of human attempts to understand the world is attribution theories. Seligman's (Seligman and Maier, 1967) experiments with dogs and his resulting theory of learned helplessness (Seligman, 1975) represented a more nomenthetic approach to understanding humans' explanatory thinking. Seligman found that dogs who received inescapable electric shock learned to be helpless and exhibited symptoms similar to clinical depression. Later research discovered that the original theory of learned helplessness failed to account for people's varying reactions to situations that cause learned helplessness. Learned helplessness can remain specific to one situation or these attributions can generalize across situations. A person's attributional or explanatory style presents the means to understand why people respond differently to adverse events. Although people may experience similar negative events, each person's interpretations of the event affect the likelihood of acquiring learned helplessness and depression (Abramson, Seligman and Teasdale, 1978). People with a pessimistic explanatory style who perceive negative events as permanent ("it will never change"), personal ("it's my fault"), and pervasive ("I can't do anything correctly") are more likely to suffer from learned helplessness and depression.

Weiner, a cognitive psychologist, developed a similar attribution theory (1979, 1985) based on research from children's academic achievement motivation. Weiner proposed that people attribute a cause or explanation to an unpleasant event. Attribution theory includes the dimensions of globality versus specificity, stability versus instability, and internality versus externality (Weiner, 1985). A global attribution occurs when the individual believes that the cause of negative events is consistent across different contexts. A specific attribution occurs when the individual believes that the cause of a negative event is unique to a particular situation. A stable attribution occurs when the individual believes the cause to be consistent across time. An unstable attribution occurs when the individual thinks that the cause is specific to one point in time. An external attribution assigns causality to situational or external factors, while an internal attribution assigns causality to factors within the person (Abramson et al., 1978).

RATIONAL EMOTIVE BEHAVIOR PHILOSOPHY

Perhaps more than any other system of psychotherapy, REBT grows out of and actively utilizes strong philosophical underpinnings. Disturbance is largely (but not completely) a function of the perceptions, evaluations, and attitudes we take toward life events—components of our personal philosophies. REBT has embedded within it an epistemology, or a theory of knowledge; a dialectic, or a system of reasoning; a system of values; and ethical principles. Let us take each of these in turn.

Epistemology: The Art of Knowing

REBT rests on some philosophical assumptions. The first of these is commitment to the scientific method. Ellis believed that applying the scientific method to one's personal life results in less emotional disturbance and ineffectual behavior. People would be better off if they recognized that all of their beliefs, schemata, perceptions, and cherished truths could be wrong. Testing one's assumptions, examining the validity and functionality of one's beliefs, and posing a willingness to entertain alternative ideas promotes positive personal adjustment. Rigid adherence to a belief or schema of the world prevents one from revising one's thinking, and dooms one to behave as if the world is as one hopes it will be, rather than the way it is. Ellis believed that people are better off if they hold beliefs flexibly and are willing to give them up if more helpful, logical, and empirically consistent beliefs come along.

REBT believes (DiGiuseppe, 1986; Ellis, 1994) that humans would function best if they adopted the epistemology of the philosophy of science, specifically the positions of Popper (1962) and Bartley (1987). Popper noted that all people develop hypotheses. Preconceived hypotheses distort the data people collect and lead to confirmatory biases. As humans, we cannot stop ourselves from forming hypotheses, nor from remembering data that fit them. This renders objective inductive reasoning impossible. The solution is to acknowledge our hypotheses and attempt to falsify them. If you fail to falsify a hypothesis you continue to hold it until a better idea or hypothesis is found. Popper maintained that knowledge accumulates quickest when people deduce predictions from their hypotheses and attempt to disprove them. REBT recommends that we adopt the Popper model of falsifiability personally for our own emotional health and as professionals to help our clients. Bartley's epistemology of comprehensive critical rationalism adds that people should use not only empirical falsifiability tests of their ideas, but any other argument they can muster to disprove their thinking. Following Bartley, Ellis believed that it is best to apply all means to challenge one's thinking as a theorist, a therapist, and an individual.

Ellis's philosophy contains elements of constructivism. Specifically, Ellis maintained that all humans create ideas of how the world is or ought to be. Ellis thought that people make up many of their beliefs. This explains why he abandoned search-ing for insights from the memories of clients' experiences or testing the veracity of automatic thoughts of past events. All these ideas could have been made up.

REBT differs from the postmodernist philosophers and the constructivist cognitive therapists such as Mahoney (1991) and Neimeyer (1993) in two ways. First, these constructivist therapists believe that the sole criterion to assess beliefs is their utility or viability. Empirical reality is not a criterion. The extreme con-structivists maintain there is no knowable reality. REBT posits that empirical real-ity is an important criterion and that one needs to assess the empirical veracity of one's beliefs along with their utility and logical consistency. Second, constructivist therapists believe that therapists should help clients examine the viability of their ideas. They would not provide alternative beliefs for clients, but would allow cli-ents to develop alternatives on their own. As a philosophy of life, REBT posits that there are some rational alternative beliefs that will promote emotional adjust-ment. Learning through self-discovery is valued in REBT, but if the client fails to generate alternative beliefs, we would offer alternatives for them and help them assess the veracity and viability of these alternatives.

How do we know a thing to be true? What are the most reliable and valid ways of obtaining knowledge? These are questions of epistemology. Each of us (and each of our clients) operates under at least one implicit epistemology.

For example, a common stance is an authoritarian epistemology; that is, some-thing is true because a credible authority says it is true. One variation on this theme is seen in religion. Many religious individuals consider revelation or divine inspiration to be a valid source of knowledge, whether the words are found in the Bible, the Koran, and other religious texts or come from the local minister, priest, imam, or rabbi. A somewhat less divine but no less dogmatic source may be a parent or teacher, prior therapist, or the vague "everyone" (e.g., "everyone knows that…").

A particularly frustrating sort of thinking might be called narcissistic episte-mology or, "It must be true because I thought of it," and "It seems right to me." A more demanding divine version of this philosophy rests on such rules as, "It's that way because I say so" or "It's got to be that way, because that's the way I want it."

In REBT, we search for more reliable and valid ways of obtaining knowledge and determining how we know a thing to be true. REBT philosophy suggests that it is through the methods of science that we can best obtain knowledge about the self, others, and the world. REBT advocates scientific thinking and an empirical stance to knowledge. For every belief expressed by a client, an appropriate REBT ques-tion would be, "Where is the evidence that what you believe is true?" In REBT, we seek to make better scientists of our clients so that they can acquire correct infor-mation, use evidence logically, and construct sound, self-helping beliefs.

Science starts with questions about what is, and then proceeds to question the relationship between events. Hypotheses are formed to answer the questions, and observation and measurement are conducted to test the hypotheses. If the observations are consistent with these hypotheses, the hypotheses are strength-ened and intellectual errors are reduced. The emphasis on the observable tends to eliminate mysticism and magic. In addition, acceptable observations are verified by more than one observer, to eliminate the use of "special powers" of intuition or inspiration.

How, then, do we know a thing to be true? We cannot know for certain. We determine the probability of its truth through repeated verification by observable data. Of course, we hope to do more than confirm isolated facts; we hope to build them into a coherent picture or theory of reality. From our theory, we can predict new occurrences of similar events and deduce new hypotheses to fit different circumstances. The important point is that we continue to question and remain open to new evidence.

Dialectics: The art of thinking

The art of logical thinking is not easy to acquire; most people seem to be expert at illogic. A typical bit of self-deprecating illogical reasoning goes like this:

> I must be perfect.
> I just made a mistake. How horrible!
> That proves I'm imperfect and therefore worthless.

Would this reasoning stand up to logical scrutiny? It would not. Where is the evidence for the statement, "I must be perfect"? There is none, although there is ample evidence that I, like everyone else, am imperfect and thus, in a sense, "must" be imperfect, not perfect.

How about "I just made a mistake"? Perhaps it can be demonstrated that I made a mistake (although I'd better be careful not to make a rash judgment here, for it may be too soon to tell whether it was a mistake), but how is a mistake "horrible"?

That I am imperfect is surely proven by my mistake, but does it follow logically, therefore, that I am worthless? Obviously not, although people who are thinking dichotomously will say that it does. In dichotomous thinking, there are only two categories, "perfect" and "worthless."

> Consider another syllogism (= logical reasoning):
> If Arthur loved me, he would call me.
> He hasn't called.
> Therefore, he doesn't love me anymore.

Can you spot the errors? Is the first premise correct? (Not necessarily.) The second statement? (Yes.) The conclusion? (Not unless the first premise is true.)

Clients are rarely aware of the major premises in their thinking or the syllogistic flow of their thoughts. More commonly, they focus only on the conclusion which, if it is distorted, is likely to produce emotional problems. Rational thinking, then, involves logical reasoning based upon empirically verified or verifiable statements. If we think rationally, we are not likely to reach conclusions that lead to extremely disturbed feelings.

Ethics

REBT philosophy suggests that ethical guidelines for dealing fairly with other people can be based upon human reason, and on anticipating and understanding the consequences of our actions. REBT theory proposes that generalized ethical principles of right or wrong are distorting and oversimplified for the reasoning adult. What is ethical is specific to each situation. There are no absolute rights and wrongs. In fact, the self-imposition of absolute rights and wrongs is precisely what leads to guilt, shame, anxiety, and depression, as well as to hostility and intolerance of other people.

Research in the psychology of moral philosophies, such as that by Kohlberg (1976), suggests the developmental nature of ethical ideas. In a typical research paradigm, moral dilemmas such as the following are presented to subjects of varying ages:

Max, six years old, was told by his mom not to touch her expensive new vase. One day, feeling particularly loving toward his mom, little Max went into the backyard and picked a bouquet of flowers for her. He carefully put them in the new vase, but a few moments later, he remembered that flowers need to have water or they'll die. So, very carefully, he carried the vase to the sink for water; but on the way back, the vase slid from his slippery wet fingers, fell to the floor, and broke. Just then, mom came into the room.

> Dilemma:
> Did Max do a bad thing?
> Is Max a bad boy?
> Will mom be mad?
> Should Max be punished?

When puzzles such as these are presented to very young children, the moral judgments are clear: Max's bad and he should be spanked! The older the subject, however, the more complex the moral reasoning, and the less clear-cut the ethical solution. Factors such as Max's motivation, the role of intentionality, the purpose of punishment, the severity of punishment, the nature of the relationship of the parties, and other complications begin to come into play. With greater maturity comes greater flexibility; the act in question is seen in a larger context. This maturity—the ability to reason in terms of situational ethics—is consonant with the principles of REBT philosophy.

It might be argued that with situational rather than absolute ethical rules, ethical behavior would break down. If there are no absolute *rights* and *wrongs*, *goods* or *bads*, what would prevent total moral chaos from occurring?

REBT seeks to help the individual use reason in solving ethical dilemmas, to evolve an undogmatic, nonabsolutist philosophy of living that is socially responsible. The ethical principles are derived from answers to the question, "Will my actions harm other people?" not "Does this act violate some God-given rule?" Ethically responsible acts are both pro-social and pro-self; that is, they harm neither others nor ourselves.

Why is it desirable to behave ethically? Without resorting to abstract morality, we can outline a number of simple, pragmatic reasons. For example, experience shows that if we treat others unfairly (lie, cheat, steal, cruelly criticize, etc.), they will eventually retaliate. What happens is obvious when you examine the norm of fair play (more technically, the "norm of reciprocity"). The norm or unwritten rule is that people should deal fairly with each other. While it is often difficult to state the specific details that constitute "fairness," people usually have an implicit understanding of what is fair in a given situation. If you break this norm, the same social processes are likely to occur as when other norms are broken. First, other people try subtly or directly to influence the norm breaker to conform. This process may include attempts to teach, threats, and even punishment. If the norm breaker continues, he or she will be expelled from the group. Because most of us have as one of our goals of happiness to relate to many people compatibly and to a few people intimately, the threat of rejection is enough to keep us from breaking norms. It is not in our best interests to act unfairly, inconsiderately, or selfishly.

On a broader scope, if you behave unethically, you help create a world in which people behave unethically, and you, in turn, will suffer in such a culture. Therefore, it is in your own best interest to promote an ethical society.

Thus, according to the ethical principles of REBT philosophy, it is wrong to exploit and act harmfully toward other people. It is wrong for the individual because it may defeat his or her goals. REBT does not specify what is right or wrong in an absolute sense, for that smacks of dogmatism. REBT holds that rigidity, authoritarianism, dogmatism, and absolutism are among the worst features of any philosophic system and are styles of thinking that lead to neurosis and disturbance.

In essence, the ethics of REBT are much like the golden rule—that is, act in ways that set good examples for other people (or, do as you would have others do).

Ethical Humanism

Virtually all Judeo-Christian religions are based on the golden rule, and the golden rule is the essence of REBT philosophy. REBT provides an ethical system for how we are to treat other people, and a nonjudgmental philosophy of accepting oneself and others exactly as they are. Nonetheless, REBT is more aligned with ethical humanism than with religion.

In ethical humanism, the reasoning individual is the source of wisdom, not almighty "God." The concept of "God" is not needed to explain the creation of things (that is the job of science), or to generate an ethical code (for that can be done by clear thinking). Ellis himself was clearly an atheist, and in several articles postulated that although religion (that is, a philosophy of life) may be rational, religiosity (that is, dogmatic and absolute faith unfounded on fact) is not merely the opiate of the masses but a major cause of psychopathology (Ellis, 1987b).

Box 1.1

A clinical example: the client was a thirty-eight-year-old Catholic woman, whose tearful presentation was soon shown to be related to a severe case of guilt about an abortion she had had—twenty years before. For twenty years, she alternately repressed her awareness of the abortion or acknowledged it with immense emotional suffering. Abortion, in her mind, was wrong; she had "killed her child," which therefore made her a murderer, a sin for which she could not forgive herself. Attempts to dispute the "wrongness" of the abortion were futile. No matter what her life circumstances had been, in her value system the choice to abort was a wrong and evil thing to have done. Attempts to dispute her devaluation of herself as a person were also futile; in her mind, the "murder" made her a "murderer." Our successful disputation asked whether it is conceivable to forgive people who acknowledge that they have made mistakes, especially when they have attempted to do penance for a bad deed. With the help of an enlightened clergyman, we reached an agreement that twenty years of self-inflicted guilt was sufficient punishment for the "crime," and that if Jesus were able to forgive the sinner it was only fitting that she follow suit. Her ability to do so was quite dramatic thereafter, and was followed soon by a long-desired pregnancy!

Even though Ellis was a humanist and atheist, one can retain religious beliefs and practice good REBT, which is what many pastoral counselors, in fact, have done (e.g., DiGiuseppe, Robin, and Dryden, 1991; Johnson, 2006; Neilsen, Johnson and Ellis, 2001; Hauck, 1985). Much of REBT philosophy and most rational beliefs are consistent with moderate religious ideas. It is possible to utilize the client's religion or the Bible in support of rational thinking and healthy behavioral change. Religion may be like a Rorschach test. People see in it that which they are inclined to see. The REBT therapist can help clients focus on the rational parts of their religion.

Values

Two explicit values in the philosophy of REBT are widely held by people but not often verbalized. These two major values are survival and enjoyment. The system of psychotherapy derived from these values is designed to help people live longer, minimize their emotional distress and self-defeating behaviors, and actualize themselves so as to live a more fulfilling and happier existence.

The underlying concept is that if people are enabled to think more rationally, more flexibly, and more scientifically, they may be better able to live longer and happier lives. Similarly, appropriate behaviors enhance survival and happiness, as opposed to behaviors that are self-defeating or socially damaging. Helping people to feel appropriate emotions, whether positive or negative, will increase their longevity and satisfaction. Thus, REBT can be used not only to reduce suffering but to promote well-being and happiness (Bernard, Froh, DiGiuseppe, Joyce, and Dryden, 2010).

Our commonly held goals, therefore, are to live the only life we are sure of having with as much enjoyment as possible, given the limitations of the human body and the physical and social world; to live peacefully within our chosen group; and to relate intimately with certain people of our choosing. These are the explicit values advocated by REBT.

Ellis and Bernard (1986) outlined several important subgoals that are consonant with the basic REBT values and that may help individuals to achieve these values:

Self-interest. Emotionally healthy people tend to put their own interests at least a little above the interests of others. They sacrifice themselves to some degree for those for whom they care, but not overwhelmingly or completely.

Social interest. Most people choose to live in social groups; and to do so most comfortably and happily, they would be wise to act morally, protect the rights of others, and aid in the survival of the society in which they live.

Self-direction. We would do well to cooperate with others, but it is better for us to assume primary responsibility for our own lives rather than to demand or need excessive support or nurturance from others.

Tolerance. It is helpful to allow oneself and others the right to be wrong. It is not appropriate to enjoy obnoxious behavior, but it is not necessary to damn the person for doing it.

Flexibility. Healthy individuals tend to be flexible thinkers. Rigid, biased, and invariant rules tend to minimize happiness.

Acceptance of uncertainty. We live in a fascinating world of probability and chance; absolute certainties do not exist. The healthy individual strives for a degree of order, but does not demand complete predictability.

Commitment. Most people, especially intelligent and educated ones, tend to be happier when vitally absorbed in something outside themselves. At least one strong creative interest and some significant interpersonal involvement seem to provide structure for a happy daily existence.

Self-acceptance. Healthy people freely decide to accept themselves unconditionally, rather than measure, rate, or try to prove themselves.

Risk-taking. Emotionally healthy people are willing to take risks and have a spirit of adventurousness in trying to do what they want, without being foolhardy.

Realistic expectations. We are unlikely to get everything we want or be able to avoid everything we find painful. Healthy people do not waste time striving for the unattainable or for unrealistic perfection.

High frustration tolerance. Paraphrasing Reinhold Niebuhr and Alcoholics Anonymous, healthy people recognize that there are only two sorts of problems they are likely to encounter: those they can do something about and those they cannot. The goal is to modify the obnoxious conditions we can change, and learn to tolerate—or "lump"—those we cannot change.

Self-responsibility. Rather than blaming others, the world, or fate for their distress, healthy individuals accept responsibility for their own thoughts, feelings, and behaviors.

Thus, the goals of REBT are consistent with its values, which are to minimize distress, maximize the length of our life, and enhance our joy in the process of living. These values are sometimes referred to as "responsible hedonism."

Responsible Hedonism

The philosophic stance of REBT also rests on Epicureanism. Unlike the blindly compulsive hedonism of the Freudian *id*, however, the Epicureanism of REBT is both guided and individualistic. Whereas according to the concept of the id we are all driven by the same impulses that originate in bodily processes, individuals in REBT are recognized as enjoying and therefore seeking a wide variety of pursuits. Epicureanism was founded around 307 B.C. and is a system of philosophy based upon the teachings of Epicurus. Epicurus believed that pleasure is the greatest good. However, the way to attain pleasure was to live modestly and to gain knowledge of the workings of the world, and thus the limits of acquiring one's desires. Acceptance of these limits results in a state of tranquility and freedom from fear and emotional disturbance, as well as the absence of bodily pain. The combination of these two states constitutes happiness in its highest form. Epicureanism is a form of hedonism and declares pleasure as the sole intrinsic good, but its conception of absence of pain as the greatest pleasure and its advocacy of a simple life make it different from "hedonism" as it is commonly understood.

Epicureanism is not just the seeking of pleasure and the avoidance of pain; such a principle would not necessarily lead to continued enjoyment. If you derive pleasure from something that has harmful side effects, you clearly will not enjoy the pleasure very long. Thus, if you drink or use drugs to excess, you may experience considerable pleasure in the short term but more pain than pleasure in the long term. Because short-term pleasures may actually work against the other main goal of survival, REBT teaches, and even advocates, moderation.

The term for moderation is hedonic calculus, a concept taken from the pragmatic philosophers of the nineteenth century. It is not a true calculus, of course, because no numeric values are assigned to our various pleasurable pursuits. Rather, hedonic calculus refers to the sensible habit of asking ourselves whether the pleasure we experience today is likely to backfire in some way tomorrow, next week, or even years from now. Conversely, if we live only for the future, we might pass up a good deal of current enjoyment, and that, too, would be irrational. So, as you can see, the pursuit of the simple hedonistic goals of survival and happiness can be quite complicated. Both immediate gratification and delay of gratification have advantages and disadvantages. REBT advocates noncompulsively seeking an optimal solution that sacrifices neither the present nor the future.

A special form of hedonism that deserves careful consideration is when one avoids pain, discomfort, and inconvenience and in so doing cuts oneself off from a desirable outcome. A person may want to do something but be unwilling to work toward a long-range goal. In REBT, this avoidance is considered to result from Frustration Intolerance (FI). Clients demonstrate FI when they refuse to do what they agree would be beneficial for them, citing reasons such as, "It's too hard," "I'd be too scared," or "I can't stand it." FI is perhaps the main reason that clients do not improve after they have gained an understanding of their disturbance and how they create it.

FI is a personal philosophy of life that states, in effect, "I absolutely shouldn't have to do anything that is unpleasant or uncomfortable, and I'd sooner maintain the status quo than risk discomfort." Although people clearly have a right to live by such a philosophy, it can create unhappiness by blocking them from goals they would like to attain.

Does the Epicureanism of REBT lead to irresponsibility and anarchy in human relations? No, not if the person has thought through the consequences of his or her behavior, which includes getting cut off from future opportunities to pursue happiness. Exploitation of other people is hardly in our long-range best interests.

Language and General Semantics

Ellis reported that he was greatly influenced by General Semantics Theory in the creation of REBT (see Ellis, 1991). General Semantics (GS) is less a philosophy than the study of language and how the structure and use of language can shape and distort human experience and communications. The seminal figure in General Semantics is Alfred Korzybski, whose most famous work *Science and Sanity, an Introduction to Non-Aristotelian Systems and General Semantics* (Korzybski, 1933) identifies the core principles of GS. As the title of this text reflects, GS advocates that humans function best and remain free of emotional disturbance by following the scientific method, which advocates cognitive flexibility, awareness of implicit assumptions, specification and testing of hypotheses, and the empirical verification of ideas. Korzybski's book title, *Science and Sanity*, could have been the source for Ellis's hypothesis that more scientific thinking would lead to emotional adjustment.

The most important premise of GS is that language is usually incomplete. Any word for an object or an action by its very nature leaves out some important features of the event, thing, or action that the word attempts to identify. This idea is captured by the GS expression, "The map is not the territory." No matter how detailed a map, it will fail to include some aspects of the area it represents. In all things, the word is not the thing it defines. In addition, no two things are exactly the same; humans categorize things. In addition, no person or thing is the same over time. Each of us changes. The person we are today is different from the person we were in the past. As the old adage goes, *you can never step into the same river twice.* Thus, each event or thing has some unique features that are lost by the mapping of events and things into categories that we use words to express. Clinically, these ideas led Ellis to be suspicious of words and to ask probing questions of his clients to uncover their clinically relevant experiences. If a client reported being anxious, Ellis did not assume that he knew what the client meant by anxious, but would follow up on the nature of the sensations, images about that particular experience of anxiety, etc. If a client reported that her hurt resulted from a criticism from someone, Ellis would not assume he knew what the upsetting element was from the criticism. Perhaps it was the tone, the gestures, the content, or the assumptions underlying the criticism that the client responded to in becoming hurt. In subsequent chapters on assessing the crucial components of the activating event, or on assessing the emotions, the reader can see the influence of GS on the process of REBT. The primary take-away-message would be words can confuse and some information always remains left out by words; clinicians need to make sure that they get that crucial information.

Korzybski also thought that identity reactions promoted by the verb "to be" in the structure of languages resulted in overgeneralization, confusion, and maladaptive behaviors. The verb "to be" implies an identity between the subject of the sentence and the predicate object of the sentence. For example, if you say, "the lemon is yellow," you think that yellowness is a crucial necessary part of the lemon. The result is that we confuse our response to the lemon, "yellow," with the lemon itself. In the dark, we would fail to notice the lemon as yellow. If you were wearing blue-tinted glasses, you would see the lemon as green; if you were "color blind," you would see the lemon as some shade of gray. There are also unripe lemons that are green and some varieties of lemons that are not yellow. The structure of our statement, "the lemon is yellow," leads us to identify yellowness and lemons as identical. A more accurate, appropriate formulation would be "I see the lemon as yellow." Here the observer is included in the statement, leaving open the option that other observers may abstract something different and that the lemon can have other attributes beside yellowness. Korzybski cautioned against the thoughtless or excess use of "is," because it implies identity, especially when applied directly to objective reality. He wrote: " . . . the use of the is of identity, as applied to objective, un-speakable levels, appears invariably structurally false to facts and must be entirely abandoned." (Korzybski, 1933, p. 751)

Moving away from fruits and colors, consider the use of the verb "to be" when describing people. "He is a failure." The person represented by "he" and "failure" are linked in identity. Failure is part of the identity of the person represented by "he." This can lead to feelings of unhealthy negative emotions and not applying effort to new tasks because failure is already part of the picture.

To avoid the confusion of identity implied in the verb "to be," Korzybski invented a new language called E-Prime, or English-Prime. E-Prime is a version of English that excludes all forms of the verb *to be*; and does not use conjugations of *to be* (*am, are, is, was, were, be, been, being*). Instead of saying, "He is a failure," one would say, "He failed at [*enter the specific task.*]" Korzybski's position on E-Prime greatly influenced Ellis's identification of the irrationality of global evaluations of human worth and his notion of unconditional self-acceptance.

Korzybski's writings on the "is" of predication encouraged me to help clients to stop using several kinds of overgeneralizations. For if they say, "I am good," they strongly imply that they have an essence or "soul" of goodness, that they only do "good" things, and therefore deserve to live and enjoy themselves. This is misleading, because they cannot prove that they have any essence (which is a very bad, vague, and mystical word); and if they do have one, they cannot show that it always, at all times, is "good." To be much more precise, as Korzybski would put it, I help my clients say, "I am a person who does good things (e.g., helps others in trouble) but who also does many "neutral" and "bad" things (e.g., harms others). I am never really entirely "good," "bad," nor "neutral."

Korzybski showed that using the "is" of predication leads us to think imprecisely. Thus, statements like, "I am good," and "I am bad," are inaccurate overgeneralizations, because in reality I am a person who sometimes acts in a good and sometimes in a bad manner. In RET, we teach our clients not to rate themselves or their being but only what they do. All self-ratings seem to be mistaken, because humans are too complex and multisided ever to be given a global evaluation (Ellis, 1991, p. 18).

We strongly recommend that the new REBT therapist spend some time reading about GS, whether it be the classic work by Korzybski (1933), or some other authors on the topic, such as Hayakawa (1962) or Johnson (1946). These books will change the way one hears language.

What Rational Emotive Behavior Therapy Is Not

Many people assume that because Ellis frequently quotes the Stoic philosopher Epictetus, REBT is a form of Stoicism. Not so! The true Stoic works to develop immunity to feelings, whether physical (such as pain) or emotional (such as mourning). By contrast, the REBT position is that rational thinking can lead to feelings, even very strong negative feelings, without resulting in disturbed feelings and unnecessary suffering. REBT is a synthesis of Stoicism and Epicureanism.

REBT also should not be confused with Rationalism, which posits that one attains knowledge by logic alone and not through empiricism. REBT does not suggest that logic can conquer all. REBT proposes that knowledge comes through logical and empirical challenges to our troubled thinking and also advocates that we had better act on our new beliefs.

It is also important not to confuse rational thinking with rationalization, a so-called defense mechanism, which is, in fact, a form of distorted thinking. When we rationalize, we invent an explanation for an action, thought, or emotion rather than face an undesirable reality—quite the opposite of rational thinking.

Box 1.2

The old Aesop's fable of the fox and the grapes is a good example of rationalization. No matter how high the fox jumped, he was unable to get at the luscious grapes, but he continued to try, becoming angrier and angrier. The only way he was able to stop his foolish persistence was to decide that the grapes were probably not ripe, and he stomped off muttering that he didn't want those "sour grapes" anyway. What might be a rational response (as opposed to a rationalization) to this frustrating situation?

RATIONALITY AS A PERSONAL PHILOSOPHY

When REBT practitioners explore a client's belief system, they will encounter some rules of living that the client has been trying to follow. These personal rules, or philosophies of living, may rest upon parental and religious teachings, widely held common wisdom, or highly idiosyncratic opinions about how life should be lived. These rules, because they are dogmatically held, rigidly self-enforced, conflicting, or otherwise maladaptive, are the basis of the client's disturbance. When personal rules of living hinder a client's attainment of the goals of happiness and survival, they are fair game for examination and change.

The REBT therapist hopes to help the client evolve a new philosophy of life, one that will help to reduce emotional distress and lead to increased happiness. The therapist holds the view that people can choose to either add to their misery with illogical and unscientific thinking or promote their enjoyment with careful reasoning from evidence. The goals of a rational philosophy are to establish beliefs and habits that are congruent with:

Survival

Achieving satisfaction with living
Affiliating with others in a positive way
Achieving intimate involvement with a few others
Developing or maintaining a vital absorption in some personally fulfilling
  endeavor(s)

Box 1.3

Philosophy in the clinic: Working at a philosophical level may be a very practical clinical strategy because it can result in deep change that affects many behaviors. If you are working behaviorally, you may have to hit each (behavioral) nail on the head separately; but if you can work philosophically, you may hit one board, which then will drive many nails at once.

REBT therapists know and help clients remember that all persons are fallible, forever destined to often fail and err. They help clients to give up their demands for perfection and to strive to develop constructive self-acceptance as well as acceptance of others. In its best form, this change comes about by scientific and logical thinking, which results in deep philosophic and attitudinal change.

The writings of Albert Ellis can be divided into philosophy, a personal philosophy of living, a theory of psychopathology, and a theory of psychotherapy. The philosophical positions described above set the foundation for theories of psychopathology and psychotherapy that we discuss in the following chapters.

2

Rational Emotive Behavior Theory

There are three main psychological aspects of human functioning: thoughts, emotions, and behaviors. All three aspects are intertwined and interrelated, since changes in one will often produce changes in the others. Thus, if individuals change the manner in which they think about an event, they will most likely feel differently about it and may alter the way they behaviorally react to it. Changes in our behavior may likewise lead to changes in our thinking; once we have done something we had been afraid to do, we may no longer think of it as dangerous or difficult.

Behavioral psychologies focus on changing environmental contingencies to alter behavior, and cognitive psychologies focus on altering thought content, but few psychologies deal with changing emotions directly because emotions are elusive and difficult to pin down. Cognitive-Behavior Therapy (CBT) focuses on the cognitive-emotive interface. However, different forms of CBT postulate different cognitions leading to disturbed emotions. Rational- Emotive Behavior Therapy (REBT) shares the focus on the cognitive-emotive interface; however, REBT differs in hypothesizing the role of demandingness and other Irrational Beliefs (IBs) have in contributing to dysfunctional emotions.

In this chapter, we review some of the fundamental principles in the theory of REBT, discuss how it relates to cognitive theory in general, and illustrate how it applies to clinical treatment.

THE SEVEN PRINCIPLES OF REBT THEORY

We can condense the main ideas in REBT to seven basic principles:

1. The basic principle of Rational Emotive Behavior Theory is that *cognition is the most important proximal determinant of human emotion.* Simply stated, we feel what we think. Events and other people do not make us "feel good" or "feel bad"; we do it to ourselves, cognitively. It is as if we are writing the scripts for our emotional reactions, although usually we are not conscious of doing so. Thus, past or present external events contribute to, but do not directly induce or "cause" emotions

in us. Rather, our internal processes, such as our perceptions, our evaluations of these perceptions, and especially our acceptance or failure to accept the perceptions—are the more direct and powerful sources of our emotional responses.

2. A second principle states that *irrational thinking is a major determinant of emotional distress.* Dysfunctional emotional states and many aspects of psychopathology are the result of dysfunctional thought processes, which can be characterized by exaggeration, oversimplification, overgeneralization, unexamined illogical assumptions, faulty deductions, absolutistic ideas, and demands that emotions, thoughts, or realities do or do not exist.

3. The most effective way to change dysfunctional disturbed emotions begins with an analysis of our thoughts. If distress is a product of irrational thinking, *the best way to conquer distress is to change this thinking.*

4. *Multiple factors,* including genetic and environmental influences, are etiologic antecedents to irrational thinking and psychopathology. Ellis repeatedly pointed out that humans have a natural predisposition to think irrationally and rationally (e.g., Ellis, 1976a; 1985; 1994; Ellis and MacLaren, 2005). He thought that humans evolved the capacity to think both rationally and irrationally about the world. Evidence for the global species wide tendency to think irrationally is supported by the ubiquity of irrational beliefs. One's culture furnishes the specific content of these beliefs.

5. Emotions exist to signal people that they have a problem that requires attention and action (Darwin, 1872/1998). Unlike most other theories of psychotherapy, REBT distinguishes between two different types of emotions in reaction to negative events: Ones that we call helpful, healthy, functional, and adaptive, and others that we call unhelpful, unhealthy, dysfunctional, and maladaptive for the individual. Most of the times individuals experience healthy and unhealthy emotions together. However, we are not aware of the mixture. The healthy emotions lead to functional, adaptive behavior, and the unhealthy emotions lead to dysfunctional, maladaptive behavior. The distinction between the two emotions is essential and provides the opportunity to only direct interventions to the unhealthy part. The unhealthy part (also in behaving) is connected with irrational thinking, while the constructive part goes together with rational thinking.

6. Like many contemporary psychological theories, Rational Emotive Behavior Theory emphasizes *present proximal influences* on emotions and behavior rather than *historical* influences on behavior. Another tenet of REBT theory is that although heredity and environmental conditions are important in the acquisition of psychopathology, they are not the primary focus in understanding its maintenance and continuation. People maintain their disturbance by continued self-indoctrination.

The rehearsal and continued adherence to irrational beliefs, not how they were acquired, leads to the present emotional distress. Thus, if individuals re-evaluated their former thinking and abandoned it in the present, their current functioning would be quite different. Negative historical events can lead to disturbance because a person learned to think irrationally about that event and actively rehearsed those thoughts over time. Ellis attributed a quote to Sigmund Freud concerning this point. "The past is important because you continue to carry it around with you." (Freud, 1965).

7. Beliefs can be changed, although such change will *not be easy*. Irrational beliefs are changed to rational beliefs by active and persistent efforts to recognize, challenge, and revise one's thinking, and to behave against the belief, thereby reducing emotional distress and increasing the occurrence of positive experiences and the achievement of one's personal goals.

COGNITIVE THEORY AND RATIONAL EMOTIVE BEHAVIOR THEORY

REBT is one of the many forms of Cognitive-Behavior Therapy (CBT). Today, CBT represents one of the most popular theoretical orientations among psychologists and psychotherapists (after eclecticism/integration) (Cook, Biyanova, and Coyne, 2009). However, CBT is a hyphenated moniker. Virtually all advocates of cognitive interventions integrate them with the behavioral interventions identified elsewhere in this book. Although CBT remains a part of behavior therapy, it has emerged from several disparate traditions within psychotherapy. The first tradition started from within behavior therapy when practitioners became disappointed with their strictly behavioral methods and theories. An influential event in moving the field of behavior therapy toward a cognitive perspective was Albert Bandura's *Principles of Behavior Modification* in 1969. The final chapter of Bandura's classic text reviewed his and others' work on the pervasiveness of learning through modeling. The research results on human learning questions the reliance on conditioning as the primary method to explain behavior change and human learning. Mahoney (1974) followed Bandura's book with several influential publications, including *Cognition and Behavior Modification,* reviewing the place of language, modeling, and cognitive factors in learning and psychotherapy. These works in Behavior Therapy both reflected and reinforced the growth of cognitive models in psychology as a whole.

In 1976, Albert Ellis organized and funded the first conference on Cognitive-Behavior Therapies, which met in New York City at the Albert Ellis Institute. Important CBT figures, such as Aaron Beck, Marvin Goldfried, Michael Mahoney, Don Meichenbaum, and George Spivack attended this conference. One of us attended as a postdoctoral fellow (RD). This conference and a similar one the following year united several theoretical positions under the term CBT.

After the conference, the journal *Cognitive Therapy and Research* began publication, with Michael Mahoney as its inaugural editor. (For more information on the history of CBT and REBT, see Hollon and DiGiuseppe, 2011.) REBT was one of the founding and central theoretical positions within CBT. However, because Ellis emphasized the role of particular kinds of cognition in emotional disturbance, REBT has many distinctive features, unique theoretical positions, and clinical strategies.

REBT THEORY OF PSYCHOPATHOLOGY

REBT theory maintains that cognitions are the most important determinant of emotions; however, REBT recognizes that there may be more than one pathway to emotional arousal. This recognition of multiple paths is exemplified in an early discussion by Albert Ellis. In 1974, Joseph Wolpe (one of the founders of Behavior Therapy) and Ellis debated the role of cognition in psychopathology and psychotherapy at Hofstra University. Wolpe spoke first. He presented a model of a human head on the blackboard and identified vision and auditory sensory pathways. He thought that there were two pathways to anxiety problems. The first pathway ran from the senses to the lower levels of the brain and the hypothalamus and on to the adrenal glands. This pathway, he said, occurred through conditioning. Exposure and systematic desensitization effectively treated disturbed anxiety mediated through this pathway. The second pathway involved information from the senses going up from the thalamic nuclei up to the cortex and back down the thalamus and onto the hypothalamus. The reaction time for this pathway was slower and required re-learning of faulty assumptions and thought. Treatment of disturbed emotions that formed through this pathway involved the testing and replacement of disturbed ideas. Thus, Wolpe had identified a conditioning and cognitive pathway for emotions. Wolpe stated that the first conditioning-formed pathway accounted for about 90% of all anxiety disorders, and the cognitive path was less important.

Ellis then walked to the podium. The audience expected him to challenge Wolpe as Al's reputation for debate had preceded him. Ellis agreed that there were two pathways mediating emotional disturbance. One was lower, quicker, and resulted from conditioning. The other pathway was cognitive, slower, and based in the cortex. However, Ellis said the cognitive pathway mediated 90% of emotional disturbance and the conditioning pathway mediated 10%. The remainder of the debate involved compromises concerning what proportions of disturbance could be attributed to the two pathways. This debate clarified that CBT and REBT existed within the larger context of behavior therapy. REBT still holds that the mechanisms of psychopathology and the mechanisms of change are multiple; different strategies are often required for effective therapy. This dual pathway theory identified in 1974 in the Wolpe and Ellis debate remains an active area of inquiry within CBT (see Power and Dalgleish, 2008). Some emotions are mediated by cognition, and others are mediated by noncognitive pathways.

INCREASING RATIONAL BELIEFS OR DECREASING IRRATIONAL BELIEFS

Humans are likely to hold both Rational Beliefs (RBs) and Irrational Beliefs (IBs) at the same time; or they will vacillate back and forth between the two beliefs. Sometimes they will report the RBs in the therapy office, but experience the IBs when they confront the problematic activating event in the real world. Presently, we (RD) are examining the ratio of irrational and rational beliefs and found that in a nonclinical sample of college students, participants endorsed rational beliefs 1.66 times more than irrational beliefs. People in therapy appear to have a higher proportion of endorsements of irrational beliefs to rational beliefs. Thus, it is not only the presence of irrational beliefs that causes disturbance. Rather, it is the absence of the counterbalancing rational beliefs. A task of therapy is to help clients discriminate RBs from IBs, and then to ask them to help reduce the proportion of irrational beliefs and increase the proportion of rational beliefs. We do this by challenging their IBs and by practicing and rehearsing philosophies that are more rational.

ADAPTIVE/HEALTHY AND MALADAPTIVE/ UNHEALTHY EMOTIONS

REBT distinguishes among disturbed, dysfunctional, unhealthy, and maladaptive negative emotions and nondisturbed, functional, healthy, adaptive, and motivating, albeit negative, emotions. Different languages vary on whether they make this distinction for the different emotions. Cultural context is important so that therapists are aware of how their language makes this distinction. Negative emotions are not evidence of psychopathology. If one experiences an activating event (A), and one thinks irrationally (B), one will experience a disturbed emotion such as anxiety, disturbed anger, depression, or guilt (C). If one then challenges one's irrational belief and replaces it with a rational belief (a new B) a new emotional and behavioral consequence will occur (the new C). If the unpleasant activating event is still present (and it usually is in our clients' lives), it would be *inappropriate* to expect the person to feel good or even neutral after achieving cognitive change. What does one feel if the intervention is successful and one thinks rationally? The answer is a negative, functional, motivating emotion.

Most psychotherapies conceptualize therapeutic improvement as a quantitative shift in the emotion. Often therapists ask clients to rate their emotion on the SUDS scale (subjective units of distress) developed by Wolpe (1961; 1990), or a score on a self-report measure of a disturbed emotional state. Therapy is successful if the SUDS rating demonstrates a lower score, representing less of the emotion. According to this model, emotions differ along a continuum of their intensity of physiological arousal and phenomenological experience.

Ellis (1994; Ellis and DiGiuseppe, 1993) proposed that emotions have two continua, one for the disturbed emotion and another for the nondisturbed emotion. When people think rational beliefs, they actually experience a qualitatively different emotion that can differ in strength. The emotions generated by rational beliefs remain in the same family of emotions as the disturbed emotion. However, they differ in many aspects, such as phenomenological experience, social expression, problem-solving flexibility, and the behaviors they generate. Ellis posited that irrational thinking leads to anxiety, depression, anger, or guilt; rational thinking will lead to concern, sadness, annoyance, and regret or remorse respectively. REBT (DiGiuseppe and Tafrate, 2007) believes that clients can learn adaptive emotional scripts, and not just change the intensity of their feelings. As a result, therapists use words carefully to describe adaptive/functional emotions and to help clients choose which emotions they could feel in place of their maladaptive, dysfunctional, disturbed emotion.

A good example of this principle might be Dr. Martin Luther King, Jr.'s emotional response to racism. Dr. King had an *intense* but adaptive emotional reaction to racism. His intense emotion led to commitment and high frustration tolerance, as well as problem-solving and goal-directed behavior. If he had encountered a psychotherapist who wished to help him experience a less intense emotion, would the world be a better place?

Dryden (2008) suggested that there is some accuracy to the traditional model of intense disturbed emotions, and Ellis's notion of two separate levels of emotional intensity. Dryden noted that very intense sympathetic physiological arousal causes cognitive constriction. Continued arousal makes one focus more on the topic about which one experiences the emotions. This restriction of focus reduces our ability to conceive of adaptive behaviors. Perhaps a functional/adaptive emotion can only be so strong before the sympathetic arousal of the emotion results in restricted concentration and leads to dysfunctional reactions. In Dryden's revised model, sympathetic emotional intensity has a role in explaining disturbed emotions. However, even when they are of low intensity, disturbed emotions are still disturbed. The rationale for this is the Yerkes-Dodson (1908) law. High levels of sympathetic physiological arousal interfere with any type of performance and lead to dysfunctional attention, problem-solving, and adaptive performance skills. Figure 2.1 displays Wolpe's traditional model of emotions, Ellis's theory, and Dryden's proposed revision. Figure 2.2 displays the Yerkes Dodson Law.

In Figure 2.3, we show the differences between Wolpe's SUDs model and the REBT model in a graph (From Backx, 2012). According to REBT, functional and dysfunctional emotions are qualitatively different, which means that there are two distinct dimensions (the functional and dysfunctional). When people react emotionally to an event, they produce a mixture of a functional and a dysfunctional emotion within one emotion family (e.g., sadness and depression). We can depict that in a graph consisting of an X and a Y-axis; the X-axis represents the intensity of the functional emotion and the Y-axis the intensity of the dysfunctional emotion. Because REBT posits that functional and dysfunctional emotions not only coexist but also are independent of each other, we can expect scores for an individual at any place on the X and Y axes. In Figure 2.3, we see a set of scores in the form of a cloud. The higher the score on the horizontal axis, the stronger the

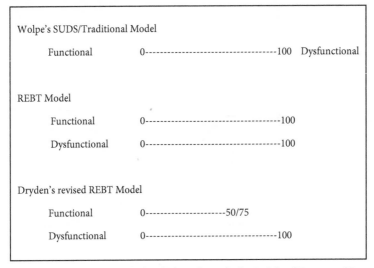

Figure 2.1 A comparison of Wolpe's, Ellis's and Dryden's Models of Emotional Intensity.

intensity of the functional emotion, and the higher the score is on the vertical axis, the stronger the dysfunctional emotion.

When we follow the interventions made by a therapist using Wolpe's model we would expect all scores to be reduced to 0 as much as possible as the arrow shows. Because there is no discrepancy between functional and dysfunctional emotions both will be reduced.

When a therapist intervenes according to the REBT model only the dysfunctional emotions will be subjected to reduction, which will result in the round arrow in Figure 2.4.

This graph also explains why it is inaccurate to believe that REBT tries to eliminate emotions. Once the scores are shifted by the curved arrow the dysfunctional emotions are reduced, but the functional emotions can still be high. Every score can be seen as a vector, which has a length and a direction. The direction represents

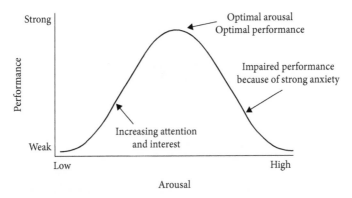

Figure 2.2 Yerkes Dodson Curve.

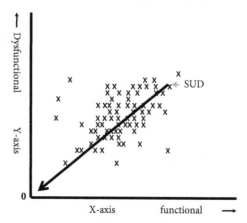

Figure 2.3 A set of negative emotions and the direction to change them according to non-REBT approaches, that is, the *quantitative* change.

the ratio between functional and dysfunctional emotions; that is, the quality of the emotion and the length of the quantity of the emotion. We only change the direction (quality) of the vector and not the length (quantity).

LEVELS OF COGNITIONS AND DISTURBANCE

REBT postulates that at least three levels of cognitions are associated with emotional arousal. These levels appear in Figure 2.5. Some thoughts occur in the stream of consciousness. Others are tacit, undeclared, and even elusive; they may even be unconscious. Still others are *schematic* in nature. The first level of cognitions lies in the stream of consciousness. These cognitions are *inferential* in nature. *Inferential* cognitions represent our perceptions of reality and the inferences we

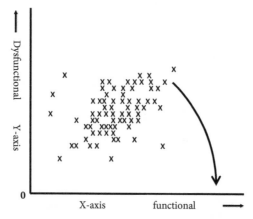

Figure 2.4 A set of negative emotions and the direction to change them according to REBT, the *qualitative* change.

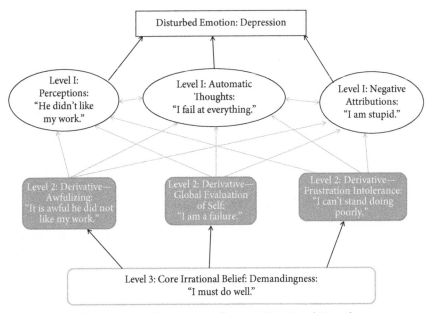

Figure 2.5 The Three Levels of Cognitions Influencing Emotional Disturbance.

draw from these perceptions. For example, suppose you are walking down the street and see a coworker approaching on the other side of the street. You wave your arm in greeting, but your gesture is not returned. You may infer from this event that your coworker saw you and decided not to greet you. You may even go further and infer that the absence of a greeting has some interpersonal meaning; perhaps the coworker is upset, or angry with you, or does not like you, or that no one at work likes you. Many of these cognitions may be incorrect inferences, which take the form of negative automatic thoughts, erroneous assumptions, global and fixed internal attributions. These inferences can be empirically tested to determine whether they are actually true. Many of these inferential cognitive constructs have been associated with emotional disturbance and psychopathology (Beck, 2005).

Inferences or negative automatic thoughts are experienced in a person's stream of consciousness and are easily tested against empirical reality. Evaluative cognitions are irrational beliefs that are derived from the more central imperative demands. Imperative Demands are thoughts about the way reality should be. They are somewhat like schema. People construct the world as they want it to be.

Let us look at some examples. Suppose you get up to give a speech in front of a group of colleagues and you experience tremendous anxiety. You observe one person yawning and a few others looking around the room. You then draw inferences: "Maybe they don't like what I have to say. They think that I'm boring." Those beliefs may be true or false, but it is the *evaluation of their possible truth* that is the focus in REBT. According to REBT, the negative automatic thought ("They don't like what I have to say.") or the belief in a lack of effectiveness ("I'm boring them.") are not necessarily sufficient to directly produce emotional disturbance.

Disturbance, in REBT, arises when you evaluate these inferences as *horrors*. Your more central evaluative beliefs may be something like:

> I must please them and earn their approval.
> If I bore them, I am a worthless, boring person.
> It is awful that people think of me as a boring presenter!

In an experimental test of this process, Dryden, Ferguson, and McTeague (1989) asked their subjects to rehearse to themselves one of two attitudes:

> "I absolutely must not see a spider, and it would be terrible if I did."
> "I really don't want to see a spider, but if I do, it won't be terrible."

Subjects were asked to imagine that they were about to enter a room and were instructed that in that room there was at least one spider. With that scene in mind, subjects answered questions such as:

> "How many spiders are in there?"
> "How big are they?"
> "In what direction are they moving?"

The results indicated that those subjects who rehearsed the "must" ("I must not see spiders and if I do it is terrible.") imagined more spiders, saw them as heading toward themselves rather than randomly moving about the room, and rated the spiders as bigger than did subjects in the other group. The "must" affected their (imaginary) perceptions.

Discriminating among inferential cognitions, evaluative cognitions, and imperative/schematic cognitions sets REBT apart from other cognitive therapies. An REBT therapist acknowledges the importance of inferential processes and uses a variety of strategies to modify those distorted cognitions, but the evaluative cognitions and the imperative/schematic are the key to understanding psychological disturbance. Thus, even if you think your wife does not love you, even if you think you will never accomplish certain feats, even though you think you lack efficacy in certain areas, you can protect yourself from undue emotional pain about these unfortunate realities if you think about them rationally and give up the demand that you *must* have your spouse's love or be successful.

REBT recognizes that these inferential cognitions are associated with pathology but does not believe that they are central. These second-level cognitions are largely *evaluative* in nature. These thoughts are closer or more central to emotional disturbance because they evaluate the importance of the inferences. In REBT parlance, these second-level cognitions are the derivative Irrational Beliefs and fall into three categories: awfulizing, frustration intolerance (FI), and global evaluations of human worth. These three types of beliefs evaluate the badness of the inference, one's evaluation of one's ability to cope with or tolerate the situation, or the worth of the persons involved. We call these beliefs derivatives because they are psychologically deduced from the more core irrational beliefs. (We will go into more detail in Chapter 9.)

The third level of cognitions involves the schematic demands. People construct the world to be the way they want it to be. Ellis identified three types of *musts* (Ellis, 1994; Ellis and Dryden, 1997; Ellis and MacLaren, 2005).

> I must...
> You must...
> The world must...

COGNITIVE MECHANISMS OF DISTURBANCE

Cognitive Appraisal Other Than Irrational Beliefs

REBT theory posits that irrational beliefs lead to dysfunctional emotions while rational beliefs lead to functional emotions. Irrational beliefs lead to all dysfunctional emotions including depression, anxiety, shame, guilt, and disturbed anger. Corresponding rational beliefs lead to sadness, disappointment, concern, apprehension, regret, and functional anger. Suppose three clients are anticipating people rejecting them, and they each hold the irrational belief that others *must* accept them, and the clients each experience one of three different dysfunctional emotions (anger, anxiety, and depression). REBT theory explains why they each experience a dysfunctional emotion. However, the theory fails to explain why each client experiences a *different* dysfunctional emotion.

David and his colleagues (David, Schnur and Belloiu, 2002) have solved this problem. They suggested that the types of appraisals identified by Lazarus (1991) determine whether a person experiences an emotion in one of the basic families of emotions (e.g., depression/sadness, anxiety/concern, anger/annoyance, or guilt / remorse). According to appraisal theory, two types of appraisals result in arousal of emotions (Folkman and Lazarus, 1991; Lazarus, 1991; Smith and Lazarus, 2001). People encounter a situation thinking they will achieve some goal. The terms appraisal or evaluative cognitions are used to define how representations of the environmental encounter are processed in terms of their relevance for attaining one's personal goals and well-being. The primary and secondary appraisal processes generate emotions. The first to affect arousal results from the appraisal that a situation or a transaction is harmful, beneficial, threatening, or challenging. Aspects of the *primary appraisal* are *motivational relevance* and *motivational congruence*. Although motivational relevance is an evaluation of the extent to which the encounter is relevant to one's personal goals, motivational congruence refers to the extent to which the encounter is consistent with one's goals.

The presence of irrational or rational beliefs determines whether the emotion one experiences is a dysfunctional or functional emotion within the family of emotions that the appraisals produced. Therefore, the appraisals identified by Lazarus would determine whether a person felt an emotion in the remorse family or sadness family. If those appraisals resulted in an emotion in the sadness family of emotions, thinking rational beliefs would lead to sadness while thinking irrational beliefs would lead to depression.

To sum up, cognitive appraisals determine whether an individual will experience an emotion in one of the basic families of emotions. The presence of rational or irrational beliefs influences whether one experiences a functional or dysfunctional emotion within that family of emotions. For example, suppose your romantic partner left you for someone else. You might experience something in the sadness family of emotions. You might think rational beliefs such as (1) Rational preferences: "This is a great loss and I will miss my lover intensely, but these things happen to people all the time"; (2) Rational, non-awfulizing thought: "Although this is bad, it is not the end of the world. I will cope the best I can"; (3) Rational frustration tolerance beliefs: "I do not like this, but I can stand the loss and I will survive this"; (4) Rational self-acceptance beliefs: "I will look to see if there was anything I did to cause the breakup and try to improve that, but I am not a worthless person because of the breakup"; and (5) Rational other acceptance beliefs: "My partner did something that was hurtful to me, but that does not make him/her condemnable." These thoughts are likely to lead to sadness, disappointment, and mourning.

If, on the other hand, you thought irrational beliefs such as (1) IB demandingness: "This must not happen. S/he has no right to leave me and s/he must not leave me"; (2) IB awfulizing beliefs: "This is the worst thing that could happen to me"; (3) IB frustration intolerance beliefs: "I just cannot survive this. I cannot stand living without my partner"; (4) IB self-downing beliefs: "This must mean that I am a worthless and unlovable person"; and (5) IB other-downing beliefs: "My partner fooled me all along, s/he is a despicable person." These thoughts would lead to anxiety or depression and the last one, other-downing beliefs, would lead to anger.

It may be more accurate to call irrational beliefs irrational schemata or imperative beliefs. REBT construes irrational beliefs as *tacit, unconscious,* broad-based schemata that operate on many levels. Irrational schemata are sets of expectations about the way the world is, ought to be, and what is good or bad about what is and ought to be. Irrational beliefs have the same characteristics as rigid, inaccurate schemata (DiGiuseppe, 1986, 1996; David, Freeman, and DiGiuseppe, 2009; Ellis, 1996; Szentagotai, Schnur, DiGiuseppe, Macavei, Kallay, and David, 2005). Schemata help people organize their world by influencing (a) the information to which a person attends; (b) the perceptions the person is likely to draw from sensory data; (c) the inferences or automatic thoughts the person is likely to conclude from the data he or she perceives; (d) the belief one has in one's ability to complete tasks; (e) the evaluations a person makes of the actual or perceived world; and (f) the solutions that a person is likely to conceive to solve problems. Irrational beliefs/schemata influence other hypothetical cognitive constructs that are mentioned in other forms of CBT, such as perceptions, inferences, or automatic thoughts, and attributions of cause. Figure 2.5 represents how irrational beliefs relate to other cognitive constructs and emotional disturbance. The model suggests that interventions aimed at the level of irrational beliefs/schemata will change other types of cognitions as well as emotional disturbance. It also suggests that interventions aimed at other cognitive processes may, but not necessarily, influence the irrational schema.

DEFINITION OF IRRATIONAL AND RATIONAL BELIEFS

Maultsby (1975), one of Ellis's earliest students, defined three criteria for beliefs to be irrational. To be irrational, a belief is illogical, inconsistent with empirical reality, or inconsistent with accomplishing one's long-term goals. These criteria are similar to those that Thomas Kuhn (1996), the historian of science, proposed that scientists use to evaluate theories. Scientists give up theories because they are logically inconsistent, fail to make empirical predictions, and lack heuristic or functional value (i.e., they fail to solve problems).

Most definitions of irrational beliefs are similar to Maultsby's definition; however, we want to focus on the centrality of the *musts*. One of us (WB) proposed that we define irrational belief as the cognitive expression of the unwillingness to accept an unwanted outcome of reality related to one's striving to achieve something positive or to block something negative. An irrational belief is a demand on reality that attempts to take away a negative outcome. The beliefs are usually formulated in "musts," "shoulds," and "oughts." A rational belief is the cognitive expression of the basic willingness to accept an unwanted outcome of reality related to one's striving to achieve or to block something, independent of how much it deviates from what one wants and independent of how strong one's desire is.

A good metaphor for irrationality according to REBT is the following: One of us had dinner at the house of his sister and brother-in-law. At that time, their child, age two years, was served Indonesian food (*Nassi*) for the first time, which he refused to eat. So we made a deal with him. If he would finish the dish, he would get his most favorite dessert, ice cream. He ate the Nassi, and we gave him his ice cream, but he refused to eat it. We did not understand. Why did he not want to eat his ice cream? It turned out that he had kept the whole meal in his mouth and had not swallowed it, because he believed that he **should not** have to eat it. He could not enjoy his ice cream because he held the unwanted food in his mouth right at the place where it did the most harm, near his taste buds. As this example shows, demanding that reality be different than it is and refusing to take it as it is, increases one's suffering.

Based on our definitions, an irrational belief has the following characteristics:

1. It is absolute, dichotomous, rigid, and unbending;
2. It is not logical;
3. It is not consistent with reality;
4. It does not help to achieve one's goal;
5. It leads to unhealthy/dysfunctional emotions.

Consequently, the features of a rational belief are the opposite:

1. It is flexible. Rational thinking recognizes that one could have many possible shades between black and white;
2. It is logical;
3. It is consistent with reality;
4. It is helpful in pursuing one's goal;
5. It leads to healthy, functional emotions, even when the person is facing negative events.

TYPES OF IRRATIONAL BELIEFS

As the reader becomes more familiar with the REBT literature and reads older books, they will notice an evolution of the concept of irrational beliefs. Ellis originally proposed thirteen different irrational beliefs (Ellis, 1962; Ellis and Harper, 1975) as independent from the constructs of other cognitive theories; the thirteen different irrational beliefs were not in any structural or categorical order. Some of them were factual errors, while others were demands, catastrophizing statements, condemnations of the self and others, or reflections of frustration intolerance. Later, several authors (Bernard and DiGiuseppe, 1989; Burgess, 1990; Campbell, 1985; Ellis, 1994; Ellis and Dryden, 1997) consolidated the original thirteen irrational beliefs into five types of beliefs: demandingness, awfulizing, frustration intolerance, self-condemnation, and other-condemnation.

An activating event could generate up to five possible irrational beliefs, the demand, and one or more of the four derivatives. The theory maintains that "demandingness," or absolutistic, rigid adherence to an idea is the core of disturbance and that the other types of irrational thinking are less central and are psychologically deduced from or created from demandingness. Below, we present each of the irrational beliefs and explain what makes them irrational.

Demandingness is an unrealistic and absolute expectation of events or individuals being the way a person desires them to be.

Awfulizing is an exaggeration of the negative consequences of a situation to an extreme degree, so that an unfortunate occurrence becomes "terrible."

Frustration Intolerance (FI) stems from demands for ease and comfort, and reflects an intolerance of discomfort.

Global evaluations of human worth, either of the self or others, imply that human beings can be rated, and that some people are worthless, or at least less valuable than others.

This model of irrational beliefs appears in Table 2.1. Along the horizontal dimension are listed five core types of irrational processes and along the vertical dimension are listed the topics about which the person thinks irrationally. The grid has led to some hypotheses about irrational beliefs involved in specific disorders. For example, human-rating IBs about the self may play the major role in depression; IBs about comfort are thought to be prominent in agoraphobia

Table 2.1. MODEL OF IRRATIONAL BELIEFS

Irrational Process

	Demandingness	Frustration intolerance	Awfulizing	Self-worth ratings	Other-worth ratings
Social relationships	Demanding about affiliation	FI about affiliation	Awfulizing about affiliation	Self-condemning about affiliation	Other-condemning about affiliation
Achievement	Demanding about achievement	FI about achievement	Awfulizing about achievement	Self-condemning about achievement	Other-condemning about achievement
Comfort	Demanding about comfort	FI about comfort	Awfulizing about comfort	Self-condemning about comfort	Other-condemning about comfort
Fairness	Demanding about fairness	FI about fairness	Awfulizing about fairness	Self-condemning about fairness	Other-condemning about fairness

Belief Content

(Burgess, 1990); and frustration intolerance IBs are often considered crucial in addictive behaviors (DiGiuseppe and McInerney, 1991).

Box 2.1

Take a minute to bring to mind several clients with whom you are now working. Jot down the name of each client and his or her presenting problem. Then try to figure out where on the grid each client's thinking falls. For example, the IB may be demandingness about comfort, demandingness about fairness, FI about comfort, and so on.

Clinical experience suggests that the content dimension could be expanded to include the factor of *control* (thereby expanding the model). Thus, "demandingness" in interaction with "control" might result in a belief structure such as, "I must be in total control of my marriage in order to feel safe"; FI × control, "I can't stand it when things happen that I can't control"; rating × control, "I think I'm worthless as a person when I can't control things"; and awfulizing × control, "It's awful when things are beyond my control."

Demandingness about the way an activating event should or should not be was the core of disturbance, and awfulizing, frustration intolerance, or condemnation of the self or others were thought to be derivatives. That is, these psychological constructs emanated from the person's demand and then influenced the person's type of emotional experience. This model has several clinical implications. First, it was important to assess the client's demandingness and less relevant to assess the presence of derivative irrational beliefs. Also, if demands were core beliefs, the derivative irrational beliefs would change once the client changed his/her demandingness. Therefore, it was more important that clinicians challenge the demanding beliefs and help the client adopt a more rational replacement to them than it was to challenge and replace the derivative beliefs. Much of the REBT literature focuses on changing demandingness.

RELATIONSHIPS AMONG IRRATIONAL BELIEFS

Presently there is some debate among CBT advocates as to the relationships among the irrational beliefs. This debate is important because the position one takes can influence which irrational belief one targets first in therapy. We will review each of these positions and their clinical implications.

Ellis (Ellis and MacLaren, 2005) argued that the demands are the core irrational beliefs and that the IBs such as awfulizing, Frustration Intolerance, and global self or other evaluations psychologically follow from the **musts**. This model is represented in Figure 2.6.

A.T. Beck (1976) and J. Beck (1995) proposed that demandingness plays a less central role in psychopathology. They posit demandingness as mediating the effect of the other irrational beliefs. This model is represented in Figure 2.7.

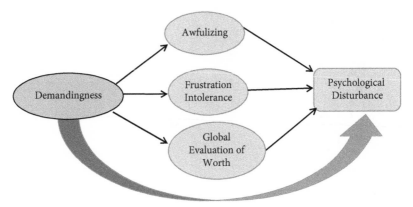

Figure 2.6 Model 1—Ellis's Model: Demandingness as Core.

In this model, the evaluative beliefs are more important and seem to produce the demandingness beliefs. If the Becks' model is correct, and demandingness serves only as a mediator, demanding beliefs would be less important as targets for assessment and intervention in therapy.

DiGiuseppe (1996) argued that because REBT theory lacked empirical support for the hypotheses of the centrality of demands, and until such time that support becomes available and convincing, therapists would best serve their clients by assuming that their irrational beliefs were independent of each other. This would mean that the therapist would assess cognitions at levels 2 and 3 and target whichever level the client reports experiencing during their emotional episode. This model appears in Figure 2.8.

What is the data for the centrality of demandingness? Bernard (1993) and DiGiuseppe, Leaf, Exner, and Robin (1988) performed factor analyses and psychometric studies and found that demandingness, awfulizing, and frustration intolerance all loaded on one factor, and global self-condemnation loaded on a separate factor. Ellis (1996) responded to this challenge by saying that it was difficult to measure the true nature and extent of demandingness with self-report measures, as is usually the case. Demandingness IBs may not be readily accessible to conscious processes. Ellis suggested that demandingness biases our responses

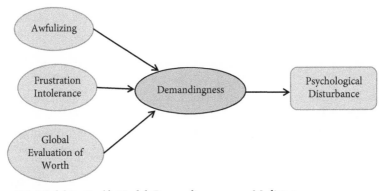

Figure 2.7 Model 2—Beck's Model: Demandingness as a Mediator.

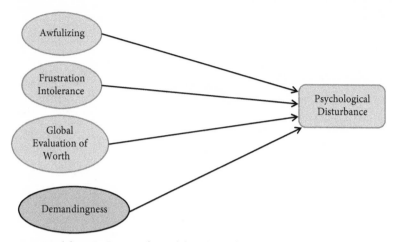

Figure 2.8 Model 3—DiGiuseppe's Model: Independence of Irrational Beliefs.

in an indirect way and this might only become visible during a clinical interview, or on more sensitive indirect measures. Ellis's idea is not unique, and it is congruent both with cognitive psychology theory and research on the unconscious processes, which have demonstrated the indirect impact of our cognitions on our behaviors (Wegner and Smart, 1997), as well as with the schema literature, which shows that it is difficult to verbally describe the deep structure of a schema (Anderson, 1990).

Szentagotai, Schnur, DiGiuseppe, Macavei, Kallay, and David (2005) researched the influence of holding irrational beliefs on memory recall as a way of demonstrating whether they functioned as deep schema. They found that demandingness and global evaluation/self-downing seem to be organized as schemas. Awfulizing and frustration intolerance function more like appraisals. In addition, demandingness seems to be strongly associated with the other irrational beliefs and this supports the REBT centrality of demandingness hypothesis. Other research has shown that awfulizing, frustration intolerance, and global self-evaluations mediate the effect between demandingness and emotional disturbance, also supporting the centrality of demandingness (David et al., 2006; DiLorenzo, David, & Montgomery, 2007; Szentagotai et al., 2005). These results provide some support for the idea that all irrational beliefs are derived from demandingness.

Not all research in this area, however, has supported the centrality of demandingness. Recently, Agiurgioaei-Boie, Agiurgioaei-Boie, and DiGiuseppe (2011) explored the relationship between the different irrational beliefs and emotional disturbance in two countries, the United States and Romania. They found the presence of a different constellation of irrational beliefs specific to each country. More specifically, in the American sample, distress seems to be strongly related to awfulizing, demandingness, and self-downing/global evaluation. On the other hand, for the Romanian sample the core irrational beliefs related to distress were frustration intolerance and self-downing/global evaluation—not demandingness.

As of this writing, we have no scientific data that targeting client's demandingness is more effective than targeting the derivatives. Additionally, we have no evidence that therapy targeting only demandingness will produce positive change in the derivatives. What are the implications of this lack of scientific consensus on the centrality of demandingness? We do believe that practitioners should follow the theory and hold on to it "lightly." This means that practitioners might investigate the presence of demands when clients are emotionally disturbed and they might wish to target demandingness first. However, we recommend that the clinician be open to the possibility that for any particular client, one of the derivatives might be the more important path to disturbance. We also believe that it is possible for demandingness to be central but for the derivative beliefs to become independent and persist even if the client changes their demandingness. The personality psychologist Gordon Allport (1937) coined the term "functional autonomy" to describe the phenomenon of psychological constructs becoming independent of the original causes for them. Sufficient rehearsal of a thought, motive, or emotion may result in it no longer requiring the original antecedents that elicited it. We think the same can happen with the derivatives.

WHY ARE PEOPLE IRRATIONAL?

If, as we have pointed out, it is self-defeating to hold irrational ideas, why do we do so? A number of factors come into play. First, common cultural stereotypes in our language, our stories, and our songs reinforce this tendency. A review of popular music, for example, found that 82% of country-western and rock songs expressed irrational philosophies (Protinsky and Popp, 1978). Second, there may be a kind of self-reinforcing thrill achieved when we are irrational. Think of the boy who has tearful hysterics because he did not make the team, or the girl who was not invited to the dance. Distortion and exaggeration can be exciting and, of course, may elicit attention or sympathy from others in our environment. Another way of looking at it may be that people experience short-term advantages by thinking irrationally. Once one thinks oneself to be worthless, one is legitimized to not put effort into achieving one's goal(s) (Backx, 2012). Perhaps the most basic reason why people are irrational, however, is stated by Ellis (1976a), who suggested that almost everyone thinks irrationally some of the time; it is the human condition. Strange as it may seem, this last explanation for irrationality may be clinically quite comforting. Such a suggestion appears to function well because it changes the attribution and allows clients to stop blaming themselves for their irrational beliefs.

DISTINCTIVE FEATURES OF REBT THEORY

Although REBT shares many features with other forms of CBT, many aspects of REBT are distinctive and separate it from other variants of CBT. These include the following:

1. REBT's Position on Human Nature—REBT believes that humans are inherently rational and irrational; and that people can augment one or

the other predisposition by rehearsal. Emotional disturbance may be influenced biologically or genetically.

2. REBT's Distinctive ABC Model—REBT draws distinctions among several types of beliefs, perceptions about the external events, inference about the external events, derivative irrational beliefs, and demanding beliefs.

3. Rigidity is at the Core of Psychological Disturbance—REBT posits that rigid thinking is the core foundation of emotional disturbance.

4. Flexibility is at the Core of Psychological Health—REBT believes that flexibility is the hallmark of psychological adjustment.

5. Extreme Beliefs are Derived from Rigid Beliefs—Cognitive errors about the world that are extreme are psychologically created by rigid beliefs.

6. Non-extreme Beliefs are Derived from Flexible Beliefs—Adaptive, accurate, non-extreme beliefs about the world result from flexible thinking.

7. Distinction Between Unhealthy Negative Emotions (UNEs) and Healthy Negative Emotions (HNEs)—REBT distinguishes between unhealthy, disturbed, and dysfunctional emotional reactions and healthy, adaptive, and functional emotions. The goal of therapy is to reduce the UNEs and replace them with HNEs.

8. Explaining Why Clients' Inferences are Highly Distorted—Inferences are driven or deducted from our core schema. If one holds a rigid demanding core schema one will generate distorted perceptions, attributions, and inferences.

9. Position on Human Worth—REBT posits that self-esteem and global ratings of human worth are dysfunctional and lead to emotional disturbance. If you can rate yourself as better than other humans, you can also rate yourself as less worthwhile than other humans. REBT posits unconditional self-acceptance.

10. Distinction Between Ego and Discomfort Disturbance and Health.

11. Focus on Meta-emotional Disturbance—REBT postulates that humans can hold irrational thoughts about their disturbed emotions, which in turn causes an escalation of the disturbed emotions. These meta-emotional disturbances distract the person from thinking about the thoughts that lead to the first disturbed emotions. Therefore, therapy preferably focuses on the meta-emotional disturbance first.

12. Choice-Based Constructivism and Going Against the Grain.

A MAJOR MISCONCEPTION

At this point, we would like to dispel a common misconception of REBT. "Rational" does not mean "unemotional." REBT theory does not say that all emotions are to be eliminated. Rather, REBT posits that it is not inevitable that one feel *terribly* upset or emotionally disturbed. A rational belief about a negative activating event will still lead to a negative emotion. Rational thoughts lead to negative functional emotions, while irrational beliefs lead to negative dysfunctional emotions. Even when thinking rationally, the individual may experience uncomfortable negative emotions—even strong ones. The distinction between the consequences of rational and irrational thinking is reflected in the *adaptability* of the negative affect rather than in its presence or absence. See Figure 2.4. If emotional turmoil blocks constructive action, it is consequently self-defeating and nonadaptive for the individual.

Emotions are important motivators for behavior as well as for behavioral change. When people experience no emotion, or, at the other extreme, experience excessive emotion, behavioral efficiency is lost. For example, an extremely anxious student may do poorly on a test; the student who has no concern at all may never be motivated to study and will do poorly. Thus, we are distinguishing between *emotional disturbance* and the presence of negative (even strongly negative) emotions, a distinction on which we will elaborate in Chapter 8.

Box 2.2

One argument raised by critics of Rational-Emotive Behavior Theory is that if people do not believe that events are "awful," they will not be motivated to change them. "Rational," however, does not mean passive acceptance of events. There are two general kinds of events: those we can possibly change and those we cannot. Accepting an unfortunate reality and not getting overly upset about it acknowledges that the reality exists, that it is unpleasant, that it would be irrational to demand or insist that it should not have happened, and that we will attempt to change it, if we can. One can certainly be vigilant in trying to prevent similar events from happening again. When we are feeling upset, however, we may not be adept at problem solving or working effectively at changing our environment.

In summary, the basic principles of REBT theory are as follows:

1. Cognition is the most important, though hardly the only, determinant of emotion.
2. Irrational thinking often produces dysfunctional emotional states. The most effective way to reduce emotional distress is to change our thinking.
3. We have a natural tendency to think irrationally and upset ourselves, which is reinforced by the environment.
4. We perpetuate our emotional distress by re-propagandizing ourselves with our irrational beliefs.
5. Changing irrational beliefs, therefore, will not necessarily be easy work and is likely to require persistence and practice.

6. Remember, rational thinking leads to a reduction in the frequency, intensity, and duration of emotional disturbance, not to flat affect or the absence of feeling.

7. In the next chapter, we discuss each of the irrational beliefs, and why they are irrational. This information will help you understand REBT theory, and lay the foundation for clinical assessment and intervention.

3

The Irrational and Rational Beliefs

In the last chapter we discussed the major theoretical aspects of REBT. In this chapter, we will try to identify why each of the four irrational beliefs is irrational and why their corresponding rational beliefs represent a more adaptive strategy. We will start with the core irrational belief demandingness and then discuss the derivatives.

DEMANDINGNESS

As we discussed in Chapter 2, more central to emotional disturbance are imperative beliefs that reflect commands that the universe be a certain way. The Oxford English Dictionary (2011) defines *imperative* as "Having the quality or property of commanding; of the nature of, characterized by, or expressing a command; commanding; peremptory." This is precisely the idea that Ellis used in describing demands. *Demands* reflect unrealistic and absolute expectations of events or individuals, and are often recognizable by cue words such as "must," "ought," "should," "have to," "got to," and "need."

REBT distinguishes between preferences and demands. Preferences are neither rational nor irrational. They just are. Therapists do not attempt to change a person's "wants," or preferences. REBT posits that no desire is a sign of pathology. People's desires do not cause disturbance. When people demand that their desires be reality, however, they become disturbed. How and why does demandingness lead to disturbance?

People construct schemata concerning the reality they encounter. Research has demonstrated that when people experience a discrepancy between their schema of the world and the reality they confront, they experience emotional arousal. We detect information that is inconsistent with our expectations. We call this the *expectancy-reality-discrepancy*. When people perceive this discrepancy, they become emotionally aroused and attempt to resolve it. Piaget (1954) noted that people resolve this discrepancy by either assimilation or accommodation. The production of a new schema is accommodation. A well-adjusted person becomes motivated by this emotional arousal and seeks out further information to revise his or her schema of the world.

Assimilation involves maintaining the schema in spite of the discordant information and changing one's perception to keep the schema. The expectancy is maintained despite evidence from reality that it is false. In science and our personal lives, people do not change beliefs for every inconsistency that arises. When significant and substantial discrepancies exist, however, it may be best to change one's schema. REBT maintains that it is the rigidity and the failure to change schemas, no matter what evidence exists for them, that causes human disturbance. Thus, demandingness causes disturbance because people use assimilation to cope with the *expectancy-reality-discrepancy*. This rigid adherence to the existing schema and continued assimilation as a cognitive strategy results in the same expectation and the continued perception of a discrepancy between what one perceives and what one expects. This discrepancy continues to arouse emotions and a sense of frustration or threat.

For example, consider the case of a couple who arrived for therapy. Victoire awoke early each morning, got ready for work, made coffee, put the milk in her coffee, and ran out to work leaving the milk on the counter to get warm. Pierre awoke several hours later, got ready for work and went to the kitchen for breakfast to find warm milk for his cereal. He became furious at her inconsiderate behavior. Victoire apologized, but continued to do the same thing. Therefore, we asked Pierre what he expected of Victoire. He said that if she loved him and was considerate she should put the milk away in the refrigerator. The disputing focused on whether Pierre set his expectations on what he wanted and thought was right or what Victoire had done.

T: How often does she do this behavior?
C: Every morning.
T: Well for how many years has she been doing this?
C: At least eleven years that she has had this work schedule.
T: So, do you base your prediction on what she does or what you *want* her to do?
C: I base it on what is right. And what is best for her to do.
T: So let me get this straight—she has done this five days a week, for forty-eight weeks (taking time off for vacation) for eleven years. That means she has done it $5 \times 48 \times 11$ which is 2,640 times.
C: Yeah, you see how inconsiderate she is.
T: But after 2,640 times you are still shocked and surprised about what she has done. If you were paying attention to what she does, wouldn't you expect her to leave the milk out by now? So are you basing your expectation on what you *want* or what she has done?
C: I guess it has to be on what I want.
T: Now how would you feel and behave differently if you based your expectation on what she did, rather than what you wanted her to do?
C: I guess I wouldn't be angry because I expect it to happen, and I would get two containers of milk!

In this example, Pierre's rigid schema of how his wife **should** behave resulted in an 11-year argument and no problem solving around the issue. We have often noticed that people do not try to solve a problem that they think should not exist. Pierre will not think of a new way to get cold milk for his breakfast as long as he believes that his wife **must** behave differently. Once he surrenders the demand and acknowledges the reality, he is freed up to solve the problem. The short-term advantage to the demand is Pierre deludes himself that the reality is the way that he wants it to be and he can continue to keep alive his desired reality.

Ellis (1994) has identified English words such as "should," "ought," "must," and "have to" as representing demandingness. These words have several meanings in the Oxford English dictionary (2008). One set of meanings concerns activities or things that are preferable, desirable, or beneficial. A second set of definitions identifies "shoulds" as the first premise in a conditional syllogism. If you want X, you should do Y. The third meaning refers to some reality. Such as, if you let go of the pen it must drop down to the desk. In English, we use the same words to represent desirable events and reality. General semantics theory (Korzybski, 1933), which Ellis (1992) claimed as a basis for REBT, posits that humans become confused and dysfunctional when they use words imprecisely. This is most likely to occur when using a word with several meanings. Thus, people make preferences into laws of physics.

Each year, professionals come from around the world to the Albert Ellis Institute for professional training. Over the last decade, one of us (RD) has asked colleagues from other countries whether their languages similarly use the same words for "should," "ought," "must," and "have to" for preferences and realities. I have received affirmative responses from professionals speaking Arabic, Chinese, Croatian, Dutch, French, German, Hindi, Hungarian, Italian, Polish, Portuguese, Romanian, Russian, Serbian, Spanish, Thai, Ukrainian, Urdu, and Vietnamese. Could humans all over the globe confuse preferences and reality and use similar words such as "should," "ought," "must," and "have to" in their languages to represent or confuse these two concepts?

Once people understand and work against the irrationality of demandingness, we say that they "accept reality." The concept of acceptance has become popular in the therapy literature. A search on *PsycInfo* of the word "acceptance" in the title of publications when psychotherapy appears in the abstract produces some interesting results. Articles with "acceptance" appeared rarely before 1985. A large increase occurred in the late 1990s, and another jump occurred after 2000. Many of these publications have resulted from the recent popularity of Hayes' Acceptance and Commitment Therapy (ACT) (Hayes, 2011). The word acceptance also appears often in articles about Dialectical Behavior Therapy (DBT). Although some differences exist in Ellis's conceptualization of acceptance compared with the way ACT (Ciarrochi, Robb, and Godsell, 2005) and DBT (Robins and Chapman, 2004) use the concept of acceptance, these differences are small and reflect a clear influence of Ellis's ideas of acceptance in modern psychotherapy. In ACT, acceptance refers more to accepting one's emotional experience and interfering thoughts and is less focused on external reality (which reflects the meta or secondary level—see Chapter 8).

Clients often resist giving up their demand and replacing it with acceptance because they confuse acceptance with approval. Dictionaries often refer to approval and agreement as synonyms for acceptance. This is an unfortunate complication of the meaning of the word "acceptance." In our use of the term "acceptance," we do not think people have to approve or agree with the negative aspects of themselves and/or their lives. We emphasize the acknowledgement of their reality, thereby circumventing emotional disturbance, and leaving clients in a better position to change what they can. It probably would have been more beneficial if the field of psychotherapy used the term "acknowledgement" instead of "acceptance."

AWFULIZING

Awfulizing or catastrophizing beliefs are characterized by exaggerated nega-tive evaluations and thoughts regarding something about oneself, others, or the world. The English language represents this idea by the words "terrible," "awful," or "catastrophic." Psychologists and cognitive behavior therapists often use the term "catastrophizing" as a verb. Such thinking often involves predicting hyper-negative outcomes to a situation that has no basis in reality. Rorer (1989) suggested that when people hold such beliefs they fail to define just what awful or terrible is, or what catastrophe will occur. They are uncertain of the outcome and define it as extremely bad. Rorer believed awfulizing is subjective. People often arbitrarily assign an extremely negative valence to an event and never test reality to see if the occurrence of the event brings such dire consequences. Mark Twain said, "I've suffered a great many catastrophes in my life. Most of them never happened" (Twain, 1971/1972). This best summarizes the empirical argument against awfuliz-ing thinking. Rational thinking would acknowledge that some things are bad, but emphasize that they are survivable. Traditionally, REBT has posited that these types of thoughts are related to anxiety disorders (Burgess, 1990; Ellis, 1962; 1994).

Challenging awfulizing beliefs can lead to an alliance rupture because the cli-ent could erroneously conclude from the therapist's comments that the therapist does not understand or empathize with the client. Clients who have experienced trauma are particularly sensitive to feeling invalidated when therapists challenge such ideas. It is best to target these thoughts when the stimuli's evaluation is an extreme evaluation, not a belief concerning a real trauma.

We have noticed that clients with catastrophic thinking vary along a continuum of negative activating events. Some clients attach such thoughts to life events that are truly not terrible. Some clients we have seen have catastrophized events such as failing a test, not getting a date, experiencing a romantic breakup, missing an appointment, looking foolish, or not having their favorite meal in a restaurant. These examples represent a prediction of the hyper-negative outcomes to a situa-tion that have no basis in reality. On the other hand, we have had clients who have displayed catastrophizing to truly bad, life-threatening, painful, or psychologically distressing life circumstances. Consider those clients we have seen with terminal cancer, developmentally delayed children, or chronic pain; or those clients who have experienced the death of a child, or who have been sexually assaulted. The nature of their thinking does have some basis in reality. These life events are very bad and in most social groups, social consensus would validate and confirm their use of the terms "terrible" and "awful." We think that therapists should evaluate the irrationality of catastrophic thinking differently in these two extreme groups.

Challenging the catastrophic thinking in the group with bad but minor events will focus on whether the event is as bad and as disruptive as the person thinks it is. In this group, we often encounter a combination of awfulizing and demandingness. It is awful that the restaurant does not have my favorite dish and they *should* have it. For the clients who have experienced a traumatic event, we recommend that you focus on the dysfunctionality of the catastrophizing and not the negative valence of the event.

Challenging the catastrophic thinking of clients with real trauma and very negative events is problematic. All of us have found that disputing such thoughts has resulted in the most negative images of REBT and caused frequent alliance ruptures with clients. Clients often have social consensus that their trauma is terrible and awful. Attempting to convince the client that their Activating Event is not as bad as they think it is, or is less than "100% bad," or just is not as awful as they think it is, have been less than helpful strategies. In such cases, we have switched our strategy to challenging the frustration intolerance or demandingness about such terrible events. Clients who have experienced true trauma often hold one of these two other IBs: "I cannot stand to live with the trauma or the results of the trauma," and "The trauma should not have occurred." Such clients can learn to believe that although traumas have occurred in their lives, they are strong enough to survive and tolerate them, and that the world is a place where traumatic things do occur.

The concept of catastrophizing is used most frequently in the scientific literature in health psychology and pain management. A recent search of *PsycInfo* for the term "catastrophizing" resulted in more than 430 scientific citations. Most of these involved the role of catastrophizing about one's pain or medical symptoms in different types of medical patients or patients recovering from surgical and medical procedures. Overwhelming evidence supports the role of catastrophizing in increasing the experience of pain and medical symptoms and slowing the recovery of physiological and motor functions from illness. The recommendation to target catastrophic thinking with such patients is strongly supported.

For example, when individuals receive in vivo exposure treatment for musculoskeletal pain, those with high catastrophizing do not benefit from the treatment (Linton, Nicholas, MacDonald, Boersma, Bergbom, Maher, and Refshauge, 2011). Perhaps the catastrophizing results in the client failing to focus on the pain and its associated stimuli, which interferes with the exposure treatment. For patients with physical injuries who are removed from the workforce, some evidence suggests that catastrophizing leads to expectations about the difficulty of returning to work (Fadyl and McPherson, 2008). Catastrophizing was a good predictor of heightened nighttime pain reported in patients who underwent knee replacement (Edwards, Haythornthwaite, Smith, Klick, and Katz, 2009). A review of studies of patients with cancer pain (Zaza and Baine, 2002) found that three out of four studies examined showed that catastrophizing leads to more intense pain in such patients, which leads to increased distress, and decreased levels of social activity and support.

FRUSTRATION INTOLERANCE

One of us (RD) predicted that fifty years after his death, Albert Ellis would be most remembered for his contribution to psychology for his theoretical and clinical concept of frustration intolerance (FI) (DiGiuseppe, 1991). Ellis (2003a; 2003b) proposed that humans have beliefs concerning how much frustration and discomfort they can and are willing to tolerate. One could consider this an expectation of one's strength or ability to sustain effort, survive, or to strive in the face of frustration, discomfort, or pain. People have beliefs regarding their strength and the effort they can muster. The disturbed emotion associated with such irrational thoughts Ellis called "discomfort anxiety." Such beliefs imply that an individual cannot stand something he or she finds frustrating or that the individual does not have the endurance to survive in its presence. For example, someone who has *too* many e-mails in his/her inbox might say, "I cannot stand having to respond to all these people. It is *too* hard to have all this work to do." These beliefs are illogical because, short of dying, one has actually tolerated whatever one claims one cannot stand. On the other hand, the emotion a person would experience to the rational thought that one is strong enough to persist despite the frustration is not represented in English or—as far as we know—in other languages. We could imagine that people in this situation would have an attitude of commitment and endurance, and the behavioral C of persistence. The ability to withstand frustration would lead to what we usually refer to as self-control.

Frustration intolerance beliefs are often triggered by negative emotional experiences and then lead to secondary emotional disturbance (see Chapter 8). Ellis claimed he borrowed the idea that thoughts about emotions and thoughts about thoughts could lead to more disturbance from Korzybski (1933). Ellis also often commented on the work of Raimy (1975) who thought that much of disturbance resulted from failures to accept emotional discomfort and from catastrophizing about one's original symptoms. Harrington (2011a) reviewed the history of this idea and noted that other psychologists have focused on the importance of displaying high frustration tolerance to achieve psychological adjustment. Freud posited that human's neurotic defenses were strategies aimed at reducing anxiety in situations that people considered unbearable. Dollard and Miller (1950) attempted to combine psychodynamic and learning theory and hypothesized that neurotic behavior was often an attempt to avoid negative experiences. They proposed the approach-avoidance conflict as a situation where people had positive attraction to a situation but also avoidance of some negative aspects of approaching the desired stimuli. Amsel (1990) proposed that frustration of anticipated rewards could lead to an aversive state. Depending on the reinforcement history, this aversive state could motivate avoidance or persistent efforts to achieve the reward. If persistence had been reinforced, the motivation to avoid this aversive state was diminished and frustration tolerance was increased. Eisenberger (1992) proposed an operant conditioning model of frustration intolerance. He suggested that all effort to achieve reinforcement involved some discomfort. Organisms had the choice to tolerate this discomfort to obtain a reward.

Although Ellis (2003a, 2003b) originally called this type of irrational belief "low frustration tolerance" (LFT), we prefer the term Frustration Intolerance (FI). The term FI appears more appropriate than Ellis's term LFT. We owe this change in name to the Australian psychologist Dr. Marie Joyce. Joyce pointed out that the term LFT can invalidate clients' difficulties (Joyce, personal communication, 1999). While Dr. Joyce was working with parents of neurologically disabled children, she found the parents had difficulty following behavior management plans. The parents often complained that the strategies were too hard and that they could not stand being so consistent with their children when they misbehaved. When Dr. Joyce challenged the parents' low frustration tolerance, they felt misunderstood. Dr. Joyce admitted that these parents had more difficulty raising their children than most other parents. In fact, they had been tolerating more frustration than most parents had. The problem was not that the parents had low frustration tolerance, but that they did not have *sufficient* frustration tolerance to accomplish a most difficult goal. They needed to have *greater frustration tolerance* than the average parent to get their children to behave better. Dr. Joyce suggested that REBT change the title of this type of irrationality to frustration intolerance. It represents the unwillingness to sustain or tolerate the degree of frustration necessary to achieve one's goals. To suggest to someone who has experienced a disability or trauma that they have low frustration tolerance invalidates the person's attempts to overcome and cope with adversity (Muran and DiGiuseppe, 1994). We would encourage clients to tolerate above average frustration to accomplish their specific goals. We acknowledge that they have to endure greater difficulty to achieve their goals.

Ellis's concept of FI is represented in other forms of CBT, including Dialectical Behavior Therapy (DBT) (Linehan, 1993). DBT posits that many symptoms of borderline personality disorder are an attempt to assuage the patient's intolerance of negative emotions. The therapy includes teaching the client strategies to tolerate such emotions. Acceptance and Commitment Therapy (ACT) (Hayes et al., 1999) has proposed that most psychological symptoms result from experiential avoidance; that is, self-defeating behaviors that avoid the internal experience of thoughts and emotions. ACT teaches the client to engage in valued, rewarding behavior despite these discomforting internal experiences. ACT does not focus on tolerating and accepting the external discomforts that might be necessary to attain the rewards as REBT would do as well (Amsel, 1990; Eisenberger, 1992). Baumeister et al. (1994) suggested it is often the discomforts resulting from threats to self-esteem that motivate dysfunctional behavior. That is, aversive feelings stemming from self-awareness of one's limitations and faults motivates people to change from pursuing long-term goals to seeking short-term relief from emotional distress.

Harrington (2005b) developed a frustration intolerance scale and distinguished among four types of FI. The first type was *Emotional Intolerance*, which reflects intolerance of emotional distress. The second type was *Entitlement Intolerance*, which reflects ideas about immediate gratification and tolerating unfairness. The third type was *Discomfort Intolerance*, which referred to ideas that life should be easy, comfortable, and free of hassle. The fourth was *Achievement Intolerance*, which reflects the frustration following failure to achieve a goal. Distinguishing these different types of FI is clinically useful because they relate to different clinical problems (Harrington, 2005b). Discomfort Intolerance was strongly correlated with avoiding one's perceived behavioral responsibilities. Emotional Intolerance was related to relying on self-medication for relieving one's emotions problems. So far, alcohol use has not been shown to have a relationship with any of Harrington's FI scales; we still need research to uncover which type of FI beliefs lead to addictive behavior. The relationship of FI types and self-harm was complex. Entitlement Intolerance led to anger and then to self-harm; while Emotional Intolerance led to anxiety and then to self-harm. The different FI types related to different emotions. Entitlement Intolerance was uniquely associated with anger; Discomfort Intolerance was related with depressed mood, and Emotional Intolerance was related with anxiety. These exact results were replicated in a Serbian sample by Stankovic and Vukosavljevic-Gvozden (2009). It is important to note that the cognitive process of FI is the same in all four of Harrington's types. It is the content of the IB that makes up the component that leads to the different clinical problems and emotions.

Harrington cautions that there can be hidden problems in challenging FI beliefs. The terms tolerance and acceptance can be misinterpreted by clients. People may misconstrue the rational antidote of FI, that is, acceptance or tolerance, as giving up, submitting, or passively accepting events. However, the rational thought that one can stand the discomfort of hard work and confronting problems can strengthen one's resolve to overcome problems and achieve difficult tasks. Clients could confuse tolerance of other people's misconduct as condoning bad behavior. In REBT, rational tolerance implies that although we may dislike a situation and want to change it, achieving our goals requires us to tolerate frustration and discomfort. Although some things might be unchangeable, or require considerable time and effort to change, we do not know they are unchangeable until we try hard to change them.

GLOBAL EVALUATION OF HUMAN WORTH

Global negative evaluations of human worth can result in depression or guilt if one applies the evaluations to oneself or in anger and contempt if one applies the evaluation to another. These beliefs in human worthlessness cannot be true because a person cannot be rated as either good or bad, as it is not possible for one to be completely good or bad due to the complexity of human beings (Ellis, 1994; 2005c). Instead, ratings should be restricted to people's behaviors. As was mentioned in Chapter 1, one can see the influence of General Semantics (Korzybski, 1933) in these ideas. It is more logical and certainly healthier to state, "I performed poorly with my teaching," instead of saying in addition, "Therefore, I am a bad person." Ellis's position was a philosophical one. He proposed that people take seriously the Preamble to the U.S. Constitution or the Judeo-Christian religious tradition, both of which state that all persons are created equal, the former by government and the latter by God. REBT tries to teach people to rate their deeds and not themselves. As Mahatma Gandhi said, "Hate the sin, but love the sinner." Self-evaluations are replaced with what Ellis called Unconditional Self-Acceptance (USA).

REBT opposes programs that attempt to build a person's self-esteem. Self-esteem is a combination of two different cognitive processes. The first is self-efficacy, which is the belief in one's ability to perform a task. If you examine the items on self-esteem scales, you will notice that many items reflect this type of statement. REBT theory has no objection to this idea because it evaluates one's behavior and not the self. The second cognitive content in self-esteem is global evaluation of the self. This idea involves conclusions about one's worth as a person. Humans (and psychotherapists) often get these two concepts confused and evaluate their worth, or lack of it, based on perceived self-efficacy or the lack of it.

Self-esteem interventions teach people either that they are special or good because they are efficacious or directly teach people unwarranted self-efficacy. That is, that they are good at certain tasks regardless of the evidence. REBT points out three difficulties with such interventions. First, such interventions teach people that they have self-worth because of self-efficacy. This may work for the moment; but what if their skills falter or they are surpassed by other more talented peers? The mental health of people who receive such interventions may be on an emotional roller coaster. They feel good when they perform well; however, that feeling is paired with anxiety based on the idea that they must continue to do well to remain worthwhile. Alternatively, they feel depressed when they perform badly because they rate themselves as worthless based on their performance.

Second, self-esteem interventions often teach self-efficacy beyond the person's demonstrated skills. Clients are likely to become emotionally upset when they no longer get feedback that they are performing effectively. People can develop an addiction to the constant need for positive feedback to keep bolstering their self-worth, which is based on their performance. Third, self-esteem programs fail to provide coping strategies for poor performance. Because most people fail some of the time on the way to success, or fail more often than they succeed, people need to cope with doing poorly. Consider some examples that you can provide for clients who believe that they must always do well to have worth. Babe Ruth, the famous baseball player, set a record for hitting home runs. He struck out 1331 times. Thomas Edison tried 89 different times to create the electric light bulb before he got it to work. Steve Jobs, the founder of Apple Computers was fired. In addition, our mentor Albert Ellis had to be rejected by 99 women before he got a date. All famous successful people have had to deal with failure. If they condemned themselves each time they failed, they most likely would not have progressed to their success. Thus, REBT works toward Unconditional Self-Acceptance (USA). USA refers to the acknowledgement of one's fallibility and flaws, without rating one's worth either positively or negatively. USA involves the focus on one's performance and using this information to decide on future behaviors without getting distracted by thoughts about oneself as a global entity. USA does not mean that one approves of, likes, or ignores one's flaws and weaknesses.

Box 3.1

Global, stable, internal attributions for failure (e.g., "I'm dyslexic," or "I'm too bad a writer to do this paper.") lead to depression because we condemn ourselves for having these qualities. This assumption results in REBT therapists using a strategy that is a little different from other cognitive therapists.

For example, if a client was brain-damaged by a stroke and could no longer do certain things, how could you help the client to feel better?

Many therapists, such as Seligman (1978) and Weiner (1985), who have advocated attributional interventions would try to show the client what s/he *could* do. However, what if s/he still could not do the things that were important to him or her? These therapists would probably try to convince the client that s/he could do *other* things. Although their strategies might be somewhat helpful, they would also miss the core philosophical point of REBT: "I'm an OK person even though I can't do [and probably will never be able to do] what I used to do and what others can do easily. I am still an OK worthwhile person."

Case Example

Here is the case of Paolo, which we will use to draw distinctions among the four types of irrational beliefs and their rational counterparts. Paolo was a thirty-eight-year-old Brazilian emigrant to New York. He sought therapy because of his anxiety and insomnia. Clinical assessment revealed that his primary imperative/demand was that his wife must love him and she must never leave him. For Paolo, the primary imperative/demanding irrational belief was "My wife must never leave me."

Paolo endorsed all three derivative irrational beliefs. For the awfulizing derivative, he thought, "It would be awful and terrible if she left me." For the frustration intolerance derivative, he thought, "I could not tolerate it if she left me, and I could not live without her." He also endorsed the global evaluation of worth of both himself and his wife. He had the derivative self-downing thought, "If my wife left me, I would be a loser." He became angry with her when she engaged in solitary activities or seemed preoccupied with other tasks. These events led him to draw the negative inference that, "She is distant because she is leaving me." He had the other downing derivative, "She is a worthless piece of garbage if she leaves me."

Paolo's irrational beliefs led to anxiety, which resulted in clinging behaviors that were pushing his wife away. He also had difficulty sleeping at night and concentrating at work during the day because his mind was flooded with irrational ideas about her leaving. Paolo experienced depression, which resulted in ignoring his wife, which was sabotaging the relationship. When he condemned her, he became angry and he yelled and screamed at her, which created further distance in their relationship. As we can see in Paolo's case, irrational beliefs are not helping him attain his goals. When people think in absolutes and become shackled by upsetting emotions, they are hardly in a position to work at maximizing pleasure and minimizing discomfort. They are directed to short-term relief of their disturbance (clinging behaviors when he was anxious, ignoring his wife when he was depressed, and yelling when he was angry) instead of achieving their long-term goals. Paolo will not be able to attain his goal of a happy life with his wife if he is continually disturbed about his wife leaving him.

Now consider the rational beliefs that the therapist constructed with Paolo. For the imperative/demand, the RB was "I strongly do not want my wife to leave me, but I can accept (not like) it if she did leave." The RB for the awfulizing derivative would be, "It would be *really* bad if she left me, but it would not be the end of my life." The RB belief for the FI derivative would be, "I would hate it if she left me, but I am strong enough and could stand to live through the pain." The RB for the derivative of the global evaluation of him would be, "If she left me that would be a loss, but it would not make me a loser. My worth as a person is not dependent on being in a relationship." The RB for the derivative belief of the global evaluation of his wife would be, "It would be painful if she left me, but I can accept her even though I do not like what she did." Compare these statements to each criterion of irrational beliefs. This can help you understand what makes rational beliefs rational.

A rational belief is internally consistent; it is logical and coherent. Note that a rational belief is not merely a logical belief; logic is necessary but not a sufficient ingredient in identifying a rational philosophy.

A rational belief is empirically verifiable; one can support it with evidence. Consider our example above: we could prove that unpleasant effects would result from the client's wife leaving him. Presumably, he would lose many pleasant things.

A rational belief is not absolute; instead, it is conditional or relativistic. A rational belief is usually stated as a desire, hope, want, wish, or preference, reflecting a desiring rather than a demanding philosophy, and it includes acceptance of not achieving the goal. Can you see how the example above reflects a preference rather than a demand? Paolo thinks, "I'd prefer it if my wife stayed in our marriage, but I can accept it if she doesn't."

A rational belief elicits adaptive emotions. Thus, RBs can lead to negative feelings that may range from mild to strong, but which are nonetheless functional and healthy and motivate coping. This is an important distinction, because a common misconception about REBT is that rational thinking leads to the absence of emotion. Quite the contrary; it is untrue that a lack of emotion would be helpful or rational. Adaptive emotions serve as motivators to problem solving. Returning to our example, when Paolo thinks about his wife leaving him, he probably feels concerned and sad but not clinically anxious or depressed. When Paolo thinks rationally, he can react by (1) looking at the activating event to see if it can be changed; (2) making the best of his life with the change; and (3) moving on and finding a new mate. Unhealthy emotions hinder these outcomes.

Rational beliefs help us attain our goals. Thus, RBs are congruent with satisfaction in living, minimizing intrapsychic conflict and conflict with the environment, enabling affiliation and involvement with others, and growing toward a vital absorption in some personally fulfilling endeavor. Rational beliefs provide us with the freedom to pursue goals in a less fearful, noncondemning fashion and allow us to take the risks that may be involved in attaining these goals. From our sample of rational beliefs, we conclude that Paolo's goal is to live as happily as possible, and this cannot be done if he is clinically depressed or suffers from anxiety. In addition, if the strong demands and negative global evaluations about his wife leaving resulted in unhealthy anger, his behavior would perhaps drive his wife and other potential mates away.

We have identified REBT theory and outlined the differences between irrational and rational beliefs. The next chapter will identify the basic techniques of REBT.

PART TWO

General Therapeutic Strategies

4

The A-B-C Model and Teaching
Clients the B to C Connection

The therapeutic system evolved by Ellis over the years is a pragmatic and efficient clinical discipline, useful with moderately dysfunctional neurotic adults, severely disturbed adults, psychotic individuals, and children as young as eight years. The therapist takes a persuasive, active-directive role, yet client and therapist share in working toward common goals. REBT uses a psycho-educational approach, and encourages the client to do reading and homework assignments to help the client incorporate the concepts and ideas that he or she learned in the therapy sessions into living and enjoyment outside them.

REBT does not claim to undo the mental and emotional effects of physiologically induced dysfunctions, such as those attributable to hormonal imbalances, seizure states, or affective illnesses or psychoses that are basically heritable neurochemical problems. It is important to note, however, that clients often have a neurotic overlay to their neurochemical problems that is amenable to rational emotive behavior therapy. For example, clients with bipolar illness, even when taking appropriate medications and not in a depressed state, often worry about when their depression will strike again. Clients with schizophrenia often feel ashamed of their hallucinations or delusions, and fear the onset of a new psychotic episode. Although REBT does not cure the underlying neurological or psychotic illness, it can be extremely helpful to teach the clients to deal with emotional problems *about* being ill and this may be helpful in managing the illness when it is active. When used in conjunction with psychotropic drugs, REBT may be distinctly valuable in helping to ameliorate the course of such illnesses (Ellis and Abrahms, 1978).

Box 4.1

As you begin to practice REBT, you will find it easier to begin with individual adult clients. REBT is useful with children, couples, families, and groups, but each of these populations or formats presents specialized problems. Trainees have told us that REBT requires their intense concentration at first, so that having children or more than one client in the room makes the job more difficult. Your learning will proceed better if, at first, you start with one reasonable, not too disturbed client. Then you can progress to more difficult clients, young clients who require more developmental considerations, and then more than one client in the room.

THE A-B-C MODEL

Ellis conceived a conceptual schema to illustrate the role of thinking processes in emotional disturbance, the ABCs of REBT. In this system, the A stands for **A**ctivating event (or activating experience), which is usually our perception of some obnoxious or unfortunate environmental occurrence. The C stands for the unhealthy, dysfunctional emotional and behavioral **C**onsequences and not the healthy, adaptive emotions and behaviors; it is this uncomfortable emotion that often propels the client to the psychotherapist's office. The B is the client's **B**elief system. The belief system consists of two parts: rational and irrational beliefs. It is the presence of the irrational beliefs and the absence or weak endorsement of the rational cognitions that will be the therapist's focus. We use the term "belief system" because people usually have an imperative/schematic demand and one or more of the derivative irrational beliefs that lead to their disturbed **C**. Because REBT philosophy assumes that a major goal in life is to be reasonably happy, it also assumes that such disturbing cognitions and emotions are incompatible with this goal. When clients believe that the **A** event is directly responsible for **C** (their emotional upsets), they are ignoring, or more likely are unaware of, the presence and impact of their cognitions, attitudes, philosophies, and beliefs on their emotions and behaviors. Clients in psychotherapy are experiencing debilitating and disturbing emotions. If they are disturbing themselves, presumably they can also refuse to disturb themselves. In other words, when bad **A**ctivating events occur, nonpsychotic people typically will feel some negative emotions. They can influence whether their emotional **C**onsequence is a disturbed, dysfunctional one, or a functional, adaptive emotion. The way they think influences whether or not they end up suffering. It is a primary task of the therapist to teach clients that their psychological problems result from the cognitive processes of irrational thinking.

This basic principle is easy enough to state and often difficult for clients to grasp. Our everyday language contains many examples antagonistic to this concept. How often do we say or hear phrases such as, "*He* made me so mad!" or "*It* has got me so upset!" In these sentences, the object or the A is the actor and cause of the emotional disturbance. Clients will not attempt to change something that their language implies is not in their control. More correctly, we could say, "*I* made myself mad about him" and "*I* got myself upset about it." How strange these revised statements sound to our ears! Yet they share an important concept: we are responsible for our own emotional disturbance. Thus, disturbed emotions are not foisted upon us, or inserted magically into us, or caused by the events around us. However, our disturbed emotions result from something we actively do. Specifically, disturbed emotions result largely from what we tell ourselves. Clients come to therapy firmly believing that A causes C, and this belief is reinforced by every significant person with whom they come into contact. You, the therapist, will be teaching a quite revolutionary idea, that B largely determines C, and your first responsibility is to help your client understand this concept.

Box 4.2

Before you become adept at teaching the **A–B–C** model to your client, you can practice at training your own ears. Eventually, when you listen to your clients, their words will sort rather automatically into the three categories.

One way to begin to train yourself is to divide your therapy notes into a three-column format. Begin now. Divide the page into three segments, and label one **A**, another **C**, and a third (perhaps larger) as **B**. You will find that clients usually begin by telling you about their **A** or **C**. Once you have filled in one of these columns, proceed to the next. Thus, if you know **A** (what happened), ask for **C** (how the client felt); if the client begins by expressing affect, the **C** ("I was anxious"), ask for the trigger or context (the A). When you have **A** and **C**, proceed to ask for **B**.

If you can make a copy of your notes on the spot, you can hand one sheet to the client and go over the columns with him or her. For example, "You see, Mary, here is the **A–B–C** model. Let's look at what I've written down today. See, these are your thoughts—and these are your feelings—and this is what happened." You will be surprised at how often clients find this organizational strategy to be helpful.

At the Albert Ellis Institute, we have created two forms that will help you learn this. The first, which appears in Appendix 1, is a sheet like the one we just described. We give it to our trainees during our *practica*. While they are listening to a peer counselling session or a recording of a therapy session, they listen to each thing a client says and assign each statement to an element in the model and write it down in the appropriate column. This active listening and quick identification of the content of the client's verbalizations helps people learn to identify the correct category. We have also developed a therapy session progress form that uses a similar system, which appears in Appendix 2. The therapist identifies the main **A**, **B**, and **C** statements uttered by the client in the sessions. They can use this to keep track of what they worked on in each session.

TEACHING CLIENTS THAT EVENTS DO NOT CAUSE UNHEALTHY/DYSFUNCTIONAL EMOTIONS

How can the therapist illustrate to clients that internal rather than external factors are primarily affecting their feelings and actions? We call the theory that **B**eliefs largely contribute to disturbed emotional **C**onsequences, the **B** to **C** connection. Clients who continue to see their Activating events as the cause of their disturbed feelings are said to hold onto the A to C connection. One way to explain the B to C connection is to ask clients how a hundred people similar to themselves would react to their problem. For example, a client has just discovered that his wife, whom he loves dearly, would like to get a divorce, and he is very depressed. The therapist might ask him how he thinks a hundred different men would react to the same event. Clients usually respond with, "Well, most of them would be depressed." (If the client says instead, "100%," the therapist can point out how unrealistic such an estimate is.) The therapist persists and asks, "But what percent would be depressed—40%, 50%, 60%?" After the client has answered, the therapist leads the client to examine other possible reactions that the remainder of the population might have. In this way, the client is faced with the fact, by his own admission, that while possibly 50% of the sample might be depressed, some of the remainder would only be sad, others would be a little displeased, some would be neutral, a few relieved, and a small percentage would be downright exuberant. At this point, when other emotional options have been set forth, the client is confronted with the crucial question, "If activating events (A) do, in fact, cause emotional consequences (C), then how do you explain that the same event can lead to so many different emotional reactions within this hypothetical sample?" Most clients respond at this point with something like, "Well, I guess A doesn't really cause C," or "They're all different, so they react differently." The about-to-be-divorced client has given the therapist an opening, for he has mildly and ever so slightly hinted that A did not cause C. The therapist can reinforce the client for reaching this insight and for doing so on his own, and then explain further, "That's correct; they're all different; they all reacted differently because they thought differently about it." The therapist can now elaborate further on this point.

A story such as the following may help to make the A-B-C connections clear: Three corporate vice-presidents were fired from their jobs at the same time, when their corporation was taken over by another company. All three executives loved their jobs equally, and all three were at the same salary level. The activating event was virtually identical for them. Do you think all three VPs reacted the same way? Actually, they did not. One said, "This is terrible. I can't stand it and I will never recover," and he felt depressed. Another said, "I don't like this, and it's a big hassle, but it will give me the opportunity and the push I needed to go into business for myself," and she felt frustrated and determined to rebound. And the third said, "Well, this is certainly really bad and certainly not what I wanted to happen, but I'll get through it in some way," and this person felt very sad and very disappointed. Can you see how these people would *feel* quite different emotions about the same events because of the way they thought about the event?

TEACHING THE CLIENT THAT OTHER PEOPLE DO NOT CAUSE OUR UNHEALTHY/DYSFUNCTIONAL EMOTIONS

Commonly, clients object that other people in their environment do, in fact, cause them to be upset. This concept is embedded in the linguistic structure of our everyday experience. "I make myself so angry when you say that" is a phrase that sounds strange, while "You make me so mad" sounds "normal."

Again, a story may help the client to see the B to C connection. Three kids have cut class, gotten caught, and are now in trouble. They arrive at the principal's office. Do they all react the same way when the principal comes out of his office and scowls at them? As it turns out, one kid is frightened, the second is angry, and the third is concerned and decides not to get in trouble anymore.

The use of hypothetical situations and analogies can help to get the point across. As an experiment, the therapist might say:

"OK, Maria, if people can cause you to have an unhealthy emotion let's see if I can do it right now." (*pause*) "Maria I really dislike you and I want you to feel depressed forever. Now—what emotion are you feeling?"

Analogies such as the following might be useful:

Maria reported that her mother complains whenever Maria wants to visit friends.

C: She makes me feel so guilty!

T: No, Maria, they are your guilt buttons. She may be pushing on them, but you're in charge of the keyboard. If you learn a more healthy way to think to yourself about what she says, she could push all the keys she wants and you would still control your emotions.

Another way of disputing the notion that other people give us feelings is to point out the incongruity between this notion and the belief that many people have, particularly religious ones, in free will. Most religions and cultures teach people to believe that human beings are different from the rest of the animals because human beings have intellect and free will. Thus, they strongly profess independent action and self-determination. The therapist could ask: "If someone made you angry, you therefore had no say in it. Well, how much do you believe in free will and self-determination?" By phrasing the question in this way, the therapist is pointing out to the client that he or she has some choice. If something negative happens, you will feel negatively about it, but you have a choice as to whether you experience a healthy, adaptive emotion or an unhealthy emotion. You can decide to be self-defeatingly angry and miserable, or to feel constructively annoyed and motivated to do something about it.

There are a number of other ways of illustrating that the A-causes-C hypothesis is incorrect. As an example of an alternate strategy, the therapist might say:

"Well, Abdul, if your father really causes your anger, we'd better terminate therapy. You see, if the cause of the anger is outside you, how can I help you? You'd better send your father to me instead, and let me change him!" Abdul might say yes, the therapist should treat his father! Then the therapist can focus on the willingness of Abdul's father to change. Most likely dad will not be willing to change to assuage Abdul's anger, and this will bring the focus back to Abdul controlling his anger.

The following example involves teaching this point to young children:

T: Jeremy, it sounds to me as if you believe everyone controls you. No matter what happens to you, it's someone else's fault. They make you angry, they make you sad, they make you unhappy. Well, I have a great idea! Why don't we create a

Jeremy videogame? You know, we'll have this character and with the controller we can make him happy, we can make him sad, we can make him depressed, we can make him dance, sing, or fight. We'll control the character just like in Super Mario Brothers. Other kids will play the game and make Jeremy react. What do you think about these ideas?

C: (laughs) That's funny. But that's not how it is. I don't sound that way!

T: Oh, yes you do. You sound as if you believe you are a videogame character and other people control you.

Ed Garcia, formerly co-director of training at the Albert Ellis Institute, used dramatic procedures to point out to his clients their self-imposed powerlessness:

C: (Complaining about how other people controlled her, made her feel badly, etc.)

T: (Opens desk drawer, pulls out a large box or bag, and hands it to client.)

C: What's this?

T: This is your power. I'm giving it back to you. Obviously you've been walking around without it for a long time. You keep telling me how this person made you angry, and this person made you upset, and this person made you love him, and this person made you this and that. You go on and on telling me how other people are controlling your life. You must have left your power here one day when you ran out in a hurry. I really think you had better take it back now. Maybe you can get some more control over your life.

Once clients grasp the idea that their thoughts affect what emotions they feel, the next task for the therapist is to show them that changing their thinking can lead to changes in their emotions. We commonly script our verbal behaviors in everyday life to affect *other* people's reactions; we preplan in order to maximize the probability that we will get the reaction we want. This planning is customary and socially acceptable. We rarely spend any time, however, examining and preplanning how we talk to ourselves. It could be pointed out to clients that how we talk to ourselves will affect our own reactions as surely as how we speak to others affects their reactions. Similarly, we often ask ourselves, "How can I say this *to him* [or her] so that my message will be clear and I will have communicated correctly?" How often do we ask ourselves the same questions about our internal dialogues?

TEACHING CLIENTS THAT PAST EVENTS DO NOT CAUSE UNHEALTHY/DYSFUNCTIONAL EMOTIONS

Often clients find it difficult to understand that the correction of current thinking patterns is a prime focus of therapy. The difficulty arises because many clients believe that their past history and experiences cause their current emotions and behavior, and thus, they believe they are either helpless to change or that they must first discover the "roots" of their disturbance. If clients have spent years in a therapy that emphasized this belief or they simply subscribe to the widespread belief that the past fixedly determines the present, it may take a lot of persuasion to change their focus. Unfortunately, it is not only former therapy clients who suffer from the belief that the past fixedly determines the present. It is this basic misunderstanding of Freudian theory that seems to have permeated Western culture. It is popularized on television and in the movies, and is heard from even very sophisticated clients. A therapist might say to a client who held this belief, "If you had a cold would it be helpful to learn where you caught it, or do you want to get over it?" A quote from Sigmund Freud is often helpful in getting clients to see the role of their current thinking about the past in maintaining dysfunctional emotions. Freud said, "The past is only important because you continue to carry it around with you." (Freud, 1965). As part of this therapeutic obstacle, clients may believe that change is impossible because of their past. A client might assert, for example, "But I can't change; I've always been this way!" The therapeutic challenge then involves correcting the client's language and thereby the concept. For example, the therapist could respond:

"You mean you haven't changed *so far.* Even if that's been true up to now, does that mean you won't change tomorrow? That's my business, you know—showing you how to change."

The literature on developmental issues in personality suggests that some aspects of our style of behavior are relatively fixed; we refer to these fixed qualities as "temperament." It would be a fruitless endeavor to try and change one's basic temperament. These qualities, which may be comprised of biological predispositions in conjunction with prolonged early training experiences in our families of origin, may mean that change is *difficult* or that it may take a great deal of *time* or require the use *of multiple strategies.* The fact that change may be difficult does not mean that change is impossible, however. Yet the client who firmly believes that he or she *cannot* change may be creating a self-fulfilling prophecy, which ironically will be self-defeating. An instructive analogy might be the therapist saying:

"If you go into a ball game believing, 'I can't win, I can't win, I can't win,' you will find that attitude very self-defeating. If you go into therapy believing, 'I can't change; my early experiences fixed me permanently,' that's also self-defeating and you may not change."

A useful challenge to the notion that the past determines present distress is to point out that although past events may have had an important role in contributing to past distress, they continue to be a problem only because the client continues to think about them in the same way. It is present cognitions, not past events, that affect us. Thus, although your mother may have worked hard to convince you that you were a worthless person, it is only because you continue to take what she said seriously *today* that you upset yourself with this notion. Merely leaving home will never solve the problem, because you will figuratively take your mother with you wherever you go unless you dispute your irrational thinking. Thus, if clients believe they are no good, and believe they hold this opinion because it was taught to them, the therapist might respond with questions such as:

"If people accepted that the present cannot be changed because of the past, would we have any new inventions, cures for diseases, or political changes?

"Do you know anyone who has overcome some adversity in life and do you know anyone who has recovered from trauma?

"How would you explain someone who has experienced prejudice and discrimination or abuse and managed to fight against it; for example, Rosa Parks, Martin Luther King, and Nelson Mandela?"

The important point, therefore, is that past beliefs continue to be a problem because clients *currently re-indoctrinate* themselves with these beliefs. An analogy such as the following might be useful to teach this point:

Suppose you had learned to play basketball very well in high school, but did not play again for twenty years. If you then went out on the court to play, you wouldn't do very well at all. You would have lost a lot of the skills because you hadn't practiced them, right? It's the same with holding irrational beliefs. If you learned to think irrationally when you were young and didn't practice it for twenty years, then right now you wouldn't be all that disturbed. But you keep practicing it over and over again, re-indoctrinating yourself, and that's what keeps you so good at being distressed!

DISTURBANCE ABOUT DISTURBANCE

A crucial aspect of REBT is its focus not only on the A-B-C structure of emotional distress but also on the client's ability to upset himself or herself about being upset. Emotions or behaviors that would be classified under C frequently themselves become new As. Essentially, clients watch themselves behaving ineptly or feeling upset and then have an irrational belief about this that generates a new dysfunctional emotion for this ineptitude. To illustrate, consider the following cycle:

Activating event (A)—Client's mother keeps bitterly complaining about the client's behavior.

Irrational belief (IB)—"Because I don't like it, she *shouldn't [must not]* do it, and she's a jerk for acting that way."

Emotional and behavioral consequences (C)—Feeling **anger** with mother and **yelling** at her.

WHICH LEADS TO…

Secondary Activating event (A_2)—The client's anger and yelling.
Secondary Irrational belief (IB_2)—"I should [must] be able to 'keep my cool',
    and *I'm* a jerk for blowing up like that at my mother."
Secondary Consequence (C_2)—Anger at self or feelings of shame.

Clients will often become anxious about their anxiety attacks, depressed about their depressions, and angry at their temper tantrums, and generally give themselves problems about their problems. REBT literature refers to this process as *secondary emotional problems, or meta-disturbance.* This idea has a long history in psychotherapy. Ellis introduced this concept into REBT back in 1979 in the treatment of agoraphobia (Ellis, 1979a). However, we (RD) recall him speaking about this in supervision in 1975. Raimy (1975) discusses this idea and may have been the influence on Ellis. More recently, the idea of secondary emotional disturbance has been incorporated into other forms of CBT, such as Acceptance and Commitment Therapy (Hayes), Dialectical Behavior Therapy (Linehan, 1993), and Cognitive Therapy (Dobson and Hamilton, 2009). We recommend that the therapist usually address these second-level symptoms first, for the added layer of distress will prevent clients from working most efficiently on the basic A-B-Cs. (Secondary emotional problems will be discussed more in depth in subsequent chapters.)

EXPANDING THE A-B-C MODEL

The ABC model of REBT helps to explain to clients the source of their emotional distress; in its expanded form, an *A-B-C-D-E* model, it illustrates how they can reduce this distress. D stands for *Disputation,* in which clients learn to challenge and debate with themselves, cognitively and behaviorally, about their irrational thinking. When successful, at E the therapist and client will collaboratively formulate a new *Effective Belief*—a more rational philosophy that results in a healthy adaptive emotion that is compatible with effective problem-solving. Thus, the REBT therapist works not only at helping to change beliefs but also at helping to change activity, and often makes use of behavioral homework assignments to accomplish both ends.

Once clients have mastered disputation skills and developed a new effective belief that represents a more rational coping philosophy, there is still work to be done; unpleasant activating events may remain to be confronted. Even when clients are not disturbing themselves, they will probably be less happy if unpleasant activating events frequently impinge on their life. Because the therapist cannot ensure that clients will always live in a stress-free environment, the preferred strategy is to teach them to cope with the unpleasant aspects of their environment. As long as they remain upset, their problem-solving skills will tend to be adversely affected, and their ability to get what they want will be impaired. After the disturbance is reduced, interventions can focus on teaching clients how to choose or change their environment to minimize aversive conditions.

REBT is based on an integration of philosophical Stoicism and Epicureanism. Many people have a misconception that Stoicism and therefore REBT advocate that people just calmly accept a negative condition and do not attempt to change it. REBT maintains that once people are freed from their dysfunctional emotions, they can work at making their lives happier and more fulfilling, and thereby become better able to achieve their goals. Thus, therapists can help clients change their life situation; however, if circumstances allow us we think it is better to help them do this *after* we change their dysfunctional emotions and maladaptive behavior. There are times when we will try to change the A before we work on the emotional solution. We might recommend this if the client is, for example, living in a dangerous situation, or is living in a situation where he or she might have legal problems and be arrested.

A goal of therapy is to have clients learn to be their own therapists. After learning to identify and dispute their irrational beliefs, clients can decide and implement the decision not to upset themselves. We now move on to discuss how the therapist teaches the A-B-Cs of REBT.

Box 4.3

New therapists often ask whether it is necessary to teach the A-B-Cs directly to the client or to include these phrases in the active therapeutic vocabulary. The answer is that it is not necessary to do so, but it may be highly desirable, because the client can use this clear conceptual schema to complete structured cognitive homework assignments and to aid him or her in generalizing beyond the course of therapy. The new practitioner is advised to actively teach the A-B-C model because it will also help the new practitioner to keep to the REBT structure. Some experienced REBT therapists, including Ellis, occasionally or often omit these descriptive devices. For the *new* practitioner, however, we strongly recommend the formal adoption of the A-B-C system for use in listening, speaking, and teaching work with clients.

A Demonstration

As an overview of the basic tenets of REBT, we include a condensed version of a therapeutic demonstration by Dr. Albert Ellis at one of the Institute's practicum courses. The client was a young professional who attended the course and wished to discuss the difficulties of beginning a new practice. In brief, the A was a desire to try new professional activities, such as giving workshops, and the C was inertia. Dr. Ellis asked the client what she was saying to block herself; the response was:

C: I might flub it.
T: And what would that do?
C: People might think I'm a crummy teacher.
T: And that would do what?
C: I wouldn't like it.
T: Just *that* evaluation wouldn't make you upset.
C: I can't stand it.
T: Why can't you stand their thinking you're a lousy teacher?
C: (long silence)... I think I have to be a good teacher in their eyes.
T: And why *must* you be a good teacher in their eyes? I'm a scientist—prove it (grinning).
C: (long silence)
T: As long as you believe that *must,* how will you feel?

C: Anxious.

T: *Must* they all like you?

C: No.

T: Then why must—

C: Because I want them to!

T: Whatever I want, I *must* get? Where will that command get you?

C: Scurrying around...

T: Right! Anxious, depressed. Now suppose you *get* it—they all adore you. You know you'll still be in trouble? (pause) How do you know you will get it the next time? Aren't you asking for, *demanding* guaranteed adoration?

C: Hmmmm. Yes.

T: You'll be anxious as long as you believe that. How could you *not* believe that? How could you get so that you desire, but don't *need,* their approval?

C: Give some workshops?

T: Take some risks, right. What else? (pause) "If they don't approve, I could stand it. What would that make me as a human being if they don't like my teaching?" Suppose you're just lousy at giving workshops? Too bad! Can you be a happy person even if certain things you want you don't get?

C: Ye-s-s-s-s. (tentatively)

T: See how mildly you said that? How could you say that even stronger? (models) "Goddamn it! I'm determined not to put myself down even if I *never* do many things well!" Rating yourself as OK is also wrong. Why are you OK? Proving you are OK is just as impossible, empirically, as proving that you're a bad person. "I am I. Nancy. Now how the hell do I *enjoy myself* without trying to *prove myself?*" You see, you can choose not to label yourself at all. You don't need a grade for yourself, a continual report card. You can rate your behaviors in the workshop, because it will be pleasurable to do well.

In this chapter, we have outlined the basics of REBT. In subsequent chapters we will expound on each of these steps. We will start by assessing the As, Cs, and IBs, and then move on to changing the IBs and Cs.

5

Getting Therapy Off to a Good Start

In one sense, therapy begins at the first moment of contact between you and your client, and develops as you and your client attend to some important preliminary groundwork in the therapeutic process. All forms of therapy include some common factors that contribute to success (Wampold, 2007). This chapter will focus on some of these factors. Included in this groundwork are two primary tasks:

Interpersonal—developing a therapeutic alliance, establishing a therapeutic rapport, and building a collaborative relationship.

Organizational—socializing the client for therapy, beginning the process of assessment, agreeing on the problem areas, and establishing treatment goals.

Each of these tasks works in the service of the other; for example, the active, collaborative setting of treatment goals begins to forge the therapeutic alliance. This chapter addresses the ways that an REBT therapist might work at these tasks to set the stage for cognitive-behavioral work.

SETTING THE STAGE INTERPERSONALLY

It might be useful to begin this discussion by asking you, the reader, to recall your own first session with a psychotherapist. If you have not had that experience, try to visualize yourself in the client's shoes. Imagine coming into new surroundings, facing a complete stranger, and then trying to discuss your most difficult or embarrassing problems. What emotions would you be experiencing just then, and would those emotions facilitate open, honest discussion with your therapist?

Box 5.1

Remember that most clients come to therapy because they are *suffering*. It is our task to find out about this suffering and figure out how we can help the client. To start, we want to provide a sense of hope and to demystify the therapeutic process for the client. It is our contention that the active-directive approach of

REBT is ideally suited to accomplishing these objectives. The typical intake process at mental health clinics usually involves multiple sessions of data collection concerning the client's history and life functioning. We believe that this process can interfere with the development of the therapeutic alliance. Do you want your therapist to take a detailed history of your life and problems, or do you want him or her to directly assist you in solving the problem that brought you to therapy? Albert Ellis always began his sessions with the question, "What problem would you like to work on?"

A good way to begin with a new client is to ask whether s/he has been in therapy before. This question can assess the client's expectations of therapy. A positive expectancy increases the chances of a positive therapeutic effect, while incongruence between the client's expectations and the therapist's view of the tasks of therapy decreases therapeutic efficacy and increases the dropout rate (O'Leary and Borkovec, 1978). We also like to ask what was helpful and what was not helpful in their previous therapy. It is helpful, therefore, for the therapist to take time to outline the general nature of REBT using a problem that the client brings. During the first session, we also discuss the collaborative nature of the therapy, how the therapy works, and the nature of homework assignments. You could say that we want to socialize the client to therapy.

A second benefit to knowing about any previous therapy the client might have had is that it can help the therapist avoid unnecessary mistakes. As a rule of thumb, avoid doing something that a previous therapist already tried unsuccessfully, or at least if you do, present it differently. If the therapist who used the technique was not skilled at it, it might be possible to try the technique again; to avoid an expectation of failure by the client, change its label. So, be sure to ask, "What did you do with your former therapist?" "What do you think helped you?" and "What do you think was not helpful?" Occasionally, the client will report, "The other therapist never talked about what was really bothering me." This may give the therapist a good opportunity to ask, "What was that?" If the client replies with a specific emotion or behavioral problem or traumatic event, the therapist may respond: "Is that an important problem you would like to work on now?"

Clients often think of therapy as pouring out their hearts to the therapist and getting sympathy. Although this may provide some relief in the manner of a confession, it can be merely palliative, for the clients will not have learned the important insight that they are responsible for their own dysfunctional emotions and that they can help themselves. Ellis (2001) often said that there is a difference between feeling better and getting better. Sympathy from a therapist or cathartic expression of one's emotions can help clients *feel* better, but it does not teach them the skills to *get* better. At the Albert Ellis Institute, we tell our trainees and clients, you have friends to help you feel better, and you have a rational emotive behavior therapist to help you get better.

Box 5.2

Take a moment to practice outlining REBT to a new client with no experience with REBT. The encounter takes place on the phone, because the potential client has looked you up on the web and wants to ask a few questions before making a choice of therapists. She says, "I see, Dr. X, that you are listed as a rational emotive behavioral therapist. I am afraid I do not know what that is. Could you tell me something about this kind of therapy?" Compose a brief response; try to answer in three sentences or less.

Ask for feedback from your supervisor, colleague, or a fellow student about whether your mini-explanation is clear as well as concise.

Especially for the new client, it is quite important for the therapist to describe the therapeutic tasks and procedures involved. It is important to take time to outline what you expect from the client (e.g., being on time for appointments, doing homework) and what the client can expect from you (e.g., introducing the client to a cognitive-behavioral model of therapy). This explanation is best given during the first session, usually after the client has presented some major problem(s).

"I'll be showing you how you can control many unhealthy emotions. I'll be doing that by pointing out some of your thinking styles, asking you to re-evaluate some of your perceptions of the world, correcting some of your belief systems, giving you homework assignments to help you change your thinking or your problem behavior, and asking you to read books and listen to recordings. Your active role in therapy is what is most important for you to reap the most benefits. I can help you and I can advise you, but you will be required to do the work."

We think it is also important to encourage clients from the beginning to express any disagreements or reactions to things that the therapist says or does. We want to support their collaborative relationship with us.

REBT is problem-oriented, and this focus can be communicated to the client in the early sessions. The therapist can suggest, for example, "You say that you've been feeling depressed lately. Let's find out what's going on there." If the client has listed a number of areas of difficulty, the therapist may simply ask, "Which problem would you like to begin to talk about in therapy?" In succeeding sessions, the therapist can begin by asking, "What problem would you like to work on today?" or "Last week, we were discussing such-and-such problem; how have you been working on that this week?" Opening remarks that provide structure are preferable to more general questions (e.g., "How was your week?"), because they set a problem-oriented tone and help keep the session focused.

Box 5.3

Many REBT therapists attempt, even during the first session, to help clients learn to conceptualize their problems in REBT terms, to uncover some of the irrational ideas that are causing their troublesome behaviors and unhealthy emotions, and to help them begin to discover what they are doing to disturb themselves. Ellis himself was particularly active and directive in his initial sessions with clients. Perhaps because of his temperament, many years of clinical experience, eminence in the field, and diagnostic acumen, Ellis set a fast pace that many new REBT therapists assume they *must* follow. Such an assumption would be incorrect, however, because the novice may not be able to replicate Ellis's performance, nor is it always desirable to do so. REBT therapists have many different yet effective styles. REBT therapists can adopt different styles with different clients to match the client's temperament. The Albert Ellis Institute has produced The Master Therapist Series that shows a number of different therapists doing REBT in their own authentic styles.

Many therapists find that an important opening question to ask the client is, "Why did you make this appointment *now?* What happened this past week that propelled you to this decision to act now?" The active-directive stance of the REBT therapist is in evidence: we want to get to the immediate problem and try to begin to be helpful. We are mindful that the client is in distress in some way.

ESTABLISHING RAPPORT

Many therapists believe that being *active and directive* is incompatible with the development of rapport; we disagree. Remember that the basis for the therapeutic relationship is not friendship but professional competence, credibility, respect, and commitment to help the client change. Thus, REBT therapists are not friends to their clients, although they could be, but rather concerned professionals. Rapport, therefore, *can* be developed when the therapist behaves directively.

This point was particularly evident to us while co-leading psychotherapy groups with Dr. Ellis. As directive as he was, the group members frequently reported feelings of warmth and respect for "Al." When questioned by us, group members reported that he demonstrated his concern by his many questions, his complete attention to their problems, his advocacy of an accepting and tolerant philosophy, and by teaching them something immediate that they could do to reduce their distress.

Special problems in the development of rapport can occur with various populations: court referrals, employee assistance provider referrals, unwilling spouses with marital problems, and especially children and adolescents. Some of these clients may not really understand the role of the therapist, and why they are being sent to see one. Others are simply not interested in therapy. Children, for example, may believe that if you are a doctor, you will jab them with needles, drill their teeth, or do the kinds of painful things to them that other doctors have done. Some reluctant clients believe that only "crazy people" go to a "shrink" and refuse to cooperate because doing so would be an admission of such a diagnosis. Still others think that you are a righteous judge or harsh disciplinarian who will humiliate or punish them for their misdeeds. In all these cases, the same directive, honest approach is recommended.

Many REBT therapists believe that the best way to establish rapport is to *do therapy* with the client. The bond will develop through the conjoint activity. Perhaps this sequence applies more to the experienced therapist. The new therapist who is awkward and unsure of his or her skills may want to begin to establish rapport not by doing therapy but rather by talking with the client about the *process* of doing therapy.

Self-disclosure by the client is a prerequisite for psychotherapy, yet self-disclosure of the sort and extent necessary for psychotherapy is considered inappropriate behavior in most other social situations. In many families, there is little talk of emotions and thought, so that prior modeling may have been lacking. In addition, the self-disclosure that is required for therapy can be suppressed by fear. For many children and adolescents, self-disclosure might be particularly difficult. It is often not until late adolescence, when close friendships or love bonds develop, that children begin sharing personal secrets. Members of various ethnic groups can also have difficulty identifying and expressing their emotions. Some cultures discourage the sharing of emotions. Clients might not be accustomed to self-disclosure or may not know how to do it.

Psychotherapists frequently fail to recognize this discrepancy in expectations for self-disclosure. Some therapists expect their clients to freely discuss personal problems, while the client may have quite a different agenda. Failure to self-disclose can be viewed by some therapists as resistance or as a symptom of deep psychological disturbance, but we suggest that the therapist avoid such preconceptions. Be willing to consider multiple hypotheses—specifically, that problems of self-disclosure may also be a result of a lack of prior modeling of this behavior, or suppression due to fear or a cultural norm.

Discomfort with self-disclosure may be particularly evident if clients view their problem behaviors as socially unacceptable. Issues such as addiction to Internet pornography, homosexuality, promiscuity, alcoholism, hoarding, obsessive-compulsive symptoms, and even suicidal ideation may fall into this category. Therapists may have to spend a number of sessions establishing a climate of trust before such problems surface. Alternatively, clients may repeatedly work on "easy" problems for most of the therapy session and, just when the time is up, "casually mention" an emotionally charged issue. With patience and gentle confrontation, the client will usually become less hesitant across sessions about bringing up major issues.

Box 5.4

Should a therapist look for the client's core irrational belief or most central problem(s) in the beginning sessions? This may not always be a good idea. Even if clients do not bring up their most serious problems and present what appear to be superficial or less distressing problems, much can be gained by the therapist applying the REBT model to these less central problems. We believe that it is easier to learn the system of identifying and changing irrational beliefs about less disturbing, less ego-involving problems. Once the client has learned to apply REBT to these less central problems, it will be easier for them to transfer the skills to the more serious problems.

If self-disclosure is initially absent, make use of reinforcement and example. Reinforce the client whenever he or she self-discloses and show by your own (relevant) self-disclosure that it is a safe and desirable behavior. In addition, we would suggest that you allow an adequate period for the client's fear to subside, which will be difficult if you are very active or appear to be impatient. In addition, we have found it helpful to inform clients that we do not have to talk about certain problems, but it is helpful to talk about what makes it so difficult to do so.

Box 5.5

Sometimes you can begin to socialize clients to REBT even before the first session, and even when they are in emotional distress. For example, in your first telephone contact, you might comment on the client's affect in a general way (e.g., "You sound like you're having a tough time.") and begin to provide some structure. For example,

"What I'd like you to do in the time between now and when I see you is to think about how to tell me what kinds of problems you're having in your life, and what kind of help you may be looking for. In addition, I would like you to keep a log. If you're feeling distressed, that is a good time for you to sit down and just freely write about whatever is going on inside you. So, if you're feeling really upset, remember that those feelings can be very useful to our work, because you will have some good material to present in our first meeting."

Relax. It is not necessary to solve the client's problems right away. In order to assess the problems, take some time to get to know the client and get an impression of his or her thinking. The client is more likely to discuss personal problems if he or she believes that the therapist is truly interested in listening.

Box 5.6

Some clients come to REBT therapy with prior expectations—especially those who have previously experienced nondirective therapy. They may talk (seemingly endlessly) about their problems. For example, a client named Jay came in week after week, describing in poignant detail the many hassles he had experienced at work, and yet how fruitless it was to think of leaving his job. He was stuck and wallowing. Clients such as Jay have rehearsed in their previous therapy the recitation of the details of their week. This leaves little time to learn new reactions to the problems they face.

REBT is an active therapy. We communicate to the client that (a) we can offer more and (b) the client can do more than cathartic expression. We convey these messages in a respectful way. Here is an example: "Jay, you've done a good job of identifying the problem. Do you think it might be beneficial if we examine what you were thinking in these situations and how you can think differently?"

SOCIALIZING THE CLIENT TO THE MODEL

As we said above, socialization can begin on the telephone, before the first appointment, by teaching clients the kind of therapy you do, informing them about what to expect in their first visit, and being open and collaborative in your style of communication. REBT is a problem-oriented approach to psychotherapy. When the therapist asks the client, "What problem would you like to discuss first?" or asks "What problem bothered you the most this past week?" a number of messages are being delivered:

You are both there to get a job done.
REBT is a focused and efficient approach to emotional problem-solving.
The process is going to be largely active and directive.

GENERAL ASSESSMENT

Clients at the Albert Ellis Institute in New York City receive a packet of questionnaires to fill out at the time of their first visit. The purpose of these assessments is to reduce the amount of session time needed to get basic biographical data, to help the client to focus his or her goals, and to provide information for the therapist to prepare a case conceptualization and treatment plan. In addition to helping the therapist to generate hypotheses about the client's problems, these data provide a baseline of disturbance against which to monitor progress.

The packet includes a biographical intake form (see Appendix 3), a Million Clinical Multi-Axial Inventory III (Millon, 1987; 1988), the Psychiatric Diagnostic Screening Questionnaire (Zimmerman and Matia, 2001) the Anger Disorder Scale-Short Form (DiGiuseppe and Tafrate, 2004), the Satisfaction with Life Scale (Diener, Emmons, Larsen, and Griffen, 1985), the Outcomes Questionnaire (Lambert et al., 1996) and the Attitudes and Beliefs Scale 2 (DiGiuseppe, Leaf, Robin, and Exner, 1989). All forms are computer-scored at the Albert Ellis Institute and returned to the therapist shortly after the client's first visit.

In many mental health clinics, clients could be subjected to lengthy social histories and routine psychological testing. Often, the client is not provided a reason why this is necessary. These standardized procedures may contribute to the well-known tendency of clinic clients to drop out of treatment very quickly, not necessarily out of impatience, but because they have lost confidence that their needs will be met. We believe that much of the information other therapists look for is unnecessary, or fails to provide us with the type of information we need in order to start therapy. Background data are useful, but following a rigid pattern of elaborate history-taking before initiating therapy may reduce client rapport. Some clients may feel threatened by an impersonal battery of standardized tests; others believe that much of the testing is irrelevant and the therapist is wasting valuable time that could be used to help them. If clients are ashamed or uneasy about exposing their problems, they are as likely to conceal them during an extensive assessment as in a shorter one.

Clients are best served by working with the therapist efficiently on an issue that they want to discuss, while the therapist transmits nonjudgmental acceptance in the hope that clients will come to view the therapist as a competent and trustworthy person to whom they can divulge their "secrets." Thus, you do not need to wait for the "real" problem or a list of all the problems before beginning the work of therapy. Take whatever activating event or emotional or behavioral consequence the client is willing to present and use it to teach the A-B-C model. In this way, the client will receive some help while being educated about REBT theory.

Because REBT is a cognitive therapy, it is to the therapist's advantage to briefly assess the cognitive functioning of the client. Psychological assessment by means of a formal battery of tests is recommended for most children, but is not essential for adults. There may be some cases involving adults, however, in which standardized tests may be helpful in attaining information on cognitive functions. Cognitive deficits can have a neurological basis that is responsible not only for the psychological problems but for any accompanying deficits in social skills as well. This neurological basis can go unnoticed unless careful detective work and psychological testing are done. Keep in mind that George Gershwin spent years in psychoanalysis for the treatment of headaches and then died of a brain tumor.

Sometimes cognitive deficits are a result of chronic substance abuse, which may be surprising news to the client who claims, for example, to have "never missed a day of work." It is generally a good practice to ask the client (even if the written intake forms include this topic) about the use of alcohol and other drugs in his or her life, and about times when greater than normal use may occur. In general if the therapist suspects that the client is not giving an accurate picture of any problem, corroborative interviews with family members are recommended.

Good diagnosis is the first step in good treatment. In REBT, the major diagnosis focuses on identifying the dysfunctional belief systems that produce emotional distress, but diagnoses of other problems are also important. From the first session onward, the therapist is building up a picture of the client's current level of functioning by amassing pieces of information about the client's life. Some of this information is gathered in the biographical data form or other pencil-and-paper measures, but much of it will emerge more informally in the therapeutic hour.

In addition to an A-B-C analysis of the client's belief system (as described in the succeeding chapters), the therapist does a careful behavioral analysis of the major problems. Good detective work is often required to establish the *antecedents* and *consequences* of specific target behaviors. For example, if the client is requesting help with obesity, the therapist can follow behavior therapy prescriptions and ask the client to keep data on where and when the client eats, what was eaten, the client's mood and thoughts when eating, and the immediate consequences (internal and environmental) of eating. The roles played by significant others in the client's life may also be important: Does the obese client's spouse encourage him or her to eat second helpings? What motivates the spouse's behavior? What would it mean to the spouse if the client shed weight?

Box 5.7

Because clients are each unique, they want different things; some jump right in and begin therapy, and others go more slowly and want to tell you more of their history. One client vigorously defended against the attempts of the therapist to "get to work," saying, "I want to tell you more about myself, my family, and my background. That way, I'll feel like you have a better chance of understanding me, and maybe I'll be better able to trust what you say."

If you are not sure what the client wants, ask him or her. You might say, "*What type of information do you think I need in order to help you?*" This question also helps make explicit the client's implicit theory of therapy. "*What do you think will help you?*" This question makes explicit the client's conception of the tasks of therapy.

Identifying and Agreeing on Problem Areas

Clients typically state their problems in vague terms or express them as external problems. For example:

I have trouble with my daughter.
I am having trouble with my social life.
We need help with our marriage; we do not communicate.

One of the first tasks in setting up therapy, therefore, is to reach an agreement on the definition of the problem(s). In REBT, we focus the client on how the problem affects him or her. In this way, we draw the client's attention to the behavioral and affective aspects of the problem, and ultimately to the B-C connection. For example:

C: My problem is that my eighteen-year-old daughter just sits around the house and plays her music and drives me crazy!
T: That sounds like it can be difficult to live with. Could you also be making a second problem for yourself? Do you demand that she act differently from how she does and make yourself angry?

Sometimes the client's concept of the problem can obscure the real diagnostic issues. Consider the client who says he has "trouble with his social life." One might assume that the affective problem is social anxiety, or the behavioral problem is a social skills deficit. A little digging, however, may reveal that in social situations, the client puts himself down unmercifully, makes bad jokes about himself, and, of course, is not pleasant company. What is the real problem? Likely, it is depression. The point is that the therapist had better ask the client to be explicit and concrete in elaborating on the nature of his or her problem. In this instance, for example, the therapist might ask, "How do you know you have a problem with your social life?" "When was the last time you had a social problem in this area?" "What was it like?" "What kind of feedback did you get from others?" And so on.

Suppose you and your client do not agree on what is the most pressing or serious problem. Suppose you believe that the presenting problem is a kind of screen or concealment of other problems. Do you work on the problems that are presented to you and show the client the REBT process—or do you try to get at the "real" problem? We suggest that you do the former. Occasionally, screen problems may be a test by clients to see if you really can help them. Cases such as these may provide an argument for why a diagnostic assessment done in the first visit might not be productive. In any case, it teaches us that assessment goes on *throughout* therapy, not just at the start. We think it is generally best to wait for the client to bring up a problem in the initial stages of therapy.

Problems can be stated tentatively to acknowledge your willingness to modify them. There is no such thing as a definitive assessment or diagnosis of the nature of a problem. Good clinicians are always willing to be wrong or to change their minds about their conceptualizations as they listen to new information. By sharing our conceptualizations with our clients, we are modeling self-disclosure, willingness to test out thinking and to be wrong, and the use of the scientific method. Sharing hypotheses builds collaboration and respect. It is advisable not to state hypotheses in declarative sentences. Use suppositional language; phrase the item as a question that needs feedback. When you say, "Sharon, I have a hypothesis that your social problem may be due to depression, and I would like to know what your thoughts are about that?" you are demonstrating respect by asking for the client's feedback.

What if the client cannot identify a specific problem? A question the therapist might ask is, "If this was our last session, what would you have liked to have achieved from therapy?" The client may then begin to formulate his or her goals for treatment, and perhaps be able to explore feelings or behaviors that are impeding him or her from achieving those goals.

If, at this stage, you have not yet reached an agreement with your client concerning the nature of his or her problem, you can suggest to the client that he or she keep a "problem diary." Encourage your client to monitor disturbed feelings during the week and suggest that he or she write them down, including when and where they were experienced. Another recommendation for clients having difficulty identifying goals is to have them complete a three-month goal sheet found in *The REBT Resource for Practitioners* (Wolfe and Bernard, 2000), which breaks down goals into behaviors to increase and decrease, thoughts to increase and decrease, feelings to increase and decrease, and sensations to increase and decrease.

Generally, we suggest that you agree on the definition of the problem with your client before proceeding to a problem-specific assessment phase. In doing a more specific assessment of the problem area, be as *concrete and detailed* as you can. Your client experiences the emotional problem and holds related irrational beliefs in many contexts. Being specific helps you obtain reliable and valid data about A, B, and C. One way to model specificity is to ask for a *recent* or *typical example* of the target problem; for example, "When was the last time X happened?"

IDENTIFYING TREATMENT GOALS

Within the first few sessions, the therapist will establish with the client the goals of therapy. Implicit or preferably explicit agreements will be made with the client so that both parties can determine when and if therapeutic progress is being made. In fact, frequent reassessment of these agreed upon goals encourages not only therapeutic responsibility but also the client's involvement and commitment to the process. A stated commitment to goals also enables the therapist to refer back to them when the client is distracted and off task. For example:

"By not focusing on X, aren't you hindering yourself from getting what you set out to achieve, Alice?" or

"How can you accomplish your goal of finding a relationship, Sam, if you don't go out and meet people?"

Most therapists follow a professional code of ethics, which implies that they work to help clients change what they want to change. The therapist's purpose is not to stamp out all irrational beliefs that clients may have, but to work on their problems as their consultant. The therapist might see major problems that a client has not identified and want to discuss the problems with the client. For example, "John, I think you have some other problems that you haven't brought up, and here's the reason why I think we could work on these." The ultimate decision, however, rests with the client.

In addition to establishing long-range goals for therapy, we recommend that you set weekly treatment-plan goals. At the end of each session, you can review each of the problem areas, determine the next step in working on the problems, remind yourself to check up on the progress of older problems, and outline the goals for the subsequent session(s). (The use of formal treatment plans is discussed in detail in Part V, "The Therapeutic Whole.").

AGREEING ON TREATMENT GOALS

By this point, collaboration on treatment goals is straightforward. In some instances, however, things get tricky. You might find that you and your client have different goals.

This often occurs in marriage counseling, sex therapy, and with clients who have anger and guilt problems. Clients might want the As changed; they might want practical or behavioral solutions. In REBT, in most cases, we approach the *emotional solution* before we target the practical or behavioral solution. In other words, we encourage clients first to work on C, and not change the A. Why do we want to work on the emotional problem first? There are three main reasons:

Disturbed negative emotion can interfere with learning. The Yerkes Dodson Law reminds us that there is generally an inverted U-shaped relationship between performance and intensity of affect. With too little sympathetic arousal, we function like "relaxed incompetents"; with too high sympathetic arousal, we struggle along as over-anxious nonlearners.

Disturbed negative emotion can interfere with the individual's problem-solving ability. Coming up with sensible solutions to life problems might therefore be impeded.

Even when functional behaviors are learned, disturbed negative emotions can interfere with the production of these behaviors. For example, Schwartz and Gottman (1976) found that problems in assertiveness are not usually a result of skill deficits but of performance inhibition.

Dealing with the disturbed negative emotions could be considered necessary, but *not necessarily sufficient:* replacing disturbed negative emotions with healthy, nondisturbed negative emotions frees the person up to deal with *practical* problems or to move on to self-actualization and improvement in the quality of life. Both are important.

PROBLEMS IN ACHIEVING COMMON GOALS

Be alert when clients phrase their goals in terms of therapeutic *process* rather than emotional or behavioral outcome. For example, "I really want to *understand* why I'm so depressed." "I want to learn what my irrational beliefs really are." Or "I want to learn how I became so irrational." These client goals are vague and both the therapist and the client are unlikely to know how to assess them and will become frustrated when they look back to determine the utility of the therapy experience.

Evaluate whether the client's goals are *realistic* or useful to them. For example, Paolo's wife had just left him, and his goal in therapy was to *be happy, not care* about his wife's abandonment, and to acquire a belief that it was *perfectly OK* that she did so. It is unlikely, and perhaps undesirable, that Paolo will be successful in this endeavor. When a lonely Saturday night rolls around, or when Paolo visits old haunts that he frequented with his wife, that cavalier attitude is likely not to hold up. The view that the separation "doesn't matter" will quickly fall apart because it does matter. If the client selects an inappropriate emotional goal, s/he will not be able to maintain it because the *a priori* beliefs to sustain it are irrational and not in accordance with reality. In order to be happy about your spouse's abandonment, you would have to believe something like, "It's wonderful that she left." That belief is inconsistent with reality, and so the goal is unattainable. The ending of Paolo's marriage was an unfortunate event, and rather than colluding in denial or emotional dissociation, the therapist could help Paolo aim for more rational and realistic beliefs that acknowledge the unfortunate reality and allow for appropriate sadness and even mourning, without despair and torment.

Sometimes people resist change because they are experiencing emotional suffering, and yet they believe their emotions are *appropriate* to hold. Those emotions are often guilt, usually anger, and sometimes depressive moods. For example, an Italian widow, whose husband had died five years earlier, was encouraged to seek therapy by her children for her depression. She was very resistant to change. She discussed with her therapist the appropriateness of grieving. She was sure that because her husband died, her life was over. The therapist asked if it would be inappropriate for her *not* to be miserable, and the client responded that she could not imagine it. The therapist teased, "You know, you could go on grieving forever!" The client seemed astonished at this comment and reflected for a moment. She then responded that some years ago, she and her husband had been touring Sicily, and the guide had pointed out a house draped in black, which was described as "the widow's house." The Sicilian woman's husband had died twenty-six years ago, and she was still grieving. This memory caused the client to muse, "I guess that *is* going on too long, and isn't appropriate." Once she decided that *prolonged* grieving was an emotional burden that she did not have to experience, she could work at re-thinking her dread about her husband's death.

Sometimes a therapeutic goal seems unattainable to clients because they cannot *conceptualize* the new emotion and might not agree that it is adaptive and more functional. Lila, for example, was sexually promiscuous and felt guilty; she initially would not agree to give up her guilt because she felt that to do so would lead her permanently to a life of sexual excess. She believed that she needed her guilt to maintain self-control. Eventually, Lila learned to differentiate feeling responsible regret from feeling guilty.

Below is another example. For five weeks, a therapist had been working with a father to help him avoid becoming enraged at his kids. In the sixth session, the father looked up in amazement and said, "Wait a second. You want me to not be angry with my kids?" The therapist responded, "You finally got it!" The point is that the therapist had not gotten it! The father believed that anger was necessary to discipline his children. The therapist had neglected to discuss with the father that other emotions besides anger could lead to responsible discipline.

Many times, clients have no *role models* for appropriate emotional and behavioral reactions. The therapist can ask a client to pick out people s/he knows in her/ his life (or public media figures) who had the same activating event but reacted appropriately, even if negatively. In this way, the therapist helps the client find a model: the client cannot work toward a goal he or she cannot conceptualize.

C: I could never be happy without a man.
T: Do you know anyone who is in that situation? Without a man, but reasonably happy?

C: No. Well…maybe.

T: Let's find that person and interview her. Maybe we can also find women who are occasionally sad without men, but not depressed. They are not always happy about it, but they function well in their lives.

Of course, the therapist should explore carefully the beliefs expressed by the models. We do not want to promote parallel irrationalities, such as "All men are vermin, so who needs them?" That role model might not be depressed because she has replaced despair with the equally debilitating emotion of unhealthy anger.

Sometimes role models can be found in specific self-help or support groups. For example, the distraught parents of a young child with Tourette's syndrome may find not only support but also models for negative albeit *nondisturbed* levels of affect in a Tourette's support group. One young mother, whose small son developed *alopecia areata* and suddenly lost all the hair on his body, found what she needed by starting an alopecia support group, using REBT as its underpinnings.

Sometimes clients believe that they are the only people who have a particular problem. This often results in self-condemnation and hopelessness regarding any solution to their problem. One of us encountered a client who felt depressed about thinking she was inferior; a problem she called inferiority feelings. She thought no one had this problem and no help was available. The therapist asked her if they could go out to the street and ask people if they had inferiority feelings, and what they did about it. Both the therapist and the client were surprised that all the people they stopped wanted to talk about it in detail. In addition, they had lots of solution for how to deal with it. She returned from this outing believing that it was hopeful to talk about this problem and that she could learn to accept herself with these feelings.

6

Basic Therapy Skills

In REBT, as in other forms of psychotherapy, certain therapist qualities can help to build rapport and maximize therapeutic gains. Below we list some therapist characteristics described by Rogers (1951) and Carkhuff (1969), and follow each with a description of how to communicate these attitudes in an REBT session.

QUALITIES OF A GOOD REBT THERAPIST

Empathy is the ability to perceive accurately what another person is experiencing, and to communicate your perception. The empathic therapist attends not only to the words of the clients but also to the nonverbal aspects of their behavior in order to perceive accurately their feeling state. Next, the empathic therapist lets the clients know that he or she is aware of the clients' positive feelings and emotional discomforts. Empathy works because the client feels accepted; it provides a corrective emotional experience; it promotes exploration of meaning; and activates self-healing, all of which improves compliance in treatment. The empathy effect size mean is .26 and explains 4% of the variance in the therapy relationship (Norcross and Lambert, 2011). Bohart, Elliott, Greenberg, and Watson (2002) found evidence that empathy might be more important to outcome in cognitive-behavioral therapies than in others. However, Norcross and Lambert (2011) were unable to confirm this in their analysis.

The empathic *REBT therapist* lets clients know that he or she understands not only what the clients are feeling but also what they are *thinking*. For example:

"It sounds like you are unhappy. Could you also be thinking it would be awful if you *did* fail?"

When both the thought and the emotion are reflected, the client can begin dealing with either; emotive reflecting alone, however, precludes this option. Sometimes clients are surprised by such dual reflections and appear assured that the therapist has "read their mind."

We take the view that demonstrating empathy toward clients serves a two-fold purpose. Empathy involves *understanding* clients, but more importantly, empathy *helps* clients by confronting and influencing them to rethink their problems and to begin to solve their problems. We have found that clients feel best understood when their problems are not only understood but also when they feel they have found somebody who is really helping them to solve what they so far have not been able to do by themselves.

Box 6.1

Often you will see rather dramatic improvements in a client's mood during the course of a session. Clinical research, using pre- and post-session measures, suggests that about 90% of the variance in this mood shift can be predicted by two factors:

The technical portion of the therapy hour, for example, the percentage of change in the client's belief system, *and*

The perceived empathy of the therapist, that is, the degree to which the therapist is seen by the client as understanding, caring, and supportive.

These are independent but additive effects.

Respect is evident when the therapist indicates a deep and genuine acceptance for the worth of the clients, separate and apart from their behavior. The mere fact of the clients' existence justifies this respect. The therapist respects the right of clients to make their own decisions, even if they appear in error, for much can be learned from failure. As a respectful therapist, you are neither rejecting nor overprotective. Instead, you foster client independence, self-confidence, and self-reliance.

The *REBT therapist* shows clients that they can be respected despite their disagreement with the therapist over certain philosophical issues. Thus, the REBT therapist clearly discriminates between the clients and their dysfunctional thoughts and behaviors. By offering Unconditional Other Acceptance, clients learn they, too, can separate their worth as humans from their behaviors and performance and embrace Unconditional Self Acceptance.

Warmth is communicated to the client by appropriate use of touching, smiles, and other nonverbal gestures of appreciation, as well as by positive comments of concern and affection for the client.

The *REBT therapist* demonstrates concern and caring for the client in the following ways:

(a) by carefully attending to the client's behavior;
(b) by frequent questions for clarification or therapeutic intervention;
(c) by recall of personal details about the client and his or her problem;
(d) by the use of gentle humor;
(e) by unconditional acceptance;
(f) and by quick, active attempts to help the client solve difficult issues.

Genuineness is conveyed by not being phony or trying to play roles. Make your verbal and nonverbal behaviors congruent. Your behavior in the counseling relationship need not be dramatically different from that outside the relationship.

As an *REBT therapist,* you can go a step further. Active confrontation requires genuineness, and genuineness, in turn, requires honesty. Thus, the REBT therapist is likely to disagree openly with the client, to ask directly for clarification when confused, and to respond to client questions without hesitation.

Box 6.2

Be careful to monitor your level of warmth, caring, and concern. Too much of a good thing can also be problematic. Therapists as well as clients are often susceptible to the "dire need for approval," and the REBT therapist takes a cautious approach, being careful to note irrational beliefs that may arise in the context of the therapeutic relationship. Unchallenged, approval needs may block clients from really working hard to change themselves or even block therapists from being firm enough to help them change! Attentive self-monitoring is essential.

Concreteness refers to specificity in the therapist's work on the client's problems. Attention to detail is evident; the therapist will ask for concrete, specific details (the what, when, where, and how) of the client's experience. Therapists often ask concrete questions for specific examples and lead the client through a comprehensive analysis of these situations.

The *REBT therapist* places importance on concrete details of the client's perceptions, cognitions, and emotions. Do not encourage the client to supply details only about external circumstances (A), but rather focus primarily on the belief system.

Confrontation refers to the therapist detecting and mentioning discrepancies (a) between what the clients are saying and what they have said before; (b) between what the clients are communicating verbally and nonverbally; and (c) between the way the clients view their problem and the way the therapist views it. Confrontation in counseling is particularly encouraged when the therapist notes discrepancies in the client's thoughts, feelings, and actions. For example, a therapist may point out, "John, you just described how your father would come home drunk and once picked up your brother and threw him across the room— and you told me that with a smile on your face. What was that about?" Or, "Mary, you began by telling me that you had a wonderful family life, but the stories you told me about your family don't seem consistent with that conclusion."

The *REBT therapist* pays particular attention to discrepancies between the client's thoughts and their reported emotions. When a discrepancy occurs, it is important to point this out to the client and ask for clarification. It is common for clients in session to report a rational belief and an unhealthy negative emotion. When this occurs, the REBT therapist explains that either the client was holding an irrational belief at the time, or the emotion the client is reporting in session was not an unhealthy negative emotion but rather a healthy one.

Confrontations take courage, and are among the most powerful and valuable tools of the therapist. For example, the therapist might suggest, "You say you aren't angry, Mary, yet you're sitting there with your fists clenched!" Or "You say you have no problems, Fred, but what are you doing here in jail?"

Box 6.3

Some areas of clinical inquiry require a gentle persistence of confrontation rather than a battering ram. A prototype of such an approach appears in work with survivors of abusive or alcoholic homes who often seem to be "super-stoics" because they cope by "not knowing." Their conversation may suggest that they live in a fantasy ("my childhood was wonderful") or in denial ("I had fun in the hospital when I was a child"), or somewhere on the continuum between repression and dissociation ("I don't remember much of my childhood").

Remember that these are defense strategies and they exist for good reasons. Defenses are attempts to avoid what seem to be "unknowable" and "unbearable" memories and affective states. Our goal in confrontation is to help these survivors of abuse to know what happened to them, to feel strong negative feelings about it, and to not be overwhelmed by those feelings.

Carkhuff (1969) has outlined various levels of confrontation strategies, ranging from very mild to frontally assertive. The *REBT therapist* typically operates at the top of this hierarchy, at the most direct levels. The approach is based on a number of theoretical assumptions: (a) unlike other therapies, there is no concept of "readiness" of the client for confrontations or insights; (b) by confronting clients with aspects of their behavior that are not in their awareness, problems can be quickly brought into focus; and (c) clients are unlikely to be devastated by confrontations and do not need to be overprotected. Thus, through confrontations, the REBT therapist actually expresses respect for the client. However, we advise establishing a good working therapeutic alliance before confrontations at the top of the hierarchy are used.

Confrontation is very difficult for many new therapists. Despite the difficulty, it can be a very effective strategy at the beginning of therapy. During the first contact with a client on the phone, the therapist can explain some of the ingredients and tenets of REBT. Additionally, it is especially useful to discuss some possible problematic events that might arise in therapy during the first session (e.g., anxiety regarding talking about their problems, other emotions of which they were unaware). When choosing to confront, it is important that the client knows that s/he is very much in charge of the whole process, including saying "no" to certain confrontations. On the other hand, it is the therapist's responsibility to question the client in case s/he does not want to be confronted. It is important to identify any irrational beliefs that may exist, such as frustration intolerance.

Sometimes a client will leave the therapist's office with the therapist's idea about how s/he makes her/himself depressed over a situation in her/his life (knowing which IB is responsible). Upon reflection between sessions, however, clients may discover that the therapist's hypothesis is not true and that their thoughts are different. It is often easy for the client to return to that issue the next session, saying: "Yes, I thought that to be the case but now that I've thought about it longer it seems to be that…." It is important to discuss with clients their ability to tell the therapist when the therapist is wrong.

Discussing this has three advantages: (1) The therapist can estimate how cautious s/he has to be in suggesting hypotheses to the client due to the client being restrained by socially desirable behavior in the session; (2) The client gets the message that the therapist is more interested in the client's problems than in the therapist's hypotheses; (3) It sets the tone for clients to be highly responsible for their own therapy.

The key to facilitating collaboration is to follow such confrontations with requests for feedback: "What do you think or feel when I say that to you?" The therapist's comment is a stimulus to elicit an emotional and cognitive response. The feedback can be used either diagnostically or collaboratively, depending on how the client reacts to the content of the confrontation and/or the act of confrontation. Different elements of the client's response can be teased apart.

Three additional qualities that are important in building rapport are self-disclosure, the use of humor, and an active-directive style. *Self-disclosure* brings human sharing to the communication. Therapists can expose their own thoughts, ideas, feelings, and attitudes at special times for the benefit of the client. For example, the therapist might say, "I know what you're going through, Joe. As a matter of fact, some years ago I went through the same thing, and here's how I dealt with it." The therapist's model may provide hope in such instances, in that the therapist is suggesting that he or she has had a similar problem and successfully grappled with it. Thus, the therapist models rationality, demonstrating appropriate thinking and behavior for dealing with a specific problem. In addition, the therapist is modeling self-disclosure and thereby demonstrating trust in the client; this behavior reverses the typical one-way street of therapy. Self-disclosure can also be a good way of teaching the model of REBT, in a coping rather than mastery style. Occasionally, a client will ask the REBT therapist if they practice what they preach. It is important to be honest with your answer. I (KD) have found clients are relieved to hear about my frustration intolerance for technology. I try to serve as a model of human fallibility, while at the same time expressing to my clients the importance of working on my own irrational beliefs.

Self-disclosure is useful, however, only when it is relevant; the therapist may check on relevancy by asking himself or herself, "What is the payoff for the client from this self-disclosure?" Keep in mind that the rationale for self-disclosure is primarily to build rapport and to model cognitive and behavioral strategies.

Box 6.4

Windy Dryden has used himself as a coping model in illustrating to clients how he overcame his anxiety about stammering. The core strategy was to repeatedly force himself to go into situations where he was likely to stammer, practicing "opening his mouth" and rehearsing the attitude, "If I stammer, I stammer. Big deal." The idea was to do this many, many times until he got used to the discomfort of doing so.

In addition, REBT therapists are encouraged to develop and utilize a healthy *sense of humor*. Obviously, the client is never the butt of a joke, but by gently poking fun at the irrational beliefs or events that the client views as catastrophes, the therapist may put problems into a more realistic perspective. For example, "You seem to have a healthy case of perfectionism. It doesn't do you much good, but it's nice to know it's well-developed!" On the other hand, in attempting to point out a client's demandingness, the therapist may suggest, "You seem to be using the Reverse Golden Rule. Remember the Golden Rule? Do unto others, as you would have them do unto you? The Reverse Golden Rule says others should do unto me as I do unto them!" As Ellis (1977c, p. 269) has pointed out, "A sense of humor, in itself, will not cure all emotional problems. But the refusal to take any of the grim facts of life *too* seriously largely will."

Box 6.5

One therapist had a client who, after the therapist's relevant self-disclosure, said, "Doctor, I'm not paying good money to hear about your problems—let's get back to mine." What we suggest, since you cannot know your client's response beforehand, is:

Do not do too much self-disclosure at the onset of therapy.

When you self-disclose, first ask yourself "Who will benefit from this story?" It is not your therapy. If only you will benefit from rehashing a story, do not share it, and move on.

Use self-disclosure in small doses, and ask your client for feedback. For example, "What do you think about that? Is there anything in my story that is meaningful for you? How could you apply that?"

PROCESSES OF CHANGE

Prochaska (1999) recognized that several different processes account for the change clients make in psychotherapy. Although REBT is concerned with primarily cognitive change, we try to incorporate all of these methods into our therapy. These methods appear below with activities that can accomplish them:

Consciousness-raising—Increasing information, by means of observations, data collections, reading.

Self-evaluation—Assessing feelings and thinking, by means of values clarification, corrective emotional experience.

Dramatic relief—Experiencing feelings about one's problems or solutions.

Self-liberation—Consciously making choices and committing oneself to following them.

Counterconditioning—Substituting alternative behavior for problem behavior.

Stimulus control—Avoiding or controlling stimuli that elicit problem behavior.

Reinforcement—Rewards for adaptive, desirable behaviors.

ELEMENTS OF THE SESSION

Within the cognitive-behavioral model, there is a session format, the purpose of which is to ensure all aspects of the therapy are accomplished for each session. This section outlines a suggested format for a typical working session. We recommend for a number of reasons that you spend some time trying to follow this outline.

Box 6.6

It is extremely important that therapists understand the powerful impact they can have on the client. The client usually exquisitely monitors the therapist's words, deeds, and facial expressions—even breathing patterns. Try not to underestimate the impact you might have, whether the client expresses it to you or not. Support, caring, and reframing in a positive manner are crucial skills, and, unfortunately, occasionally missing or neglected in skill-focused clinical training. Be sure to get some supervision on the interpersonal aspects of your work as you go along.

First, a session format is helpful to clients whom you are inaugurating into treatment. Many clients take comfort in knowing what to anticipate each week in the structure of the therapy hour. The predictability of the session format helps alleviate some of the intrinsic anxiety that therapy often brings. In addition, many new therapists (or "old hands" who are attempting to learn a new model) find this structure helpful because they have so much to think about that they often feel overwhelmed, and the structure simplifies the framework.

OUTLINE OF A WORKING SESSION

1. Old business from the previous session
2. Checkups: mood, symptoms, medication
3. New business: any major life changes
4. Check on homework
5. Setting the agenda

DOING THE WORK ...
1. Summary of work done
2. Assignment of homework and identification of barriers to completion
3. Closing questions

Note that "work time" is sandwiched between two sets of setting-up and wrapping-up tasks. In order to maximize work time, these other items should be brief. You might aim to set up the session in approximately ten minutes and allow ten minutes to close it. In a typical 50-minute therapy hour, therefore, you may really only have 30 minutes of work time. This realization may help you to keep your agenda for each session to realistic proportions.

REBT is as structured as any other active-directive therapy, and the outline above can help you to do more structured work. If the beginning and the end of your therapy sessions are tidy, the middle working part will go much more smoothly. The therapist skill that is required here is *agenda setting*.

The idea behind agenda setting is that the session must be blocked out in terms of tasks that need to be done. Agenda setting prevents the tendency to let the session meander wherever the client's opening comments happen to take it. Frequently, these opening remarks are more like social chitchat and avoid the emotionally charged material the client wants to discuss. If the therapist is following rather than leading the session, it becomes the client's task to break the social mold and redirect their attention, which the client may be reluctant to do in order not to appear rude or disinterested. Albert Ellis was careful not to begin his therapy sessions with open-ended questions such as "How was your week?" He set the agenda by asking his clients, "What problem would you like to work on today?"

Box 6.7

Sometimes new therapists object to agenda setting because it runs counter to the helping skills they have been cultivating. Here, for example, is an extract of a dialogue between a student of REBT and his supervisor:

Student: I find it so hard to get the client to stop talking and just fix the agenda. It feels so rude. Therapy has had the kind of flavor that says: "This time is yours and you can use it any way you want, to talk about yourself, and so on."

Supervisor: It *is* hard. It is against your social skills training. It feels businesslike. However, I find that once clients understand that this is a structured kind of therapy, they usually appreciate the structure. They socialize to it quickly if the therapist is consistent. They quickly learn that what will happen is the therapist will say, "Do we have any leftovers from last time? How did your homework assignment go? Are there any crucial events I should know about? What else goes on the agenda for today?" Soon the client will get into the swing of this and will usually come prepared with agendas. Those clients with whom we have done the most focused work have walked in with notes or index cards containing their agendas.

Our working model suggests items on which the therapist can check, in order to negotiate with the client what the focus of the day's work will be: "How much of the session shall we spend on 'this' or 'that'? Is there anything else we should talk about today?"

The skilled therapist will be able to lead the client quickly through these checks, using each point to decide whether an item needs to be addressed in the *working part* of the session. Setting up the session this way gives you time to do some work, at the end of which you stop and roll the session back to the beginning and say, "OK, here's what we did; was it helpful or useful?" "What will we give you for homework? Where shall we start next time?"

Agenda setting is a skill that requires training, supervision, and lots and lots of practice. It is important to avoid having the client digress in the therapeutic hour before you agree on the items for the agenda. Once the agenda is set, it is then more productive to let the client talk and the therapist listen.

Let us take each of the items on the outline in turn.

1. *Old business.* The therapist may say something like, "Margo, did you have any negative thoughts or feelings left over from our last visit that came up after we parted company?" Note that the therapist is asking a more focused question than "Any old business?" Specifically, he or she is asking for problems because problems are what the pair is there to work on. At the end of the previous session, the therapist asked if there were any immediate reactions, so he or she does not need to ask that again. After the session has "percolated" for some days—are there any *delayed* reactions that need to be added to the new session's agenda?

2. *Checkups.* The therapist checks on the client's current mood in a variety of ways. For example, you may ask the client to complete the Outcome Questionnaire, Beck Depression Inventory (BDI) (Beck, Steer, and Brown, 1996), or some other self-report measure while in the waiting room. Alternatively, the therapist can ask the client to do a mood log or to keep a record of anxiety attacks over the week and use this checkup time to glance over the log. If a particular symptom has been troubling the client (e.g., sleep disorder, medication side effect), the therapist can simply ask about the particular symptom. In any case, once the client acknowledges a mood or symptom issue, the therapist's task is to ask, "*Would you like to put that on our agenda for discussion today?*" The client's response may be surprising if you ask this question directly. Clients frequently will say, for example, "No, I don't want to work on that; I want to talk about what my boss said to me!" If the therapist disagrees (e.g., thinks the client is avoiding a discussion of (say) a panic attack because that, in itself, arouses anxiety), then he or she may question the client's decision. The point is that checking on the client's current mood is phrased as an inquiry because what the therapist and the client are working on at this point is to collaboratively set the agenda.

3. *New business.* The therapist will ask, "Are there any major life changes or events that I should know about before we go on?" This question serves many purposes. It can prevent "door-knobbing," that uncomfortable occurrence when the client says, while opening the office door to leave, "Oh, by the way, doctor, I got fired. ..." Or, "The biopsy was positive. ..." Or, "I'm pregnant." Knowing the social happenings of the week can also change the meaning of the client's symptom report by providing a context in which to understand it. Most important, when answered in the affirmative, this question allows the therapist to ask, "*OK, does this go*

on our agenda for today?" Remember, at this point what we are doing is
setting the agenda.

Box 6.8

Student: Suppose the client says, "I'm in crisis and I just want to talk to you right
now and tell you what happened"?
Supervisor: Then that is the agenda!

---

4. *Homework check.* This is a particularly important item, because unless the
   therapist makes an inquiry, the client is likely to decide that the homework
   is not an important part of the therapy process, which in REBT is certainly
   not the message we want to communicate (see Chapter 16). The therapist
   can check briefly by making a few inquiries, such as: "Did you have a
   chance to do your homework? How did it go? Was it a useful assignment?"
   The trick here is to avert a prolonged discussion of the homework by being
   businesslike and reminding the client, "If there's a lot about the homework
   to discuss, *shall we put that on our agenda for today?"*
5. *Setting the agenda.* At this point, the therapist may have some items on the
   agenda and can more broadly ask if there are any other items that belong
   on the list: "Is there one particular problem you want to talk about, or shall
   we pick up where we left off at the last session?" The therapist may also
   have to prioritize and negotiate with the client if there are many items. The
   agenda may have too many items to discuss in the allotted time. In that
   case, the therapist may ask the client, "If we only have time for one item,
   which one shall we focus on?"

After the setting-up questions, the work time left may be twenty to forty
minutes, depending on the total session length. That may seem like a short
therapy time, but the therapist will probably find that time can be more efficiently spent because the preliminary structure has been done.

6. *Summary of work done.* The summary items at the end of the session are
   as important and informative as the setting-up questions. Good teachers
   know that it is useful to review the lesson just taught while it is still fresh
   in the student's mind. This end-of-session summary can be done by either
   the therapist or the client and take just a sentence or two. It serves to wrap
   up and replay the major task or learning theme of the "work time" part
   of the session. It might sound like, "OK, Sean, let's wrap up. What we did
   today was to review how your need for approval caused you a problem in
   the workplace, and you not only disputed those irrational demands, but
   practiced more assertive communication, right?" If the client is the one
   to do the summarizing, the therapist can get a good idea of how well the
   client understood the work.

Box 6.9

REBT differs from traditional, more nondirective therapies. In nondirective work, the client often emerges from a session not able to describe what was accomplished in therapy. Even at the end of a course of therapy, clients often cannot clearly state the nature of the work. Our contention is that being able to summarize and articulate the work of a therapy session significantly assists clients in remembering and utilizing therapy in their everyday lives.

If the client's summary is vague (e.g., "We just kind of talked through the problem again." Or, "It just felt good to be here."), the therapist will want to add some structure so that the client has something to hold onto as an outcome of the hour spent together. A few clarifying questions or simply a restatement by the therapist may help.

7. *Assignment of homework.* If it has not already flowed naturally from the working part of the session, the therapist, the client, or the two working in collaboration may assign homework. The homework provides a review or rehearsal of the session's work, or extends the client's understanding of some area under discussion. The various kinds of homework assignments used in REBT are discussed more fully in Chapter 16, but for now be aware that homework is an integral aspect of REBT. There is a strong positive relationship between progress in therapy and working on homework outside the therapist's office.

8. *Closing questions.* The therapist will ask for positive and negative reactions in turn. To assess the positive reactions, the therapist may say, for example:

"What did you find useful today?" *or*
"What do you think was the most helpful thing we did today?" *or*
"Was there anything I did or said today that you found particularly helpful?"

This is important and potentially useful feedback for the therapist, so ask the question more than once, if necessary, in order to encourage the client to be clear and concrete.

To assess negative feedback, the therapist might say:

"Is there anything that happened today that leaves you feeling worse?" *or*
"Is there anything I did or said today that you feel bad about?" *or* "Did anything rub you the wrong way today?"

If this is the first session or two, the therapist might encourage the client to share negatives: "John, if there *were* any negative moments, would you be *able* to share them with me? Would you give yourself permission to tell me, in the future, if I say or do anything that rubs you wrong? It's really important and helpful to this process if you'll do that, ok?"

Obviously, a number of messages are communicated this way: (a) feedback helps the collaboration; (b) it is acceptable to have negative feelings in therapy; (c) it is good to tell your therapist about them; (d) exploring negative feelings can help; and (e) the therapist can handle hearing negative feelings without becoming angry or hurt.

When the client expresses negative reactions, the therapist may have time to deal with them immediately (e.g., by clarifying, teaching, or apologizing) or may simply put those reactions on the next session's agenda (e.g., "Thanks for telling me that, Linda. How about starting with that next time, since we are out of time today?" or "Could we put that on next week's agenda?").

Note that not every session must follow this model. A model is just that: a *model*, not a "must." It serves as an example, not a rigidly adhered to requirement. Some sessions are devoted to getting the client's relevant history, listening sympathetically, giving counsel, or providing information. There is a range of good practices of REBT. Some rational emotive behavioral therapists work with very short agendas. Albert Ellis, for example, typically began by asking about the homework. He also gave his clients the assignment of making brief notes during the week about anything that really bothered them (e.g., anxiety or depression) and about any time they defeated themselves behaviorally (e.g., procrastinated or behaved phobically). In this way, clients largely structured each session by bringing in these notes and spending much of the session discovering, first, what they told themselves (B of the A-B-Cs of REBT) to make themselves disturbed; and, second, what they did (or now can do) to become more rational (e.g., disputing their IBs and acting against them).

Some therapists eschew the concept of a structured therapy hour altogether. However, we strongly urge you, as a *new REBT therapist,* to use this model faithfully, and to see whether it proves useful for you and your clients. As in many fields of endeavor, such as art, music, or cooking, it is a good idea to begin by following the basics. Sketching from a still life, practicing scales, and following written recipes give students some fundamental skills upon which creativity can later embellish. As a creative therapist, you can emerge with a model quite different than the one outlined above. If so, and it really works for you and your clients, great! The point is to be authentic in your style and approach to the therapeutic session.

Box 6.10

Here is another conversation between a supervisor and a student of REBT that may answer some questions you have about the outline of a session.

Student: Do you follow this structure with all of your clients?

Supervisor: I try to do so with most clients, especially at the beginning of therapy. I have a tendency to loosen up after a while and get sloppier. I always regret it when I do. When I organize sessions, they come out better.

Student: How do you know they come out better? It is not like research. When things work out better, how do you know it is because of the therapy? Do you just *think* it comes out better because you have followed the structure you laid out … or is it true?

Supervisor: I get the data from which to say "better" when I ask the closing questions. When I run very structured sessions, there is practically no latency; clients are bubbling over to tell me what was useful. They can toss it off 1-2-3 because it is organized in their minds, too. When I run looser sessions you can see them falter, and they may say something like, "Well… it was good to talk about the problem." I have to help them fish to take something home in an organized way at the end because I have not structured it well during the session.

PART THREE

The A-B-Cs of REBT: Assessment

7

Identifying the A

THE EXPANDED A-B-C MODEL

When clients describe a troublesome event in their lives, the therapist can think of it as containing up to six elements: (1) what happened; (2) how the client *perceived* what happened; (3) what the client *inferred* about what happened; (4) how the client *evaluated* what happened; (5) the client's acceptance or nonacceptance of the evaluated perception and inferences of what happened; and (6) the client's emotional and behavioral reactions. There will always be at least one of the first three, one of items four and five, and always number six. The first three elements are aspects of the A—the Activating Event; the latter two relate to the client's belief system. Items four and five represent the B—irrational or rational beliefs and the final element, six, is the C emotional or behavioral consequences. If at A the client reports, "She said a horribly critical thing to me," the client is confusing five elements. The issue of what actually happened involves an objective description of what was said and the tone and manner in which it was said. That the comment was a criticism is a perceptual issue or an inference, and whether it need be viewed as horrible that she was criticized is on the one hand an evaluative issue (I do not like it) and on the other hand an imperative attitude (she should not do that).

We are drawing distinctions, therefore, among confirmable reality, perceived reality, and inferential reality. *Perceived reality* is reality as clients describe it and as they presumably believe it to be. *Confirmable reality* refers to a social consensus of what happened. If it were possible for many observers to have witnessed the same event, and they all described it the same way, we would have obtained confirmable reality. In our example above, if a group of people had heard the exact words and the manner in which they were said to our client, and a high percentage of the onlookers perceived the event as an insult, we would conclude that in confirmable reality the woman had indeed insulted our client. *Inferential reality* would be a conclusion the client makes based on what she perceived. The thought, "She does not like me." might be an inference drawn from the fact that "she criticized me." This inference is a thought the client creates about an imagined activating event. Whether the imaged/inferred event is true or not, the client reacts to it with emotional disturbances and therefore we treat it like a real event. People often confuse inferences and irrational beliefs. However, REBT considers them two distinct components of cognition.

To avoid confusion, realize that the term "belief" or "believe" is commonly used in English to refer to descriptive cognitions, inferential cognitions, evaluative cognitions, and imperative cognitions. For example, a client named Dan attended an event where Sue was present and she did not look at him. If many other people noticed that Sue did not look at Dan, this would be the confirmable event. Dan reported in therapy, "Sue is avoiding eye contact with me." This descriptive cognition happens to be part of the activating events. Dan went on to say, "Sue isn't looking at me because she's upset with me." This is an inferential cognition that is also part of the activating event. The *perceptual* and *inferential* cognitions are thoughts; they are about events and considered part of the A. Dan then said, "It's terrible that Sue is upset with me." This is an evaluative cognition that in REBT is a derivative irrational belief. Dan revealed in the session, "Sue should not be upset with me." This is the imperative/demanding belief that is the core B. **To maximize clarity, REBT uses the term "belief" to refer only to evaluative/derivative cognitions and imperative/demanding cognitions.** It will become clear in the next several chapters that it is important to make a distinction between these types of cognitions when the client uses the word "belief." We want to stress that perceptions and inferences are cognitions; however, they are not the type of thoughts REBT focuses on. They are thoughts about the existence of reality.

In effect, the A-B-C model of REBT can be described as follows:

A-*(confirmable)*—the activating event as it could be validated by a group of observers;

A-*(perceived)*—what clients perceive happened in the activating event; that is, their subjective description of it;

A-*(inference)*—the conclusion about what the client thought happened or could happen;

B-*(evaluative/derivative)*—the clients' appraisal or evaluation about what they perceived, inferred happened and/or about themselves or other actors in the event;

B-*(imperative/demanding)*—what the client thought must happen, or must not happen;

C-*(emotional consequence)*—the emotional consequence(s) about what happened or could have happened;

C-*(behavioral consequence)*—the behavioral consequence(s) about what happened or could have happened.

For example, our client Dan also presented a problem of depression because "nobody in my office likes me." Further questioning revealed that co-workers interacted with him primarily about business matters; they infrequently chatted or invited him to lunch, and when they did so, he refused. Thus:

A-*(confirmable)*—"Few people ask me to lunch or attempt to socialize with me."

A-*(perceived)*—"People are not including me in social interactions."

A-*(inferential)*—"I think that no one likes me."

B-(evaluative/derivative)—"It's terrible and awful that no one likes me!"; "I can't stand it that no one likes me."; "I'm a loser because no one likes me."

B-(demanding/imperative)—"People MUST like me."

C-(emotional consequence)—Depression.

C-(behavioral consequence)—Social avoidance.

A crucial distinction to understand at this point is that the client's perception of the activating event does not in itself cause the upsetting emotional reactions. In the example above, Dan could conclude that no one in his office liked him, yet not upset himself about that perception. How would he do so? He could choose not to *evaluate the* A as something terrible. Thus, if at B, he believed that being rejected was merely unfortunate or perhaps (less probably) that not being in the social circle had certain advantages, he could, at C, feel quite differently about the situation. Although the A–(perception) or A–(inference) does not cause C, the client who misperceives A *and* holds irrational demands and derivative beliefs is more likely to be upset than the client who is merely irrational at B. Thus, if Dan thought that almost everyone disliked him and he irrationally demanded that they do like him, and he evaluated that as terrible or intolerable, he would be upset more often than if he did not hold that particular perception and inference at A. If Dan held those A–(perceptions) and A–(inferences), he would have more cues to set off his irrational thinking.

The client who thinks rationally at B, but who continues to distort reality at A can still experience healthy negative affect and act adaptively. Let us return to the example above. If Dan believes that it is only a preference to be liked and he does not *have to* be liked and that it is not awful but highly regrettable that people at the office do not like him, he will still experience a negative emotional response, such as displeasure or disappointment. Thus, the cognitive elements of the A do have an effect on the C, albeit a less significant?dysfunctional? one. Therapeutic work on these cognitive distortions is, therefore, an appropriate endeavor. We make the distinction between the *philosophical, elegant* solution and the *inelegant, cognitive* solution to therapy. Targeting these cognitive elements of the A (A–perception and A–inference) would be the inelegant solution and not the first or primary choice in REBT. We might target these aspects of A *after* we intervene at the philosophical elegant solution of changing the B imperative/demanding and B evaluative/derivative. Helping Dan make new friends would be the *practical solution* that we refer to in Chapter 4.

Box 7.1

Before going on, we encourage you, the reader, to test your understanding of the crucial distinction between A and B. Examine the following client statements. For each, discriminate between the activating event and the IB. The answers are at the end of the chapter.

"I did poorly on that exam. Oh, I'm such a loser!"

"No one talks to me. I just can't stand being so alone!"

"My mother's always picking on me. I know she hates me!"

"Doctor, the most terrible thing happened last week. My wife told me she wanted a divorce."

"I ate like a pig! You see, I know now that I'm really no good."

"I only make $100,000. Do you call that success? Only a loser makes that little money."

"I'm on top of the world when I'm with George because it makes me feel good enough when he loves me."

What are the options available to the therapist if our client Dan above presented with both categories of cognitions A–(perception) and A–(inference) versus B–(imperative/demanding) and B–(evaluative/derivative cognitions)? Two strategies can be recommended. First, cognitive therapists (Beck, 2005) would begin by challenging the accuracy of the client's perceptions and inferences of A. Therefore, if Dan stated that nobody liked him, a cognitive therapist would challenge the accuracy of this statement, calling into question the word "nobody" and the criteria that Dan uses to determine how others feel about him. According to this model, if Dan no longer thought that people disliked him, he would feel better regardless of how he evaluated being disliked. If the therapist challenges the A–(perceived) or A–(inference) the therapist will provide models for the client to challenge the A rather than to do the more difficult work of challenging the B.

The cognitive therapy position is to intervene by first tackling the distortions of the A–(perceptions) and the A–(inferences). As we mention in Chapter 4, Ellis (1977a, 1979a; David, Lyn, and Ellis, 2010) referred to these attempts to correct perceptions and inferences of A as the *empirical* or "inelegant solution." Ellis considered it inelegant because this strategy does not provide the client with a coping technique to deal with his or her distress should reality ever match or approach the client's distorted version of it. For example, although unlikely, it is entirely possible that our client Dan above will indeed find himself in a social environment in which no one likes him. He would be prepared to endure such a fate if, in fact, he believed it to be highly regrettable rather than "horrible." Many Cognitive and Cognitive Behavioral Therapists choose to use this approach as their first choice.

The second strategy comes from REBT and suggests that the more philosophical elegant solution is to enable the client to *assume the worst* and feel healthy, adaptive, but still negative emotions even if it were true. If the client insists that no one likes him, Ellis might have said something like, "Well, we don't know if that's true, but let's just assume for the moment that it is. What do you tell yourself about that?" The assumption in this therapeutic approach is that if the client can deal with this distorted view of the A, the therapist's focusing on the reality will be more manageable.

Which is the better way to proceed? There are no empirical answers because the crucial experiments have not yet been done. In addition, the question itself is perhaps misleading because both Ellis and Beck ultimately do lead the client through an assessment of the accuracy of A.

If the therapist elects to challenge the perception of or inference about A as an initial maneuver, we recommend that the therapist do so thoughtfully. Some clients could react to an early challenge to their perception and inferences by feeling threatened, misunderstood, invalidated, and unsupported by the therapist. Such interactions could weaken the therapeutic alliance.

In summary, the REBT practitioner believes that assuming the worst and aiming for a philosophical elegant solution is valuable because the A situation for the client might be true now or become true in the future, and if this is so, the client will have coping strategies. Consequently, we recommend that the new practitioner follow Ellis's model, reserving the challenge to the client's perception of or inference about the A until some work on disputation of the irrational belief has been done. Some helpful hints on how to intervene "at the level of the A–(perceptions) and the A–(inferences)" are found in Chapter 17.

CLARIFYING THE A

Unnecessary Detail about the A

As we stated in Chapter 1, clients typically come to therapy because they feel or behave in a disturbed manner (C) and believe that they are feeling and behaving disturbed because of some event (A). Usually clients have little difficulty in describing A and often want to spend a great deal of time sharing the details of the event with the therapist. Elaborate detail about the A might be unhelpful. REBT thinks it is unhelpful for three reasons. First, there is only so much time in a session and only so much money for therapy sessions. The more the therapist and client focus on the details of the A, the less time they have to focus on identifying, challenging, and replacing the B. As we uncover **B**s that are more central to the client's problems, we will spend more time discussing them. Second, allowing the client to spend much time on the details of the A reinforces the belief that cathartic expression is curative. Rumination about the details of the A can make the client's disturbance worse and reinforce the idea that the A causes the C. Third, the reality of the A can often not be determined. We just can never have the data to determine whether people at work really dislike you, or whether your spouse speaks to you in a hostile manner.

Communicating this focus without appearing to be dismissive or unsympathetic is difficult, particularly with clients who have an expectation that it is appropriate or curative to present elaborate detail about their past or present troubles. Historical As can never be changed, of course; only the client's demands and evaluations of them are available for discussion, and evaluations can be presented succinctly.

Box 7.2

The types of clients who have a tendency to report excessive detail about the A include:

Those with Obsessive Compulsive Personality Disorder (DSM-IV);

Angry clients, particularly those in couples therapy, because they want to convince the therapist that their partner (the transgressor) is at fault;

Clients with a history of more traditional psychotherapy;

Avoidant clients;

Children and adolescents have a tendency to provide a lot of detail. In work-ing with this population we recommend that you allow them to do so in order to enhance the fragile therapeutic alliance;

Clients with low motivation for change;

Perfectionistic clients who believe you need to have all the details to help them.

Here is an example of a dialogue with a client who gives too much detail about the A:

T: Well, Jose, what were you upset about this week?

C: Well, Doctor, let me tell you exactly what happened. It all started Saturday morning. I went over to visit my wife and children. I got out of my car and my kids came over and greeted me with a big hug. I wasn't doing all those things that usually upset my wife. I went into the house. I didn't say anything about the newspapers being all over the floor or the house not being clean. I did not say any of those things as I usually do. Then I said to my wife... (the client goes on for fifteen minutes describing all the details of what happened and what did not. He finally concludes) and after I begged her to take me back, she did not!

This therapist has allowed too much detail from Jose. Jose's final point is really the most crucial one and is really the A about which he is upsetting himself. One strategy to get to the crucial aspect of A would have been to stop Jose's mono-logue earlier and direct him to focus on the most important crucial aspect of this sequence of events, as in the following example:

T: Well, Jose, what were you upset about this week?

C: Well, Doctor, let me tell you exactly what happened. It all started Saturday morning. I went over to visit my wife and children. I got out of the car and my kids came over and greeted me with a big hug...

T: Is that what you were upset about?

C: No! Let me tell you some more.

T: Before you do that, Jose, let me point something out to you. You often give me many details that are interesting but not necessary in helping me understand just what you are upset about. Try to tell me exactly what you were upset about in this story about your wife.

C: But if I don't tell you what happened, how will you understand me?

T: We can go back and get the details later, but for now, just try to help me under-stand what you were most upset about. It might help to tell me what happened just before you got upset.

Notice that in this dialogue the therapist tries to help Jose focus on the crucial aspect of the A that appears to be the detail that occurred closest to the emotional reaction.

A second strategy to deal with verbose clients is to train them to monitor and condense their own stories by giving them feedback that their present mode of communication is inefficient. With the client above, the therapist could allow the story to run its course, and then intervene in the following manner:

"Jose, you've just given me a great deal of information and detail. I am confused about what is the most important part. Could you go back and tell me just what the reason you got upset was?"

Note the manner in which the therapist allows the client to review his own report and learn to succinctly extract the relevant information. If the client has mistaken the forest for the trees and cannot summarize the relevant incident, the therapist can reflect the critical portion for the client and thereby model condensed speech. For example,

"Jose, it sounds to me that you're upset because even though you've tried to change, your wife won't take you back. Is that it?"

Critical Characteristics of the A

Clients often give us As that are part of stories that include many elements. The therapist needs to clarify what the critical characteristic of the A is. By this, we mean what about the A was the element that triggered the B that resulted in the dysfunctional C. Failure to make this distinction can result in your searching for irrational beliefs that are associated with stimuli that are not upsetting for the client.

We have identified two types of situations that are likely to hide the critical component of the A. The first involves As that are part of a sequence of events and the second involves As that are one of a number of parallel presenting stimuli. A good example of the sequentially hidden As often arises in phobias and anxiety. Marielle said she was afraid of subways. Although this statement can initially seem specific, careful probing revealed a critical activating event. We asked Marielle what it was about subways that triggered her fright. She responded that it was the feeling of being closed-in. We then asked what might happen if she were closed in? Marielle feared she might faint. What might happen if she fainted? She answered that people on the train might judge her poorly. Thus, in this example, Marielle's basic fear was of disapproval, not of trains. Notice that in this example we kept asking questions in a sequential fashion. Each stimulus was part of a chain of events that led to the critical aspect of the A.

Vagueness in Reporting the A

Occasionally therapists will encounter clients who have difficulties in presenting A, being either vague or denying that a specific event triggered some B that, in turn, triggered their disturbed emotions and behaviors. Possible reasons for this vagueness can include

Fear of Therapist Disapproval—Clients might be afraid that what they reveal will elicit disapproval from the therapist.

Experiential Avoidance—The client might fear facing certain events and talks around them to avoid the fear.

Lack of Introspection—Some clients are not aware of what they upset themselves about and they can lack insight, have poor introspection, or they might not have spent much time thinking about the problem. For these clients, spending more time talking about the A can be helpful.

Difficulty in locating A is common in clients who have psycho-physiological disorders, such as migraine or tension headaches. A client might complain of headaches, for example, but insist that nothing is wrong in her life. Now, REBT as a cognitive-change therapy depends on two antecedents: (1) the belief that it is acceptable to self-disclose; and (2) the ability to recognize that a psychological problem exists. The lack of the former antecedent can be approached by remaining empathic, while actively listening over a number of sessions. The second antecedent can be approached in two ways. The first strategy is to ask the client not for problems but for information on how the client could make his or her life even better or could become more self-actualized with their headaches. Second, the therapist can help the client learn problem identification skills and help him or her to recognize areas of conflict in interests, desires, and so on. The most constructive approach to problem identification entails getting a behavioral analysis. For example, clients with headaches might be asked to keep a log in which they record overt and covert antecedents (events, thoughts, and feelings) as well as consequences of each headache episode. As these data accumulate over a number of weeks, patterns will usually unfold. Research supports the efficacy of this strategy (Finn, DiGiuseppe, and Culver, 1991).

Some clients sound as if they are experiencing an "identity crisis." When asked why he came to therapy, Ted might respond, "To find myself—who am I?" The REBT therapist would respond by asking the client to change the question "Who am I?" to "What do I enjoy and what do I value?" Little progress will occur unless the therapist can determine what the client would like to do that s/he is not doing.

Therapists would do well to communicate to the client that they do not teach self-discovery but rather self-construction. REBT views the client not as an entity to be found, but as an evolving process. Once we discover what the client is not doing, we would identify what the client is feeling that stops him/her from doing what he/she would like to be doing. Doing a desired activity then becomes the activating event. The thought of doing the desired activity then elicits irrational beliefs and dysfunctional, unhealthy emotions.

The use of pinpointing questions is helpful. For example, Joan, a depressed client, claimed that she is depressed "all the time." The following questions can help her achieve some focus on her affective state: "When did the depression begin?" "What time of day are you most often depressed?" "What seems to make the depression worse?" If the client reports that she does not know, the therapist can ask, "Can you give me your best bet about what events, thoughts, or feelings make it worse?" If this tactic fails, having the client log their mood and corresponding events might again be useful.

Some clients come to therapy with what therapists call an *existential neurosis* (Frankl, 2006). For example, Kenji complained, "Life is meaningless." A therapeutic clarification might entail asking, "What would it take for your life to be meaningful, or, what would you have to do to give your life meaning?" Clients like Kenji might be harboring the irrational notion that they need to be pursuing noble motives or prestigious goals in order to be happy. Their mundane, everyday existence or their failure to pursue their motives and goals would be the Activating Event.

The most severe problem of identifying A is the client who does not do so at all. They are unaware of what triggers their beliefs and emotions. A client, Robert, reported that he had been depressed for weeks but he had no idea why. Clients faced with this problem frequently choose to reduce their discomfort by creating an attribute for their depression. Understandably, the conclusion that they often arrive at is that they are simply "depressives," thus giving themselves a new A about which they further depress themselves. When Robert does not identify an A at all, the therapist can frequently be helpful by asking pinpointing questions, such as, "Has anything changed in your life in the past few months?" Or "Do you anticipate any changes in your life in the next several months?"

In summary, when the client's description of activating events is confused, vague, or absent, the therapist might keep in mind the following suggestions:

Talk in the client's language in drawing the data from his or her experience.
Ask the client detailed questions.
Ask for recent examples.
Avoid abstract language.
Request logs of events and emotional experiences.
Keep the client on track, not only to reduce the problem of scattered focus but also to serve as a model for the client.
Ask about recent or impending life changes.

Too Many As

Many clients come to therapy with multiple problems and a wide array of activating events to discuss. The initial therapeutic focus is on selecting a target problem on which to work. Therapist and client could list problem areas, and they can have a collaborative discussion about which problem to start with. Unless you have a good rationale to begin with one problem, it is best to start with one problem the client chooses to work on. Occasionally, therapists might wish to make the choice. They could wish to select a small problem with minor affective consequences because (1) they think they can best teach the REBT principles in a less complicated area; or (2) they believe that progress can be made in very few sessions to enhance the client's positive expectations and participation. The therapist might also wish to make the choice regarding what to work on when a problem exists that, if not resolved successfully or soon, the client will experience a cascade of subsequent serious problems. For example, James was arrested for domestic violence for hitting his live-in girlfriend and had an order from the court to stay away from her. He had anger problems with other people in his life and wanted to discuss in therapy his anger with his mother for taking his girlfriend's side. He continued to call his girlfriend to beg for her forgiveness. The therapist decided that James's upset about not having his girlfriend's forgiveness was clinically more important than his anger with his mother. If he sought forgiveness from his girlfriend he would violate the court order and be arrested. This would cause more serious problems for James. The therapist sought to explain this rationale to attain agreement on the immediate session goal and maintain the therapeutic alliance.

Is it wise to allow the client to bring up new problem areas before some resolution of old ones is achieved? Usually, yes, because the clients typically spend only one hour a week in therapy and 167 hours in their normal environment. New problems and crises are bound to arise, and therapists who rigidly insist on sticking to the previous week's agenda might not only fail to be helpful but could jeopardize their relationship with the client. As a caveat, however, the therapist could be watchful for diversionary tactics by the client. Is the presentation of a new problem a way to ward off discussion of difficult or troublesome topics? For example, a compulsive overeater might bring up a number of other problem areas to avoid the work of dieting; the diversionary behavior could thus be another example of frustration intolerance. If the client repeatedly brings up new problems over a number of sessions, the therapist would do well to confront the client directly by pointing out and discussing this aspect of his or her behavior.

In some cases, the therapist might note a common theme in the new problems or a correlation between them and the original or core problem, and can use the new material as a wedge to get to the core. Consider, for example, the case of a young woman, Amy, who presented problem after problem—with the common theme of failing. She reported not being able to do well at a job interview because she believed she did not deserve the job. She described sabotaging love relationships because she believed she was not good enough for her partners. She told of alienating friends because "no one could like a person like me." Amy seemed to believe that it was good for her to be in pain. After several sessions of listening to these activating events, the therapist asked her if she recognized the common theme in all of these examples—that she had to suffer because she was not good enough to reap any of life's rewards. Amy replied that, in fact, she did recognize that theme and recalled how the other members of her immediate family had suffered greatly. Her sister died after a very painful car accident; her mother died after a bout with breast cancer; and her father after a sudden heart attack. Only she had remained alive and apparently believed that it was only right, proper, and moral for her to suffer as well.

THE C BECOMES AN A

One of the most important activating events that the therapist will quickly seek is *secondary disturbance or meta-problems.* In other words, the client's symptom

$$A_1$$
$$B_1$$
$$C_1 \implies A_2$$
$$B_2$$
$$C_2$$

Figure 7.1 The Emotional Consequence Becomes an Activating Event.

(e.g., depression) becomes a new A and itself requires an REBT analysis. Ellis (1979a, 1979d) was influenced to add this concept to REBT by the work of Raimy (1975) who coined the phrase "phrenophobia," fear of going crazy. He estimated that at that time 77% of the clients seen in an office practice had such thoughts and feelings about their primary problems (Raimy, 1975).

This concept is presented in Figure 7.1. A hallmark of rational emotive behavior therapy is its focus on these higher-level problems as *a first* order of business. The cycle of events can proceed as such:

A—Original symptom (e.g., depression)
B—"Isn't it awful that I have this symptom!" "I mustn't feel this way!" "I must be able to get over my problem quickly and easily."
C—This produces more anxiety, guilt, or depression.
The client can become upset about Bs or Cs in such a cycle. For example, clients could become angry or depressed about their irrational beliefs:
"There I go thinking irrationally again. Damn it, I'll never stop. What's the matter with me? I should've learned by now...."

Similarly, clients could become anxious over the physical signs of anxiety, a problem that is particularly prominent in agoraphobia (Goldstein and Chambless, 1978). These clients appear to focus on the physiological symptoms of anxiety and believe that they are signs of impending death, doom, or unbearable discomfort:
"I'm terrified of panic. When I get in the car and I feel the anxiety come, I know I won't be able to stand it! And I think I must not be anxious."

Clients commonly upset themselves over their behavioral difficulties as well. Thus, the drug addict might suffer equally from guilt addiction, and the overeater typically overindulges in self-blame.

Primary focus on such secondary problems might be particularly important when dealing with seriously disturbed or psychotic clients. Psychotherapy of any sort might be difficult or even prove ineffective in ameliorating primary symptoms such as thought disorders or endogenous depressions that might be a function of biochemical imbalances (Davison and Neale, 1990). Often, however, there is a neurotic overlay or secondary symptom; for example, depression about manic-depressive episodes. A useful therapeutic goal might be to help clients learn to accept themselves with their handicaps instead of depressing themselves about such handicaps. The same principle is true, of course, with less seriously disturbed clients. Consider Sam, a compulsive overeater. His overeating is the behavioral C that he and his therapist work on. However, whenever he breaks his diet and over-eats, he immediately begins to cognitively castigate himself, which inevitably leads to the meta-problems of uncomfortable feelings of guilt or shame. Once he is feeling badly enough, he tends to "do something nice for himself" in an attempt to assuage his guilt and shame, and that "something nice" could very well be another hot fudge sundae. The meta-problem causes Sam to engage in the very behavior that is the target of the primary A-B-C. Breaking the meta-level shame and guilt cycle is a prerequisite to helping Sam stay on task to achieve his long-range goal of weight loss.

Box 7.3

Secondary problems are particularly troublesome in clients who have begun to understand their REBT. The more sophisticated they become, the more upset they get with themselves for overreacting. The particular emotional problem these clients feel is *shame*.

It might seem like a paradox, but half the goal of therapy is to change dysfunctional negative feelings and the other half is to accept oneself with these negative feelings. It is important to know which of the two goals you are working on at any time.

The REBT therapist will usually try to determine whether the client has a secondary emotional problem about the primary one by *asking directly*. For example, if the primary problem is anxiety, the therapist might ask, "How do you feel about being so anxious?" It is also important to determine whether there are secondary emotional problems about *appropriate* negative emotions, such as sadness. If the secondary emotional problem interferes significantly with the client's ability to deal with the primary problem, or if you can show the client why it makes more sense to deal with this second layer first, then that will be the initial contract. Because people usually have beliefs about their primary problem, it is a good habit to ask the client what problem they want to work on. We would go with their choice unless we had good reason to convince them to do otherwise, and at which point we would explain our rationale. When we are discussing the secondary level problem, it is easy for the client to go back and forth between the two levels. The therapist needs to monitor which topic is being discussed and stay on track. Sometimes the track changes, and even though the client appears to be speaking on one level, you realize he or she is actually talking about a problem on the other level. When you notice this pattern, you need to point it out to the client and discuss which topic is the more clinically relevant to discuss.

Once a second-level disturbance has been identified as A, therapy proceeds in the usual fashion: C is clarified, irrational beliefs are identified, and the client is assisted in disputing them.

The Elusive A

We see a common unsuccessful maneuver by therapists in supervision. The therapist has difficulty identifying the activating event when clients want to stop a compulsive behavior (e.g., smoking, drinking, overeating, procrastinating) or engage in a beneficial behavior (e.g., exercise, treat others kindly, eat healthy). The client states his behavioral goal (e.g., "I want to stop smoking."). The therapist asks the client when the last time was he smoked and follows up by asking how the client felt when he failed at the behavioral task. The client reports a negative emotion about having failed at changing his behavior. The therapist looks for the irrational belief behind this negative emotion. The therapist has identified a secondary, meta-A-B-C without first identifying the primary A-B-C. This intervention could be correct, but it fails to target the client's stated goal of changing his behavior.

T: What problem would you like to work on today?
C: I want to stop procrastinating and finish my dissertation.
T: When was the last time you procrastinated?
C: I wanted to work on it last night but I watched TV instead.
T: How did you feel after you procrastinated?
C: I felt bad.
T: Ok—let's look at what you were telling yourself about procrastinating to feel bad.

In this example, the meta-emotional reaction (i.e., bad) is not specific enough. The therapist could have persisted for a clearer description of the C. The entire focus is on the secondary meta-emotion. The emotional reaction at failing to control one's behavior can be often a healthy, functional, albeit negative emotion that could motivate the client to learn and practice new self-control strategies. It is important to discriminate between healthy and unhealthy second meta-emotions.

NOTE
Answers to Box 7.1:
Activating event- I did poorly on that exam.
Irrational belief- Oh, I'm such a loser! (Ratings of worth)
Activating event- No one talks to me.
Irrational belief- I just can't stand being alone! (Frustration intolerance)
Activating event- My mother's always picking on me. I know she hates me!
Irrational belief- None present.
Activating event- My wife told me she wants a divorce.
Irrational belief- Doctor, the most terrible thing happened last week. (Awfulizing)
Activating event- I ate like a pig!
Irrational belief- You see, I know now that I'm not really good. (Ratings of worth)
Activating event- I only make $100,000.
Irrational belief- Only a loser makes that little money. (Ratings of worth)
Activating event- I'm on top of the world when I'm with George.
Irrational belief- ...it makes me feel good enough when he loves me. (Ratings of worth)

8

The C: The Emotional and Behavioral Consequences

Why do clients come to therapy? Usually because they are feeling badly, they are in emotional distress, or they are behaving badly. A therapist does not want to lose sight of this focus. Clients usually do not come in to talk or to rid themselves of irrationalities. Many are not even aware of their irrational thinking. The C, the emotional and behavioral Consequences, brings them to the therapist's door. We want to stress that in Rational Emotive Behavior Theory the Consequences are emotional *and* behavioral. The psychological construct of emotions includes not only the feelings, but also the action tendencies that are part of the experience. Many emotion theorists see the behavior as part of the emotion (Frijda, 1986). In REBT, we consider the C to be the emotion(s) that is (are) experienced, the behavior that the client does, or both. Throughout this book when we talk about assessing the C, we mean both the emotion experienced and the behavior. Although the majority of the discussions will focus on negative emotions, the same principles can be applied to positive emotions. Humans can have healthy, functional, positive emotions as well as unhealthy, dysfunctional, positive emotions. Pride is an example of a healthy, functional emotion, compared with the unhealthy, dysfunctional positive emotions such as conceit or pompousness.

More REBT therapists have found that clients can clearly explain their emotions about certain Activating events. In fact, clients usually begin sessions by discussing their emotions. Thus, the client might reply to the question, "What problem would you like to discuss?" by saying, "I feel very depressed lately." If the client does not volunteer the emotion, the advised strategy, in accordance with REBT's emphasis on active-directive intervention, is to ask. After the client has described the activating event, the therapist typically asks, "Well, what emotion do you experience about that event or situation?"

More experienced therapists might have a clinical hunch about the client's emotional state and phrase the question in another way such as, "Are you feeling anxious about that?" This technique might also serve as a strong rapport builder, for clients could conclude that the therapist truly understands their problem. We advise against telling your clients how they feel, however. Phrase your comment as a question and be prepared to change your mind when you have sufficient data that your hunch is wrong.

The more experienced therapist will recognize that certain emotional states are frequently associated with specific clinical problems. For example, avoiding certain situations usually indicates anxiety; verbally abusive behavior generally points to anger; lethargy or inactivity probably means depression; self-injurious or self-deprecatory behaviors indicate guilt or shame; and a recent loss is likely to lead to grief.

Box 8.1

When his clients had trouble in identifying a specific emotion, Albert Ellis encouraged them to "take a wild guess," a method that surprisingly yields quite useful information about C.

In other words, experienced therapists can use four sources of information to infer the presence of emotional states. These include (1) cues from the client's posture and behaviors; (2) the client's vocal reactions such as their tone, metaphors, and language; (3) the common emotional consequences to life situations in the client's culture; and (4) deductions from REBT theory, so that from knowing a client's belief system one can infer a specific emotion.

A general rule of thumb to remember is not to ask your client questions that reinforce the "A causes C" confusion. As supervisors, we frequently hear new REBT therapists phrase questions such as, "How does *that make* you feel?" An alternative question that does not imply that the A causes the C would be, "How do you feel when that happens?" "What is your emotional reaction to that event?" or "What do you make yourself feel about that event?" We recognize this slight but ever so important change in the therapist's wording might feel awkward initially. Rephrasing your question to emphasize the client's emotional responsibility takes practice for new REBT therapists.

DISTURBED VERSUS UNDISTURBED EMOTIONS

A crucial focus of REBT theory is the distinction between healthy functional, negative emotions and unhealthy, dysfunctional, negative emotions. Not all emotions are disturbed or are targets for change. REBT theory does not say that negative emotions are undesirable; in fact, they are an essential part of our ability to adapt and cope with negative activating events. Emotions tell us that we have a problem that needs attention and a reaction (Darwin, 1872). An unhealthy, dysfunctional negative emotion impedes clients' ability to achieve their goals, to react to problems, and to cope with adversity, and often results in self-defeating behavior. In addition, some emotions are physiologically harmful—such as anxiety, which can lead to psychosomatic disorders (e.g., colitis, duodenal ulcers, and hypertension), or intense and damning anger, which at least knots up the stomach. Thus, while it is quite appropriate for a client to feel sad—even very sad—about a loss (e.g., when a parent dies, a spouse leaves, or a child becomes ill), when the sadness is prolonged or debilitating and becomes depression, it becomes a potential target for therapeutic intervention. At some point, we would say that it is more than a negative functional emotion, that it is a disturbed negative emotion.

It is sometimes very difficult to discriminate between a negative but adaptive emotion and a disturbed emotion, but here are some suggestions to differentiate them, qualitatively and quantitatively:

Phenomenologically, an adaptive emotion might not be experienced internally by the person as "suffering," although it might be intense and negative.

Physiologically, a disturbed affective response might be much stronger, accompanied by intense or prolonged autonomic nervous system hyper-reactivity.

Behaviorally, the disturbed emotion leads to self-destructive behaviors or blocks problem-solving behaviors so that the person remains "stuck." As a social stimulus, the disturbed emotion has a higher probability of eliciting punishing or avoidance behaviors in others, rather than empathy or supportive nurturance.

Cognitively, disturbed emotions are distinguished by the irrational thoughts that go along with them.

Box 8.2

The English language is notoriously impoverished in emotional language. In addition, many of us are raised in homes in which emotions are not discussed. At the dinner table, mom or dad might ask what we did during the day. However, only the rare family follows up by asking how you felt about what you did. Some cultures impose a virtual prohibition on expressing emotions, particularly for men; this lack of emotions is described as alexythymia (Lane, Ahern, Schwartz, and Kaszniak, 1997). Alexythymia is a psychiatric term that derives from the prefix "a," meaning "without"; "lex," a stem from which we get the word "lexicon," indicating "language"; and the suffix, "thymia," meaning "mood." Thus, the term implies being without a language to describe mood.

Without a lexicon in a topic, it is difficult if not impossible to express ourselves, and certainly, we have trouble indicating subtle shadings of meaning. Semanticists have taught us that the absence of a rich vocabulary also tells us about how the culture values the topic. The science of General Semantics has taught us that it is difficult if not impossible to make discriminations when we do not have words to describe what we are differentiating.

Even our clinical language is confusing. Consider the word "depression." William Styron, the Pulitzer prize-winning author, states: "I want to register a complaint about the word depression. [It is] ... a term with such a bland tonality that it lacks any magisterial presence, used indifferently to describe an economic decline or a rut in the ground, a true wimp of a word for such a major illness" (Styron, 1990). Similarly, can we distinguish between a depressed mood, grieving, a depressive syndrome, and depressive illness?

Sadness is a mood state, a normal reaction to negative life events, which usually remits without undue laboring. Grieving [is] a more prolonged and intense mood typically precipitated by a major loss... [in which] the focus of the client is on the loss rather than on the self and self-blame.... More than a blue mood, the syndrome of depression is a cluster of symptoms that might include an overreaction to a negative Activating Event, and other cognitive, emotive, behavioral, and physical symptoms.... [Then there is] depression, an illness. Actually, this title would more accurately be, "depressions: a spectrum of illnesses [which seem to be largely heritable and usually recurrent] (Walen and Rader, 1991, pp. 232–3.)

Clearly, we had better teach our clients a vocabulary and a set of discriminating words so that we can be sure that we understand each other!

Although the discrimination between disturbed and nondisturbed emotions is, in our view, one of the most helpful aspects of REBT theory, it is also one of REBT's most problematic aspects because of the difficulty in establishing an operational definition of these terms. Even so, the distinction between disturbed and nondisturbed Cs can serve to give a clear focus to one of the main goals in therapy: transforming suffering into appropriate, adaptive, albeit negative emotions. In addition, the therapist can acknowledge the severity of a negative activating event, communicate empathy for the problem the client faces, and address the reality of dealing with difficult, prolonged As without colluding with the client's "awfulizing."

We suggest that you adopt the typology and vocabulary of common emotional expressions presented in Table 8.1 so that you and your clients might better discriminate among appropriate, helpful, adaptive, undisturbed, healthy emotions, and inappropriate, harmful, maladaptive, unhealthy, and disturbed ones. The terms in Table 8.1 provide a start toward facilitating clearer communication. Because many languages are not designed to discriminate well between functional and dysfunctional emotions, some of the pairs of healthy and unhealthy counterparts could look more different in strength than in quality (e.g., annoyance—anger; or concern—anxiety). Therefore, it could be useful to speak of healthy fear as opposed to unhealthy fear or healthy anger as

Table 8.1. A VOCABULARY OF APPROPRIATE AND DISTURBED EMOTIONS

Healthy and Functional	Unhealthy and Dysfunctional
Concern	Anxiety
Sadness	Depression
Annoyance	Clinical anger
Remorse	Guilt
Regret	Shame
Disappointment	Hurt

opposed to unhealthy anger. One pair, sadness as opposed to depression does not have this problem and everybody can see that one can be very sad without being depressed.

TROUBLE-SHOOTING PROBLEMS IDENTIFYING THE C

A common problem for therapists is the failure to accurately identify the client's C. Sometimes this problem arises because therapists simply do not take the time to label emotions clearly or because therapists assume that they and/or the client intuitively understand what C is. Such an assumption is often wrong, of course. More often, problems in identifying C come not from the therapist's negligence but because emotions are a difficult and confusing problem for the client to identify. The following sections might help the therapist to trouble-shoot some of the reasons for the client's difficulty with identifying the C and offer some ideas to help explore and identify the client's emotions.

MIXED FUNCTIONAL AND DYSFUNCTIONAL EMOTIONS

Some emotional experiences are a mixture of healthy and unhealthy ones. Therefore, identifying such emotional experiences can be difficult because one has to identify the two components of the functional and dysfunctional emotion parts. Clients who are not familiar with this distinction will talk about one emotion. A good practice within REBT is to discriminate between the two types of emotions, because we leave the functional emotion unchanged and only focus on the unhealthy one (Backx, 2012).

GUILT ABOUT C

Trouble in identifying the C might stem from guilt; clients might be unwilling to label their emotion if they are experiencing negative emotions/meta-emotions for which they denigrate themselves, thus causing a second C (i.e., "C becoming an A"). We saw an example of this in the case of Talya, the wife of a devoted rabbinical scholar. She often felt compelled to interrupt his studies to remind him of his responsibilities to his congregation, such as visiting the sick or the bereaved. He would do as she suggested and received the thanks and approval of his flock. She, however, being quiet and shy, was perceived as aloof, and received no credit for her contributions to the congregation. Talya stated her problem vaguely as wanting more support, understanding, and appreciation; yet she could not define a specific C other than reporting she felt she was overlooked and taken for granted. These statements are A–(perceptions) and A–(inferences). Further exploration revealed that Talya's underlying C was anger. However, as the wife of a clergy, she believed she could not feel such an emotion. Her guilt about her anger prevented her from sharing this emotion with the therapist, let alone her husband.

What might the therapist do in such cases to encourage the client to face the emotion? Iris Fodor (1987) suggested that Gestalt exercises might be helpful to REBT and CBT therapists in general to help clients reveal their emotions. Ellis (2002) used the Gestalt exercises in marathon groups for the same purpose. Using Gestalt or psychodrama exercises, such as the empty chair technique, could have helped Talya, the rabbi's wife. We could ask her to imagine her husband or one of the ungrateful parishioners sitting in an empty chair. She might then be engaged in a dialogue in which she plays one or both parts, perhaps moving between the two chairs as she exchanges roles. Loosening the usual stimulus constraints in this way might increase the likelihood that she will acknowledge her anger.

Box 8.3

A very powerful way to help clients become aware of their emotions is visual imagery. Ask the client if she would be willing to close her eyes. Tell her you will be giving her some very open-ended instructions and that you do not want her to report her thoughts or give you many words. Instead, ask her to be very still and wait until a picture or image comes to her mind. Very mild direction in the case of Talya for such an image might be, "Let an image of you and your husband come to mind." or "Imagine you are among the members of the congregation."

Often, therapists can use this extraordinarily evocative and emotive procedure, particularly when they probe the image by follow-up questions such as what is going on, what feelings are being expressed in the image, and what bodily sensations the client is experiencing. These images will help identify the emotion.

Try modeling. The therapist might say, for example, "Talya, do you know anyone else in a similar situation? What do you think they would be feeling?"

Try using humor. Be deliberate in your exaggeration, gently poking fun at the situation, or make a humorous analogy. The therapist might set the climate for a less threatening acknowledgment of Talya's anger. Examples: "I guess you really are a saint; some people would be boiling mad!" or "It's great how you let them ignore you; everybody loves that!"

SHAME ABOUT C

Clients might not be in touch with their emotions because of a tendency to intellectualize their predicaments. Such individuals will avoid labeling their emotions and instead describe the situation or offer rationalizations for their behavior. They might even deny that they experience emotions at all. Underlying this emotional anesthesia might be the belief that the expression of emotion reflects a sign of weakness to others. Avoidance of emotions prevents the client from being judged negatively by others and feeling shame.

The key concept here is that the therapist wants to communicate that all emotions are justified in the sense that they exist. Emotions are neither acceptable nor unacceptable for any external event, because emotions are internal and come from what a person is saying to himself or herself about the outside events.

Machiavelli (1532/1998), in his famous book, *The Prince,* taught that it might be in one's best interest to withhold information from others on how one is feeling. We would want to help clients understand when it might be in their best interest or not to reveal their emotions. However, they need not feel ashamed or be condemning of themselves if others think less of them for having an emotion.

LITTLE OR NO EMOTION IN THE SESSION

The therapist might encounter clients who express no emotions in the sessions. Assuming that the absence of emotion is not a psychotic symptom, the therapist might want to check out two possible hypotheses about such clients.

1. Clients might believe that they are "supposed to be serious" in therapy. That is, therapy is a solemn occasion requiring hard work and a no-nonsense attitude. In such situations, the therapist will want to disabuse clients of such notions by direct suggestion, modeling, and use of creative strategies to elicit more emotion and put the client at ease (e.g., encouraging disagreement with the therapist, or asking clients to pantomime their problems or express them in song or poetry).
2. The therapist's behavior might elicit little emotion and might even inhibit its expression. For example, the therapist might be making long-winded speeches, asking closed-ended questions, stacking questions, moving too fast, or confusing the client. Listen to recordings of your therapy sessions with such clients and observe your own remarks that precede instances of minimal emotion. Try to encourage verbal expression by asking simple, open-ended questions (e.g., "And then what?").

FEAR ABOUT EMOTIONS

Clients might not be aware of their feelings because they fear the emotion; the problem might be one of avoidance of emotional states. For example, feeling depressed is an uncomfortable or even painful experience. The client might avoid discussing life situations that are evocative of this emotion. We have seen clients who are fearful of their anger outbursts, fear depression, and fear their anxiety and phobias. The problem in this case seems to be one of discomfort anxiety and frustration intolerance, in which clients convince themselves that the emotional turmoil is more than they can stand. Avoidance of emotions because they are too painful can cause many psychological problems such as agoraphobia or substance abuse (Hayes, Wilson, Gifford, Follette, and Strosahl, 1996), and procrastination (Steel, 2007).

The important clinical strategy is helping clients realize that their own fear of their emotions blocks and prevents them from facing and resolving their problems. Consider the case of Felix, a prominent professor who came to therapy with vague complaints about a stilted life and the desire to become more self-actualized and happy. Felix described his wife with flat, unemotional language. He described her as being over-involved with her career, her parents, and the children. However, Felix did not sound close to her. In addition, Felix described an extramarital affair as his soul mate. His happiest times were with his mistress. Felix felt angry with his wife for allowing distance in their relationship. However, he was afraid to admit these problems.

T: Felix, you seem to describe your happiest times as when you see your girl-friend. Moreover, when you speak about your wife, you sound cold and distant. I am wondering how you feel toward your wife.

C: I really did not come here to discuss this.

T: I know. I think you would be happier if I did not notice your feeling toward your wife.

C: Yeah, that would be a lot easier. I guess I love her, but sometimes I think she stopped loving me.

T: So is this something you might want us to discuss?

C: (Exhales deeply) That might open a whole can of worms that I don't want to face.

T: So you are aware that you are avoiding your feelings about your marriage and your affair?

C: It is just so scary to think about it. We have kids and a history together. I am just afraid to examine how I feel about her because of all the things that might unravel.

T: It sounds like you are just too frightened to look at your feelings. But, if you let that fear win, you might never solve any of the problems that brought you here.

Identifying Felix's fear about examining his emotions placed this meta-emotion on the top of the agenda.

CONFUSING THE A, B, AND THE C

People in our culture frequently confuse thoughts and feelings. Sometimes you might ask a client to describe a feeling and he or she will respond with a belief. For example, the client might say, "When she said that, I felt dumb." At other times, you might ask a client to identify a belief and get a feeling for a response. You might ask, "What were you thinking then?" and the client might respond, "Oh, I was thinking I was anxious."

A difficulty that new therapists and clients often share is discriminating **B**s from **C**s, and this problem might relate in part to the imprecision in our language. The word "feeling," for example, could have many different meanings in everyday speech:

Physical sensation—"I feel cold."
Opinion—"I feel that taxes should be lowered."
Emotional experience—"I feel happy."
Evaluation—"I feel that it's terrible."

The therapist can carefully listen for clients' meaning of "feel" and encourage them to use the term to describe emotional consequences rather than opinions and evaluations. This distinction will help clients detect the difference between their beliefs and emotional **C**s, which will be of great value to them when they attempt to dispute their irrational beliefs. Thus, when clients mislabel B as a feeling, it is often useful to stop and correct them. The important point is to listen to the client's answer to your question. Make sure s/he is answering the question you asked.

CONFUSING THE A AND THE C

Although REBT has taught you to distinguish between A and C, many of your clients will not make such distinctions. Frequently when you ask clients what they were feeling, they will give you an A–(perception) or A–(inference) as the answer. Remember our discussion from Chapter 3 that these components are actually cognitions, but they are not the beliefs that we think are crucial to disturbance in REBT. They are part of the A because they are potential events about which the clients get themselves upset. Here are some examples of responses we have heard clients give to questions about their feelings, responses that were actually not emotions but A–(perceptions) and A–(inferences).

I feel ignored.
I feel disrespected.
I feel unloved.
I feel left out.
I feel betrayed.
I feel powerless.
I feel I am not smart (pretty, sexy, sophisticated, thin) enough.

In each of these examples, the client has used the verb "feel" to identify a perception or inference about a potentially true situation. The clients have used the verb "feel" but have not described the emotional Consequence. The strategy we recommend in such situations is as follows. The therapist would reflect back and acknowledge that the perception or inference the client has reported might be true or could happen. The question to follow would be, "What emotion would you feel or experience if that were so?"

T: How were you feeling then?
C: I felt betrayed.
T: Well, let's suppose you *were* betrayed. What emotion would you have felt about being betrayed?
C: Well, I suppose angry.

Sometimes clients persist in answering questions about the C with synonyms for events about which they are upsetting themselves. For example,

T: How were you feeling then?
C: I felt betrayed.
T: Well, let us suppose you *were* betrayed. What emotion would you have felt about being betrayed?
C: Well, I felt deceived.
T: Well, let's suppose you *were* deceived, what emotion would you have felt about being deceived?
C: I felt they were disloyal to me.
T: You know Roxanne, betrayal, deception, and disloyalty are all events that you thought happened to you, but they are not emotional reactions. Emotions are experiences like anger, joy, sadness, anxiety, and shame. So, what emotion did you feel about being betrayed and deceived?

Another example is a client, Tom, who felt fear that people would reject him because he thought he was inadequate in many ways. Tom was depressed because he condemned himself for not being more successful and popular. When we asked Tom, "How were you feeling on the day you did not apply for the job?" and he responded, "I felt dumb," we recognized that Tom (1) has most likely strong feelings of anxiety and depression; and (2) he possibly could be making a self-deprecatory statement about himself. However, before trying to test these two hypotheses, we pointed out to Tom that "dumb" is not an emotion but reflects a thought or inference he concluded about himself, one which he was frightened would cause people to reject him. Dumb was not the emotion. It is important to make this distinction because Tom might have attempted to dispute his feeling of "dumb" or to justify his belief that he is dumb because of this so-called feeling. Thus, in the example above, the therapist would point out to Tom that he does not *feel* dumb; he feels anxious and depressed about believing that he is dumb. The stage is now set for working on this irrational belief.

DESCRIPTIVE DEFICITS

When asked how they are feeling, clients can be confused about their emotion. The confusion might be because they lack an adequate emotional vocabulary to express themselves. In general, the more the therapist can help clients label their emotional problems, the more easily they will be able to grapple with them. Again, if a client can only describe him or herself as feeling "down," the therapist can inquire if he understands the word "depression." In other words, the therapist might want to take the opportunity to expand the client's vocabulary. A side benefit of this procedure is increasing the client's ability to profit from bibliotherapy, because most self-help books use terms such as "depression," "anxiety," and so on.

The therapist might help clients label their emotions by instruction and modeling. Initially, the difference between positive and negative emotions might be suggested (e.g., "Did you feel good or bad?"), after which more descriptive terms might be suggested and discussed. Some of the following exercises might be useful either in session or as homework assignments: *Here are the names of some emotions or feelings:*

happy   sad
angry   disappointed
proud   hurt
embarrassed   curious
scared   frustrated
nervous   guilty
relaxed   anxious
Pronounce each word to yourself; say it aloud.
Do you know what each word means?
Pantomime (act without words) each of the words that you know. (People express the feeling in different ways, so there is no right way to do it!). Are there any other feelings you can think of? If so, write them down.
Orally or in writing, complete the sentence, "I feel ___" in as many ways as you can.
Start a diary of "I feel" or "I felt" statements. At first, just write the statements. Later, begin to add, "When such and such happened, I felt ___." For example, "I felt anxious when I started writing this diary." Finally, keep a log of your emotional experiences through the day.

Another reason clients confuse their emotions is that they are experiencing several emotions about the same event. Although we have an A-B-C theory, this does not mean that clients will have only one of each element in their experience. In clinical practice, it is more likely that multiple elements exist at each level. A client might have A to B to C_1, C_2, C_3. It is important to check with the client that they have identified the various emotions they experienced in response to the activating event. Do not assume that the first emotion reported is the most clinically relevant one.

Let us return to the client, Felix, mentioned above who had a fear of examining his emotions toward his marriage. His Primary A was that his wife worked a lot and displayed very little affection toward him. Once the therapist successfully identifies this meta-fear, the session can focus on this primary problem. He reported feeling confused about what he felt. The therapist offered Felix the possibility that he had more than one emotion. Could Felix identify all the feelings he might have toward his wife? Once he was free not to have one correct answer, Felix identified several emotions. He felt angry with her for not being affectionate. He felt guilty that perhaps her lack of affection resulted from his own inadequacy. He felt hurt that perhaps she did not love him anymore. He felt fearful that she would leave him and he would be alone. He also felt shame that he would be disgraced if she left him. Once this list was identified, the therapist asked Felix which emotion they should work on first.

Notice that each emotion has a slightly different crucial component of A. Felix's anger emerged from the A–(inference) that she did not love him. His guilt was triggered by the A–(inference) that he was responsible for her lack of love. His fear was elicited by his A–(inference) that she would leave him and he would be alone. Finally, his shame was related to the A–(inference) that others would view him negatively for being divorced.

DICHOTOMOUS THINKING

Many clients categorize emotional states dichotomously; for example, they might believe that the only emotion they can feel is an unhealthy, dysfunctional negative emotion or a neutral feeling as if nothing happened. In fact, clients have choices about which qualitatively different emotion they might experience. Let us suppose that a client has experienced a loss. Within the larger category of sadness, which is one of the basic human emotions, she could feel sad, depressed, despondent, or disappointed. Some of these choices are healthy/functional emotions that will help the client resolve the loss. Others are unhealthy/dysfunctional emotions that will lead to disturbance and failure to resolve the loss. Therapy focuses the client on realizing that people have options regarding what they can work to feel (Dryden, DiGiuseppe, and Neenan, 2010; DiGiuseppe and Tafrate, 2007).

Box 8.4

Your client can report feeling "frustrated" at C. Technically frustration refers to the blocking of goals and is an activating event rather than a feeling (DiGiuseppe and Tafrate, 2007; Miller et al., 1958; Trexler, 1976). However, the word frustration can refer to an emotion or feeling of disappointment that is a weak version of anger. We think that the original meaning of blocking of goals is the correct one. However, therapists need to be clear, and ask their client which usage the client intends. You might say to your client, "'Frustration' often means a blockade of a desire. That is something that blocks or frustrates us from getting what we want. When you were frustrated by your receptionist yesterday, what emotion did you feel—anger, annoyance, disappointment, or indifference?"

If the client can envision and label various types of emotions, he or she might also be able to envision ways (cognitions) to arrive at a more desirable or adaptive feeling state. The therapist might, for example, present a group of emotional labels to the client and help him or her to classify the words as unhealthy/dysfunctional or healthy/functional emotions. It can then be pointed out that rational thinking usually leads to healthy/functional emotions (such as intense regret or sorrow), which are adaptive, and irrational thinking leads to strong and debilitating emotions.

MISLABELING EMOTIONS

Clients often mislabel their emotional states, so that it is a good rule of thumb to clarify the emotional referent. The therapist would be wise to ask routinely for some explanation or expansion of the client's emotional label (e.g., "What do you mean by guilty/anxious/bothered?") and, if the client seems to be in error, point it out (e.g., "Sam, it sounds more like you're angry than anxious."). Emotions that clients frequently seem to mislabel are guilt or anger, which are confused with anxiety.

Some clients, more often men, and people from some other cultures, are likely to somatize their feelings rather than clearly label the emotion. When asked how they are feeling, such clients might describe having "tension in my neck," thus describing the physiological sensation rather than the emotion.

UNCLEAR LABELING OF EMOTIONS

Clients might use a label that, although clear to them, might be unclear to the therapist. For example, Junko said, "I was so indignant!" Do you understand precisely what she means? Is this level of affect mild, moderate, or intense? Is it an adaptive or maladaptive emotion? Does it stem from a rational or irrational belief? The answers to these questions can become clear by asking Junko clarifying questions such as, "What do you mean when you say 'indignant'?" or "That sounds like you're angry; what do you feel, think, or do when you are indignant? How angry are you?" Common examples of unclear labels include:

I feel bad.
I feel upset.
I feel distressed.
I feel stressed out.
I feel uptight.
I feel overwhelmed.

Therapists can help with clarification by asking directly, "When you say you feel upset, do you mean you feel angry?" or "When you say you feel overwhelmed, are you overwhelmed with depression? Or sadness?" Therapists might also ask a multiple-choice question, such as, "By 'stressed out,' do you mean you feel anxious?

Or depressed? Or angry? Or guilty?" Writing this simple emotional menu on a chalkboard or even an index card can help the client clarify his or her current mood and provide a teaching model for future communication.

Sometimes clients will assert that they cannot find the exact right word to describe their emotion. You might help by suggesting that they show you how they feel by using their facial movements or body postures, and modeling yourself just a bit to break the ice. This strategy of using exaggerated kinesthetic facial and body cues might give the therapist a clue as to what the emotion might be and help the client by evoking a keener awareness of the emotional state.

A preliminary goal for such clients might be to appreciate the extent to which all people react emotionally. As a homework assignment, the therapist might request clients to write down all the different "I feel ___" or "I'm in a ___ mood" statements that they hear others make in the course of a week. They can also monitor their own statements of this sort. In addition, the therapist could make use of the three techniques described above.

LACK OF APPARENT DISTRESS

Occasionally, one will interview clients who rattle off a list of problems, but they are not in distress about anything. Research has documented that there are clients who come to therapy with very low levels of disturbance; and they tend to get worse as the session progresses. The therapist might want to consider the following possible explanations for those seeking therapy but displaying low levels of disturbance. Perhaps the client (1) is truly not in distress, but is seeking some type of growth or actualization experience; (2) has come to therapy for companionship rather than help; (3) is worried about not being "normal" and has come to therapy to seek reassurance; or (4) is defensive and engages in avoidance of negative emotion. If no emotional distress is apparent, confrontation might be recommended. The therapist could discuss one or more of the above explanations with the client so that appropriate goals for action might be set.

Avoidance maneuvers pose perhaps the trickiest problem, for if clients' behaviors effectively prevent them from experiencing unhealthy, negative emotion, both they and the therapist will be in the dark about C. If an emotional consequence is not evident but clients describe troublesome behaviors, it is often helpful to apply a learning theory model to the behavior problems. Behavior is maintained either by its pleasurable results or by the avoidance of negative stimuli. Often the negative stimuli are the clients' own hidden emotions. Sometimes direct confrontation might break the blockade, as in the following instance. A possible solution is to ask clients to imagine they are doing or confronting the things that they avoid. A client, Jerry, was avoiding taking a major licensing exam, yet claimed he felt no anxiety about it.

T: Jerry, if that were so, if you had no anxiety at all, why would you avoid taking the test?

C: But I don't experience any anxiety now.

T: Right, because as long as you stay away from that test, you avoid experiencing your anxiety. Do you see that something is blocking you from getting too close to the exam, and that something could be anxiety? Now what do you think would happen if you took the test and failed?

C: Well, I am not sure.

T: OK, can you imagine that you wake in the morning and are in the exam room faced with taking the exam. How do you feel in that image?"

C: Well, I won't like that.

Often, a more extensive use of projective fantasy is called for to discover what the client fears. We recall a client, Grace, who reported that she was concerned that she was dating only married men. She denied any particular negative emotion and stated that she was simply more attracted to married men. The therapist guided her through a fantasy in which she imagined herself out on a date with an attractive man who suddenly announced that he was single and who found her to be the most desirable woman he had ever met. Here we asked Grace to confront in imagery what the therapist hypothesized Grace was avoiding.

In another case, an obese client, Kees, reported that he had no dysfunctional emotions. The therapist hypothesized that Kees avoided dating, and that his excessive eating and weight was a mechanism to avoid interaction with potential lovers. Kees had no reaction to the therapist's hypothesis. The fact that he was so neutral to the idea was unusual. The therapist asked Kees to fantasize about being very slim and out on a date with an attractive man. Kees began to squirm when the therapist mentioned this idea. When he began the image, he became red and said he felt "uncomfortable." In both instances, the imagery exercise allowed the clients to access interpersonal anxiety, which their avoidance behaviors (dating married men or being overweight) had successfully blocked. The anxiety then became the focus of therapy.

A client, Charles, came to therapy but reported that he experienced no specific emotional problems except exhaustion. He complained of feeling tired almost all of the time, and no matter how he slept, he never felt truly rested. Medical evaluation revealed no physiological basis for his fatigue. His physician referred him to therapy. Extensive questioning revealed that Charles had a demanding yet fulfilling job, enjoyed a full social life, and was active in athletic events. In all respects, he appeared to be "living the good life." On closer questioning, however, Charles reported that he did not always enjoy all of his activities and occasionally did not want to do them. Because the intrinsic pleasure of the activity was not always maintaining his behavior, the therapist hypothesized that some of his busy schedule was actually avoidance behavior. The therapist asked Charles to fantasize a typical day in his life, and to omit one of his activities. After each imagery scene, Charles reported, much to his own surprise, feelings of guilt. Further analysis revealed an irrational notion of self-worth based on accomplishing all that he thought he *should* do. Thus, he avoided the underlying emotion of guilt by maintaining an extremely active life.

A similar problem is often encountered with clients who report an inability to control addictive behaviors such as drug abuse, smoking, drinking, and overeating.

They might not acknowledge any emotional problems that increase the frequency of their addictive behaviors, although they do sense guilt over having done them. With such clients, the therapist might ask them to imagine that they are sitting in front of the food or cigarettes and deny themselves these pleasures. Clients usually report a very uncomfortable feeling akin to intense agitation, heightened arousal, muscle tension, or jitteriness. This emotional consequence, a result of their irrational belief that they need to have what they desire, might have remained out of their awareness because they were so successful at avoiding the unpleasant feeling by quickly devouring what they desired. Such an imagery exercise might help clients get in touch with their **Cs**.

EMOTION IN THE SESSION

Whether or not clients are able to identify emotional reactions in relation to their life events, the therapist will want to attend to emotional cues within the therapy session. Body position, tensed muscles, clenched teeth, breathing changes, perspiration, facial expression, moisture in the eyes, giggling, and so forth can reveal the relevant emotions. A good therapist can read clients' body and facial expressions and will make associations between what is said or not said and clients' expression of emotion. This is a crucial skill for identifying emotions and becoming a good therapist. Do everything possible to enhance and practice this skill.

When you see these signs of emotion, you might want to begin to do an in-the-moment A-B-C analysis. Do not make the mistake of avoiding working with emotions expressed in the session. Therapy does not always have to deal with problems of past or recent history. Reflect what the client is expressing and use that as a start of your analysis. Below is an example of such an interchange:

T: Sally, I notice that your eyes loom red and your posture seems dejected.
C: Oh, you are right! (sobs)
T: Sally, you seem to be feeling upset right now. I wonder if you could tell me what emotion you are feeling.
C: Well, it is so hard. My whole life is ruined. I have nothing to live for.
T: I understand. It seems that you are feeling depressed about that.
C: Yes.
T: Well, why don't we talk about that now rather than the other problems you brought up? Because as long as you believe that, you are going to feel depressed and cry.

AGREEING TO CHANGE THE C

Once clients have acknowledged and correctly identified the distressing emotion, they have a decision to make. Do they want to keep experiencing or change this emotion? For example, they have the right to keep or give up their anger, anxiety, or depression, and the pros and cons of their choice might be an interesting topic for discussion. Emotions after all, have their advantages; they communicate what is going on within us to others, and others could respond in ways we like. Sometimes people have what therapists call "secondary gain" for their emotions. These gains or advantages are often immediately reinforcing, but the negative consequences of the disturbed emotion make them self-defeating.

Identifying and challenging one's irrational beliefs only makes sense if one holds some prerequisite beliefs. These include:

1. My present emotion is dysfunctional.
2. There is an alternative, culturally acceptable, and more functional emotional script to experience in response to this type of activating event. It is better for me to give up the dysfunctional emotion and work toward feeling the alternative one.
3. My beliefs cause my emotions.
4. Therefore, I will work at changing my beliefs to change my emotions.

Convincing the client of these four ideas will motivate clients who are reluctant to change their emotions to engage in the REBT process. This model facilitates agreement on the goals of therapy and moves clients to the action stage of change.

We have presented a model to establish these insights as a way to motivate change (DiGiuseppe and Jilton, 1996; DiGiuseppe and Tafrate, 2007). The steps involve asking clients to assess the consequences of their emotional and behavioral C in a Socratic fashion. This helps clients identify the hidden costs and negative outcomes of their emotions and behavior. Next, the therapist presents alternative emotional reactions that are culturally acceptable to the client. Because people learn emotional scripts from their families, and learn that some emotional scripts are acceptable to their cultural group, it is possible that a disturbed client has not changed because he or she cannot conceptualize a healthy/functional emotional script to experience in place of the disturbed emotion. Therapists can explore with the client alternative emotional reactions that are culturally acceptable. Next, therapists help the client make the connection that the alternative script is more advantageous to the client. Once the client reaches this insight the therapist teaches the B to C connection to the client and can move on to identify the IBs.

Consider the example of Tamara, an angry young mother. In many ways, Tamara's anger worked for her; when she yelled at her son about his messy room, he quickly tidied up. The display of anger also was intrinsically reinforcing; after Tamara had a temper tantrum, she felt a pleasant state of fatigue and relaxation akin to the aftereffects of exercise. Quite simply, it felt good when she stopped. In addition, Tamara provided her own cognitive self-reinforcement for her abreactive display (e.g., "I did the right thing by getting angry!"). Thus, interpersonal, kinesthetic, and cognitive factors operated to help maintain her angry feelings and behavior. To help overcome these factors, the therapist could suggest that (1) Tamara could consider the long-range consequences of her behavior. Certainly, her displays of anger did not endear her to her son. (2) She was providing a poor model for her son. (3) There were more helpful ways of achieving a release of tension, such as relaxation exercises. (4) There were more effective ways of controlling her son's behavior. (5) And, her cognitive statements were misplaced and stemmed from an exaggerated and unflattering sense of righteousness.

Box 8.5

One strategy used by REBT and CBT therapists to increase the client's motivation to change is the two-column format (e.g., Burns, 1980). The therapist can assist the client in developing a list of advantages and disadvantages in changing a particular emotion. Here, for example, is one client's (partial) list of pros and cons in giving up her chronic anger at her husband:

Advantages of eliminating anger	Disadvantages of losing anger
I would have more energy.	I will become a doormat.
Long-term health consequences would be improved.	It works. I would be giving up a useful tool.
It would be better for the kids.	I might be manipulated.
I would be less jealous of other couples.	I do not have any other way of getting my needs met.
I would feel proud of myself.	I will not be standing up for my principles.
I would be more comfortable in my own home.	

We recommend that you have your clients list the pros and cons for *both* the short-term and long-term. Can you imagine the work that this client has to do before she will agree to reducing her anger?

A more subtle source of gain can sometimes be operating; a debilitating emotion is maintained to avoid an even more distressing one. Consider, for example, the case of a mother who lost custody of her children to the father, an event that precipitated intense and prolonged depression, which the client seemed unwilling to surrender. What would it mean to this woman to give up grieving? Apparently, she believed that it would prove her an uncaring and uncommitted mother, a concept that induced an even more intense feeling of guilt. Once this irrational belief was successfully disputed, however, the client could agree to work at relieving her depression.

Clients might decide to remain upset rather than do the hard REBT work of disputing. In essence, they might be saying either, "That's the way I am." or "I can't change." or "I've always been this way." or "It's more rewarding [or easier] for me to be upset." Once identified, these hypotheses can be tested, perhaps by simply requesting that the clients do an experiment that will allow them to test their hunch: "Is it, in fact, true that you cannot change or that it's easier to be upset?"

The point to keep in mind is that there might be many reasons why the client is reluctant to change C, some of which the therapist might be able to challenge. If the client does not want to change C, however, rational emotive behavior therapy usually cannot proceed.

BEHAVIORAL ASPECTS OF C

So far, we have discussed clients presenting primarily emotional problems. As we stated in the beginning, emotions produce action tendencies that are meant to resolve threats or problems. Behavioral reactions are part of the C and in all cases we want to be careful to assess what clients actually *do* and not just what they feel. Sometimes their behavior might be in the foreground and is more important than the emotion. Such behavioral **C**s are procrastination, addictions, compulsive behaviors, and defensive avoidance. Often new REBT therapists focus so much on what clients feel that they ignore or miss a behavior problem because they have not considered a behavior as part of C.

REBT falls under the category of the behavior therapies. As such, it is important to identify behavioral goals that clients will work toward. Change in feelings without change in behavior would be an unsuccessful treatment. In addition, clients can claim to change their feelings, but if there is no corresponding change in behavior, one must question the accuracy of the emotional change. The discussion *a priori* and *post hoc* A to B to C in Chapter 7 emphasized this point.

TEACHING TRANSCRIPT

In the following therapy transcript, the therapist is confronted with a client who describes experiencing a number of unpleasant emotions, and the therapeutic task is to label them, rate their severity, and rank-order them for investigation.

TRANSCRIPT SEGMENT

T: Hello, Ashwin. What problem do you want to work on today?

C: My wife says I am depressed, and she is very concerned about me. I have very confused moments. The reason I originally felt suicidal—I don't even know how to express the feeling that I had, because I know if I really wanted to commit suicide I would have accomplished it.

Note that the client really has not answered the therapist's question.

C: Well, I felt this way, if it happened, if the eight pills had done the job that would have been OK, and if they didn't, fine.

T: But you were not going to ensure that they did by taking twenty-five or thirty?

C: Exactly. That is how I felt.

C: Well, after my first divorce, I was uptight and I thought about it. Twice, in fact.

T: How are you feeling today?

Here the therapist returns to the client's feelings after making reasonably sure that suicide was not imminent.

C: Extremely anxious.

T: Anxious?

C: Yes.

T: Usually, most people who attempt suicide are depressed, but you are anxious?

Notice that the therapist is working from a conceptual schema and checking the client's response against it.

C: Yeah, I am pretty anxious.

T: How anxious do you feel?

C: Well, when I become nervous my back goes out.

T: You get muscle pains?

C: That is why I am wearing my girdle now. I went out Sunday night, and I didn't do anything physical. I just bent over and it went. So, I know that is an indication that something is not right.

T: Have you been to a physician about your back problems?

C: Yes. I slipped a disc about fifteen years ago. It has been a chronic thing. Many times, I think it is due to muscular strain because I do work physically. And sometimes this has nothing to do with any...

T: Well, it could be just muscular tension. So, you do get muscular tension and get tight?

C: Well, I was not aware of it, but it has really become more of a chronic situation. My children live in Canada and that is when it really started to become chronic, when they moved to Canada. Mary brought it to my attention.

T: How long ago was that?

C: Four years ago.

T: So, for the last four years your anxiety has been getting worse.

C: Only when I know they are coming in.

T: When they are coming, you get more anxious. How frequently does that happen?

The therapist is acknowledging and accepting the client's feelings while gathering additional information about the client's life situation.

C: Well, they are supposed to come in twice a year. This year it has been only once and they will be coming again in three weeks. It is starting to build—the anxiety is started.

T: So, as your children come closer you get anxious, or frightened, as if there is something you will not be able to cope with, and you feel immobilized? Or do you mean that as the kids get closer, you get concerned about it, become committed to action, and still feel in control? Or do you mean that you are just excited about it?

C: No, I am really anxious, panicky.

The therapist has just modeled the key differential issue for this client: the discrimination between disturbed emotion (anxiety) and a functional healthy version of it (concern or excitement).

T: Now, can I ask you something else? What is it about your children coming that frightens you?

C: Well, let me say, anytime anybody mentions my children to me I sort of swell up. (Client gets tears in his eyes.)

Note that the therapist will deal with this in-session emotion.

T: So, that sounds like you are feeling sad. So, there is some sadness along with your anxiety.

C: Maybe it is because what I do is I become afraid and I think about what I am going to feel when I see them—also when they leave.

T: So, in other words, what you're doing right now is experiencing or imagining your feelings when they come off the plane or when they go on the plane and you feel sadness then—and you're feeling anxious about the sadness?

The therapist hypothesizes that a C has become an A, and he asks for feedback about this hypothesis.

C: Right.

T: Which one of the problems do you think is more important, then, the anxiety, or the sadness?

C: That is a very interesting question.

T: Both emotions are there.

C: What I am trying to find out myself is if it has a totally self-pity type of feeling I have. I don't know. I have been trying to analyze that for four years.

T: Let me ask you this: Do you have any anxiety about other issues besides your children?

C: Yes. What brought about the suicide attempt, let us call it that for the moment...

T: The attempt.

C: Might have been due to many other things. That is, like anything I have to do I have to work very hard at; nothing comes easily for me.

T: Even killing yourself! You cannot even do that easily, right?

Note the therapist's attempt at humor and how the client received it.

C: I could have if I really wanted to. That might be part of many of my problems. However, I was married eighteen years the first time. And for literally
seventeen of the eighteen years, I felt I had a very happy marriage. I was very
content. And we, my ex-wife and I, became friendly with another couple and
before I knew it, my best friend and my wife took off together. I found out the
hard way—detective, the whole thing. And I thought that after I had overcome
the initial shock that I would never trust another woman again. I was very
secure and all of a sudden not only did I lose my wife, I lost a friend, I lost my
children—it was a three-way disaster.

T: Can we stop?

C: Yes.

T: When you think about your children and you feel the sadness when they visit,
does it also remind you of the sadness you felt at that particular time?

C: No.

T: Does it remind you of how vulnerable you are?

The therapist is working from a hypothesis that the client, in the face of serious
problems, has an irrational belief that he cannot cope.

C: Oh yeah, because in a way, I blame myself for losing my children. I am not happy
about losing my ex-wife because I loved Carol very much. There is no priority. It
is just that I lost my children and there are no feelings going back to that point.

T: You agree with me that when you think about your children coming, you
remember the vulnerability you had. Now is it vulnerability toward losing your
children or the vulnerability of losing your wife?

The therapist has just heard the word "blame" in the client's remark but is holding
that concept for a later intervention.

C: No. Just the sadness that it's just a temporary thing I have with my kids and I
feel myself becoming distant on both sides—their distance and my distance.
It's such a brief period that we see each other.

T: So what you are sad about is that you don't see your children a lot.

C: Right.

T: Let me stop and redefine your words. You said that you feel sad. I agree that
you do, but are you feeling just sad? Or are you feeling sad and depressed? It
is normal to feel sad about negative events, but you might be feeling a more
disturbed emotion that we call depression. Which are you feeling? Do you feel
just sadness, or sadness and depression?

C: Well, let's bring a little guilt in there…

The therapist is not letting the client deflect the conversation. He is finishing the
work on sadness about the children and, while he has heard the comment about
guilt, he is saving it for a later point in the session.

T: I guess it might be important for us to discriminate—and maybe what you are
feeling isn't just sadness but is really, largely, depression. Because I think, any

man would feel sad about losing his children the way you did—and sadness now. But they would not be as debilitated as you are. So, the sad feelings you are probably always going to feel. You are going to feel sad about not having your children...at least I hope so. You are not going to be cold-hearted, and I do not think I could help you to be that way; even if I could, I do not think I would want to. However, the point is, your problem is not sadness. That is normal. It is depression. You are depressed about this. And, I think it is important that we use different words, rather than just sad. Now, what is the guilt factor?

The therapist has discriminated and helped the client correctly label his emotions. Not only the high intensity, but also the guilt and self-denigration and the suicide attempt, are clues that his problem is depression, not merely sadness.

C: In whatever my ex-wife needed—it was mostly the financial area—I overindulged her. Our lifestyle went far beyond my financial means because I felt it was what she needed. And, I work hard, many hours, and I go home and go to sleep. Get up and go to work, go home, and go to sleep. That was the vicious cycle, except for the weekend. I used to look forward to the weekend like it was a vacation of two months coming up instead of only a few days—just so I could spend time with our friends and enjoy my life. The guilt comes in where I was not smart enough to realize that there is more to life than just working.

T: And because you did not realize that, what happened?

C: She found the fun part of her world with my friend.

T: Because you were not there, she went somewhere else, and if you were smart enough to know better, you would not have lost your children?

C: Exactly.

T: You think you are really stupid, don't you?

This is an attempt at humor and was said with a grin.

C: No.

T: You are really beating yourself up about it.

C: Well, I am beating myself up about it because I was almost falling into the same problem in my new marriage again. And, I was not quite aware of it and I am very confused about it. Because what I started to say before and I want to get that part out of me, what brought on this attempted suicide was my lack of confidence in living—and friends. I don't have a true friend, even after this past weekend.

T: You don't trust them, as you do not trust women?

C: Exactly. Except might be, after this weekend, I have found a new friend. It's about time. But Mary has always made me feel fidelity, honesty, on a conscious level, and that I'm number one, and no other man will ever come between us. And I was very comfortable. It took a lot of work for me to believe again. And unfortunately, a very ridiculous situation came up. Mary was depressed about not being able to find a job. This has been going on for two years now. And, last week, I don't know how the conversation came up, Mary said to me, she could even go to bed with a guy if he would get her a job—the right job.

T: She was after his connections?

C: Yeah. In the meantime, my mind has really had it. So, I told Mary how I felt and that weekend was a disaster. I couldn't cope with the fact that my wife would go to bed with another man at any price.

T: It appears to me, at least in REBT terms, there are several activating events, several emotions, going on at the same time. Some of them being depression, some of them anxiety, and some of them guilt. The activating events appear to be seeing your children, missing your children, and having left your children or causing that to happen; and another is a futuristic one that your wife would leave. From what you tell me, it appears that the thing that upsets you the most is something that is right now. That you are afraid your wife will leave. And, any slight indication that that might come true really leads to an awful amount of anxiety. And, it appears that when you think about your children, possibly you think about how your wife left you suddenly, and if it could happen then, well…

Even though this was a first session, the therapist introduced REBT to the client through the books he had read. Note that the therapist summarizes the complexity of the client's problems and is hypothesizing that the client believes that he caused his former problems and might do so again with his present wife.

9

Assessing the B

FINDING THE IRRATIONAL BELIEFS

Clients' irrational belief systems are not easy to identify. These thoughts are greatly overlearned cognitive habits that have become automatic. They are tacit, implied, and unspoken assumptions that often fail to reach consciousness. Irrational thoughts and other schematic thoughts are well-rehearsed and for reasons of cognitive economy, they operate quickly and out of our awareness. The Soviet developmental psychologists Vygotsky (1962) and Luria (1969) traced in children the development of self-talk. At the earliest stages of verbal development, children's behavior is controlled by the overt vocalizations of others. Somewhat later, children can be heard giving themselves similar behavioral directives aloud. Ultimately, their self-talk is completely internalized. With repeated practice, not only is the need to focus on the internal commands reduced, but also a kind of short-circuiting apparently takes place so that individual elements of the thoughts are subsumed under larger headings. This last point will perhaps be clearer if you recall learning to drive a car or watching your child learn to tie his or her shoes. In both cases, a complex task is initially broken down into smaller units of instruction and communicated by someone other than the learner, then usually verbalized aloud by the learner, repeated subvocally, and finally integrated into a continuous whole that can proceed without conscious attention. The thought processes that precede emotive reactions presumably follow similar, although perhaps more subtle, developmental patterns. Thus, a clinical task may be to help clients identify and verbalize their thoughts, beliefs, attitudes, and philosophies. REBT postulated that IBs are unconscious not because our psyche banishes them out of awareness because they are unacceptable, but because they are over-rehearsed and reach a stage of automaticity (DiGiuseppe, 1986).

Because of this aspect of irrational beliefs, they do not come easily into clients' awareness. When you ask clients what they were thinking when they experienced an emotion, they will report stream of consciousness thoughts such as A–(perceived) and A–(inferential) or what cognitive therapists call automatic thoughts. Some additional assessment and exploration is necessary to discover clients' IBs. Sometimes when therapists query clients about their thinking, they respond with emotions ("I think I'm sad/anxious/apprehensive," etc.). The therapist's task is to go beyond clients' feelings and A–(perceived) and A–(inferential) to the irrational thoughts.

Therefore, once the therapist has identified the relevant Activating events and Consequences, we then move to explore the **B**s. To start this process, ask the client what they are thinking after the A or before or during the C. Some questions you could ask are:

- "What was going through your mind when that event happened?"
- On the other hand, if a client is emoting in a session, you could ask, "What is going through your mind right now as you experience that emotion?"
- "What were you telling yourself about the event when you had that feeling?"
- "Were you aware of any thoughts in your head when you felt that way?"
- "There goes that old tape in your head again. What is it playing this time?"
- "What was on your mind then?"
- "Are you aware of what you were thinking at that moment?"

For the reasons stated above, the answer to these questions will usually be A–(inferences) or automatic thoughts. Therefore, we suggest you ask more specific questions such as:

- "What were you telling yourself about the A (plug in the client's specific A) that made you feel C (plug in the client's specific C)?"
- "What were you demanding should happen when you were upset?"

Clients who answer these questions with IB–(imperatives/demands) such as *shoulds, musts,* or IB–(derivatives) have better insight into what they are thinking and you will be able to move through the steps of therapy quicker.

Several strategies can lead clients from their A–(inference) to the tacit irrational beliefs.

Clients' Awareness through Induction. In many forms of CBT, therapists have clients report their inferences and attempt to challenge the truth of these thoughts. If therapists do this for enough sessions, the client will have had the experience of associating their problems with these inferences. Just by this repeated revelation, the client can come to see that there is a pattern or common theme in their inferences. Seeing these themes among many specific inferences helps clients inductively become aware of their core imperative demands that cut across the accumulated inferences.

Below is an interchange between a socially anxious client named Miguel, who became aware of his irrational beliefs on his own after seven sessions of challenging his inference that corresponded to his anxiety.

C: You know, I am thinking that people will reject me. Each week I come here with a different event where I was scared. And I always think people will not like me.

T: I agree; that is an accurate observation. For seven weeks, you have presented predictions of people rejecting you that have not been true.

C: Maybe I predict that people will reject me because I think it would be so devastating if they did. Somehow, I think I need them to like me!

From the many individual episodes of anxiety and thoughts of social rejection, Miguel used inductive reasoning to draw a general conclusion. This technique allows clients to self-discover their core irrationalities on their own, if it will happen at all. It works. However, it takes many sessions just to identify the IBs before you even get to challenging them. This is an effective, but less efficient strategy. The advantage to this strategy is that it relies on self-discovery. If you believe that self-discovery is a crucial component in psychotherapy, this strategy makes the most sense. Some psychotherapists value self-discovery over guided discovery. The issue of whether self-discovery is a more effective means of change remains open to debate. Research on learning through self-discovery has not shown this to be a uniformly superior strategy. It works well for some things, but fails to be a good strategy in learning things such as mathematics. Imagine that they let students discover the solution of differential equations by themselves. Whether it is a better strategy than guided-discovery in psychotherapy is still an empirical question. Self-discovery might work well with bright, articulate clients. When we are working with a less intelligent, or nonintrospective client, as is frequently the case, the fumbling of the client for self-discovery can result in a more protracted period. As we wait for the client to self-discover, they continue to suffer.

Inductive interpretation. A somewhat more active procedure utilizes interpretation by the therapist. After collecting and challenging a large number of A–(inference), the therapist can point out common themes that the inferences contained, and, by interpretation, suggest possible core irrational beliefs or underlying schema. This strategy, however, is relatively time-consuming. It presents the problem of how many examples of the client's emotional episodes and A–(inferences) is necessary before the therapist has a sufficient sample of episodes to draw a correct conclusion. How many are necessary for an adequate sample: three, five, or seven sessions worth of material? Another problem with this strategy is the manner in which the interpretation is offered. We usually avoid the use of the term interpretation. Interpretation in psychotherapy involves the conceptualization of the client's problems by the therapist, and the therapist sharing it with the client. However, the therapist is often right. Used in this context, the practitioner might be tempted to think that the amount of material they collect upon which to base their interpretation ensures their accuracy. Interpretations are still educated guesses or well-formed hypotheses; and as such are subject to error. Let us continue with the case of Miguel and show how a therapist could use this strategy.

C: This week I went to a family engagement. I did not know many people there from my wife's family. I was so anxious again. And I just thought they were judging me.

T: Miguel, for weeks you have come in reporting being anxious in social situations. Each time you have had thoughts that people would be judging you negatively and would dislike you. Tell me if this makes sense. Perhaps you think you need other people's approval and you think you are unlikeable.

This procedure usually works. Therapists are good at inferring client's core irrational beliefs from a large sample of A–(inferences). Again, our question is whether the time it takes to collect the sample is an efficient use of therapy time. We think not.

Inference chaining. A psychologist from Florida named Bob Moore developed this technique. Here, the therapist identifies the A–(inference) and offers the hypothesis that the A–(inference) could be true. The therapist asks the client one of two questions. "What do you think would happen if that were true?" or "What would that mean to you if it were true?" Shorter versions of these questions would be, "What if that were true?" or "What would that mean?" Each question can yield new A–(inferences) and these types of questions are repeated until an irrational belief appears. The therapist keeps phrasing questions until the irrational belief is conscious. Below is an example of a dialogue with our socially anxious client, Miguel, that demonstrates inference chaining.

C: I have that business event to go to next week, and I know that those people are not going to like me.

T: Well, we do not have any evidence for that. However, let's suppose that would be the case. What would happen if they did not like you?

C: I would fail to make contacts and would lose business.

T: Well, I am not sure it would mean that, but let us assume you are correct and you do not make contact and you do lose some business. What would that mean?

C: Well, if I fail at business, I would have less money and not be able to keep up with my friends and then they would dislike me.

T: Well again, you are jumping the gun. We do not know if all that would happen. But if it did, and you lost these friends, what would that mean?

C: Well I would be a total loser. I mean you **have to** be liked to be somebody.

In inference chaining, the client draws out the core irrational beliefs from their own experience, although the therapist directs the client's search for the core beliefs. This strategy has the advantages of efficiency and the advantage of self-discovery. Inference chaining rests on the Socratic dialogue technique, which is a time-honored method of teaching through self-discovery. Clients are often surprised when they hear themselves speak at how much information can be elicited by these inference-chaining questions. We often find that clients reveal core irrational beliefs that surprise them. This demonstrates that they were unaware of the core irrational beliefs before the questioning.

Similarly, a chain of time-projection questions may be useful. Below is another example of inference chaining where we tried to ask time-sequenced questions. This client, Vladimir, was jealous of his wife. He constantly thought that she would leave him, and he was spying on her actions to catch her cheating.

C: This week I had such a fight with my wife when I took her cell phone and checked whom she was calling.

T: What were you feeling when you decided to check her phone?

C: I was feeling anxious and jealous that she was talking to other men.

T: Vladimir, we have no evidence that she is talking to other men. But, what would happen if she was frequently talking to other men?

C: That would mean that she does not love me anymore.

T: Well, we don't have evidence for that yet, but suppose that happened. Suppose she did stop loving you? What are you afraid might happen next?

C: She might leave me.

T: Yes, that would be very bad, but let's suppose it happened, what is the worst thing that could happen if your wife did leave you?

C: I might not find another woman. My God!

T: But let's suppose you never did find another woman. What is the worst that could happen then?

C: I would be alone. And, that can't happen and I **couldn't stand it** if I was.

Many therapists are often tempted to stop at each A–(inference) and challenge it. We do not want to get distracted by challenging the sometimes outrageous and improbable A–(inferences) that are discovered along the chain. They sidetrack us from getting at the core IB. The therapist can continue pursuing the chain to target the IB that is identified at the bottom line. Our clinical experience suggests that it is best to go right to the end of the inference chain and challenge the IB uncovered by the last A–(inference) there. Stopping to change all the A (inferences) and their respective IBs along the chain can be distracting. And the therapist is less likely to get to the most important core IB. Sometimes the most important A–(inference) might not be at the end of the chain, and the therapist can discover which A–(inference) is the most important by reflecting back to the client on the A–(inferences) uncovered in the chain and asking him/her which one is most related to their disturbance.

In the example above, the therapist continues to probe for the client's core irrational beliefs by asking questions and, along the way, uncovering their IBs. Clients may begin by complaining that they want their mother, their spouse, their children, their boss, and so on to do what they want ("I want things to be the way I want them to be.") The therapist's next question in the case of Vladimir might be, "Why can't you stand not having a woman in your life?" "Why must you have a lover in your life?" If the therapist continues to ask why Vladimir must be loved, still more irrational beliefs could be revealed. In this example, the client may state that he believes that it would be awful if his wife did not care for him, because it would prove that he was worthless. His belief in his worthlessness would be the core IB.

Client Awareness through Use of Conjunctive Phrasing. Related to inference chaining is the use of conjunctive phrases to complete the inference chain. In this technique, instead of reflecting and posing a question, the therapist responds to the client's identification of an A–(inference) with a phrase that encourages the client to continue speaking. For example, after the client's A–(inference) the therapist would say, "…and that would mean…" or "…and then…" or "…and therefore…" Imagine that the therapist erases the period at the end of the client's sentence and inserts a conjunction to continue the line of thought. Ellis often employed this strategy. One reason it might be efficient is that it can be less distracting than a full reflection, which the client would then have to process for its accuracy before continuing the phrase. The client maintains momentum and stays focused on the line of thinking on which he or she had been engaged. Again, we will use an example of how this technique would work with our socially phobic client, Miguel.

C: I know they are not going to like me.
T: … and then…
C: I'm not going to make any business contacts.
T: … and that would mean…

Another simple alternative for the therapist is to use a sentence-completion phrasing:

C: I'm going to make less money and fall behind my friends.
T: …which means….
C: I'm a loser. I **have to** be liked to be somebody.

We have found that the more verbal, insightful, and intelligent clients respond better to the use of conjunctive phrasing; and the more concrete and literal-minded clients do not do so well. People with less introspection and verbal skills seem to do better with the more structured technique of inference chaining.

Sentence Completion Chain. Another variation of inference chaining is the inclusion of a sentence completion technique to form a sentence completion chain. In this technique, when the therapist uncovers an A–(inference), she or he places the inference into a sentence stem such as, "The worst thing about _____ is…" If a new inference is uncovered, the process is continued with the same sentence stem. We will show how this technique would be implemented with our socially anxious client, Miguel.

C: I know they are not going to like me.
T: The worst thing about them not liking you is?
C: I might not make any business contacts.
T: And the worst thing about not making business contacts is?
C: I'm going to make less money and fall behind my friends.
T: OK, the worst thing about making less money and falling behind your friends is?
C: I am a loser. I **have to** be liked to be somebody.

The sentence completion technique keeps all of the advantages of all the inference-chaining strategies. However, the higher degree of structure makes these advantages available to a wider range of clients who require structure.

Deductive Hypotheses Driven Assessment. If the self-discovery methods of inference chaining fail to uncover the client's IB, several more directive techniques are available. The first of these is offering hypotheses to the client. Karl Popper's (1968) philosophy of science, which we discussed in Chapter 1 has had a large influence on REBT. Popper said that people cannot help but formulate hypotheses about questions they are investigating. Think about it; how long does it take you to formulate a hypothesis about a new client's diagnosis, or a new client's IB? We bet a matter of minutes. Popper believed that science progresses fastest when the scientists acknowledge their hypotheses and attempt to disconfirm them. Popper's philosophy would posit that clinical knowledge about a specific case would develop fastest if the clinician acknowledges his/her hypotheses and attempts to disconfirm them. Clinicians do not objectively hold hypotheses. A clinician's hypotheses influence what questions they ask and what they remember. Therefore, it is best to acknowledge the hypothesis and develop a line of questioning that will provide data to disconfirm the hypothesis.

Clinicians can formulate hypotheses based on their clinical experience, their knowledge of the person, their knowledge of psychology and psychopathology, and their knowledge of REBT and other forms of CBT. Rather than allow the generation of hypotheses to only be automatic, think through the information mentioned above and try to come up with the best hypotheses concerning your clients' IBs.

Once you have formulated the hypothesis, offer it to the client. We have several suggestions on how to offer hypotheses to clients. First, use suppositional language. Most people do not like to be told what they are thinking. So, avoid declarative sentences. Second, give up narcissistic epistemology (epistemology is the philosophical study of how we know things). That is, give up the philosophical position that you are such a brilliant clinician that your ideas must be correct. We all make mistakes and we all need to acknowledge that. Third, ask the client for feedback. Clients are the ultimate arbiter of the correctness of their experience. Fourth, observe the client's affect when they respond to such queries. Listen to their tone of voice and watch body language. This will provide you with important information concerning whether the IB you proposed to the client aroused some emotion.

Here is an example of how a therapist would use the hypotheses driven assessment strategy, again with our socially anxious client Miguel.

C: I went to a social engagement the other day and I was so anxious.
T: Were you aware of what you were thinking?
C: No. I was not aware of any thoughts. I guess I am just not aware of what I have been thinking. I have been scared of people rejecting me for so long; it is just part of me.
T: OK Miguel, thanks for clarifying that. Let's consider another idea. Could you be thinking something like, "I have to be thought of as a successful person."
C: No, that does not sound like me. I do not have to be great, just be accepted in the group.

T: OK, how about the idea, "I'm a loser, and can't stand to be rejected. I **have to** be liked to be somebody." How does that sound?

C: (His shoulder and neck muscles tighten and he answers in a noticeably fearful voice). Yeah, at least someone has to accept me. I need to be accepted in some group.

Asking for the Must. Based on REBT, we would postulate that an imperative/demand drives the emotional disturbance. So, we can ask the client what they are demanding in the situation in which they are upset. For example, if the client is reporting anxiety about potential criticism from others, rather than asking, "What are you telling yourself about this criticism?" you might ask, "What demand could you be making about criticism from others?" or "What kind of person would you think you are if others criticize you?" Again, we will apply this technique with our client, Miguel.

C: I know they are not going to like me.

T: OK, what demand are you telling yourself about people not liking you that is making you anxious?

C: I am not going to make any business contacts and I will make less money.

T: Yes, that might be true, but again what are you *demanding* should happen that is making you anxious?

C: I must make money to keep up with my friends.

T: And if you don't make more money, what are you telling yourself must happen with your friends?

C: I **must** have them like me and if they don't, I am loser. I **must** be liked to be somebody.

Choice-Based Assessment of IBs. One of us (WD) invented an assessment technique to identify a client's IB that is particularly effective. We call this the choice-based assessment technique. We present an example of how to use this method in identifying the client's premise and provide a commentary on the thinking that underpins the therapist's interventions. We then outline the points to follow with your clients when using this technique. There are several steps to use in the choice-based assessment. These include (1) assert the client's preference about A and elicit the client's agreement; (2) state that the client could hold one of two beliefs that account for his or her emotion or behavioral problems at C and ask for permission to present them; (3) state the client's C and then present the two beliefs. One will be a rigid, absolutistic belief and the other will be a nondogmatic preference; (4) ask the client which belief accounted for his or her unhealthy dysfunctional C. Note that this technique also could be used in assessing your client's IB–(derivatives).

Below is an example of how to apply this technique with our client Miguel:

T: Now we know that it is important to you that your boss is not cross with you. Is that right?

Here the therapist asserts the client's preference. This underpins both his rigid belief and his undogmatic preference.

C: Yes, that is correct.
T: OK. Can I suggest two beliefs that you could have been holding at the time you were anxious? Can I outline them and then you can tell me which belief related to your anxiety?

Here the therapist is drawing on REBT theory and thus is using a theory-driven method of inquiry.

C: OK.
T: At the time when you were anxious, was your anxiety based on belief number 1: "It's important that my boss is not cross with me, and therefore *he must* not be cross with me," or belief number 2: "It's important that my boss is not cross with me, but that does not mean that he must not be cross with me"?
C: Definitely, belief number 1.

The last three techniques we have suggested to assess the IBs are very active and directive. Some therapists are reluctant to be so directive because they think that these techniques put words into their clients' mouths. Some therapists object because they believe that the only insights that clients can use are those that the clients have reached through self-discovery. One could suggest that the therapist could be reinforcing the client for irrational beliefs that he or she might not really hold but that they agree with to please the therapist. However, the alternative disadvantage is remaining stuck, with no IBs to challenge; the therapy, in that case, might not help the client. Be respectful of your client and remain aware of your fallibility. Whenever you are wrong, use that information to help reformulate a new hypothesis.

The advantage of such questions is that they effectively orient clients toward looking specifically for irrational beliefs. If it is clear that clients' emotional responses are unhealthy and self-defeating, what you will likely find is that the clients experience a clear recognition when the therapist directs them to search for *shoulds, musts,* or related demands.

MULTIPLE IRRATIONAL BELIEFS

A key point to remember is that the emotional and behavioral consequences usually have multiple determinants. Too often, the new REBT therapist forgets this principle of psychology and thinks that the client's C will be linked to one IB. The therapist obtains the C (emotion or behavior), finds one IB to target, and considers the case closed. By allowing the client to talk freely or by persistent questioning, the therapist can find that the client's C results from several IBs, often with spiraling, lateral, or hierarchical connections.

Do not be surprised if you encounter clients with a group of Bs, or a "regular B-hive." A client could have two *musts* and each could be associated with more than one derivative. The therapist can jot down the IBs as they emerge and then present the list to the client for discussion and evaluation. Perhaps the therapist can point out any common themes; if there are none, client and therapist can work together to hierarchically arrange the IBs for change. It is important that the therapist obtain the client's agreement on which IB to target first. Failing to do so could disrupt the therapeutic alliance. So, if you have failed to discuss which IB to target, and the client appears irritated or confused, go back and ask the client what s/he is feeling and how you can help reformulate the goals and tasks of the session. Doing so can restore a ruptured alliance.

Let us return to the jealous client, Vladimir, discussed above. When Vladimir thought that his wife was cheating and might leave him, he had three demands. First, he thought that she should remain faithful to him even if she did not love him IB–(imperative/ demand #1). This demand elicited the derivative IB that she was a worthless person if she did not remain faithful IB–(derivative #1/global rating). These thoughts lead to his anger. Vladimir's jealousy was linked to two demands. First, he thought that he *needed (must have)* her to be happy and to live with him IB–(imperative/demand #2). This demand was associated with the derivative IB that he could not stand living without her IB–(derivative #2/frustration intolerance). He also had the demand that he *must* be the type of person that she would love IB–(imperative/demand #3). He had to be as good looking, sophisticated, and intelligent a man as she wanted. This demand was coupled with the derivative IB that he was worthless if he could not be what she wanted in a man IB–(derivative #3/global rating). Complex cases such as Vladimir are what therapists usually encounter.

The first step in identifying the core IB is to make a decision on whether Vladimir wants to work on his anger or anxiety. So start by selecting one C.

C: I am so angry, and so jealous. I feel one or the other emotion all the time.
T: OK Vladimir, think for a moment which of these two emotions you want to work on first, the anger or the jealousy.
C: How do I make that decision?
T: Well, you could chose to work on whichever one is the most disruptive to your life. Or, you could pick the one that might be easiest to change first.
C: Well, I would pick the one that is the most disruptive. I get no work done because of the jealousy. So let's work on that first.

Once the therapist and client have agreed on what emotion to address, they have reduced the number of IBs to target by a third. Next, the therapist will guide Vladimir to decide which jealousy-related IB to target.

T: OK then, we will focus on the jealousy.
C: Yeah, that's good.
T: Well, you said that you had several beliefs that preceded your jealousy. Can I review them?

C: Yeah, go ahead.

T: First, was the demand that you needed her to be happy and to love you. Second, you think you cannot stand to live without her. You also think that you must be the type of man that she would love. Last, you think that you are a worthless loser if you cannot be what she wants in a man.

C: Wow, those are all really upsetting just listening to you recite them.

T: Yes, but which one do you think we should try to change first. Again, we can try to change the one that might be easiest to change first, or we could pick the one that is most upsetting, even if it is hardest to change.

C: Let's go with the most upsetting one.

T: And which one would that be?

C: I just cannot stand the thought of living without her. I need her so much.

T: OK, so help a bit more here. So, is it the thought that you cannot live without her, or the thought that you need her which is most upsetting to you? Notice that the thought that you cannot live without her is related to the demand that you must have her or that you need her.

C: I just cannot stand not having her in my life.

T: OK, let's look at the idea that you cannot live without her, and then we can work on the demand that you must have her.

In this dialogue, the therapist has gone from six IBs to one. Several remarks might be helpful to understand the REBT process. Therapist and client have several choices to pick from; the most frequent IB, the one most strongly endorsed, the most closely connected to the dysfunctional emotion, the easiest to change, or the one that seems centrally linked to all the others. We do not have sufficient research to guide us in choosing which irrational belief to target to attain the best therapeutic outcome. We think it is best to go with the client's choice to maintain cooperation unless the therapist has a compelling reason to make a different argument to the client.

It is possible that choosing any IB to target for change will have a ripple effect in reducing the endorsement of all or some of the others. It is possible that there is one central or core IB from which all the others are derived and that targeting this belief resolves all the client's problems. This search for the "Holy Grail" of IBs sometimes becomes the obsession of therapists. We just do not know yet whether such core IBs exist, or how to identify them, and whether targeting them for change leads to pervasive improvement in the others. If targeting the core belief does not lead to pervasive change and the client changes only that first targeted IB, the therapist will know because the client will remain disturbed. It is equally plausible that each IB becomes rehearsed and stands on its own. Remember Allport's concept of Functional Autonomy. Allport believed that some psychological constructs can develop because of their link to a central or core idea, emotion, or behavior. However, as they play a role in a person's life, they become independent of the construct to which they were first linked. Functional autonomy implies that the therapist might have to work on all the client's IBs. In the case of Vladimir, the therapist would target each of the six beliefs. So knowing the number and extent of the client's IBs is important to plan the course of treatment.

Now that Vladimir and the therapist have agreed on an IB to target, they can move on to work at changing the belief, which is the topic of another chapter.

ASSESSING IRRATIONAL BELIEFS ASSOCIATED WITH DILEMMAS

New therapists often have problems identifying all of the IBs when clients have difficult life choices to make and they are blocked from deciding a path of action by strong dysfunctional emotions. Suppose a client comes to therapy for help in making a decision. The client has two or more alternative paths. It is not the therapist's job to pick a choice for the client, but to help the client identify IBs that prevent him/her from selecting one or the other path. One IB could elicit an emotion that blocks one path and another IB elicits a different unhealthy emotion that blocks the other path, and so on for each path. These IBs could be about giving up one possible solution or about the possibility of losing something that would have eventually turned out to be good. A third possible IB that can block decision-making is the belief that "I must make the right decision." The therapeutic goal is to uncover all these IBs so that the client can engage in problem-solving, to weigh the pros and cons of the alternatives, and to make a decision for her or himself, and to live with it. This is a problem for therapists because clients may present vague complaints of feeling ambivalent, or report the disturbed emotion associated with one of the alternatives. How does the therapist proceed so that he or she can target the irrationalities associated with all alternatives? Targeting the irrationality of only one option could unblock one choice only and leave the other alternative(s) emotionally blocked; thus preventing a real analysis of the pros and cons of each option. The therapist can easily fall into the trap of uncovering the IB that is associated with the dysfunctional emotion that blocks the path that the therapist values and would chose for her or himself.

We recommend that when clients present problems of choice, the therapist follow a sequence of tasks.

- First, ask the client how they would feel if they made the wrong decision. If this a disturbed emotion, assess the possibility that the client believes that s/he must make a perfect decision and replace that thought with the rational belief that there are no guarantees of perfect decisions.
- Second, clearly identify all of the choices the client could make, even ones that appear unlikely to be chosen.
- Third, ask the client to identify what emotions s/he would feel upon choosing each alternative.
- Fourth, assess the irrational beliefs associated with each of the emotions.
- Fifth, ask the client not to make a decision until the therapist and client have examined each of the irrational beliefs that elicit each disturbed, blocking emotion.

- Sixth, proceed to target each of the IBs for intervention until the IBs associated with each blocking emotion are successfully changed.
- Seventh, after the IBs and emotions are changed, the client can analyze the pros and cons of each alternative.

Consider the case of Mark, who came to therapy for help in deciding to stay married to his wife, Paula. Mark presented the problem clearly in terms of his strong desire to leave because of a long list of her faults. Staying with her meant that he had to accept her fallibilities. Mark was paralyzed by his demand that he had to make the right decision. Once we dealt with the fact that no guarantees were available, we proceeded to identify the emotions associated with leaving Paula and staying with her. Mark said he felt scared of staying with Paula. This emotion was elicited by the irrational belief that he would be missing the best relationship that he could possibly have. Because Paula had some flaws, he would be denied a great wife. He thought that he deserved (*must have*) the best, most loving relationship possible. When he thought of leaving Paula, he felt guilt and shame. Although Paula had a short temper and a sloppy nature, she loved him and wanted to be with him. In addition, separation and divorce would upset their children. He thought he *must* stay with Paula to make her happy and prevent the children from being hurt. After we challenged Mark's IBs, he was able to experience functional, healthy concern about not attaining great happiness, and not guilt or shame but regret and disappointment about possibly leaving. He then reviewed how he could make the best of staying and what his real chances for happiness were if he left. So far, he has remained with Paula.

Another way of dealing with a dilemma comes from decision-making theory. Often we use the method of weighing the pro's and con's. We can also look at what one decides eventually compared with what will turn out to be the right and wrong decision later, say five years from now. We can make a matrix like the one in Figure 9.1.

The two cells with an OK in them are not problematic. The ones with an X in them are. Now you can ask the client, "You see two different wrong decisions. Which of the two do you want to avoid most? Or, which of the two do you think you can live with more easily?" This allows the client to look at the dilemma in a different way than with pros and cons, and it helps the client to open his or her

		Five years from now it turns out that the right decision was	
		Staying in the marriage	Divorcing
Decision I take	Staying in the marriage	Okay	X
	Divorcing	X	Okay

Figure 9.1 Comparing the actual decision with what turns out to be the right decision five years from now.

mind to which possibly wrong decisions they could tolerate. We advise using this after the REBT work has been completed as described above.

GUIDES TO FINDING THE IRRATIONAL BELIEFS FOR SPECIFIC EMOTIONS

In order to use the hypothesis driven assessment and choice-driven assessment strategies to identify a client's IBs, it would be helpful to know what irrational beliefs are usually associated with which emotions. In each of the IB assessment strategies mentioned, the therapist knows the emotion but hypothesizes the IB. So, we will identify the IBs associated with the major emotional disturbances. The reader might be overwhelmed with what seems like an infinite number of connections between **B**s and **C**s. You may be reassured to find, however, that specific common thoughts generally lead to specific common emotions. By way of illustration, we will present the irrational beliefs that underlie eight major emotional dysfunctions: anxiety, depression, guilt, shame, dysfunctional anger, jealousy, envy, and hurt.

Box 9.1

When clients have trouble identifying cognitions, the therapist can suggest a variety of thoughts, urging clients to signal or stop when one "feels right." You can explain to clients that because they have helped you to identify their feeling, there are a limited number of thoughts that they could be thinking with that emotion. Your job is to help clients to listen to their own cognitions, or to let you suggest a few and then tell you if any of the suggestions seem to fit.

Anxiety. Anxiety results from future-oriented cognitions; people are rarely afraid of events in the past. The therapist would do well, therefore, to ask future-oriented questions: "What do you think might happen?" or "What kind of trouble are you anticipating?" What is usually heard in response is some form of catastrophizing or awfulizing. Fears may range from specific and isolated to pervasive and vague (so-called free-floating anxiety). The two most common fears, according to Hauck (1974), are the fear of rejection and the fear of failure, followed closely by the super-fear—the fear of fear itself.

There are three cognitive steps to anxiety:

1. (Inference)—Something bad might happen.
2. IB–(demandingness)—It must not happen.
3. IB–(derivative)—It would be awful if it did; Or—I would be worthless if it did happen; Or—I could not stand it if it did.

The first statement might be a good prediction based on valid evidence, although the therapist would do well to check this out. The bad "something" that clients are anticipating might be an external event, their own thoughts about some potential failure, or their own anticipated emotional experience. If we assume that the client is correct about a bad event occurring, the client's first irrationality appears at statement 2, the clearly irrational "should" or "must," as if the individual had command of the universe and could prevent bad events from happening. At statement 3, we see the irrational evaluation of the event or the person in the Activating event, which tends to keep the individual thinking in a demanding way about the future, as if doing so will magically ward off disaster.

Depression. Beck et al. (1979) outlined a cognitive triad that descriptively identifies depression. The elements include a negative view of the self, a negative view of the world, and a negative view of the future. These views are similar to and overlap the dynamic irrational beliefs that REBT theory (e.g., Ellis, 1987a) suggests are the main causative agents in depression:

A devout belief in one's personal inadequacy
The "horror" of not having what one "needs"
The "awfulness" of the way things are

Hauck (1974), in his excellent book on depression, divides the problem of depression into three types of thoughts, each with its underlying irrational structures. Depression can be caused, first, by self-blame. The thinking pattern that leads to self-blame is generally as follows:

1. A–(inference)—I failed, or possess some flaw or fault.
2. IB–(demandingness)—I should be perfect and not do bad things or have such a flaw.
3. IB–(derivative)—I am, therefore, a bad person and I am not deserving.

The second cause of depression is self-pity, whose irrational core is:

1. A–(inference)—I have been thwarted in getting my way.
2. IB–(demandingness)—I must have what I want.
3. IB–(derivative)—I cannot stand the loss I have experienced. Or "Poor me!" I am inadequate.

Finally, one can become depressed by other-pity if one focuses on bad things that have occurred to a loved one or a disaster that happened to a large group of people, and believes the following thoughts:

1. A–(Inference) Bad things are happening to other people when they don't deserve it.
2. IB–(demandingness) These bad things must not happen to others when they do not deserve it.
3. IB–(derivative) The world is a terrible place for allowing such suffering and bad things to happen.

Guilt. Guilt cognitions have two components. First, clients believe that they are behaving badly, or have done something wrong, or are in violation of their moral code. They might or might not have behaved badly, and their moral code could be too severe and logically inconsistent. However, this would not be the primary focus of REBT. A person's bad acts could be sins of commission or sins of omission. Second, they believe that they *must* behave by the moral code. Third, they condemn themselves for doing the wrong thing. These last beliefs are the core that REBT would attempt to change:

1. A–(inference) I violated my moral code.
2. IB–(demandingness) I must always live by my moral code.
3. IB–(derivative) I am condemnable because I violated the code.

The first statement may be an accurate assessment of reality according to the client's value system or it may be an exaggerated error. Considered alone, it is a statement of self-responsibility and can be useful in changing the client's behavior. This type of statement, therefore, might not be the target of change in REBT. Statements 2 and 3 add an extra, unnecessary idea, however. Consider the difference if, instead of statement 2, the client said, "Yes, I did the wrong thing. I really regret that, but people make mistakes from time to time, and I'll try my best not to do it again." Thus, true guilt always includes the component of self-condemnation and self-denigration, which sabotages emotional or behavioral improvement.

Shame. Shame is another dysfunctional emotion and it is often confused with guilt. Guilt and shame differ in one crucial way. In guilt, the IB involves self-condemnation for violation of a moral code; in shame, the person is upset about public rejection that follows the public moral transgression (Ard, 1990). To experience shame requires several different thoughts. The first is that the person has violated a public moral code. Second, is the belief that significant others or the social group know about the infraction and will negatively judge and reject the person because of the moral transgression. Third, the client has the belief that s/he should not have violated the moral code and that others should not reject her/him. Fourth, the client believes that it is awful that others reject him/her, or that s/he cannot stand to be rejected. Fifth, the client believes that being rejected by others means that s/he is no good? An example of the thoughts in shame would be as follows:

1. (Inference)—I have violated a moral code and others know it or will know it.
2. (Inference)—Others will negatively judge me and condemn or banish me because of my moral transgression.
3. IB–(demandingness)—I should not have violated the moral code; or, Others should accept me despite my moral transgression.
4. IB–(derivative)—The group is correct. I am condemnable; I cannot stand being condemned by, rejected by, or banished from the group and it is awful that they reject me.
5. IB–(derivative)—The group is right. I am condemnable and therefore I am no good.

Dysfunctional anger. The word "anger" is used to describe a broad range of emotional reactions, some of which are appropriate and helpful. Clinical dysfunctional anger, on the other hand (i.e., hostility, rage, or contempt), is an emotion that interferes with goal-directed behavior. DiGiuseppe and Tafrate (2007) and Ellis and Tafrate (1997) describe anger cognitions as a series of Jehovian commands and demands. The first step consists of defining rights and wrongs, reflecting an absolutist kind of moral indignation. The second step is the absolutist should, "You should act correctly." or "You shouldn't act that way." The third step is other-condemnation: "They are worthless for acting that way." or "You're a bastard!" and "You deserve to be punished and damned!"

1. A–(inference)—Someone behaved badly or violated my rules.
2. IB–(demandingness)—They must behave as I think they should.
3. IB–(derivative)—They are no good and deserve to pay for acting badly.

In addition, we recognize "ego-defensive anger." Some clients become enraged over other people's criticism of them. It is commonly believed that anger is triggered by low self-esteem, self-condemnation fear that another's criticism reflects one's own inadequacy, for which one condemns oneself (Beck, 1999). Substantial research has shown that angry and aggressive people do not suffer from low self-esteem but that they actually have high unstable self-esteem or narcissism (Baumeister, Smart, and Boden, 1996; Baumeister, Campbell, Krueger, and Vohs, 2005); DiGiuseppe and Froh, 2002). Anger appears to be caused by the belief that others do not see the person as great as they see themselves.

1. A–(inference)—Others have not treated me with the respect, deference, or admiration that I deserve.
2. IB–(demandingness)—Others must treat me with the respect, deference, and admiration that I deserve.
3. IB–(derivative)—I cannot stand being treated with less respect. They are condemnable for treating me with less respect, deference, or admiration than I deserve.

Sometimes the anger is related to beliefs that the criticism is unwarranted because the client believes that they should not make any mistakes.

1. A–(inference)—They criticized me and think I made a mistake.
2. IB–(demandingness)—They must not see that I made a mistake. People must see me as perfect.
3. IB–(derivative)—I cannot stand for people to see me as imperfect. They are no good for thinking I am fallible.

Unhealthy jealousy. Jealousy involves the perception of a threat of losing something that you already have. Usually people experience jealousy about the threat of losing a relationship with a romantic partner to a third person. The actual emotional experience could be fear of losing the relationship or anger at the competitor or interloper who threatens to win the love of the person's partner. An example of the thoughts involved with unhealthy jealousy that is close to fear would be as follows:

1. A–(inference)—My partner is showing interest in another potential lover. I could lose him/her to that person.
2. IB–(demandingness)—My partner must not leave me. I must have him/her.
3. IB–(derivative)—I could not stand to be without my lover. I would be a failure or loser if my lover left me for that other person.

An example of the thoughts involved in unhealthy jealousy that is close to anger would be as follows:

1. A–(inference)—That person is interested in taking my lover away from me and s/he might succeed in seducing my partner.
2. IB–(demandingness)—S/he must not try to seduce my partner. And my partner must not succumb to the interloper's advances.
3. IB–(derivative)—The interloper is a condemnable person and deserves to be punished. My partner is condemnable for being interested in the interloper and deserves to be punished.

Unhealthy envy. Unhealthy envy is similar to and often confused with unhealthy jealousy. The theme of unhealthy envy is that another person possesses and enjoys something desirable that the person does not have. The emotional experience in unhealthy envy is close to that of unhealthy disturbed anger (DiGiuseppe and Tafrate, 2007). An example of the thoughts involved in unhealthy envy would be as follows:

1. A–(inference)—That person has highly desirable resources that I could use.
2. IB–(demandingness)—I must have what that person has; I deserve it.
3. IB–(derivative)—That person is worthless and not at all deserving. I can't stand being without valuable resources that others have.

Hurt. Hurt is an emotional pain and anguish characterized by the theme that others have treated the person badly. There is also a tendency to become stuck in thinking about past hurts. The hurt person expects others to make the first move toward repairing the relationship, and sulks and makes little or no attempt to communicate with others. There are several possible thought patterns associated with hurt. Sometime the inference is that the person was treated unfairly.

1. (Inference)—The other person treated me badly and very unfairly.
2. IB–(demand)—I should not have been treated that badly and very unfairly.
3. IB–(derivative)—I cannot stand being treated so badly; and the other person is condemnable for treating me so unfairly.

Sometimes the person is upset about being alone, uncared for, or misunderstood.

1. (Inference)—Others do not care for me, understand me, or pay enough attention to me.
2. IB–(demandingness)—Other people must care for me, understand me, and attend to me.
3. IB–(derivative)—I cannot stand being uncared for and unattended to or misunderstood; and others are condemnable for not caring for me. Because they do not care for me, there is something wrong with me.

A variation in style. Some CBT therapists, as distinguished from REBTers, stress the idiosyncratic nature of the client's cognitions. In addition, they try to describe the client's cognitive world without any categorization of the thoughts, by using the client's language exactly as stated. The client is urged to speak from the direct experience of his or her thoughts, rather than talking about those thoughts. For example:

Not: I was thinking about how stupidly I acted.
But, "What a jerk I am!"

Similarly, the more broadly stated silent assumptions are gathered in the client's own language, rather than formed into categorical *musts* or *shoulds*. For example:

"I need other people's approval to feel good about myself."
"I may not be an adequate human being."
"Others will be critical of me and won't accept me or respect me unless my work is of a very high standard."

There are advantages to both the use of REBT terminology and use of the client's own words. In our clinical teaching experience, the structure of irrational beliefs laid out in REBT theory helps therapists-in-training to look for and recognize their clients' irrational processes. As REBT therapists become more experienced, they can move from the language of REBT theory toward the idiosyncratic language of the client without losing sight of REBT constructs. For example, the experienced therapist can detect a client's demandingness even if a "should" or "must" has never been spoken.

Therefore, language that reflects demandingness without using the words *should, ought, must,* or *have to* could be:

He is supposed to do that.
I expect him to do that.
I insist that he do that.
Of course, I anticipated that he would do that.
I thought I could count on him to do that.

I cannot believe he did not do that.
Why doesn't he do that?
Why are people so stupid?

Demandingness is an idea. It is usually conveyed in English with the words "should," "ought," or "must." However, other words could be used. The same is true for frustration intolerance. This idea of not being able to bear more frustration is usually conveyed in English with the phrase, I can't stand it." Alternatively, clients might say:

I have had *enough*.
That was *too* hard.
I *have had it* with him doing that.
It is *unbearable* that he did that.

The use of the client's own language frequently seems to make the disputing process more meaningful to the client. Our recommendation is to learn the REBT constructs and as much as possible to use the clients' language with them.

OTHER GUIDELINES

In the previous sections, we described how the REBT therapist uses the client's specific C as a clue in identifying the relevant irrational beliefs, and uses A–(inferences) as guideposts to underlying belief structures. In addition, as you gain experience as a therapist, you will find that particular clinical problems are commonly associated with specific belief systems. Clues to irrational beliefs could be found in the A that the client describes or in characteristics of the client that you note. In other words, in searching for the irrational cognitions with which clients upset themselves, you may begin with cognitive schemas of types of clients derived from cumulative experience with similar cases. These schemas can serve as initial hypotheses. Although it is beyond the scope of this book to suggest all of the common schemas, an example can help illustrate their form.

If the client is a mother who is experiencing a great deal of anxiety or dysfunctional anger at her children for their misbehavior, the key irrational belief underlying the problem could be one of self-worth. The mother could have not only identified the children's behavior as bad but could also have overgeneralized, concluding that she is a bad mother and, therefore, a worthless person because her children behave badly. Thus, she could have rated and devalued herself based on the behavior of her children. In working with mothers, whether their children are infants or independent adults, the therapist can keep such a schema in mind as a hypothesis.

The development and use of such schemas will evolve as you accumulate professional experience. Also, it is important to consider the ideas you apply to specific cases based on such schema as hypotheses that you need to test. You can find that you have many such decision-making schemas already. The point we wish to stress, however, is that schemas suggest hypotheses, not facts. In other words, we advise you to present your schemas in suppositional language to your clients, and to empirically validate your hypotheses by data from the client before you proceed further with therapy.

WHEN ALL ELSE FAILS

Not all clients can identify IBs that they have before or during their emotional episodes or dysfunctional behaviors. This can occur for two reasons. First, some people might just be poor at identifying their cognitive process. Just as we have referred to alexythymia in Chapter 8, so too people with poor introspection might have difficulty becoming aware of the thoughts associated with their disturbance. The identification of these thoughts would entail recalling what happened when the disturbed emotion or behavior occurred. Humans most likely store such experiences in episodic memory, and these experiences are probably not stored verbally. People have to experience the memory and translate their thoughts into language. Our clinical experience has suggested that people with low introspection or poor verbal skills have the most difficulty reporting the IBs or any other CBT construct as associated with their disturbance.

Also despite REBT theory, it is possible that some emotional disturbances are not mediated by thoughts. In Chapter 2 we mentioned Power and Dalgleish's (2008) SPAAR model, which proposed that there are at least two pathways for external stimuli to the eliciting of emotions. One pathway is through classical conditioning and involves immediate, mostly subcortical connection. Some people might not experience thoughts with their disturbance because this classical conditioning pathway mediates the emotional disturbance. Our experience suggests that people with Acute Stress Disorder or PTSD sometimes fail to report any thoughts associated with stimuli that were associated with their trauma and their fear.

So what do we do? At some point, the therapist takes the client's failure to identify thoughts at face value and moves on. At this point, the therapist can use REBT theory to suggest rational alternative beliefs that could counteract the client's disturbed emotions. The therapy would not involve disputing the IBs, since none have been identified. Nevertheless, therapy can progress and provide rationales for the new RBs and many exercises to practice them.

TEACHING TRANSCRIPT

The following transcript illustrates a therapist assisting a client in identifying his IBs and teaching the client to discriminate between rational and irrational beliefs.

The client, Sam, is a thirty-eight-year-old married man whose five-year-old daughter has a habit of waking in the middle of the night and calling for her mother. On a recent night, Sam became angry. He flew into the child's room, picked her up by the shoulders, shook her, and yelled at her, "Shut up, you little brat! This is ridiculous! And I won't stand for it!"

T: It sounds like you were angry to go in and shake her.

C: Yeah. And I yelled at her.

T: Yes; and how did you feel about your yelling afterward? (Therapist assesses for meta-emotional problem.)

C: Pretty rotten.

T: What do you mean, rotten?

C: I felt guilty. (Client reveals meta-emotional problem.)

T: OK Sam; what problem do you want to work on—the guilt or the anger?

C: I want to work on the anger so I do not do that to my daughter again.

T: OK, Sam. Let's go back, if we can. There you are, resting in bed, and you hear that whiney voice, "Mommy, mommy. ..." What thoughts go through your head? What are you saying to yourself? (The therapist assesses thoughts.)

C: I have had it with that kid. I'm just going to walk right out on her if she gives me any flak.

The therapist's initial query about thoughts resulted in behavioral not cognitive information. The therapist persisted and again asked for thoughts.

T: Well, that is a prediction you made about how you would act. But, before you came to that, you must have had some other thoughts. If we could read your mind, like some printed script, what were some of the words? ... What were you saying?

C: Damn it. I don't want to have to go through it again.

T: (repeats) OK, good. What else were you saying?

C: I don't need this aggravation. I get up early in the morning. I am going to go in there and she is going to tell me to get out. Then my wife is going to go in and she is going to get upset and be a grouch the next morning.

Note that the client continues to provide predictions but has not yet identified any IBs.

T: You are anticipating all kinds of things. Is that what rolled through your head? Now, suppose for a minute that the situation had been a little different: your kid was throwing up, and she almost never throws up. Would you have had the same kind of thoughts?

C: No, I don't think so.

T: OK, so was there something else going on here? In terms of anticipating that this could go on forever.

C: Yeah.

T: Well, what did you say about that?

C: Here we go again. It is never going to end. I do not know what we can do to make this kid sleep through the night. She keeps us up all the time.

T: So you were pretty helpless. You really didn't know what to do. You know, Sam, in addition to that, I think some other things might have gone through your head ... because if that were all that went through your head, you would have only felt annoyance. That would have been very understandable. You would have said, "Oh, no. I have to get out of this warm bed and calm her down now, damn." You would not have been very happy, but you would have done it, or at least have tried to, and if it did not work, called your wife. But that isn't exactly what you did, is it? What happened then?

C: I went in there and started shaking her, and yelled, "Stop it, stop it, stop it ... I can't stand it!"

T: Ah. So, you had some more powerful thoughts passing through your head. I can't stand it. You shouldn't have done this to me. What is the matter with you?

C: Uh hum (nodding assent).

T: Those are the kind of things that were going through your head?

Note that the therapist asks for feedback to corroborate her hypothesis.

C: Uh hum.

T: OK, Sam. Now I am going to say something to you that may surprise you. That is, it is not so much that your daughter was crying in the night and interrupting your sleep that enraged you. It is what you said to yourself about that irritating event. Now, if you lined up a thousand judges, everybody would agree that this is an irritating event. Nobody wants to get up in the middle of the night, night after night. So, for you to feel irritated, that is functional. But in order for you to get so upset that you actually wanted to go in there and throttle the kid or choke her or hit her with something.... See, you didn't just say, "Oh, gosh, here we go again." Which one of those things I said before ... which one do you think really triggered you?

C: I think, "I can't stand it anymore."

T: (repeats, twice, with emphasis) OK, now I am going to say something pretty strange to you. (pause) Did you stand it?

C: I got through it. I didn't like it.

T: That is right; you did not like it. But, you did not die, though, right?

C: (inaudible murmur)

T: All right. See, you made an irrational statement to yourself. "I can't stand it." Could you also have been thinking, "She must not do this to me." That is what gave you your dysfunctional anger. By "irrational," I mean destructive and hurtful. Causing you to go in and commit an act that you were sorry about later. You told me that the next day you felt guilty and wished you had not done it ... it was overkill. Here was a kid howling in the middle of the night, and your overreaction certainly did not help that problem any, and can even have made the situation worse. So now, we have two problems instead of the one problem. But, do you understand what I am saying to you?

C: Yeah. I am telling myself that I cannot stand something. I guess what you are saying is that when I say that, I make myself more angry?

T: Absolutely. You got it! You are the one ... you're the author of your own feelings. Now that is a kind of a profound statement. I am going to say it to you
again ... because it permeates a lot of your life and how you deal with yourself
and other people. You are the author of your own anger. Do you believe that?

C: You're saying that she gets me irritated, and I get myself angry.

T: You actually—technically—irritate yourself about it, but I think most people
would think it natural, because you are, after all, human. It is perfectly reasonable for a person who is trying to get some sleep and has to go to work the next
day, if he is awakened by a daughter who is not a baby and who has a bad habit
of doing this. To feel irritated is OK. But the fact that you lost control over
yourself and actually went in and tried to throttle her in the night ... that you
did because of your thinking. She really did not have anything to do with that.
And it is what you said in your head about the crying in the night that really
got you so upset that you lost control of yourself. See, that is what we are labeling dysfunctional. You lost control of yourself. That is not a good feeling to go
through life with—letting other people pull your strings. And I would like to
help you understand that, so that you don't feel helpless about controlling your
anger.

PART FOUR

Therapy: Getting Down to D—Disputation, and E—the New Effective Response

10

Cognitive Change Strategies

Identifying the **A**s, **B**s, and **C**s is necessary, but changing the beliefs through steps D and E is the work of therapy. Disputation is a debate or a challenge to the client's irrational beliefs and can include cognitive, imaginal, emotive/evocative, and behavioral components.

Initially REBT theoreticians and practitioners focused on the importance of disputation as the most important change process. However, since the last edition of this book, REBT practitioners have focused more on the importance of teaching new rational alternative beliefs at step E as well. Two studies found that teaching the new alternative belief was more effective than just challenging the Irrational Beliefs (Moriarity, 2002). In addition, a survey of REBT trained practitioners revealed that they thought that teaching the new beliefs was the most important process of therapy (Beal and DiGiuseppe, 1998).

We have identified three basic strategies to disputation or changing the belief. The first involves indentifying the A-B-C and then proceeding to challenge the irrational belief that was identified. The therapist proceeds through many different types of disputes and debates and then helps the client construct a new rational alternative belief. This was the primary strategy most often used by Albert Ellis. The second strategy involves the therapist teaching the distinction between RBs and IBs first, and then proceeding to dispute and debate the client's IBs and reinforcing the alternative RBs. A third strategy would involve teaching the distinction between IBs and RBs and then moving on to have the client rehearse and adopt the new alternative RBs. We do not yet have research to support which of these strategies is the most effective. We suspect that each strategy might be the most effective for specific types of clients. For some clients, one problem will improve most with one strategy, but the same strategy will not work with another problem, with which another strategy is more effective. We encourage you to try to master all three strategies and then keep track of which strategy works best for which clients or for which type of problems.

WHAT TO DISPUTE

REBT therapists never challenge or dispute a client's emotions. Emotions are experiences, they are not a matter of fact or opinion and therefore not debatable.

In fact, one of the key differences between cognition and emotion is that emotions are not debatable.

Challenging an emotion invalidates the client's feeling. It also communicates to the client that they should not feel the emotion or should change it without any skills or techniques to do so. Consider this example: If I say I am *cold*, and the other two people in the room say they are *hot and sweaty* and point out that the temperature in the room is 100 degrees, I still feel cold. The others' feedback is functionally irrelevant. "I'm *cold*" is not disputable, any more than emotions are. When others argue with my experience of being cold, they are really saying, "There's something wrong with you for feeling *cold*," and "You really shouldn't feel *cold*." Now substitute some emotion for the experience of "cold," and you can see how invalidating it would seem to clients to have their experience and sense of reality challenged. Emotions are to be respected. They are the client's experience and are not to be challenged.

Recall that when clients give us dysfunctional cognitions they will be one of three broad types: A-(inferences), IB-(demandingness) that are imperative or schematic in nature, and IB-(derivative). The theory postulates that the A-(inferences) arise from the core/imperative cognitive schemas. Therefore, we challenge these core thoughts directly and not the inferences. REBT therapists aim disputations at either the IB-(demandingness) or the IB-(derivatives). Some REBT practitioners believe that we should challenge the IB-(demandingness) first and then the derivatives. Others believe that we should challenge whichever IB most resonates with the client's experience.

When disputations target the clients' A-(inferences), we term this an inferential or inelegant dispute. The cognitive errors will likely involve errors of induction, in which clients make overgeneralized conclusions based on insufficient data (e.g., "Because he didn't call me, he doesn't love me."). When the client's attributional set is dysfunctional—that is, problems at A are seen as internal, global, and stable—it might be helpful to get the client to reinterpret the problem as temporary, external, or limited in scope (Weiner, 1985). Assume, for example, that I observe that a number of people in my audience are not attending to my lecture and my mood plummets after I make the attribution that the audience is inattentive because I am boring. An inferential disputation would temporarily reassure me that it is very early in the morning and people probably have not had their coffee yet. Nevertheless, I still might be boring, and more evidence will accumulate that people do not like or attend my lectures. As this evidence accumulates, the reattribution strategy will no longer work. What if my next lecture is in the evening and people still do not pay attention despite my supplying them with significant amounts of caffeine? The feared bad event could always happen. Arguing that it has a low probability of occurring or that it occurs because of some reason other than my performance does not give the client a way to cope with it if it does happen and might hinder progress in therapy, because temporary solutions fail to change the client's underlying core, imperative, and derivative beliefs.

Disputations targeted at the irrational beliefs of the client are referred to as philosophical or elegant disputes. They are philosophical because they get to the core assumptions and foundational beliefs of the client. They are elegant because they work in many situations especially when the worst thing really happens.

Box 10.1

When we teach new students, we often observe that they identify their clients' A-B-Cs, but do not move one to disputation or suggest alternative RBs. Instead, they return to explore more A-B-Cs. They have quickly and efficiently outlined a simple A-B-C. Instead of moving into D and E, they return to assessment (e.g., "...and what else were you feeling?"). Perhaps one of the reasons for this error is not knowing how to dispute or feeling uncomfortable challenging the clients' thoughts. A second reason is that students fear that clients will interpret the debate on their thoughts as an attack on them as a person.

A strategy that helps is to use a setting phrase. For example, you can simply repeat an irrational belief of the client and then say: "OK, now that we have found that this specific belief is causing you trouble, let's examine this belief."

If you still feel unsure of how to begin, you might follow the setting phrase by putting the problem in the hands of the client, "Do you see any ways we could begin to change that belief?"

COGNITIVE DISPUTATION

Cognitive disputations are attempts to change the client's erroneous beliefs through philosophical persuasion, didactic presentations, Socratic dialogue, vicarious experiences, and other modes of verbal expression. One of the most important tools in cognitive disputation is the use of questions. We pointed out previously that it is generally good to avoid asking "why" questions when assessing **A**s, **B**s, and **C**s; in disputation, however, "why" questions might be particularly fruitful.

In this section, we will present categories of disputes and specific questions to present to clients. These disputes are culled from disputations by Ellis (1962, 1971, 1974b, 1979b) and other therapists at the Albert Ellis Institute in New York City. We present them as examples to get you started. Note that by relying on such questions, the therapist is making the client do the work and thereby become more likely to internalize a new healthy philosophy.

We use Thomas Kuhn's (1962) model from the philosophy of science to guide the disputation process of REBT. Thomas Kuhn was a theoretical physicist, historian, and philosopher of science. He reviewed the strategies of thinking and of examining evidence that lead scientists to change their theories over the centuries. Kuhn called grand scientific theories paradigms. He believed that a paradigm was a set of beliefs that influenced the data that one perceived, the inferences that one drew, and the data one considered important. Irrational beliefs are like paradigms, but they are personal views about one's construction of reality at certain moments. As we have pointed out above, they influence the inferences and attributions that we make about the world. Kuhn (1977) also believed that scientists (and people) ignore the evidence against their beliefs until the evidence is so overwhelming that change happens suddenly. We have this model of change to the therapeutic process (DiGiuseppe, 1986). The clinical strategies suggested by this model include

- Collecting data on the hypotheses and predictions made by the irrational beliefs/schema and testing them empirically.
- Challenging the logical consistency of the irrational beliefs/schema to see whether it really explains the important events it is designed to explain.
- Checking the irrational belief/schema paradigm to see whether it is consistent with other important sets of data to see how consistently it explains other life events.
- Checking the heuristic value of the irrational belief/schema paradigm by assessing its effect on the quality of the client's life and its utility in attaining the client's personal goals.
- Repeating these steps sufficiently so as to create considerable tension in the client that the irrational belief/schema paradigm is a viable construct.
- Helping the client construct alternative rational belief/schema paradigms to replace the irrational personal paradigm.
- Reviewing the empirical evidence that was used to disconfirm the previous irrational paradigm to see whether the present rational paradigm is more consistent with the data.
- Making predictions from the new rational paradigm and seeing whether these are empirically supported.
- Reviewing the effects on the person's life to see what difference will be made by adopting the rational paradigm and seeing whether these lead to an increase in the quality of life and attainment of more of the client's personal goals. That is, assessing the new rational belief's heuristic/functional value.

Disputing, then, is not just empirical verification or logical challenging, but a complicated process whereby the logical consistency, heuristic/functional value, and empirical evidence are used to evaluate the theory and the alternatives. Each of these cognitive disputes is described below. We do not mean to imply that they should come in any order. Presently there has been very little research on the differential effectiveness of these disputes. However, our survey of practitioners trained at the Albert Ellis Institute indicated that they believed that the heuristic/functional were the most effective.

Below we will present some questions that are examples of logical, empirical, and heuristic/functional disputes. When you read these examples think of the following case and how the questions challenge this client's irrational beliefs. Barbara is a nurse who works in a busy ward of a hospital on a large team of healthcare providers. She has ideas of how the team could work more efficiently but fails to assertively offer her suggestions. When the therapist asked Barbara how she would feel if she did speak up, she reported that she felt fearful and anxious that her peers would reject her ideas and would think she was stupid and intrusive (A–Inference). She revealed these irrational beliefs:

- IB–(imperative/demand)—Because I want my peers to respect me, I must be respected by them.
- IB–(derivative/ awfulizing)—It would be awful if my peers disliked me.
- IB–(derivative/self-worth)—I would be worthless if they did not respect me.
- IB–(derivative/frustration intolerance)—I cannot stand it if they do not respect me.

Logical Disputation Questions

The first group of questions asks for semantic clarity and logical consistency in the client's thinking and can be used to challenge any IB. The discussion of semantic clarity is necessary and precedes any discussion of the logic of any position.

- What do you mean by that word "must"?
- What do you mean by the word "awful"?
- What do you mean by the word "worthless"?
- What do you mean by "I can't stand"?
- You said that because you want your peers to respect you, they must respect you. Is that good logic?
- How do you get from wanting them to respect you to the belief that they must respect you?
- If you heard someone else making a similar argument that because she wanted something, that it must be, would you be convinced?
- Why is it illogical to say that because you want your peers to respect you, they must respect you?
- Explain to me how you become worthless because they do not respect you?
- Why does it have to be so, just because you want it?
- How is it inconsistent to believe that because you want their respect you must have their respect?
- Does it logically follow that because you want them to respect you, they must respect you?
- Does it logically follow that you become worthless based on their respect for you?
- What is wrong with the notion that you are a worthless person?
- What is wrong with the notion that you would not stand it?
- How does it follow that you will not be able to stand not getting what you want?
- You might not like it if your colleagues do not respect you, but does it logically follow that you cannot stand it?

These questions focus on whether the client's irrational beliefs follow from the reasoning that the client uses. For example, when most clients are asked, "Why must the world be the way you say it must be?" they proceed to explain how it would be more desirable for them. Ellis's classic dispute points out that because something is more desirable, it does not logically follow that the world must provide what is desirable. Desirability and the client's reality are not related to each other; to proceed from desiring to demanding is to use a logical non sequitur.

Some therapists like to ask the direct question "Why must it be …?" or "Why *must* it not be …?" when the client and therapist have formulated a clear imperative/demanding cognition as the cause of the C. It is surprising how successful this question can be, as well as how much information it can yield and how therapeutic it can be.

Other disputes focus on the logical inconsistency among different aspects of the client's belief system. For example, Barbara condemns herself for not accomplishing a specific goal or reaching a specific aspiration. She could be asked (a) would you condemn others for failing to reach that same goal? On the other hand (b) would you condemn others for failing to reach their own goals? Clients often respond "no" to such questions. Moreover, we respond "How is it logical, to condemn one person for failing, but not another person for the exact same thing?" The logical inconsistency can be repeatedly illustrated with such questions and comparisons.

Empirical or Reality-Testing Disputation Questions

The second group of questions requires clients to evaluate whether their beliefs are consistent with empirical reality. For example, most "demanding" beliefs can be shown to be inconsistent with reality. No matter how strongly clients believe that the world "must" be the way they want it to be, the universe usually does not change to match the "must." Content analyses of Ellis's therapy recordings indicate that he often used this argument. He asked clients what reality is, and then pointed out that it is not consistent with their "must."

Clients who endorse frustration intolerance beliefs can be shown that even though they think they cannot stand the occurrence of A, they have, in fact, "stood it" repeatedly. Questions can require the client to evaluate whether future events will occur, and, if so, whether they will be as unpleasant as the client anticipates. Self-downing beliefs, in which the person condemns himself or herself as totally worthless, can be shown through questioning to be incorrect, because all people do some things well. Below are some examples of questions to test the consistency between a client's belief(s) with empirical reality.

- You have been demanding that they respect you for years. Has that demand changed them in any way?
- So they have disrespected you despite the fact that you demand that they respect you.

- Where is the evidence that your colleagues must respect you?
- Where is the evidence that you are worthless to society, the universe, or anyone because your colleagues disrespect you?
- If your colleagues have disrespected you, and you are still here, have you stood it?
- Assume that they do disrespect you, what is good and worthwhile about you now that they are disrespecting you?
- What do you do well even as they are disrespecting you?
- If these colleagues disrespect you, do you have value for any others in the world?
- What would really happen to you if your colleagues disrespected you?
- What is the most difficult adversity you have survived in your life? Client answers ...
- Well, you survived and stood it. Now how does that compare with their not respecting you?
- So, have you survived or stood anything worse than their disrespecting you?
- Let's be scientists. What do the data show?
- What good things could happen even if they disrespected you?
- Can you be happy even if you do not get what you want?
- How will your world be destroyed if they do not respect you?
- Where is it written that your peers must respect you?
- Where is it written that you need your peers' respect to be worthwhile?

Pragmatic Disputation Questions

The third group of questions does not challenge the logic or test the reality of the clients' thinking, but instead persuades clients to assess the hedonic, pragmatic, or heuristic value of their beliefs. Remember, rational beliefs help one attain one's goals. Therefore, beliefs can be evaluated on this functional criterion. Does a particular idea help the client to solve a personal problem? Attain a desired goal? Provide other positive consequences? Mitigate emotional turmoil? Below are some pragmatic disputes that could be used with the client, Barbara.

- So you believe that they must respect you. How much money has that made you?
- How has the demand that they must respect you gotten them to respect you?
- When you condemn yourself for not being respected, how does that help you get what you want? Or to be effective?
- So, you think it is terrible that they do not respect you. How is that thought working for you?
- "Whatever I want, I must get." Where will that command get you?
- Is it worth it for you to hold on to the belief that "I must be respected"?
- When you think that way, how do you feel? ... And is that feeling helpful to you?

- Does that thought motivate you to get to work?
- What happens to you when you think that thought?
- Why do you hold onto a belief that causes you so much trouble?
- Can you list all of the ways that your belief has helped and hurt you to accomplish your goals?

Caveats for Cognitive Disputing

When you challenge clients' IBs, allow the client time to contemplate your questions fully. New therapists often find these silences aversive, especially if they mistakenly believe that they must be directive at all times. Silence, in this instance, can indeed be golden. This suggestion implies that you will be careful to ask only one question at a time; no barrages, please. If you stack the questions, the client does not have the opportunity to think through your disputes. Take your time and become comfortable with the client's silences. In social situations, silences are uncomfortable and indicate a break in the conversation or a poor connection between the speakers. In disputation, a silence means the client is thinking about your question. The longer they remain silent the more cognitive restructuring is taking place. A good barometer of an effective disputation question is how long it takes the client to answer. If they answer immediately, they might not be rethinking, and you might not have asked a penetrating question. So attend to the latency of the client's response after your questions. Long latencies can be good. Do not provide answers to your own questions until you give the client a chance to reach for his or her own answers.

Be aware, however, that disputation questions can lead to discomfort for some clients, primarily because many of the questions have no immediate or common sense answer (e.g., "Where is the evidence for that belief?" None exists.). Therefore, although you are waiting for the clients' responses, observe any nonverbal signs of discomfort that might be exhibited during this period. If your clients are exceptionally distressed, ask them what feelings they are having and find out what irrational beliefs they are telling themselves. Perhaps they are awfulizing about not knowing the answers to your questions or realize that they are thinking in an unhelpful way. They might feel uncomfortable that you are asking them to give up a familiar idea. If any of these are true, they might not be attending to the points you are making during disputation. Uproot these irrational beliefs before you continue with the original disputation.

Clients frequently respond to disputing questions by giving you evidence in favor of the rational belief. For example, when the therapist attempts to dispute the concept of awfulness (e.g., "Where's the evidence that this is so terrible?"), the response of the client will usually be to justify why the situation is undesirable (e.g., "Because I don't like it!"). In this example, the client is failing to discriminate between undesirable and awful. The most common error made by a new therapist is to be stumped by the client's reasoning. Instead, the therapist can point out to the client that his or her retort provides evidence for the rational statement, but is not an answer to the original question. The therapist repeats the question until the client comes to the appropriate conclusion that no evidence exists for the IB. Consider this interchange with the client, Barbara, mentioned above.

T: But what evidence do you have, Barbara, that you must have their respect?
C: Because, well I want them to respect me. And, I will feel better if they respect me.
T: Barbara, that is evidence for why you want it. Because you want it and would feel good if they respected you, but the question is why must they respect you?
C: Because I have a lot to offer and I have good ideas. I deserve their respect!
T: Barbara, it could be true that you have great ideas and make a great contribution to work. However, that is only further evidence that it is unfortunate you did not get their respect. Why must they respect you even if you are making a great contribution and have great ideas?
C: You mean that they do not have to respect me even if I deserve their respect?
T: That's right, Barbara! They are who they are, and they feel what they feel and although you might have great ideas and could make a contribution, we cannot make them respect you.

In the above example, the therapist validates that not getting the respect would in fact be bad, but that does not mean that it must not exist. In general, it is good to realize that when clients say that something is terrible or awful that they often are saying two things: (1) something is bad or even very bad; and (2) that therefore it must not exist. We want only to direct our interventions to the second one and leave the first one alone. For example, when someone has experienced a very bad life event, such as a soldier who experiences the death of his comrade beside him, he will say that it was terrible. When you dispute this with: "How is it terrible?" The person could answer: "What do you know about such an experience?" Challenging the awfulizing can be invalidating to the client and they might be very resistant to the intervention. So, we can help such clients by saying, "Although such things are very bad, they still do happen. Now will it help you to acknowledge that such bad things do occur." In cases of trauma, we do not recommend disputing the awfulness of the trauma but encourage the client to accept or acknowledge that the trauma did happen.

Clients will often persist in providing similar answers far longer than Barbara did. The therapist can continue to go over the distinction between the rational and irrational beliefs until the client understands it. This could take several sessions.

Question Core/Imperative IBs and Derivative IBs

We noted earlier the importance of questioning your client's irrational beliefs in the form of both her/his core/imperative (rigid belief) and at least one of his/her three derivatives from that premise (awfulizing belief, frustration intolerance belief, or depreciation belief). If you decide to question the demand before beginning to question a derivative from the demand, persist until you have shown your client that there is no evidence in support of his/her demand. Similarly, if you have chosen to question your client's rational belief first, show her/him that there is evidence in support of the RB before moving on to question the main derivative from the rational belief.

Switching from demand to derivative (and from derivative to demand) can be confusing for the client. However, if you have persisted in questioning a demand and it becomes clear that your client is not finding this helpful, you can redirect your focus toward a derivative and then monitor your client's reactions. Some clients find it easier to understand why these derivatives are irrational than why their *musts* are irrational. In the same way, if your client finds it hard to understand why her preference is rational, then it might be more enlightening for him/her to concentrate on discussing a derivative (e.g., self-acceptance) from the demand.

STYLES OF COGNITIVE DISPUTING

A second dimension of cognitive disputation strategies is the style of the argument. Therapists can provide each of the above arguments in didactic, Socratic, metaphorical, humorous, vicarious, and self-disclosing styles.

Didactic Style

Didactic strategies include the use of mini-lectures, analogies, and parables to teach a point. Lectures, as we suggested earlier, are best kept brief and could be useful when new ideas are being presented to the client. As the client becomes familiar with REBT, the amount of time spent on didactic teaching can be gradually decreased over the sessions. When you do didactically teach, try to assess whether the client understands the concept you are teaching. A good way to do this is to follow didactic discourse with some Socratic dialogue. There is wide latitude for creativity in devising or borrowing stories to teach how the client's reasoning is faulty and what alternative philosophies can replace it. Some examples are provided in the following sections, in which suggested disputations for core irrational concepts are outlined.

Although REBT therapists prefer the Socratic style, asking questions does not always prove productive. If not, you might have to shift to give more lengthy didactic explanations concerning why an irrational belief is self-defeating and why a rational belief is more productive. Indeed, you will probably have to use didactic explanations to varying degrees with all of your clients at some point in treatment.

When you use didactic explanations, be sure that your clients understand what you have said by asking them to paraphrase your points. You might say, for example, "How would you say that?" Observe your client's nonverbal and paralinguistic signs of understanding (e.g., head nods, "hmm-hmms") as evidence that they have understood you. Such questions help your clients to become active participants in didactic explanations of REBT, and not passive recipients of the information.

Socratic Style

Many forms of psychotherapy, especially forms of CBT, use the Socratic Dialogue and its sequencing of questions to guide clinical interviews, foster self-discovery, and promote change. Some scholars consider Socrates the first psychotherapist (Chessick, 1982). Socrates saw the purpose of his teaching as deepening a person's self-awareness, self-acceptance, and self-regulation (Overholser, 1996) and promoting virtue and self-development (Overholser, 1999). The importance of self-awareness emerges in the statement attributed to Socrates, "the unexamined life is not worth living" (Lageman, 1989). Socrates viewed himself as a gadfly that irritates the horse and keeps it moving without guiding or directing it. Socrates used an analogy for human thought as a winged chariot driver struggling to use reason to control his two horses, one noble, rational, and calm, while the other was unruly, impulsive, and emotionally reactive. The struggle of the charioteer serves as a metaphor for our clients' struggle to use their rational thinking to control the irrational beliefs and emotions. The goal of the Socratic Method is to teach students to internalize the questioning process (Areeda, 1996). This sounds remarkably close to the objectives of REBT. By constantly questioning our thinking, we develop and reaffirm philosophies that are more rational, experience healthier emotions, and achieve a more adaptive life.

Overholser (1993a; 1993b; 1994; 1995; 1996; 1999; 2010) has written extensively on the Socratic Method in psychotherapy, and in CBT in particular. He has identified several components of the Socratic Method for therapists to follow from the work of the ancient Greek philosophers. Overholser's works provide an excellent guide to integrating the Socratic Method into clinical practice, and we strongly recommend that you read his works. Overholser's components of the Socratic Method include (1) systematic questioning (1993a); (2) inductive reasoning (1993b); (3) exploring universal definitions (1994); (5) disavowal of knowledge (1995); (5) self-improvement (1996); and promoting virtue in daily life (1999).

Systematic questioning involves a planned sequence of questions that guide the dialogue. Therapeutic questions encourage the exploration of different topics and strands of evidence and result in the accumulation of relevant information about the topic at hand. Systematic questioning allows clients to actively think differently and examine personal issues, values, and assumptions. Questions can vary by the form, content, and process used to structure a series of questions (Overholser, 1993a). The form of a question influences the type of answer that is elicited. Socratic questioning is not legalistic interrogation (Areeda, 1996). It avoids stacking questions for the client to answer at once, so s/he feels as though the therapist is playing "Guess what I am thinking."

The Socratic Method helps clients and therapists engage in collaborative searches for information and an understanding of each client's experiences.

Overholser recommends using open-ended questions. Open questions ask the respondent to *think* and *reflect*. They ask for *opinions*, and they put control of the conversation to the *respondent*. These questions allow for multiple possible answers. Open-ended questions encourage creativity concerning what line of experiences and evidence are examined, and often results in the therapist and client taking a new perspective on the problem. Although open-ended questions are preferred, Overholser (1993b) suggests that when clients are stuck and fail to answer, therapists can switch to leading questions to push the dialogue forward. A leading question includes an implied assumption. For example, the question "Did that thought help you in that situation?" assumes that the thought led or contributed to the outcome of being upset. An explication question involves stepping backward when the client answers, "I don't know." When the therapist asks, "What did happen when you had that thought?" and the client replies, "Well, it was not a good outcome," but does not identify the outcome, the therapist might just ask: "So what did happen after you had that thought?" or "Did you accomplish your goals after that thought?"

The Socratic Method also uses inductive reasoning to reach conclusions. The questioning guides clients to examine aspects of their lives and collect information. Inductive reasoning makes generalizations based on individual instances. In this sense, it is contrasted with deductive reasoning. Inductive reasoning helps clients form new generalizations through a gradual accumulation and systematic review of evidence (Gambrill, 1993). Inductive reasoning involves analyzing similarities and differences among specific experiences to extract a general principle about a class of events. In psychotherapy, inductive reasoning helps clients develop appropriate expectations and coping strategies at an abstract level.

Defining terms can be the beginning of disputing. Universal definitions describe the characteristics of a thing that are sufficient to capture the essence of a concept (Overholser, 1994). We strive for definitions of words that describe a concept in such a way that the concept remains unchanged when specific instances or examples of the concept vary. For example, "love" can be defined broadly as to feel tender affection for somebody such as a close relative or friend, or for something such as a place, an ideal, an animal, or a person. When a client says that someone does not love him or her because the person did not like everything the client does, the client is placing a new characteristic into the definition. This new definition could set such a high standard for love that few people, if anyone, could be said to love the client because almost no one could like everything the client does. The process of formulating definitions helps clients evaluate the appropriateness of the terms they use and the generalizations they make. "So, what do most people mean when they say they are worthless?" Definitions are important because language influences our perceptions, descriptions, and understanding of the world (Efran et al., 1990).

The definition process usually begins with refuting a critical evaluation of the client's generalization. When the client uses a term to classify a broad category of events, the therapist requests a clear and unambiguous definition of the term.

The questioning process often reveals confusion in the client's original generalization and its definition. Therapist and client work together to find the limitations or exceptions to the client's definition. Acceptable definitions must meet certain criteria. The definition should not use figurative or metaphorical language. Therapists can ask clients to clarify their term (e.g., "What do you mean when you say you are worthless?") and explain how they use a term. Such dialogues examine the client's definition to identify where and how it might be inadequate. In true Socratic style, the dialogue aims to refute the client's original definition, delimit overgeneralizations, and gradually collect examples that help the client develop a new and more useful definition (Chessick, 1982; Sternberg, 1998). This aspect of the Socratic Method incorporates the aspects of General Semantic theory that we discussed in Chapter 1. People often use words indiscriminately and do not examine their meaning nor do they often perceive the effect that labeling people and events with certain terms has upon them. By exploring the definitions of terms, much of the client's overgeneralization, self-condemnation, and catastrophizing can be eliminated.

Disavowal of knowledge is another characteristic of the Socratic Method (Overholser, 1995). Classical scholars refer to the disavowal of knowledge as "Socratic ignorance." A Greek citizen once declared, "No one is wiser than Socrates" because Socrates was the rare person who admitted he was ignorant. Socrates claimed to have no knowledge, but he had respect for the inquisitive abilities of the mind. Socratic ignorance helps both therapist and client to respect the limits of their knowledge. They recognize that they do not know what is best for the client, or what experiences the client has had that are relevant to solving the problem at hand. Even if therapists think they do know an answer, they rely on their client's ability to reach the conclusion independently. Most people tend to notice, accept, and remember information that supports their beliefs while they ignore, avoid, or belittle information that does not match their view. Clients can learn to evaluate the (1) quantity, (2) quality, (3) diversity, and (4) coherence of the evidence for and against their beliefs.

In order for the process to be effective, all four of these components need to work together. Therapy can focus on client self-improvement, with an emphasis on self-awareness, self-acceptance, and potential self-regulation of affect and behavior. In addition, therapy discussions can explore the meaning of virtue, including wisdom, courage, moderation, justice, and piety.

Overholser (1995) recognized that Socrates used his teaching method to promote self-improvement. Socrates divided self-improvement into three main components: self-awareness, self-acceptance, and self-regulation. The most relevant to our present discussion is the use of the Socratic Method to promote self-acceptance. Self-acceptance can be achieved after a thorough and rational review of the client's strengths and weaknesses. Through questioning, therapists can help clients to find their natural skills, talents, and traits to help them grow into useful qualities and productive habits. The Socratic Method adheres to the metaphor that "you can only help an acorn grow into an oak tree" or the ancient view, "do not force a cobbler to become a soldier."

Box 10.2

One of Ellis's first trainees and early supervisors at the Albert Ellis Institute, Ed Garcia, used an exercise with new therapists to teach Socratic Dialogue. He asked them to conduct an *entire* therapy session using only questions and avoiding any declarative sentences. Record a session and notice how close you came to this goal. We are not recommending that all therapy sessions only take the form of evocative questions. Too many questions could prove irritating to clients if they believe that you have something to say and are "beating around the bush" instead of saying it directly. This exercise is designed to give you practice in the art of Socratic Dialogue.

Humorous Style

Another widely used form of cognitive disputation and a primary tool of REBT is humor. Ellis (1977c) was noted for his use of this style, not only in front of audiences but also in individual, group, and conjoint sessions. There is no rule that therapy must be stodgy, dull, or super-serious.

Ellis always thought humor was a critical part of psychotherapy and used it as a means of attitude change. Humor is the tendency of particular cognitive experiences to provoke laughter and provide amusement. The term derives from the *humoral medicine* of the ancient Greeks, which taught that the balance of fluids in the human body, known as humors (as in the Greek word *chymos*, literally juice or sap), controlled human health and emotion.

Cognitive scientists (Hurley, Dennett, and Adams, 2011) have noted that most theories concerning humor focus on the content of why we find certain things funny. However, the more intriguing questions concern why humans find *anything* funny and have a sense of humor at all. From an evolutionary perspective, what is the survival value of humor? According to their new theory, Hurley et al. (2011) see humor as a means of correcting our false assumptions and thinking errors. The primary purpose of the human brain is to make sense of our daily lives by designing schema and assumptions based on sparse, incomplete information. However, mistakes in our schema are inevitable and even a small faulty assumption can lead to costly mistakes. Humor is the reward we get for seeking out and correcting our mistaken assumptions. A cognitively based psychotherapy focused on correcting faulty thinking welcomes humor as a natural error detector.

Watching comedic and humorous videos increases self-control (Tice, Baumeister, Shmueli and Muraven, 2007). Humor works best when it contrasts ideas, contrasts different meanings for the same word, and exaggerates aspects of an idea of meaning.

Though ultimately decided by personal taste, the extent to which an individual will find something humorous depends upon a host of variables, including geographical location, culture, maturity, level of education, intelligence, and context. For example, young children may favor slapstick. Satire may rely more on understanding the target of the humor and thus tends to appeal to more mature audiences. Nonsatirical humor can be specifically termed "recreational drollery." Many theories exist about what humor is and what social function it serves. The prevailing types of theories attempting to account for the existence of humor include psychological theories, the vast majority of which consider humor-induced behavior to be very healthy; spiritual theories, which may, for instance, consider humor to be a "gift from God"; and theories that consider humor to be an unexplainable mystery, very much like a mystical experience.

The root components of humor are (a) being reflective of or imitative of reality, and (b) surprise/misdirection, contradiction/paradox, or ambiguity. The methods of humor include hyperbole, metaphor, reduction ad absurdum or farce, reframing, and timing.

Once you get used to using humor carefully, you and your client could enjoy your hours together more. The use of humor does entail one caveat: the target of the humor is always the client's irrational belief and not the client. It is important to assess your client's ability to use and understand humor, and his/her ability to understand the target of the humor. The therapist might want to discuss the use of humor with the client prior to utilizing it.

With some clients, a productive way of making the point that there is no evidence for irrational beliefs is to use humor or humorous exaggeration. As Walen et al. (1992) note:

If the client says, "It's really awful that I failed the test!" the therapist might respond, "You're right! It is not only awful, but I do not see how you are going to survive. That is the worst news I have ever heard! This is so horrendous that I cannot bear to talk about it. Let's talk about something else, quick!" Such paradoxical statements frequently point out the senselessness of the irrational belief to the client, and very little further debate might be necessary to make the point.

Metaphoric Style

Metaphors are the concept or process of understanding one thing in terms of another. A metaphor is a figure of speech that constructs an analogy between two ideas. The analogy is conveyed by the use of a metaphorical word in place of some other word. For example: "Her voice was a sonata." Metaphors compare things without using the words "like" or "as." Metaphors involve the transfer of meaning from one element to another. Scholars, authors, and teachers have used them for centuries as a method of teaching and communicating in many fields. Ortony (1975) noted the mnemonic function of metaphor by pointing out that the memorability, compactness, and vividness of metaphors are what make them a highly effective learning device. This general facilitation view defines metaphors as high-imagery words that are more memorable and has received empirical support (Reynolds and Schwartz, 1983; Paivio, 1986).

Psychotherapists have used metaphors since Breuer and Freud (1895/1955) started the "talking cure"; and there are many different ways that they can be used.

(See Muran and DiGiuseppe, 1990 for a review.) Clinical experience suggests that clients often become overwhelmed by cognitive restructuring and fail to remember all the relevant challenges to their IBs and the RBs. Muran and DiGiuseppe (1990) suggested that the mnemonic functions of metaphors ameliorate this process because of their usefulness in learning. This mnemonic function allows for the synchronous organization of information into large, integrated chunks.

Successfully challenging any particular dysfunctional thought in therapy often involves a creative search for metaphors that have symbolic significance or personal meaning for the client and, therefore, could have high persuasive impact. This search might involve joining a client's own use of a metaphor and reframing it according to a particular disputational strategy. DiGiuseppe and Muran (1992) identified several rules for selecting metaphors for use in therapy. These include

(a) clearly defining the concept that you wish to communicate or teach;
(b) attending to the client's language and search for an arena which he/she understands and has comfortably mastered;
(c) searching for an analogue construct in the client's arena of knowledge that includes the core elements of the concept that you wish to teach; and
(d) if none exists or comes to mind, start over with a new arena about which the client has knowledge.

For example, a client with athletic experience or interest recently asked one of us for more direction and specific advice on how to respond to a practical problem. The therapist tried a way to explain a therapist's role; that is, a therapist teaches clients skills to solve life's problems without making the actual decisions for clients. Because of the client's active involvement in sports and her use of other metaphors in the athletic sphere, the metaphor of "coach" came into the therapist's mind. The therapist explained that the therapist was like a coach, teaching skills and making sure that the athlete practiced. A coach, however, cannot compete for the athlete. A therapist can likewise teach a client what steps to go through to make decisions, but cannot make them for the client. Here, the abstract concept embodied in a familiar arena (i.e., a coach in athletics) was applied to a new arena (i.e., a therapist in therapy) to help the client understand a new concept (i.e., the therapist's role). This successfully resolved the issue of the client seeking advice on practical decisions and facilitated learning the skills to think through her choices.

Movie characters can also serve as metaphors for use in therapy. Films provide visual, experiential story lines that people can recall to suggest new ways of thinking whenever they remind themselves of the character or plot. Consider the following example of an angry young man and the use of the 1972 movie *The Godfather*, directed by Francis Ford Coppola. Vito aspired to be a fighter and a tough guy. He frequently got into fights that he did not win because he would challenge anyone, even if he was outnumbered. The therapist (RD) struggled to teach Vito two concepts, the difference between adaptive anger and rage, and that people did not have to respect him and his family, even if he wanted them to do so. Vito loved *The Godfather* movie. The therapist suggested that Vito was just like the Godfather's son, Sonny, played by James Caan. Sonny was quick to anger and thought people, especially his brother-in-law, must respect the family, especially Sonny's sister. The competing families knew of Sonny's quick, impulsive temper and staged a fight between Sonny's sister and brother-in-law. When the sister calls Sonny to tell him of the fight, Sonny gets angry, runs to his car and drives to her rescue. The route to his sister's is through a tollbooth, and there the other family soldiers are waiting for Sonny and shoot him hundreds of times. The therapist reminded Vito of the story and asked him to focus on his favorite character Sonny.

T: And what happened to Sonny when he lost his temper?
C: Well, I guess he acted impulsively and that did him in.
T: So, do you think and act like Sonny?
C: All the time.
T: And does it work for you?
C: No, this week I got my ass kicked because I started with a group of guys in the next neighborhood.
T: So, perhaps you will end up like Sonny?
C: It could happen.
T: Well, what if each time you thought people were challenging your honor or reputation you think of Sonny. Did his anger work for him?
C: Not at all. It got him killed.
T: And did Sonny's thoughts that others must not disrespect him help him?
C: No, that helped get him killed.
T: So what if each time you perceive that someone is challenging you, you think of Sonny.
C: Yeah, I could think, "What happened to Sonny for thinking that way?" That would get me to stop and think differently.

This reference to the character "Sonny" consolidated all the information about the dysfunctional nature of Vito's anger and the heuristic disputes mentioned above. "Think of Sonny" brought all this information to his mind and helped Vito move on to more rational alternative responses.

As you progress as a therapist you will accumulate metaphors that you use to help clients give up dysfunctional beliefs and adopt new ones. Stott et al. (2010) have provided many examples of metaphors to use in a wide range of situations in general CBT.

Be Creative

The more experience you gain in questioning irrational and rational beliefs, the more you will develop your own individual style of questioning. You will build a repertoire of stories, aphorisms, metaphors, and other examples to show your clients why their irrational beliefs are self-defeating and why rational alternatives will promote psychological health.

For example, in working with clients who believe they must not experience panic and could not stand it if they did, one of us (WD) uses a technique called the Terrorist Dispute:

> I say, "Let's suppose that your parents have been captured by radical terrorists, and these radicals will release your parents only if you agree to put up with ten panic attacks. Will you agree to these terms?" The client usually says, "Yes." If so, I will then say, "But I thought you couldn't stand the experience of panic." The client usually replies, "Well, but I would do it in order to save my parents." To which I respond, "Yes, but will you do it for your own mental health?"

Another creative questioning strategy is what we call the Best Friend Dispute, an approach that is useful for pointing out to clients the existence of unreasonable self-standards.

> Imagine that your client has failed an important test and believes, "I must do well, and I am no good if I don't." Ask her whether she would condemn her best friend for a similar failure in the same way she condemns herself. Normally, your client will say no. If so, point out that she has a different attitude toward her friend than she has toward herself. Suggest that if she chose to be as compassionate toward herself as she is toward her friend, she would be better able to help herself solve her own emotional problems.

Vicarious Modeling

Therapists can frequently teach clients that many people in their environment have similar activating events and yet do not suffer from unhealthy dysfunctional emotions, because they do not adhere to the same IBs. Clients can learn much through vicarious modeling; clients can become aware that others are not devastated by similar problems. Clients can then apply this knowledge to themselves. The process can also sensitize clients to look for data in their environment that they could have selectively screened out. Vicarious modeling is a good strategy to use when clients' As are virtually universal, such as romantic breakups. We have all lived through them. One of us recently treated the mother of a child with Giles de la Tourette's syndrome. She was unfamiliar with the disorder and horrified by the child's bizarre behavior, convinced that her child was the only case in the world. Through some investigation, the therapist found an association for parents of children with Tourette's syndrome and advised the mother to attend a meeting of this group. This experience provided the woman with a coping model. At her next therapy session she concluded, "I guess people can learn to adjust and live with it." One of the benefits of groups is Yalom's Universality Principle, that humans are not unique in their suffering (Yalom and Leszcz, 2005).

CONSTRUCTING ALTERNATIVE RATIONAL BELIEFS

Challenging, questioning, and arguing against an IB is only part of the process. People will not give up an idea or behavior unless they have a replacement for it. Kuhn's analysis of the history of science shows that people often know that their contemporary theories are flawed and inconsistent with reality. However, they hold on to them because they lack an alternative idea to replace the faulty one they believe. An example involves Charles Darwin and the theory of evolution. Before Darwin set out on his travels on the *HMS Beagle*, scientists knew for years that the existing theories in biology were flawed. Darwin did not discover any new data that weakened the existing ideas. He did develop a new idea. And once that new idea of evolution was cast, the debate was on. New ideas do not come along very easily. They come from human creativity and dialectics of debating a new idea and the old ideas. In behavior therapy, it is well established that it is difficult to suppress or eliminate a dysfunctional behavior. The best strategy is to reinforce a new alternative and incompatible behavior. REBT also believes that clients are more likely to surrender their IBs when they have new alternative RBs.

The question remains: Do new ideas develop through teaching or self-discovery? The idea that self-discovery is a superior way to learn originated with the developmental psychologist Jean Piaget. Despite his enthusiasm for this means of learning, little research has confirmed the superiority of learning through self-discovery (Brainerd, 2003).

Learning through self-discovery appears to be valued in counseling and psychotherapy. Some psychotherapists would provide clients with feedback that their ideas or behavior are incorrect or dysfunctional, and wait for the client to conceive a replacement idea or behavior. REBT practitioners think it is more efficient to help the client adopt an alternative based on its philosophy.

We have no good data that self-discovery leads to more adaptive or enduring new philosophies. Also, discovering new RBs takes time, and while the therapist waits for the client to discover the new idea, s/he continues to suffer. We do not have the unlimited resources of time and money to pursue self-discovery. In the wake of no evidence that self-discovery leads to more enduring, deeper, or adaptive new beliefs, REBT advocates that therapists teach the client a new rational philosophy. However, self-discovery might be of value. So the therapeutic dilemma is how long to wait for clients to self-discover their new alternative beliefs.

We recommend that therapists always ask clients what new beliefs they could have or have had that would be associated with a more functional, nondisturbed emotion. If the client could identify this thought, we would then discuss how it could be more beneficial for them. If they could not, we might ask them to pick a model of someone who copes well with the situation that upsets them, and after identifying a coping model ask the client how they think (or know) that the model thinks differently from them. Again, if they can come up with a rational alternative belief, we will work to rehearse and strengthen the client's endorsement of that belief. However, if these strategies fail within a reasonable frame of time to uncover a new belief, we would suggest one. We recommend that therapists offer new RBs as hypotheses, and seek the client's feedback on whether that belief makes sense to them. We have found that clients often rephrase the new RB into their own words (See Chapter 12).

LEVELS OF ABSTRACTION

The goal of disputation is to change clients' negative dysfunctional thinking in such a way that they can relieve the emotional disturbance from which they are suffering. The level of abstraction at which such change takes place will vary from client to client. For example, I might not "get" the most elegant and comprehensive idea that I don't need anyone's love and approval, but I could be able to "get" the idea that I do not need the love and approval of a particular person. Although the latter idea is less inclusive, it is nonetheless rational and elegant; it would be consistent with happy living if I did not have that particular relationship in my life. Usually, we do not need to go to the most abstract level of the irrational belief, because it is unlikely that the individual will ever have to cope with it in reality. For example, it is unlikely that an individual will achieve no success at all or receive no love within the space of a lifetime.

Consider another example. If Ralph is angry with his spouse for not having dinner on the table when he thought she should, we could identify many levels of irrational thinking that lead to his dysfunctional anger:

- My wife must have dinner on the table when I want her to.
- My wife must do chores the way I want her to.
- My wife must do things the way I want her to.
- Family members must do things the way I want them to.
- People in my life must do things the way I want them to.
- All people must behave the way I want them to behave.
- The world must be the way I want it to be.

These thoughts illustrate a continuum of abstraction and represent a ladder of abstraction of IBs. They illustrate why the level of abstraction is clinically significant. If our client only believed the first irrational idea, he would react to a few future activating events, but the more abstract the IBs he subscribes to, the more potential distress he might suffer. As a parallel, the less abstract the rational belief, the less generalizable his coping will be.

Clients usually report beliefs at the lower end of the abstraction continuum. These lower-level beliefs are more readily experienced and admitted by the client, and thus might be more accessible to change. The client's ability to generalize from a specific example to new situations will be enhanced if the therapist works at the more abstract levels. Our suggestion, therefore, is that therapists conceptualize the IBs and dispute them up and down the ladder of abstraction as the therapy progresses.

Let us return to Ralph's situation. If Ralph's therapist begins disputation at a concrete level ("My wife must have dinner on the table when I want her to"),

Ralph is likely to gain some control over his dysfunctional anger in a frequently occurring event and thus be reinforced for making progress in therapy. Later, the therapist might want to explore with Ralph whether he has other demands of his wife or other people, and that the world does not have to be the way he wants it to be. Thus, by moving up and down the ladder of abstraction, the therapist will ensure that Ralph learns to deal with specific activating events and can apply the REBT solution to other similar aversive events; and that he understands the rule behind the reasoning and can apply it to other aversive events.

Additional Aids to Disputing

An important prerequisite for successful disputation is the therapist's ability to think rationally about the client's problem. How can therapists dispute something they believe that really must not happen? First, we advise therapists to ask themselves, "Why must this not happen?" If they are not convinced, how will they ever convince the client? One therapist, for example, found herself overwhelmed by a client's fears of sexual rejection after a mastectomy. Only after the therapist had philosophically accepted that such losses can happen and that people can lose a breast was she able to calmly help her client to the same conclusion.

We think it is helpful to practice the disputation process and prepare before each session with clients. Beal, Kopec, and DiGiuseppe (1996) created a chart of different types of disputes and asked trainees to complete the chart on a client before the session began. They found that such practice increased the trainees' sense of self-efficacy in the disputing process. Table 10.1 presents the form they used in their research. A blank form appears in Appendix 3. After reading the sample provided in Table 10.1, the reader can print several copies of the form and complete them for specific irrational beliefs for the clients you are presently treating. If you do this for several weeks, you might notice that you are getting better. You might also feel more confident in the session and pay better attention to what the clients are saying because you will be struggling less on how you will dispute the beliefs and support the new rational beliefs.

When you are ready to challenge the beliefs, make sure you target the appropriate philosophical concept, not the metaphor in which it is expressed. For example, if a client says, "I failed—what a horse's ass I am!" it is easy to point out that he is mistaken since he clearly does not possess the characteristics of equine buttocks. The philosophical point might be missed, however, because the client's misconception about human worth being dependent on accomplishment is still intact.

Once you have uncovered a core IB, realize that it will take a significant amount of time to dispute it. Inasmuch as the essence of REBT is to change irrational beliefs, D is obviously the most critical part. Do not be afraid to repeat a disputation over the course of many sessions if necessary. There are several ways to assure plentiful time for disputation. One way to increase disputing time is to avoid taking on a new problem in a session if you have not finished disputing an older problem from a previous session. You can begin your next session by asking

Table 10.1. Training in Disputation Strategies (From Beal, Kopec, and DiGiuseppe, 1996)

Example 1—Disputing the Irrational Belief: "I'm no Good if My Friends Look Down on Me."

Disputing Strategy

	Logical	Empirical	Functional	Rational Alternative
Didactic	If your friends look down on you, then what they do is to observe parts of you and conclude that those parts are "bad" (undesirable to them). Then they jump from those parts to the conclusion that "all of you is no good." That is bad logic!	You are made up of many parts. Even if some of the parts are "faulty" there is no evidence that "all" of you is faulty!	It looks like holding that belief gets you a lot of negative emotions, anxiety, and depression.	It seems to me that a more rational belief could be: "I am a complex, unratable, fallible human being even if my friends disapprove of me."
Socratic	If your friends look down on you, then what they do is to observe parts of you and conclude that those parts are "bad" (undesirable to them). Then they jump from those parts to all of you is no good. Is that logical? Why not?	Is there any evidence that a part can define a whole?	What does holding the belief: "I'm no good if my friends look down on me" get you?	What do you think would be a more helpful and adaptive (rational) belief that you can create right now about yourself in the situation where your friends are looking down on you?
Metaphor	Let's suppose that I own the "car of the year." However, it has a defective spark plug. So by your logic, the whole car is "no good," right?	Clearly, some people, even very important and influential people thought Jesus Christ was "no good." Even so, was that evidence that he was no good, or just their opinion?	Abraham Lincoln took a major stand when he freed the slaves with the Emancipation Proclamation. Many of his friends looked down on him. Where the United States would be today if he held your belief?	Many famous movie stars and celebrities held the belief that they were no good if their friends or the public looked down on them. Some even committed suicide. Think how their lives would have differed with a more rational belief?

Disputing Strategy	Logical	Empirical	Functional	Rational Alternative
Humor	If I were the president of the United States, or the Pope, and I reasoned that way, that would make it sound logic, right?	If I thought you were a giraffe, would your neck grow?	By your definition then, if your friends looked up to you, then you would be "good." Hitler's friends and followers deified him. Did that make him good?	With my friends opinion of me and $2.50 I can ride the subway. Wow!

EXAMPLE 2—IRRATIONAL BELIEF TO DISPUTE: "BECAUSE I WAS REJECTED IN THE RELATIONSHIP, I'M UNLOVABLE AND A FAILURE!"

Disputing Strategy

	Logical	Empirical	Functional	Rational Alternative
Didactic	It doesn't logically follow that just because the relationship ended, you're a failure as a person.	There is absolutely no evidence to support the belief that just because one person ended a relationship with you, that makes you a failure as a human being. In fact, you are just a person whose relationship ended.	It seems that as long as you keep telling yourself you are a failure because your relationship ended, you will suffer deep depression. It is not helping you to keep downing yourself and rating yourself.	It seems to me that it would be better to unconditionally accept yourself as a person of worth whose relationship may have failed. Moreover, that does not make you a failure as a person.
Socratic	Is it logical to believe that just because a relationship ends, you or anybody else is therefore a total failure as a person?	Where is the proof to support the belief that just because the relationship ended, you're suddenly a total failure and no-good-nik as a person?	How does it help you to keep thinking that because the relationship failed, you are a failure? (Where does that belief get you? As long as you keep thinking that way, what happens to you?)	What do you think would be a more helpful and truthful (rational) belief that you can create right now about a failed relationship and your acceptance of your self?

(continued)

Disputing Strategy

	Logical	Empirical	Functional	Rational Alternative
Metaphor	If a baseball player has a .300 batting average that is very good, right? However, that means the player has not gotten a hit 70% of the time. So, not succeeding in some circumstances doesn't logically make the player a total failure.	Where's the evidence that says that the student who fails one quiz or test will therefore fail ALL tests and will therefore be a total failure as a student and a person?	If Thomas Edison had told himself that he was a total failure when his early experiments with electricity failed, what would it have gotten him (and us!)?	Many famous movie stars, musicians, etc. have believed that they MUST be successful in all endeavors or else they are failures, and some committed suicide. Think how their lives would have been different with more self-acceptance.
Humor	So you are saying that because I experience failures in relationships that I am a failure too! Oh no! If I am a total failure because some relationships don't work out, I better stop practicing psychology!	Elizabeth Taylor MUST be a total failure because she has had quite a few marriages. Is that true? Is it true that if a person has not experienced a failed relationship, they must be God?	Marie Antoinette may have been the perfect partner, and look what it got her!	If you died and went to heaven, and told St. Peter of your failed relationship, would you be sent directly to Hell? Or would he probably remind you that you are still a person of worth, even in a failed relationship.

the client if he or she recalls the problem, outlining the **A**s, **B**s, and **C**s quickly, and launching immediately into disputation. Another strategy is to take the new problems brought in by the client and show how they relate to his or her core IBs, and then proceed with the disputation.

Whenever possible, it is important to work first with the client's motivation before beginning a disputing strategy. Point out to the client the benefits of changing his or her beliefs—especially the benefit of feeling less emotional distress. This strategy depends, of course, on assuring that the client does want to change C. If the client has an anger problem, for example, the therapist might first inquire, "Can you see any advantages to being (less angry) annoyed rather than angry?" After these are listed, the therapist might ask, "Can you think of any ways to feel annoyed (less angry)?" When motivation is established, the client might be more receptive to a cognitive or behavioral intervention.

Thus, among the disputing techniques to help the client challenge distress-producing **B**s are those that first point out the lack of value of the distress. Again taking anger as an example, the therapist might state something like the following:

"Let's first take a look at whether your anger is working for you or against you. What does rage do? It sets the stage for a fight! In addition, it is not good for you; it gets your juices flowing, makes you feel more irritated, and so forth. Now concern or annoyance, on the other hand, serves as a sensible cue for you to say, 'How can I change this? What can I do to help the situation? Perhaps if I explain to him ...?' See, now we are talking about strategies. And if a strategy does not work, what would you do? You would go back to the drawing board and try another. You see, you can do that kind of problem solving once you're not in a rage."

If your clients are unsure about whether they want to change their behaviors or emotions, try to determine other motivations that might be serving to maintain the pathology. A good technique to help clients become aware of the reinforcers operating to perpetuate a problem is the following sentence-completion item from Lazarus (1972): "The good thing about ... [e.g., procrastination] is ... " Repeat this phrase until the client has exhausted all suggestions. If clients cannot think of anything to say, urge them to say something anyway, the first thing that comes to mind. Stress that they need not believe what they say, nor does it have to be true of them. The therapist could even suggest a sentence-completion line as a model to get the client started. The therapist would do well to listen for a pattern in the client's responses, for not only might the client's statements indicate reasons to keep the distress, but new irrational beliefs might emerge as well.

Disputation is hard work, for what you are trying to do is shift the client's position on major philosophic issues that they have often rehearsed for a long period. Accomplishing this task requires many trials and a great deal of persistence on the part of the therapist. Like any good persuader, therapists had better believe in what they are saying, and demonstrate this belief by their persistence and enthusiasm for their position—rationality.

Persistence, however, does not mean a continual hard sell; some challenges are subtle and can take place even when the therapist is being supportive or reflective.

If you are in the early stages of therapy and attempting to build rapport, you might wish to be supportive but at the same time not reinforce irrational beliefs. For example, if your client says, "I need …," you can reflect by saying, "I know that … is something you want very badly." The therapist is thus modeling a more rational statement while conveying understanding of the client's plight.

Box 10.3

Remind your clients that it is important not merely to be aware that one's thoughts are irrational, but to actively dispute these thoughts outside of the therapy sessions. In addition, it is important to actively construct and forcefully rehearse new rational beliefs to replace the old irrational ones. (See Chapter 12)

New therapists frequently assume that generalization of behavior change will automatically take place. Although we believe that generalization is one of the advantages of cognitive interventions, we do not assume that it occurs without effort. As with behavior therapies, generalization requires planning. Thus, it might be desirable to dispute the same irrational notion across many situations, even though the irrational beliefs, the disputation, and the resulting rational beliefs could be the same in each example.

A prototype of the generalization problem is the male client with sexual difficulties, for whom a hierarchy of anxiety-arousing situations has been constructed. The client might have progressed through several exercises, such as sensate focus or masturbation training, during which he successfully counteracted his irrational beliefs about failure and performance. At the top of the hierarchy, when he is instructed to resume having intercourse with his partner, he might completely reinterpret the situation and resume his irrational catastrophizing. He then might be saying to himself, "This is the Real Thing; now if I fail, it will indeed be terrible!" Thus, although you might have helped him counteract his irrational beliefs at lower points in the hierarchy, you cannot assume that his rational beliefs will generalize to the next step. In this example, the therapist specifically questions the client about his cognitions during the various performance stages.

In addition, do not assume that if clients are thinking rationally in one problem area, they are doing so in other problem areas as well. For example, Margaret could present several problems at once: anxiety in social situations, guilt about sexual performance, anger at her boss, and so on. Generally, it is wise to work on one problem at a time. If the therapist chooses to work on the anxiety in social situations and helps the client to rid herself of all of her irrational beliefs in this area, there is no guarantee that she will automatically begin thinking rationally about sexual guilt or about her anger at her boss. These other problem areas will probably require separate work.

One strategy to maximize generalization benefits is to help clients believe that they are responsible for their own success. A number of studies in the behavioral literature have indicated that internal rather than external attribution for success at an endeavor is an important cognitive factor in generalization (Ruth and

DiGiuseppe, 1989). If clients believe that their success was attributable to internal factors, they are more likely to believe that they have control over future problems and to apply what they have learned in therapy to new problems.

A final suggestion, before we turn to a case example of disputation, is to use as many disputing strategies with each client as possible. Lazarus (2009) has proposed that the more modalities therapists utilize (cognitive, experiential, imaginal, and behavioral) the more effective the disputation will be and the longer lasting its effects. We have found this to be a helpful suggestion.

Box 10.4

Dispute with respect. We are not making fun of client's erroneous or self-defeating thinking, but working to repair or modulate it. First, however, we accept and study it. IBs are there, presumably, for a good reason.

For example, one client had lost her parents at a very young age and been sent to live with her grandparents, who soon died, so that she ended up with distant relatives. Her silent conclusion, based on the data of her life, was that love, trust, or closeness was the "kiss of death." Small wonder that she had difficulty establishing intimate adult relationships, including a therapeutic rapport. The work of therapy consisted of respectfully understanding her early experience, as interpreted by a frightened young child, which led to her illogical core belief. Gradually she learned to reinterpret her experience, reassure herself, and trust in her ability to love and, as an adult, to tolerate the potential for loss of a love object.

A CASE EXAMPLE OF DISPUTING

A transcript of portions of a sample session conducted by Ellis will demonstrate the process of disputing. This transcript is adapted from a public demonstration in which a participant asked to work with Ellis. The first problem dealt with the individual's nervousness at being on display.

Getting at the B
T: What do you think you're telling yourself to make yourself nervous?
C: I'm an idiot for being up here!
T: You're an idiot because ...
C: I might reveal sensitive areas of myself and I would feel uncomfortable.

Clarifying which IB is more prominent
T: And you should feel comfortable? Is that what you're saying? Or you should not reveal yourself at all?
C: Not at all.
T: If you reveal yourself, what? What are you predicting would happen if you reveal yourself?

C: An outburst of emotion … I would feel embarrassed.

T: So you might act foolishly in front of these people, right?

C: Yes.

T: Well, if you did, why would that be upsetting? Anxiety-provoking, if you did?

C: Can you restate the question?

Client's confusion is probably an index of his anxiety level.

T: Yes. You are saying, "I might act foolishly in front of this audience." But you'd never get anxious just from that statement. That's just an observation or prediction. But how are you evaluating yourself if you do act foolishly?

C: I don't understand.

Repeat

T: Well, just that statement alone doesn't cause an emotion. Something follows. You might be saying, "I might act foolishly, and isn't that great! I might act foolishly, and that would be good practice at acting foolishly!" And then you wouldn't be anxious, right?

C: Right.

T: But you're saying, "I might act foolishly, and isn't that what?" You're not saying, "It's great!"

C: I need to not act out of character.

T: "And if I act out of character—what?"

C: I might act fearful.

The derivative component of IB is still missing.

T: "And if I act fearful, what?" You see, you're still not giving me the evaluation of you or the situation. "I would like it? Dislike it? Be enthusiastic? I would be?" What's your evaluation of you or the results of acting foolishly?

C: It would make me feel unstable.

Therapist clarifies that "unstable" is not an emotion but an A–(inference).

T: So, "I would be an unstable person if I act foolishly up here?" Or, "They would think of me as an unstable person?"

C: Yes.

T: But that is a hypothesis about how you behave, not an irrational belief.

Inference Chaining—Assuming the worst

T: Well, let's suppose they do think you are unstable! Let's suppose they say, "Oh, shit, he's unstable." Now, you don't know that they'd say that! They might say, "Oh boy, he's got the guts to go up there and I'm scared shitless. But let's suppose they do say you're unstable. What's the horror of that?

C: That would support what I already think.

T: "That I am unstable." Well, how are you evaluating your so-called instability?

C: As a negative.

T: "I don't like this characteristic?" But then you'd only feel concerned. You wouldn't feel embarrassed or ashamed. You'd just say, "Well, I have a negative trait called instability." Do you see that you're saying something stronger than that to make yourself anxious?

C: Could it be rejection possibly?

T: Yes. "Because if I'm rejected ..."

C: Then I'm different from them.

T: "And if I'm different from them ..." What are you concluding from that?

C: I'd be lonely.

Rephrasing C as an A to show the A-C connection

T: "I would be quite alone." And how do you feel about being quite alone?

C: Depressed.

Therapist summarizes the A-B complex.

T: Yes. So if I hear you right, you're saying, "If I act foolishly up here, it would prove I'm different. Other people would know I'm different. They would probably boycott me to some degree, and I couldn't bear that—that would be awful." Is that right?

C: Yes.

T: All right. But even if that occurred ... and we don't know if it would occur ... why would it be horrible? That they thought you were boycottable and you were alone? Why would that be awful?

C: The evidence is my past experience. By being different, I was alienated.

T: But why was that horrible? Let's assume that that occurred. You were alienated and left alone. Why was that horrible?

C: I feel like I need someone to share things with.

T: Prove it! Prove that you need someone.

C: (pause) There is no evidence.

T: But if you believe it, how will you feel?

C: Terrible.

T: That's right! You've defined these things as terrible, and if you gave up those definitions, you'd feel all right. How do you feel right now about being up here?

C: A little looser.

T: Do you realize why you are feeling a little looser? Do you know why that is so?

C: I have more of an I-don't-give-a-shit attitude.

T: All right. That's good. And, you've gotten distracted somewhat. Instead of focusing on the audience, you're focusing on what we're talking about. Now, what other problem would you like to discuss?

11

Challenges to Specific Irrational Beliefs

DISPUTING THE CORE ELEMENTS OF IRRATIONAL BELIEFS

In Chapter 10, we present many ways of categorizing irrational beliefs. In searching for a systematic way to present disputing strategies to new students of REBT, we decided to teach how to challenge the core elements of irrational thought rather than each of the specific IBs. If you recall, the four basic irrational processes are:

Demandingness—the belief in universal musts, that the world must be the way one wants it to be.
Awfulizing—the belief that some things are terrible, awful, or catastrophic.
Human worth ratings—the belief that people can be rated globally as bad or worthless.
Frustration Intolerance—the belief that one cannot bear hassles, unpleasant emotions, or what one does not like.
Let us examine each core element in turn and some ways to combat them.
Demandingness
Listen for the following words in the client's speech: "must," "got to," "should have to," "ought to," "necessary."
These can be heard in "I" statements ("I have to…"); "you" statements ("you've got to…"); or ("he should…"); or "the world" statements ("it's got to…"). Shoulds are often stated about past events in problems of depression, anger, and guilt (e.g., "He shouldn't have done that.") but refer to present or future events as well in cases of anxiety (e.g., "I must not make a mistake.").

Should statements are internally illogical and reveal a philosophy of demand rather than preference. The irrational component, therefore, is the client's insistence that events or people's behavior be different. Clients upset themselves by the logical fallacy that "because I want X, it must be so," or as Ellis had put it, "My will be done!" It is as if clients believe that they can control the universe, which is perversely thwarting their efforts. These demands produce what Karen Horney (1945) called "the tyranny of the shoulds."

Three Steps for Disputing Clients' "Musts"

We have frequently encountered the problem that clients interpret the therapist's challenging of their musts as a challenge to their wants. This results in clients thinking that the therapist believes they have no right to their desires and creates a rupture in the therapeutic alliance. Consider this interchange with a client, Toan.

C: I just want my wife to show some interest in me and feel a little romance. Is that too much to ask? Shouldn't she show me a little affection?

T: Toan, why must your wife behave romantically?

C: (Sounding annoyed) Are you telling me you don't think romance is important in a marriage? It's not OK for me to want this? You don't want romance in your marriage?

Our client Toan has misunderstood the challenge to the "must" as a challenge to the "want." Because clients, as Ellis used to say, escalate a want into a demand, they frequently are not aware that there is a difference between their want and their demand. They hold them as one thought such as, "I want/demand that X be." Because the "want" and the "demand" are identified as equal, the client can believe that a challenge to one is a challenge to both. If the client thinks we are challenging his/her want s/he might feel invalidated. REBT postulates that desires are neither rational nor irrational, and neither right nor wrong. When clients make their desire into a demand, they produce disturbance. We want to make it clear that we never challenge the desire. How do we make this clear to clients like Toan?

First, the therapist explains to the client the distinction between wants and musts. Wants and desires can be almost anything. However, what "must" be is limited by the rules of physics. We teach the client that these are two different things. Second, the therapist affirms the want or preference; the desire is appropriate and not open to debate. Third, the therapist challenges the must. Consider this interchange with Toan.

T: Well, you have a point, Toan. Let me make this clear. It does not matter what I want; what matters is what you want. And you are correct that it is normal for you to want your wife to be romantic. The wanting it is not what is making you angry. The wanting it and the demanding it are too different things.

C: How's that?

T: Wanting has to do with your preferences; demanding something has to do with insisting that the world not be the way it actually is. Now, I think anyone would accept that you want your wife to be romantic, and that you highly value romance in marriage. And most people might want the same thing as you.

I have no debate with that. But what I would like you to focus on is why she has to comply with your desire just because you want it.

C: So you're saying just because I want it and it is normal to want it, she does not have to do it?

T: Yes, exactly.

When the therapist makes this distinction between desires and demands, he or she can move on to challenging the client's demands by asking questions such as:

Why is that "must" a nutty thing to say to yourself?
What law of physics exists that says it should be?
Explain that to me—why does she have to?
How does your wanting it prove it must be?

Moral Laws. Many people believe that there are "musts" about human conduct. After all, that is why we have the Ten Commandments, the code of Hammurabi, and other moral codes. Rational emotive behavioral philosophy does not question the advisability of creating or following such codes of conduct. However, it does acknowledge that these are laws devised by humans. They were not devised by nature. Even though moral codes are desirable, it does not logically follow that people must abide by them. Obviously all of us break these codes at times ("Let him who is without sin cast the first stone."). If these rules were part of human nature, they would not have been set down by moral philosophers but rather by ethologists. Thus, people would automatically exhibit moral behavior because they must do so by their very nature, and to do so would not be considered "noble." Most religious systems, although advocating a code of ethics, recognize an individual's choice in living up to it. Rational emotive behavioral theory distinguishes between the advisability of a particular behavior and the individual's potential to choose; he or she can decide not to do what is desirable and advisable. The rational individual appreciates that even the Ten Commandments can be interpreted as conditional shoulds, not absolutes. Depending on your frame of reference—if you want to be happy in heaven or have an easier time of it here on earth—then you probably should honor your father and mother.

Recall our discrimination between absolutist musts and innocuous musts. Clients confuse the two in their everyday problems; for example, "I have to go to work," "I have to take my medicine," or "I have to call my mother." You can point out to clients that human beings rarely act without first deciding to do so. Words such as "must," "have to," and "got to" imply that we are being forced to behave in a certain way, which, in fact, we choose to do. By using these terms, we place ourselves in a victim role and allow ourselves to indulge in self-pity. Instead, we could substitute more correct phrases, such as "I want to" or "I choose to." For example, if the client says, "I have to go to work," the therapist can retort:

"Well you do not have to. You could go fishing or to the ball game, or stay in bed if you wanted. If you do go to work, you are going because you choose to go. It is just that you are not willing to accept the consequences of not going to your job. You see, you do always have a choice." We try to reserve the use of the term **must** in therapy for those demands that are absolutist and not the conditional **should** and it is important to teach the client the distinction between the two.

I Must

Must or should statements about oneself usually imply a demand for personal perfection; clients with this belief are remarkably intolerant of their human fallibility. The primary dispute in this case is to teach the client that fallibility is characteristic of the human species. Technically, we do not make mistakes, but choices. It is only with the information available in hindsight that we can characterize a choice as a mistake if the consequences do not work out well. Although improvement is something for which we all can strive, perfection has yet to be achieved by humans; pencils have erasers for good reason!

When clients are distraught about having exposed their humanness by failing at some endeavor, the therapist might intervene with statements such as the following:

> "You shouldn't have acted that way and messed up? Well, why should you have succeeded? True, it would have been nice or advantageous; that we could prove. But there is no reason that because you want to succeed that you must succeed. True, it would have been preferable; but why must you always succeed? There's no law of the universe that says you should."

It is highly advisable for the therapist to act as a contrast model in this disputation, as in the following dialogue:

T: It is not OK to make mistakes or bad choices. Well, I have made hundreds of bad decisions! Are you saying that I should have not ever made mistakes as well?
C: Well, no. I was not thinking it applied to you.
T: I am allowed to make mistakes, but you are not?
C: Well, I had not thought about that.
T: So there are two sets of rules in the world? One set of demands for you and one for the rest of us. Who made these rules?
C: I guess I did.
T: If you made the first one, can you legislate another set of rules to be fair to yourself, so that you can get to live under the same set of rules as the rest of the world?

The key ingredient in this disputation is to point out to clients that they are being what Ellis called "profound *must*urbators (people who think in terms of "must")." We are provided certain standards of behavior by our culture; "*must*urbation," however, escalates these standards into a must. Consider the following therapy excerpt:

T: That's a self-demand. Why must you be a loving person? Why must you be successful at intimacy?

C: Because I want to!

T: "And I must be everything I want to?" You see, you're taking a good value and turning it into a crazy demand. "Because it might prove better, I must do it." Wouldn't it be nicer to feel good and not suffer from such crazy ideas?

Similarly, in the case of a young woman, Samanda, who was enmeshed in value conflict about having an extramarital affair:

T: What did you tell yourself to make yourself feel guilty?

C: I'm doing something immoral and I shouldn't do it.

T: Granted. You have been doing wrong by your standards—but you also feel guilty. Why should you feel guilty about doing wrong? Many people do wrong and don't feel guilty about it.

C: Because my husband and I have such a good relationship. I shouldn't do it.

T: Well, there are no "*shoulds*" in the universe. You have been doing it and you have the capacity to choose to keep doing it. If you are waiting for the *musts* of the universe to get you to behave morally, you will have a long wait because there are no such shoulds. I think your demand that you "must not do this" stops you from thinking about how you can choose to behave. Could you think instead, "I have a choice. I could choose to do it. But what is the right thing for me to *choose* to do."

C: Well, I have not thought about that as my choice. I have just thought about what I must do.

T: You have three choices here: you can change your values, change your behavior, or change your evaluation of your behavior. And they're not mutually exclusive. In other words, you get to decide what you do and there are moral rules that guide our behavior. But those moral rules cannot make us follow the rules and do the right thing. We decide if we live by the moral guideposts or not.

It is also important to point out to clients that there are good reasons to give up *must*urbation; it not only promotes emotional turmoil but also makes us behaviorally less efficient. Let us look at three different therapists commenting on this issue:

Therapist 1: There are no musts in the universe. Suppose you were saying, "I have to be rational! I have to be rational! I have to be rational!" That would be irrational, and how do you think you would be feeling?

Therapist 2: You are saying that you have done something wrong and should be condemned for it. Well, we will go back to the first part later, but for the moment, let's assume that it's true. Why would you have to condemn yourself, put yourself down, for that reason? What does guilt do to change the situation?

All it does is make you entrench and fight, rather than analyze and see how you can fix the situation.

Therapist 3: If you're driving poorly and you say to yourself, "What a loser I am for driving so poorly!" how does that help you to drive better?

Another aspect of the search for perfection involves clients' demands for the Perfect solution to their problems. Clients often come to therapy in the midst of a dilemma, or to put it more psychologically, they are caught in approach-approach or avoidance-avoidance conflicts. They expect a perfect, problem-free decision from themselves, and when they fail to come up with one, turn to the therapist. It might be unwise for the therapist to suggest a possible course of action, for that could perpetuate the notion that another human being can provide the perfect solution. In addition, the client will not have learned some important skills: decision-making, for example, weighing pros and cons, and constructing a "hedonic calculus"; understanding the reasons for being stuck at the decision point (e.g., "I might make the wrong decision and I must make the right decision"); and learning to cope with imperfect solutions.

The last problem often comes up with clients who report being unhappy about a love relationship in which they feel trapped. For example, a wife reported that she was desperately unhappy in her marriage and wanted to leave her husband, but was blocked by a number of factors:

She might later discover she regretted her action.
She might hurt his feelings.
She might not make it on her own emotionally.
She might never find another partner.

In addition, she might believe that it was wrong to leave a marriage ("Didn't the vows say until death do you part?"), so that there was a value conflict as well.

Obviously, there are many irrational ideas to challenge in this woman's situation. The therapist could teach her, first, that she was not totally responsible for the feelings of others; for if she hung onto that belief, then the only way out of her dilemma would be to devote her life to keeping her husband happy. In considering the moral connotations of her behavior, the therapist might point out that right and wrong are not useful indices of behavior; what are useful are the consequences. Ellis's parable of the two Zen Buddhists might be helpful here:

Two Zen Buddhists were out walking. One was an old master and the other was a young novice. They came to a stream that had flooded its banks. Beside the stream stood a beautiful young woman who said, "Look, Masters, the stream is flooded. Would you help me across?" The young monk shrank away in horror because he would have to pick her up to carry her across, but the old one calmly picked her up and carried her over the stream. When they were over, he set her down and the two monks went on. The young man could not get over this incident, however, and finally said to the older, "Master! You know we're sworn to abstinence. We're not allowed to touch a beautiful young woman like that. How could you take that luscious young woman in your arms and let her put her hands around your neck, her breasts next to your breast, and carry her across the stream like that?" And the old man said, "My son, you're still carrying her!"

Thus, as with the old monk, one can choose to do something "wrong" and not feel guilty; or not do something wrong, as with the young monk, and even so plague oneself by it. Does the client want to stick to her values and be miserable, or does she want to be happy even if it means changing her values? Another technique that the therapist might employ is distancing. The client might be asked, "How would you advise your best friend if she had the same problem? Would you suggest that she remain in the marriage and make herself miserable?"

Ultimately, however, the client would be wise to confront the fact that she seems to be demanding that her decision be perfect—absolutely correct and without any negative consequences. Obviously, few of life's decisions fall into this category. What she does have are three options:

> Remain in the marriage and be miserable.
> Remain in the marriage and work at not being miserable.
> Leave the marriage.

What clients often want in making such decisions are new options. For example, the client above might say, "I could stay in the marriage if only my husband were different." It would be easy to make decisions if one could construct realities and produce the best possible alternatives, but there are times when one can only choose from limited options. The therapist might point out to this client that, as in a TV game show, she has a choice of door 1, door 2, or door 3. There is no door 4.

Options do not come with guarantees; even if the therapist had some gilt-edged Happiness Guarantees printed, they would not help. Whatever clients decide will imply some risk, and clients can choose to either avoid risks or accept them as creative challenges. So, there are no perfect solutions.

Other People Must

The second direction "must" or "should" statements take is in demands for perfection in other people's behavior. There are three aspects to this dispute: other people have free will, and we do not have perfect control over them; negative consequences are often attached to attempts to control other people's behavior; and there are negative emotional consequences for insisting that others behave as we would like.

The client usually adds two additional points as well, such as, "How could they act that way?" and "Why do they act that way?" The answer to the client's first question, although it might sound glib, is quite simple. How could they act that way? Easily! Why do they act that way? This question can lead to an interesting discussion of why others act wrongly. Among the possible answers are that they are ignorant, misguided, suffering from an incapacity; or simply that "wrong" behavior pays off in some way (perhaps it serves to upset the client, which could be reinforcing to someone else). We might summarize these reasons as stupidity, ignorance, disturbance, or utility. Understanding the reasons for other people's behavior could be an important step in helping the client to tolerate that behavior. Understanding another person's behavior, however, might not produce change. Regardless of why the other person behaves as he does, he or she still behaves that way.

When the client is demanding that another person act differently, the therapist might respond:

"Where is the evidence that X shouldn't act that way? There is none. In fact, he did act that way. To demand that people must not act in a certain way is silly, because once they have done something, they must do what they have done."

It makes much more sense for the client to search for evidence that X should, in fact, have acted as he or she did:

"What is the point of being angry when someone acts the way they act? When a dog acts like a dog, we are not surprised. When a cat acts like a cat, we are not surprised. Why are you surprised when your husband acts like your husband? He has a track record. That does not mean he cannot change. But why should we be surprised when he shows us his usual behavior, especially when he does not seem interested or motivated to change? We can ask for change in another's behavior, but it's silly to demand it."

Here is an example of Ellis disputing the same should:

C: He shouldn't do that!

T: Yes, I understand you do not like his behavior, but why is that a nutty thing to say to yourself?

C: But he was wrong!

T: Let's assume that he is wrong. Why is it still incorrect for you to say that?

C: I don't know.

T: Because, you do not run the universe. He has a right to be wrong; every human does!

As pointed out earlier, there seem to be no absolute rights and wrongs, merely situationally determined choices. In addition, REBT holds that whether a decision is right or wrong is independent of the client's right to choose; one can even choose to do a wrong act.

The therapist can also point out to the client that attempting to control the behavior of others might produce further difficulties:

T: What does it mean to control other people? Usually we use negative means, such as punitive responses, whining, passive resistance, tantrums, and so forth. But, no matter how it is done, we know one thing about human behavior: anyone who is at the mercy of another person will tend to hate that other person. So the more you try to force your husband into loving you, the less likely you are to get what you want from him. In fact, the only certain control you have is over yourself.

C: But he is so unfair!

T: OK, it is not fair. That is correct. Where is it written that it should be? You're saying, "He must, he must, he must." Now, let me ask you, what control do you have over him? And what good does it do you to sit here and eat yourself up over it? Let's agree. It isn't fair. Now, you only have control over one person. What do you want to do about it?

Finally, the therapist will point out that as long as the client holds onto a demanding philosophy, the emotional upset will probably remain:

"You have a right to ask for change. But you might not get what you want. Your job is to stop evaluating yourself based upon your ability to control others' behavior."

The World Must

Clients also demand that they control inanimate objects, social institutions, and fate. How often have you heard clients wailing, "It shouldn't happen to me—it's not fair!" The primary dispute is that the world doesn't have to be the way the client wants it, and in fact, the world is the way it is for complex, often unknowable reasons, and it need not be any different. The following analogy is frequently used to make this point:

"Let's suppose that I am sitting in my office on a hot, sunny summer day, and I start fantasizing about how much I would rather be skiing than working today. If I walked to the window and started shaking my fists and demanding that it be cold and snowy outside so I could go skiing, you would look at me as if I were a little crazy. You might tell me that it is foolish to demand that it be snowing and cold outside. Well, you'd be right; it is silly to demand that the universe be the way I want. Obviously, the physical, astronomical, and meteorological factors that cause it to be sunny and warm outside have occurred, and my demandingness and temper tantrums obviously can't change these things. Is this similar to what you're doing about your problem? Aren't you also making such demands?"

This analogy can obviously be used to dispute all types of should statements; for example:

"If it is silly to demand perfect control of the weather, it's equally silly to demand perfect control of other people and even yourself." If the client is demanding to control something about the self, he or she might object:

C: I see what you mean about external events, but I should be able to control myself.
T: Well, but you do have some control. Your mistake is insisting on total control, when, in fact, you are a fallible human being. So, it really is like trying to control the weather, do you see?

Needs (Things I Must Have)

Need statements can be viewed as a special subclass of musts, for clients are failing to discriminate between what they would prefer to have and what they must have in order to live and be happy. The primary disputation in dealing with need statements is to show clients how to take their own language seriously and literally. There are relatively few things that we absolutely need in this world: a little food, liquid, air, and shelter are biologically necessary for survival. No one knows what factors are necessary for psychological adjustment, although clients who are having relationship difficulties are quick to claim that "all you need is love." The psychology literature indicates that children and young animals require some love and affection in order to thrive, but we have no evidence that a single adult has ever died without it. Love is highly desirable, both to give and to get, but we do not literally need it. As long as clients believe that they need it and talk as if they need it, they will behave as if they need it, and that's where the trouble begins. A first step, therefore, is to help clean up the client's language.

The ability to discriminate wants from needs is not taught by our society, but it can be learned even by young children. In the following therapy excerpt, the client is an eleven-year-old girl who is having trouble making friends at school:

T: Do you need to play with them?

C: Yes!

T: What does "need" mean?

C: You have to have it.

T: A need means this: What are some of the things that you need? You need water. What happens if you don't have water?

C: You die.

T: That's right. You need air. What happens if you don't have air? Same thing.

C: You can die.

T: That's right. What happens if you don't have food?

C: Die.

T: That's right. Can we say that you need food?

C: Yeah.

T: And water?

C: Yeah.

T: And air?

C: Yeah.

T: That is correct. Do you need video games?

C: Well, almost, I guess no.

T: But sometimes you say you need to play video games, don't you?

C: Yeah, because I like to.

T: Yeah, you like to and you want to, and then you think you need to do it. But that's not a need, is it?

C: No.

T: No, it's not. Do you need candy canes and ice cream?

C: No.

T: You don't need them, but you want them, don't you?

C: Yeah.

T: But you don't need them, do you?

C: No.

T: OK, do you need a new bike?

C: No, I got one already.

T: But what if your bike got broken, then would you need a new bike?

C: Yeah.

T: No, you would want a new bike, but you wouldn't need it. I mean, you wouldn't die without it, would you?

C: No.

T: You could keep on living without a new bike?

C: Yeah.

T: It might not be as much fun as having a new bike, but you could live, right? Do you need a new pair of sneakers if your old ones have a hole in them?

C: No.

T: So do you see the difference between a want and a need? What's the difference? You try to explain it to me.

C: A need is what you need to help you to live.

T: A need is something you've got to have to live.

C: And a want is that you want to have it.

T: That's right. You'd like it, it's enjoyable. Now, how about, "Lisa wants the kids in school to like her." Is that a want or a need?

C: Want.

T: It's a want, right?

C: Right.

T: So we talked a little bit about wants and needs. Now, what happens if you tell yourself "Oh, I need to have so-and-so play with me in school—I need to have her like me." How do you think you're going to feel if she doesn't like you?

C: Sad.

T: Sad. Like sad a whole lot or sad a little bit?

C: A lot.

T: A lot. How about if you said, "I need to have Kate like me. I need to be her friend."

C: I want to be her friend.

T: "I want to be her friend." Oh, but isn't there a difference? If you said, "I need to be her friend" and she wasn't, how would you feel?

C: And she wouldn't?

T: And she wouldn't. And you said, "I've got to have her friendship—I need it to live—and she won't be my friend."

C: Sad.

T: You'd be very upset. So what if you said to yourself instead, "I would like to have Kate like me. I want to be her friend, but if she's not going to be my friend, I can live without it." Would you be sad a little bit or sad a lot?

C: Sad a little.

AWFULIZING

Disputing this IB essentially entails attacking the notion of "awfulness." People often use words such as "awful," "terrible," and "horrible" loosely. Ellis first got his clients to agree with this definition: "awful" means many things—totally bad, the worst thing that could ever happen, the equivalent of being tortured to death slowly. When therapists question whether an event described by a client is truly awful, many clients defend their evaluation as follows:

T: OK, let us suppose that you were rejected and you were alone. How would that be awful?

C: Because of the depressed feelings in my gut; I'd feel terrible.

T: But you have that backward! The bad feeling comes from what you are thinking. Suppose you just defined it as a pain in the ass: "Isn't it too bad that she doesn't like me?" Do you think you would still have that depressed feeling in your gut?

C: No.

T: See, if you gave up the awfulizing, you would give up the depressed feeling. You would still feel sorry and regretful even perhaps very sorry and regretful, but not depressed. Now, where is the evidence that it would be awful, horrible, and terrible if you were rejected?

One way to convince a client that "X" isn't awful is by comparison: "Can you imagine anything worse?" or "If this is so unbearable, would you commit suicide over it?" A more concrete anti-awfulizing exercise would have the client construct an "awfulness scale" from 1 to 100. Thus, if 100 is the worst possible event imaginable (e.g., dying of cancer after having one's arms and legs amputated), where would the client place a particular problem? It might become clear, for example, that having a spouse with a bad temper is more accurately placed at about 20 to 30.

Box 11.1

Some therapists begin disputation by asking the client whether the event under discussion is more correctly placed in the category of "pain-in-the-neck bad" or "end-of-the-world horrible." Turning it into a forced choice might help the client get started on the work of de-horriblizing.

A variant of this strategy is to ask clients if they can imagine "X" being worse. For example, "Merv, now that Joyce has left you, it sounds like you feel this is one of the worst things that could happen in your life. I wonder if we could look at how bad it really is. For instance, losing Joyce might be coupled with losing your house, or having one of your children become seriously ill, or losing your job. Do you think it would help you to keep this loss in perspective if you reminded yourself that troubles can—and often do—add up?"

In working with children, Virginia Waters often used a similar device, the "horribles" list. On a blackboard or large sheet of paper, have the children list all the "horribles" or "catastrophes" they can think of. (Given the recent spate of films and TV shows about catastrophes, this is easily accomplished.) After listing 9/11, Hurricane Katrina, and the devastation in Haiti, the therapist "remembers" one more, the child's complaint (e.g., "Tommy sat in my seat."). It will probably not be necessary to point out that this item does not belong on the list. This exercise is used quite successfully with adults as well.

Clients might also do their own anti-awfulizing if the therapist guides them through the following questions: "What are the real and probable consequences of the bad situation?" "How long will they last?" "How will you be able to bear them?" "Let's work out the details of your plan." Inviting clients into the system in this way is much more preferable than an anti-awfulizing speech. Such a device not only serves to de-escalate catastrophes but enables clients to show themselves the reality of the situation and to work out coping strategies to deal with it.

In a recent group, one of the members asked, "What does REBT tell you to do about really bad events? Are you supposed to feel good about bad things?" This is a common question asked not only by lay people but by professionals as well. Clearly, the answer is "No!" Unlike "positive thinking," REBT does not take the position that every cloud has a silver lining; some are storm clouds through and through. We might not have a choice between a good and a bad event, but merely between two bad alternatives. How, then, can REBT be of help? By helping the client not to make a bad event worse by catastrophizing.

Suppose that A is truly very bad (e.g., a spinal cord injury, loss of a limb, death of a child): What can the therapist do? First, acknowledge that the A really is painful and that most people would indeed feel badly about it and advise the client to allow for a grieving process. After some time goes by, most people can move forward with life and develop attitudes or philosophies that help them cope with bad but unchangeable As. One might always feel strong negative but functional emotions about the trauma for some time or the rest of one's life. The therapist can convince clients that holding onto their thinking is not in their best interests. Again, clients might not have the choice of something bad versus something good, but only between two bad things. However, the client has some control over how she/he feels about her/his options. Accepting the bad things that have happened, whether they are an exaggerated evaluation or not, is the key word to minimize disturbed feelings one might experience.

Consider a case example. The client was a young man, paralyzed with a spinal cord injury, who in addition developed duodenal ulcers and muscle spasms. Nothing could be done to repair the spinal cord injury, but by becoming overly upset about his condition, the boy significantly increased the problem of spasms. In such a case, giving up his depression about his injury could directly affect the client's well-being. He had enough bad things to deal with and certainly did not need to add depression.

Perhaps there is a relationship between helping the client to accept a problem, such as a physical disability, and the acceptance of death. As Kübler-Ross (1969) has suggested, acceptance is not a simple process but rather a series of stages. There are many feelings to be dealt with (e.g., anger and fear), and denial could be very strong. Acceptance of death as a series of stages is a conceptual schema; not all clients go through all of the stages, or follow them in any fixed order. However, REBT could be useful in facilitating the process of moving from one stage to the next.

Many therapists tend to awfulize about clients who have a serious disability or terminal illness. These conditions are not, in themselves, reasons for emotional turbulence, however. In fact, research indicates that most people with terminal illnesses are not chronically upset but instead are quite adept at mobilizing coping mechanisms (Sobel, 1978; de N. Abrantes-Pais, et al., 2007; Livneh and Cook, 2005; Livneh et al., 2006). The therapist, therefore, needn't assume that distress is a normal reaction.

In addition to acknowledging the reality and painfulness of an activating event, the therapist can focus on clients' abilities as well as their disabilities. Although this dual focus might not be wise as an initial maneuver, as therapy progresses it is important to discuss with clients, "What can you do with what you do have?" Clients, after all, might be irrationally concluding that because they have problems, their life is over and no possibility of enjoyment remains. The useful principle here is containment of the disability to specific areas rather than overgeneralizing its effects.

In this regard, the REBT therapist would do something that other therapists might not consider: acknowledge a situation as being very bad.

There are also pragmatic reasons to give up awfulizing. First, the high anxiety levels associated with catastrophizing impede problem-solving. By decreasing anxiety, clients increase their ability to deal with difficult events. If clients awfulize about an impending problem, the therapist might point out that worrying only makes it worse, since they are living through the problem twice—both in anticipation, and when it actually occurs. If the discomfort is inevitable, clients might as well enjoy themselves as long as they can.

Awfulizing philosophies are usually associated with states of high anxiety, a common result of which is avoidance behavior. The problem with avoidance is that although it is temporarily effective in reducing anxiety, this very effect reinforces more avoidance behavior.

If, for example, one had an irrational fear of stepping on dandelions, one might easily avoid the problem by walking around a single dandelion, with little cost to one's freedom. However, one small, neglected dandelion rapidly multiplies into many problems, and soon a fearful person will find himself severely constricted, every pathway in the field blocked with multiple dandelions. (LeDoux, 2000).

Pay attention to avoidance behaviors; sometimes clients will avoid positive events in order to ward off imagined future distress. A common example is seen with clients who avoid intimacy even though they highly desire it. They refuse to get into love relationships for fear that, at some future time, the relationship might end. Because they've defined the ending as awful, they have chosen to deprive themselves of present possible pleasures. Awfulizing, in this case, results in considerable cost to the client.

An important behavioral dispute used by rational emotive behavior therapists to combat awfulizing is to have clients face their problems head-on, thereby disproving their hypothesis that the consequences are unbearably bad. Ellis referred to such behavioral disputes as "risk-taking" experiences.

Ellis anticipated a research-based trend in behavior therapy by his insistence on the desirability of encouraging clients to take risks. By forcing themselves to do the very things that seem "too hard" or "too scary," clients will be able to abandon their notions of awfulness. In fact, Ellis believed that more traditional and gentle techniques, such as systematic desensitization or relaxation training, can be iatrogenic (i.e., keep the client disturbed) in that they reinforce clients' avoidance of discomfort and strengthen FI cognitions. Ellis asserted that we coddle clients and thereby help them to remain emotionally disturbed. The most efficient way to overcome fears and avoidance habits is often to "close your eyes and force yourself to jump in with both feet." In other words, REBT recommends a flooding or implosive model of treatment, starting at the top rather than at the bottom of a fear hierarchy. Research (e.g., Marks et al., 1971; Rachman et al., 1973) supports this contention, and the shift from imaginal to in vivo desensitization and from progressive to flooding techniques illustrates that the Zeitgeist is moving in the direction taken by REBT. See Chapter 16, in which risk-taking homework exercises are described.

Box 11.2

Many new REBT therapists take the concept of Awfulizing to its extreme with the result being alienation of the client. In cases of terminal illness, rape and assault, and natural disasters to name a few, it is recommended that the therapist avoid disputing the "awfulness" of the event, but rather focus on disputing the functionality of awfulizing about it. What is deemed "awful" and "terrible" by clients is arbitrary and they might conclude that the therapist does not understand them or their situation, with the chance of premature termination. Although Ellis might have challenged the belief that the Holocaust was awful, we recommend therapists avoid this provocative confrontation. Ellis's clinical expertise and experience enabled him to use such extreme examples with his clients. It is our experience that most REBT practitioners, no matter how seasoned, would not be as well-received by clients using such extreme examples.

HUMAN WORTH

In his original writings on this topic, Ellis dealt with clients' denigrating statements of themselves and others ("I'm a worthless loser." or "He's no good.") by analyzing human worth in the following way. Logically or scientifically there is no way to prove conclusively that one human being has more worth in the universe than any other. Because there is no way to evaluate differences in human worth, one is left with the null hypothesis that all people are of equal worth. A problem still remains with this formulation, however, since the assumption of a quality called "worth" implies the possibility of its opposite, "worthlessness." Ellis later refined his theory to eliminate the entire notion of worth, replacing it with unconditional self-acceptance.

Beliefs about self-worth appear to be among the most difficult to change. Self-acceptance could be difficult to communicate to children, who are surrounded by adults who persist in global ratings of the child (e.g., "good girl" rather than "good behavior"). It is often still more difficult to convince adolescents that they do not need the adulation of their peers. An important concept to teach in this regard is that people's opinions about one's worth are not facts. This discrimination could be pointed out by referring to nonpersonal issues. For example, the therapist might point to his or her wristwatch and suggest that it is the most beautiful watch in the world. Does this make it so? What the therapist is teaching is the difference between an opinion and a fact. The therapist's statement, more correctly, means, "I judge this watch to be the most beautiful." If the client understands this concept, it might then be possible to move to personal opinions, as in this example:

"Let's say that your friend thinks you're a turkey. Does that make it so? If all your friends said you were a turkey, would you be?"

In other words, self-worth need not depend on getting the support or admiration of others; even of deities ("Jesus loves me, I'm OK."). We can skip these intervening variables and simply choose to accept ourselves. All self-worth statements are, in fact, overgeneralizations; this logical fallacy is corrected in the following dialogue:

C: I'm such a loser!
T: You're a loser? You seem to have trouble with your terminology. The label you just gave yourself suggests that some essence of you is rotten, not just your act. You've defined yourself as a rotten person. If that's true, you have to do rottenly, and do so exclusively and forever. That would be your fate. Don't you think you are over-generalizing?

Let's elaborate on that last point. It is important to teach clients the difference between being a louse and acting lousily. In other words, clients are not their behavior. One way to teach this concept is to help clients monitor their language so that they change their labels for themselves (i.e., nouns) into verbs. Thus, instead of saying, "I'm a bad mother," it is more correct to say, "I've been doing some bad mothering." The first statement is clearly an overgeneralization because it would be virtually impossible to find a person who committed only negative mothering acts. Even Harlow's "monster mother" monkeys were observed to fondle their infants occasionally (1958). The reason we urge clients to change their self-labels into verbs is that self-labeling statements use a linguistic structure that always overgeneralizes. The verb "to be" in the English language implies unity between the subject and the object of a sentence. "I am a psychologist" implies unity between "I" and "psychologist"; most of us, however, do many other things besides function in a therapeutic capacity. The basic argument is that people are far too complex to be judged within a single category. Their very complexity renders them un-rateable. Thus, Ellis suggested that clients "give up their egos," not in the sense of their executive selves but of rating themselves.

The following analogy is often employed by rational emotive behavior therapists to illustrate human complexity.

"Imagine that you have just received a large basket of fruit. You reach into the basket and pull out a beautiful red apple, and then a ripe juicy pear, and then a rotten orange, and then a perfect banana, and then a bunch of grapes, some of which are mushy and rotten. How would you describe the fruit? Some pieces are good and some are not good; you'd want to throw away some of it. And how would you label the basket? You see, the basket represents you, and the variety of fruits which vary in ripeness or rottenness are like your traits. Rating yourself by a single trait is like saying that the basket is bad because it contains one piece of bad fruit."

Wessler devised a schematic diagram that illustrates the absurdity of self-rating. Note the two intersecting continua in Figure 11.1. Many people's self-esteem ratings are contingent on the state of the horizontal axis. When things go well, they rate themselves highly (Point 1); when things go poorly, they give themselves a low rating (Point 2). What is wrong with this concept is the very act of globally rating oneself; "wonderfulizing" is as irrational as self-deprecation. Rating is a foolish venture, for as soon as external conditions deteriorate, you'll slide down the "irrational diagonal." The more rational perspective is to stay at the center point on the vertical axis, regardless of your position on the horizontal one. Thus, since rating oneself up implies the possibility of rating oneself down, the more elegant solution is to give up rating oneself altogether.

A general strategy, consistent with the concept that clients themselves do most of the hard work in therapy, is that instead of trying to prove to clients that they are not failures or worthless, have them try to prove to you that they are. Not

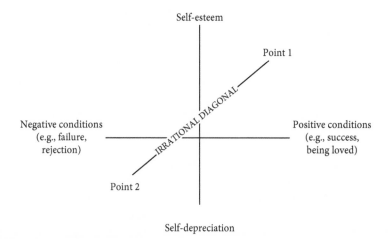

Figure 11.1 The Self-Rating Fallacy.

only is this strategy easier for the therapist, also it often provides the meaningful insight that "self does not equal one's behavior" to the client. Again, the issue is to avoid self-rating and to substitute self-acceptance or self-tolerance.

T: All right, Jack, prove to me that you're a failure.

C: But I've just told you all the things I failed at.

T: That's true, Jack, but how does that make you a failure?

C: But I've messed up so many things!

T: I know that, Jack, but don't you see what you're doing when you call yourself a failure? You're making a prediction. To be a failure means that you'll always have that characteristic, and you're only doomed to fail at whatever you try.

C: That's what's upsetting me—that I'll always fail.

T: But you can't be a failure because we do not know that you will always fail, and we have evidence that you have not always failed in the past. You see, if you were an apple, you would always have had and will continue to have the characeristics of an apple. You could not change, and that is not true of failure. So you prove to me that you always have and always will fail!

C: (laughs) I guess I can't.

T: OK, so you see, failing is something you do some of the time; it is not what you are.

A difficult issue for many clients is accepting their physical attributes, and perhaps surprisingly, this problem seems to be as prevalent among men as among women. Trying to convince clients that their perception of physical reality could be distorted seems to be an exercise in futility. After all, when clients look into the mirror and don't like what they see, they are making an esthetic judgment. Matters of personal taste are difficult to challenge. The problem is that in addition to acknowledging that the mirror image is not what they would prefer, clients awfulize and refuse to accept themselves. Here is a sample therapeutic challenge to this refusal; note the therapist's acceptance of the client's perception.

T: OK, you have sunken eyes. What are you doing with that piece of information? Are you telling yourself that you must be miserable with yourself and your sunken eyes?

C: Well, I could always find someone who likes sunken eyes (laughs).

T: And what are you saying now? Again, you're looking for external validation of yourself. Can you accept yourself with sunken eyes?

The client initially suggested that sunken eyes would be acceptable if she found someone who liked them; however, this would be a poor solution because it implies conditional acceptance. The therapist encourages her to continue to work at self-acceptance regardless of the approval of others.

Thus, physical appearance could be one area in which reexamining A might sometimes be unprofitable. Acceptance of qualities that cannot be changed is important, although if some physical attributes can be corrected (e.g., with plastic surgery or contact lenses) the therapist might certainly encourage clients to change what can be changed.

Many clients upset themselves about their appearance and condemn themselves when they are rejected by potential romantic partners. These clients believe that if they are not considered physically attractive to a particular partner, they are totally unattractive and worthless. A food metaphor might be useful in disputation:

T: So, Audrey wasn't interested in you. What does that mean about you?

C: Well, I guess I'm telling myself that no one will have me. I'm worthless.

T: What makes you worthless?

C: Well, she doesn't want me.

T: Well, that could relate to her taste in mates. It's sort of like food. Do you like chicken?

C: Yeah.

T: How about fish?

C: Yuck. I never touch the stuff.

T: Well, what does that say about fish? Or chicken?

C: Well, nothing, I guess.

T: That's right. Even though you don't like fish, lots of other people do. And just because you like chicken, that doesn't mean it is great food, or that other people should like it. People's views of you are just like food preferences. What they like says more about their taste or preference than it does about you. So, what does it mean that Audrey doesn't want you?

C: I guess (smile) I'm not her kettle of fish!

A special subclass of irrational beliefs concerning self-worth is the problem of competition; some clients believe that they must not only be competent but that they must be more competent than others. Their ability to feel comfortable depends on doing better than others and therefore involves both self-rating and other-rating. If they evaluate themselves against others and fall short, they feel depressed, jealous, or envious. Comparing oneself with others is a normal part of life and could even be desirable for improving one's performance. It becomes problematic, however, when the client overgeneralizes and uses the comparison in a self-derogatory way.

One suggestion to such clients is that they hardly change in any way each time they engage in comparisons; for example, "If you're 5' 2" and you meet someone 6' tall, does that make you shorter than you were?" or "If someone else gets a higher grade than you, does that make you stupid?" A more elegant solution, however, is again to work at giving up the concept of rating altogether. The therapist might point out that, after all, the basic goal in life is to enjoy oneself, not to prove oneself to the self, others, or the heavenly hosts.

We include at this point two sample disputations, one didactic and the other more evocative, on the general issue of self-worth.

A Didactic Disputation

I am going to suggest something rather surprising to you. Know what it is? You are neither a wonderful, bright, marvelous, intelligent person, nor the opposite—a terrible, awful, stupid, irresponsible idiot.

You're neither of those things. You're a human being. And you belong to the human race. And to be human means that you have some strengths and some weaknesses. That in some ways you're probably quite intelligent, and coupled with that is a tendency to make human errors. Because that's also what it means to be alive and to be human.

And if we are going to get you better, we had better go after your belief system. You are holding onto one now that insists on categorizing you as OK—not OK, stupid—smart. You think that you are a simple little commodity and you belong in either this box or that box.

And I am suggesting to you that there is no box that could describe you. You're a complicated person; all humans are. That you could do an "A" paper, and from it you don't need to leap to the conclusion that therefore you're a wonderful, bright, intelligent, perfect person. You're no such thing.

If you handed in a paper and it was not such a hot paper, you could do at least two things. You could say, "Oh my God, I'm stupid, I knew it, I knew it, I never should've handed it in. Now I see the evidence, just what I've always thought, I'm no good. Donna belongs in the Stupid Box." Or you could say, "Well, I'm only learning how to write stories. That's what I'm here for. I'm not already perfect or I'd be the professor. And she's not perfect either or she would be a famous writer! That doesn't mean she doesn't have something to tell me, so that the next one I write I do better at."

"So what" could be two favorite words to tuck in your pocket to say 100 times to yourself in the next week? "Well so what if it isn't an A + ? What does that mean if it isn't a perfect paper? It just means that it isn't a perfect paper, and it doesn't mean another darn thing beyond that." "So what," however, doesn't mean "It's not important at all," but simply "It's not all-important."

An Evocative Disputation

T: You really believe that you are a worthless person. By definition, that means that you're always doing things poorly. Can you prove to me that that's correct?

C: But I've failed at so many things.

T: Just how many?

C: I've lost my job, my wife is threatening to leave me, I don't get along with my kids—my whole life's a mess!

T: Well, let me make two points. First of all, that's not every aspect of your life. Second, you seem to take total responsibility for all of those events, rather than only partial responsibility.

C: But even if I'm not totally responsible, I'm still a failure.

T: No. You've failed at those things. There are other things you haven't failed at,

C: Like what?

T: You still manage to get up every morning, you keep up appearances, you manage your finances well considering your economic plight—there are many things that you do well.

C: But they don't count!

T: They do not count to you right now because you're overly concerned with negative issues, but they certainly do count. There are lots of people who don't do those things well. Are they failures?

C: No, but…

T: You know, Jack, you sound very conceited.

C: What do you mean? I've just been telling you how lousy I am!

T: The fact that you hold two different standards tells me how conceited you are. You hold much higher standards for yourself than for anyone else, which implies that you think you're much better than others. It's OK for those lowly people to have problems, but not a terrific person like you. Isn't that contradictory to your notion that you're worthless?

C: Hmmmmm.

T: How about instead of rating yourself as worthless, you just accept the failings that you do have and try your best to improve them?

C: That sounds sensible.

T: Let us take one of those problem areas now and see how we can improve things.

FRUSTRATION INTOLERANCE

Ellis has conceptualized the need for comfort as a core element of irrational beliefs. These common phrases could indicate discomfort anxiety (Ellis, 1978):

> I can't bear it.
> I can't live with (or without) it.
> I can't stand it.
> I can't tolerate it.

People seem to believe that they cannot tolerate pain, discomfort, or adversity; their willingness to bear discomfort is not necessarily directly correlated with the nastiness of the aversive event. Usually, in fact, they report that they "cannot stand" what they do not like. We referred to this problem earlier as low frustration tolerance, or simply FI.

There are two ways to combat FI: cognitively and experientially. In cognitive disputation, the therapist challenges clients to prove that they cannot bear something. Obviously such proof does not exist. Saying that they can't stand it is silly, because they can stand it (although they might not like it) and even be happy despite it. FI demands are similar to Ellis's discomfort anxiety statements above. Clients insist that they must not be inconvenienced, made uncomfortable, or denied, and if they are it is awful. The following dialogue illustrates a challenge to these notions:

C: I can't stand it when my mother acts neurotically.

T: (with exaggerated intonation) "I should have had a happy adulthood. I'm so richly deserving, I should have had a happy time." However, she might never change. What are you going to do about that?

C: Nothing.

T: Could you say to yourself, "Isn't it interesting that she's doing her number?" You could readjust your thinking so you're not making nutty demands. You see, it's akin to standing at the window demanding that it not be raining. If environmental events are impossible to control, the same goes for people's behavior. Getting angry isn't going to make it different. It might be better just to accept the reality.

Dryden, DiGiuseppe, and Neenan (2010) suggest using "the terrorist dispute" to help clients understand that they can tolerate what they think of as unbearable, and that the situation could even be worth tolerating:

T: OK, Morris. So we're clear now that what's frightening about going to the party is the prospect of spilling your drink and drawing people's critical attention to you.

C: If that happened, I couldn't stand it. I'm getting anxious now even thinking about it.

T: So, in your mind it would be unbearable.

C: Right.

T: Well, let's see if you're right. Do you love your children?

C: Of course I do. What kind of question is that?

T: Well, bear with me for a moment since I want to help you really think about whether your explanation of the scene we've just identified as "unbearable" is correct, OK?

C: OK.

T: Right. Now, let's imagine that a group of terrorists capture your children and their ransom demand is this: "If Morris goes to twenty parties, spills a drink at each one, thereby attracting the critical attention of others, we'll release his children. But if he doesn't do this, we'll keep them forever." Now would you do as they say?

C: Of course I would.

T: But you've just told me that even if you spill a drink once and are criticized once, that would be terrible. How can you do something that is so unbearable?

C: I'm beginning to see what you mean.

T: What would you tell yourself about doing this task twenty times that would enable you to do it?

C: That it's bearable.

T: That's right, that it is tolerable and presumably that it's worth tolerating in order to save your kids.

C: Right.

T: Now if you would do it twenty times to save your kids, would you risk doing it a couple of times for your mental health?

C: Yes.

T: And don't forget to practice convincing yourself that if the worst happens and you do spill the drink and attract criticism from others, that it's bearable and not unbearable.

Experiential disputes of FI provide clients with homework assignments in which they actually practice the events they previously defined as unbearable. This practice can take the form of a generalized exercise such one used by Bill Knaus:

"Focus on an itch you are experiencing somewhere on your body right now and refrain from scratching it for thirty seconds—and now another thirty seconds…"

Or use one specifically tailored to the client's presenting problem. For example, if clients become angry in certain situations, they might be asked to behaviorally dispute their anger by staying in the very situation that provoked it and practicing "standing it," such as purposefully exposing themselves to an obnoxious individual at whom they were angry. Rational emotive imagery might also be useful:

T: Let's go through the scene. OK, imagine yourself at your mother's front door. At the first sign of emotion, ask yourself what's going through your mind.

C: I'd better just pretend not to be angry.

T: Well, instead of just sitting on your feelings and denying them, ask yourself, "What would it take to get myself annoyed but not angry?"

Thus, the client can accomplish both a rehearsal desensitization (behavioral) and a repertoire of rational coping statements (cognitive).

FI could prevent clients from reaching many life goals, primarily because they refrain from putting in the hard work necessary to achieve those goals. The therapist can point out that there's seldom "gain without pain." Learning that they can stand discomfort helps such clients to face adversities more easily, take greater risks, and work harder to maximize their productivity. Thus, reducing FI and attacking the need for comfort could help one write that new book, leave a spouse, start a new business, or accomplish whatever one's personal goals might be.

12

The Effective New Belief (EB)

STRENGTHENING THE CONVICTION IN THE NEW RATIONAL BELIEF

In this chapter, we discuss the next step in the A-B-C-D-E model, the E, constructing and rehearsing the Effective New Belief (EB). Thinking differently about the same adversity is at the core of the REBT therapeutic process. Some REBT therapists believe that the disputation phase (the D) is the most crucial part of the change process. Others believe that generating and rehearsing the EB is most crucial. Disputing and challenging IBs alone does not necessarily result in the generation of new thoughts. However, without challenging the IB, clients would feel little motivation to change their thinking. Some clients will benefit more from the disputation process, and others will benefit more by rehearsing the EB. We advise doing both the disputation and the formulation of the EB. However, if clients disputed successfully and then failed to generate a new EB to replace the IB, it is doubtful that they would get better.

Building a replacement belief is a crucial aspect of change. In Behavior Therapy, it is a well-established principle that the best way to change a behavior is to pair the eliciting stimulus with a new behavior that is incompatible with the old one. Punishment of an old behavior is not sufficient to eliminate it. New responses are needed (See O'Donohue and Fisher 2009). Kuhn (1962), in his classic work on the history of science, documented that people continue to believe in discredited theories that they know are wrong until they discover better ideas. Substantial *evidence against* an idea does not stop one from believing in it. A better idea does.

Challenging or disputing (D) the IB represents just one step on the way to thinking, behaving, and emoting differently. Without continuing beyond what we have accomplished so far in the A-B-C-D sequence, we would leave the process unfinished at a crucial moment. Challenging at D helps clients to rethink the former beliefs that led them to emotional disturbance and troublesome behavior. By realizing and understanding the B → C connection, clients become aware of the disadvantages of holding onto those thoughts, i.e., what negative effects these beliefs have on their feelings and behavior. They then want to change their beliefs because they see how illogical their thoughts are, how they conflict with empirical reality, and how dysfunctional their attitude is to accomplishing their goals.

At E, the change in beliefs takes place from imperative, dogmatic, inflexible, and irrational thinking into accepting, flexible, and rational thinking.

DISTINCTION BETWEEN RATIONAL BELIEFS (RB) AND EFFECTIVE NEW BELIEFS (EB)

We think it is important to distinguish between a RB, Rational Belief, and an EB, Effective New Belief. The RB refers to beliefs that are rational from logical, empirical, and philosophical perspectives. We can say that the RB is the cognitive wording of the original want or desire. The EB refers to new beliefs that the therapist and client create *after the disputing* (D), and serves as a counter-belief against the existing IB that the client held. Therefore, the EB is first a rational belief and second serves as a counter, persuasive belief that neutralizes and replaces the IB. The EB serves to oppose and counter the existing IB that brought on the client's disturbance.

WHAT WE WANT TO ACCOMPLISH WITH THE EB

People usually have RBs alongside IBs (Ellis, 2002). Problems occur when the irrational beliefs persist and the person believes the irrational beliefs more strongly than the rational ones. One strategy to change the balance between the irrational and the rational beliefs is to weaken the irrational beliefs. That results from the disputation process by aiming critical questions at the IB.

Another strategy to change the balance is to strengthen the RB about the adversity. Strengthening the RBs about the activating events is the focus of the EBs. The EB not only strengthens the RB, but also further weakens the IB. We weaken the IB, not by asking questions, as we did in disputing, but by rehearsing strong statements that oppose, counter, offset, and contradict the content of the IBs. All people will lapse into thinking their IBs and experiencing unhealthy emotions and self-defeating behaviors. This chapter provides techniques to effectively counter such lapses.

INGREDIENTS FOR FORMULATING AN EB

Several steps are necessary before the therapist and client can formulate an EB. The first prerequisite is to have identified an IB that sufficiently explains enough (more than 50%) of the emotional or behavioral problem of the client. That means that you have identified an imperative demand, and/or one or more of the three derivatives that triggers the client's unhealthy emotion and self-defeating behavior.

Second, the client understands and is convinced of the $\mathbf{B} \rightarrow \mathbf{C}$ connection. If clients fail to acknowledge the $\mathbf{B} \rightarrow \mathbf{C}$ connection (while understanding the IB is irrational), they will not be motivated to construct, learn, or rehearse EBs.

A third prerequisite is a **good disputation**. If the therapist has only superficially challenged the IB, clients might not doubt their IB sufficiently to want to change it. The tension, doubt, or uncertainty caused by the disputes motivates clients to change their beliefs and to think of alternatives. Therefore, the better the disputes the more clients will be willing to invest in a new belief.

Fourth, a thorough understanding of what is irrational about his/her belief is necessary to counteract that belief by an EB. It is important that clients understand these ideas and are prepared to target the most malignant part of their thinking.

REPLACING IRRATIONAL BELIEFS WITH EBs

When these prerequisites are met, the therapist could ask the client what s/he could think in place of the IB. The therapist can expect many answers from clients. The specific answer the client gives indicates how well s/he understands the mechanism behind her/his problem. When clients fail to generate a useful counter belief, they mostly fail to negate the core irrational elements of their IB. The following case example with our client Olivia provides an example of how therapists can identify the EB. Olivia, a twenty-three-year-old graduate student in engineering, demands that she not experience the discomfort and bad feelings associated with failure at school. She has high demands concerning her getting good grades.

T: Now you see how your thinking leads to the problem, and that your beliefs about exams do not make sense. What can you think instead to counter that disturbing belief and will not lead to your self-defeating behavior and/or unhealthy emotions?

C: Well, I could think that it is *not that bad* if I do not get passing grades.

T: Yes, but it could actually be that bad. However, focusing on the "badness" alone is not the primary cause of your problem. So what can you say that really negates the IB that you *must* do well?

C: You mean the idea that I must not fail the examinations?

T: Yes, how does thinking it is not so bad to fail help you to replace that demand?

Of course, many clients could provide an answer in the right direction. Be prepared that some clients cannot think of a negation of the IB–(imperative/demand). In the case of Olivia, the therapist continued as follows:

T: What is the negation of "I must pass the exam"?

C: I want to pass the exam.

T: Yes, that is a desire and if that is all you thought it would be a rational belief. However, it is not the negation or the opposite of "I must pass the exam!" What would be your answer to the question "What is the negation of—I must pass the exam"?

C: Well, I do not *have* to pass the exam.

T: Correct! Now would that be a helpful belief?

The difficulty clients have in giving up the irrational belief is a reason to allow the negation of the IB a prominent place in the formula of the EB, as we will see below.

WITH WHAT DO WE REPLACE THE IRRATIONAL BELIEF?

It is important to realize that clients often fail to discriminate between a desire and a demand. When they strive for a goal, it appears to them as if they cannot desire without demanding, and on the other hand demanding means desiring. Of course, this is not the first moment in therapy that we explain that desiring something differs from demanding it. However, that does not guarantee that clients will think, feel, and behave in accordance with this concept. Therefore, in constructing the EB, we emphasize discriminating between *desiring* and *demanding* to ensure that the desiring is strengthened and the demanding is weakened.

Clients could understand REBT principles when they try to replace their demands with preferences. They go from "I must pass that exam," to "I do not have to pass that exam," to "I want to pass that exam." Nevertheless, this might not be enough to counteract the irrational belief (i.e., demand). If you give the client a sentence expressing just the want, they could escalate the want back into the demand again. We want a replacement belief that *acknowledges the want and counters and opposes* the IB, and blocks the tendency humans have to escalate the "want" to a demand. The Australian psychologist Burgess (1990) made this point evident when he attempted to construct a scale measuring rational and irrational beliefs. He worded the rational beliefs in terms of "wants" such as "I want to pass my examinations," and the counterbalance IB items were worded as demands such as "I must pass my examinations." The supposedly rational items, which reflected just a preference, were highly correlated with the demanding items. In addition, the rational preference items correlated with measures of disturbed emotions almost as strongly as did the demandingness items. Thus, when people read the preferential items, they often subconsciously and automatically completed the item with a demand. People failed to distinguish preferences from demands. DiGiuseppe and colleagues (DiGiuseppe, Leaf, Exner, and Robin, 1988) suggested that you need rational items that included the preference and the negation of the demand. Such items would lead to compound sentences that included the preferential and a counter-demanding attitude. The new rational items would read as follows, "I want to pass the exam, but I realize that I do not have to pass because I want to do well."

Therapists can help clients replace IBs not only with a preference, but also with a statement that opposes and counters the irrational belief. In the case of Olivia, who wanted to do well on an exam, the new EB would be, "I want to pass the exam, but I do not have to pass it just because I want to." The new replacement belief we encourage clients to think has a counterpoint of the want → demand escalation.

Below is the strategy we recommend to formulate the EB. To avoid an alliance rupture, we target whatever IB resonates with the client. This could be the imperative demand, or it could be a derivative. We provide examples for cases in which the emphasis in the rational thinking is on countering the imperative demandingness aspects of the IB (also taking into consideration derivative beliefs), and if the client identifies more with one (or more) of the derivatives, we provide examples for cases where the emphasis is on countering the derivative IBs, but also take into consideration the imperative. Finally, we identify steps to formulate the EB when the IB was uncovered using the choice-based assessment discussed in Chapter 9.

REPLACING AN IMPERATIVE IRRATIONAL BELIEF WITH AN EB

A three-step procedure can help formulate the EB. In each step, we will deal with the different effects that will occur by countering the IB.

I. Because the client still endorses the IB when you start constructing the EB, we counteract the IB first as a negation of the *must*. Our client Olivia's IB was, *"I* **must** *pass the exam."* We would start the EB with the negation, *"I do not have to pass the exam,"* or *"I can accept that I might not pass the exam regardless of what might happen."* Notice that "regardless of what might happen" helps the client to be open to every possibility. Once Olivia convinced herself that it was not *necessary* that the "wanted situation" *must* happen, she could *desire* passing the test rather than *demand* it: that is, she could drop the *must*. The act of striving to achieve the preference/desire is open to failure, or to only partly reaching the goal, which is not the case with the demand.

II. Then the desire follows, "Although, I really want to pass the exam." Because clients have difficulty discriminating their *demands* from their *desires*, they could get the impression that REBT involves them surrendering their goals or no longer striving to achieve their goals. This could lead them to resist the EB. We can help them by emphasizing their striving for their goal. We do this by adding the following phrase to the EB: "Therefore, I will work very hard to pass the exam." So far, we have counteracted the demand, and have emphasized the original desire not mixed with a demand. This last part can activate the client to strive for the desire by whatever behaviors that are needed to accomplish it.

III. Because the existence of the IB–(imperative/demand) results from a derailment of the (strong) desire, we expect the derailment to happen here again. This strong restating of the desire could help reestablish the demanding IB. Therefore, we add the possibility of not succeeding and repeat it to maximize the acceptance of it; it would be followed by a rational evaluation that counters an irrational derivative IB that the client would be most likely to endorse. This leads to the following phrase added to the EB, *"..., but if I do not pass the exam, I do not pass it and I can live with it/ I can stand it/ I can bear it/ It does not make me or somebody else a worthless individual or the world a rotten place."*

The following dialogue from our client Olivia above shows how she failed to discriminate between demanding and desiring when constructing an EB.

C: I do not want to resign myself to failure and give up on passing the exam.
T: I agree, and that is not what I want you to do either. That is one of the reasons why you had difficulty giving up your demand. You think that if you give up your demand then you have to give up your desire, and give up working on achieving your desire. Giving up your demand differs from resigning yourself to failure, and giving up working hard to get it. I am only suggesting you stop putting energy into the emotional upset that results from the demand and then results in negative consequences for you, and does nothing to help you accomplish what you want.

To summarize the steps for formulating the EB for an IB–(imperative/demand): (a) negate the must; (b) affirm the desire; (c) develop a behavioral approach to accomplish the desire, and then negate the must again and (d) work against frustration intolerance (FI), catastrophizing, or the denigrating of the self, other(s), or the world that could interfere with accomplishing the desire.

REPLACING A DERIVATIVE IRRATIONAL BELIEF WITH AN EB

Next, we examine EBs that counter IB–(derivative beliefs). Let us stay with the example of our client Olivia and her theme concerning her failure to pass the exam. Suppose she has self-downing beliefs about failing, and thinks, *"I must pass the exam, or else I am a worthless person."* One alternative EB would be a statement that affirms her self-acceptance such as, *"I can accept myself/I am not a worthless person, even if I fail the exam."* In addition, we can think of three alternative EBs that directly counter her IB of self–downing and that are stronger than this EB.

I. The first would counter the belief that she is worthless if she fails, such as, "I really want to pass the exam, but if I fail the exam, I am not worthless and I can accept myself."
II. A more fundamental EB acknowledges and counters the link between the demand and the self-downing: "I do not have to pass the exam, but I really want to pass it; and if I fail, I am not worthless."

III. We can complete this EB as we did before with the IBs-(imperative/ demands) by adding an attempt to achieve that desire: "I do not have to pass the exam, although I really want to pass it. Therefore, I will work hard to pass it. However, if I still fail it, I fail it. That does not make me worthless and I can still accept myself." Notice that the EB is a complex statement, of more than one sentence in length. This long EB is necessary to help the client learn all of the distinctions between irrational and rational thinking.

The generation of EBs for an "other-downing" derivative could be as follows. Suppose Olivia also became angry with her professor who designed and administered the exam. Her IB is "Because I did not pass the exam the professor made, s/he is a worthless person." One alternative EB would be a statement that affirms the acceptance of the other as a person, who in this case made a difficult exam: "My professor (who made the exam) is not a worthless person/I can accept him/ her as a person even if I failed the exam."

I. One EB would counter the other-condemnation belief that the professor is worthless because s/he made a difficult exam, such as, "I really want to pass the exam, but if I fail the exam the professor made, s/he is not a worthless person/I can still accept him or her."

II. A more fundamental EB that acknowledges and counters the link between the demand and the other-downing derivative would be, "I really want to pass the exam my professor made, but I do not have to; and if I fail the exam my professor made, s/he is not a worthless person/ I can accept her/him as a person."

III. In addition, we can complete this EB by adding an attempt to realize the want. It then becomes, "I really want to pass the exam my professor made, but I do not have to pass. Therefore I will work very hard to pass the exam, but if I fail it, I fail and that does not make the professor a worthless person/ I can accept the professor as a person."

We can do the same thing for EBs that counter and replace awfulizing IBs, such as, "It is awful if I fail the exam the professor made." A brief EB would be, "It is unfortunate if I fail the exam the professor made." Again, we think that this type of EB allows for the possibility that the client will escalate the negative evaluation of the situation into a catastrophe and think, "It is terrible and awful if I fail the exam the professor made." A better EB would be,

I. "It is not awful or terrible if I fail the exam the professor made, although I really want to pass the exam; if I fail to pass the exam the professor made, it is unfortunate." This wording counters the catastrophizing process. A belief that counters the link between the awfulizing and the demand would be as such:

II. "I do not have to pass the exam the professor made, although I really want to pass it, but it is not awful if I fail it. It would be unfortunate and disappointing."

III. Again adding an attempt to behaviorally realize the "want" makes the EB, "I do not have to pass the exam the professor made, although I really want to pass it. Therefore I will try very hard to pass the exam, but if I still fail, it is disappointing and not awful if I fail."

To complete the process, we would construct EBs to counter the *frustration intolerance derivative beliefs*, "I cannot tolerate/stand failing to pass the exam." Here the weak version of the EB acknowledges that the person can stand or tolerate failing to pass the exam as in, "I can stand it if I fail the exam the professor made."

I. An EB that counters the frustration intolerance belief would be, "If I fail the exam I am strong enough to stand that and I can tolerate the failure, although I really want to pass the exam."

II. An EB that also counters the link between the demand and the frustration intolerance derivative could be, "I don't have to pass the exam, although I really want to pass it. But if I fail the exam, I am strong enough to stand that and I can tolerate the failure."

III. Adding an attempt to behaviorally achieve the "want," makes it:

"I don't have to pass the exam, although I really want to pass it. Therefore I will try very hard to pass the exam, but if I fail the exam, I fail it, I am strong enough to stand it, and I can tolerate the failure."

Notice that in all the EBs above we added at the end an attempt to behaviorally achieve the "want." That is not always possible. Consider, "I really want it to be sunny tomorrow." We cannot say "...and therefore I will work very hard to make it sunny tomorrow." In such cases, we formulate "And if it rains tomorrow, it rains tomorrow and I can stand it/ live with it/ it is not awful."

CONSTRUCTING THE EFFECTIVE NEW BELIEF FROM A CHOICE-BASED ASSESSED IRRATIONAL BELIEF

When therapists use the choice-based technique for assessing and disputing irrational beliefs, they formulate part of the EB already when they complete the assessment of the IB. We have discovered during the assessment of the B, that some crucial aspect of the A is important to the client; for example, in the case of Olivia, it is passing the exam. Expressing what is important to clients in the form of desires would result in an RB such as, "Because it is very important to me, I really want to pass the exam." Starting off from the desire, the two choices we offer to the client come from either adding the imperative part (the absolute must) to it or by adding the accepting part (the flexible "I do not have to"). Choice number 1 will have the IB: "Because it is important to me, I really want to pass the exam and therefore I absolutely must pass the exam." Choice number 2 will be, "Although I strongly want to pass the exam because it is very important to me, I do not have to pass it." After having disputed choice number 1 by comparing it with number 2, and having chosen together with the client the rational and flexible alternative choice number 2, we still do not have the full EB as described above.

The full rational counter thought in this case would be, "I really want to pass the exam because it is important to me. However, I do not have to pass it, although I want it very much. Therefore, I will work very hard to pass the exam. However, if I do not pass it, I will not pass it and I can live with that (anti-FI), and that will never make me a lesser person (anti self-downing), and does not make the professor a lesser person (anti other-downing), or the world a rotten place to live in (accepting life conditions)."

When we finish disputing using the choice-based assessment of Bs, we are half-way to formulating the EB that replaces an IB–(imperative/demand).

New REBT therapists often require practice constructing the many forms of EBs to counter their clients IBs. In session, we often do not have the time to think reflectively through what the EBs will be. Practitioners can practice generating all of the types of EBs discussed above. Table 12.1 includes a table that the reader can use to practice generating EBs. We have provided a completed version of the form with all of the EBs for a set of irrational beliefs. Appendix 5 provides a blank version of the form. We recommend you print this table and write in the EBs to counter the IBs of several of your clients before your next session with them.

We have provided several EBs to counter the same IB, and the novice therapist could have some difficulty in determining which one to choose. We have discussed the difference between an elegant and an inelegant solution as being the difference between challenging irrational beliefs and only challenging the inferences and attributions the client makes. Here the difference consists of the comprehensiveness of the EB with which we replace the IB. We have seen that clients differ in how they use the forms of EBs we have offered. Try not to begin with the simplest and weakest of the possible EBs. See how far you can get with the client and look for your client's reaction to the EB. Some clients object to a more simple form of the EB. In these cases you can go to a stronger EB. Other clients might have reservations against the more compound EB. You can offer such clients a simpler one besides the one you gave them already, encouraging them to try to use both.

HOW TO RECALL THE COMPOUND SENTENCE

We recognize that some practical problems exist concerning the EBs we have outlined. They are all compound sentences, and as such could be difficult to hold in short-term or working memory. If clients fail to hold the EB in working memory, they will not be able to rehearse the EB and will be unlikely to retrieve the EB when they face a troubling activating event.

Table 12.1. Complete Form for Creating Effective Rational New Beliefs

Effective Rational New Belief

Irrational Belief	Imperative cognition: Demand or must	Derivative cognition: Self-downing	Derivative cognition: Other-downing	Derivative cognition: Awfulizing	Derivative cognition: Frustration Intolerance
I must not stammer when I give a speech or others will think I am no good and that makes me less of a person.	1. I can accept and allow myself to stammer as much as I do while I speak.	1. I very much want not to stammer while I speak, but if I stammer, I am not less of a person/I still accept myself.	1. I very much want to not stammer, but if I stammer when the others watch me while I speak, it does not make them worthless.	1. It is not awful if I stammer when I give a speech, although I very much want not to stammer. If I stammer, it is just unfortunate.	1. I can stand to stammer when I give a speech, but I very much want not to stammer.
I cannot stand to stammer when I give a speech and it is awful if I stammer when I give a speech.	2. I can accept and allow myself to stammer while I give a speech, although I want very much not to stammer. I will do my best not to stammer.	2. I can accept and allow myself to stammer while I give a speech, although I very much want not to stammer. But if I stammer, I am not less of a person and can still accept myself.	2. I can accept and allow myself to stammer while I give a speech, although I very much want not to stammer. But if I stammer that does not make the others worthless.	2. I can accept and allow myself to stammer when I give a speech, although I very much want not to stammer. But if I stammer, it is not awful, unfortunate, and disappointing.	2. I can accept and allow myself to stammer when I speak, but I very much want not to stammer. But, if I stammer, I can tolerate the failure.
Because I stammer when the others watch me while I speak, they are worthless.	3. I can accept and allow myself to stammer while I give a speech, although I want very much not to stammer. I will do my best not to stammer, but if I do stammer that does not makes me less of a person.	3. I can accept and allow my-self to stammer while I give a speech, although I very much want not to stammer. I will try hard not to stammer, but if I stammer, I am not less of a person and can accept myself.	3. I can allow myself to stammer when the others watch me while I speak, although I very much want not to stammer. I will try hard not to stammer, but if I stammer, that does not make the others worthless.	3. I can allow myself to stammer when I give a speech, although I very much want not to stammer. I will try hard not to stammer, but if I stammer, that is not awful just unfortunate and disappointing.	3. I can accept and allow myself to stammer when I speak, but I very much want not to stammer. I will try hard not to stammer, but if I stammer, I can tolerate the failure.

An effective way to help clients remember the EB is for them to rephrase the statement in their own words. Consider this instruction to a client: "The words in the EB might not yet be yours. So, can you put it in your own words? I will check to see if you keep the same meaning in the EB."

To help clients rehearse the EB for critical moments, as well as other moments they will need to cope, we ask them to print out the EB at home on an index card. They can bring it with them to the next session and carry the card with them wherever they go. We ask them to put such cards in other places that will provide easy access for them to rehearse the EB before they confront a troublesome A. Clients can also send the EB to their smart phones and have the message pop up when they need to read it. They can program their smart phones to have the message appear at regular intervals to rehearse it, or at times that they anticipate troublesome As for which the EB could help them cope. They can use the EB as a message in their computer screen saver.

Therapists can help clients overcome the length of the EB by explaining to them that the compound sentence is a kind of broad-spectrum antibiotic: it covers almost everything but you do not need it all at the same time. Therefore, a small part of the total EB might do the work. However, keep the compound EB in mind in case that particular part is not sufficiently working anymore.

TESTING THE NEW BELIEF

After generating an EB, it is important to determine what the client can do with it and what the EB can do for the client. Some clients find it difficult even to say the EB aloud because it is so antagonistic to what they feel. When clients cannot say the EB, we had better go back to the B → C connection to clarify to them again, how they disturb themselves by holding onto the particular IB. When they try to say it but cannot get the words out, we keep them on task until they can say the EB aloud. In addition, returning to some parts of the disputation phase might be helpful in such a case. Again, we can ask the client what would be a radical negation of the IB when they see that their belief is irrational and does cause the C. We could find another EB that is more acceptable to the client but still congruous with REBT theory. Our experience suggests that in most cases clients eventually will say the EB aloud; however, they do not feel comfortable with it. Repeating the EB a few times very convincingly to the therapist may help. The therapist could ask the client to assert the EB as if they were an attorney in a courtroom pleading a case of a client. In addition, therapists can explain again to the client that the process of change is not easy and involves moments of discomfort such as this one.

Next, we want to assess what happens to the clients' emotions and behaviors when they rehearse their new EB. The results could vary. Some clients will say that it does not make any difference to them when they say the EB. Most of your clients will experience some effect on their emotions or behaviors. "It really gives me more room." or "If I would believe this, I would not postpone as much as I do." Explain to clients that using the new thought more often can help to increase the relatively small change in feeling or behavior they experience in the session. It will be particularly efficient when clients use the EB at moments they think of the event (A) or when a similar event takes place.

Clients can continue to not experience any difference in their feelings or actions even after saying the EB. Several factors can cause the absence of the desired effect. First, clients might not say the EB convincingly. Listen carefully to whether the client is saying the EB forcefully as if s/he is convinced of it. Often clients say it with a voice indicating it is not yet part of them or with an intonation that conveys they are only saying it for the therapist. Clients could object that it is not natural for them to think of the EB yet, and that they cannot say it convincingly. The therapists could ask them to act as if it is part of them and as if they were convinced. If they do so, they might be surprised how much effect this (unexpectedly) has on their feelings or behavior. A good example of how unexpected the effect of saying an EB forcefully can be for a client is the following story.

A group therapy client could not say an EB forcefully in the group; and the group members challenged her and suggested that she bring to the next session an audio recording of her saying the EB forcefully. The next session she came with the audio recording and said that something "strange" had happened. She had made the recording at home and did her best to say the EB forcefully into the recorder. The result was the same as she had experienced so far, namely there was no effect on her emotions. Because the group had been so forceful in suggesting that she record the EB, she wanted to know that the recording was OK. So, she played what she had just recorded. To her big surprise, hearing her voice coming out of the loudspeaker speaking the EB convinced her; she suddenly felt a real effect on her depression. It is sometimes worthwhile for clients to make a recording in which they say the EB forcefully and see whether that will help convince them, or to explore other creative methods, such as saying the EB aloud in a mirror or trying to convince somebody else of the EB.

Second, clients could object to part of the EB while liking and benefiting from other parts. The therapist can determine which part is helpful by carefully questioning the client concerning which part of the EB the client has reservations about. Such discussions could lead to uncovering another IB. In that case, the therapist has to start all over again with the newly discovered IB and dispute it.

Finally, there is the possibility of resistance stemming from FI or impatience. Consider this dialogue with a client.

C: I can still feel my anxiety about it!

T: Yes, I would expect that, but this assignment is meant to be a first step in the change process. So did you feel any difference at all when you rehearsed the new belief?

C: Well, yes, I feel some difference, but not much!

T: That is exactly what we are looking for. There is no need for things to change all at once!

This dialogue shows an important part of the problem in not changing—the secondary or meta-level. "I cannot stand that my problem is not solved immediately and completely." Another way clients may present their FI is by saying:

C: Yes, I can see that if I could think like that, it would help me. But how do I think like that?

T: You are talking about your thoughts as if they are not part of you, as if you are hit by a ray from Mars. Do you think you can do anything about what you think at all? Do you have the option to think differently?

C: I probably can, but that does not mean I will immediately believe it.

T: That is not required. It is only that you *work on* convincing yourself.

WHY DO CLIENTS USE IRRATIONAL BELIEFS?

Clients often are aware of the negative effects of their thinking on their feelings and behaviors, yet keep on thinking the IBs. To help clients counter their IBs, it is useful for them to understand why they hold onto beliefs that harm them. Often it is possible to discover the advantages clients experience from their irrational thinking. However, it is usually more difficult to find such advantages than finding the irrational beliefs themselves. Irrational beliefs often result in short-term gratification and middle- and long-term trouble. "I cannot stand this, it must not be so difficult," is an example. Such an irrational belief creates a mindset that something that is very difficult to do cannot be done, because it is so difficult. Therefore one does not have to do it. For the short-term, the client escapes the difficulty and frustration of doing it. This avoidance of the problem represents a short-term advantage. The middle- and long-term disadvantage is of course that the client does not do what s/he wants to be done and what is in his/her own best interest.

A client, Marjolein, believes that nothing bad must happen to her boyfriend. This results in anxiety. She realizes that by her thinking she cannot influence what happens to her boyfriend, nevertheless she keeps thinking this way. When she tries to rehearse the EB, "I can accept that something bad (as bad as it is) might happen to my boyfriend," she hears herself saying right afterward, "No, that must not happen!" She asked her therapist why she keeps thinking this way.

T: There could be some advantage to thinking that way besides the disadvantage of your anxiety; otherwise you would not continue to think that.

C: I don't see the advantage.

T: Let's assume you do not think "Nothing bad must happen to my boyfriend." What will happen to you?

C: If something bad would happen to him, I would feel very upset because I let it happen.

T: So, you see that you keep thinking that you can influence bad things by not accepting them?

C: Yes, but I know that is not true.

T: But you do not think, feel, and behave as if that were true. You cannot let go of that thought, because you do not accept your inability to influence what happens.

C: Exactly.

T: How would you feel if you could fully accept that inability?

C: Terrible. I would have to let go of my boyfriend. And I cannot!

T: You do not want to. But you are able to. So, you think that as long as you do not let him go in your head, he cannot and will not go away in reality either. Isn't that the advantage of holding onto your anxiety provoking belief? You do not have to open yourself up to the possibility of losing your boyfriend, the idea you believe is unbearable.

C: So the belief that "it must not happen" protects me against the idea that it can happen. That is not very effective in the long run! But now I see why I hold onto that belief

T: Now you can choose to really get rid of that idea and your anxiety.

HELPING CLIENTS TO USE THE EB

Understanding the EB and feeling its results is one thing, training oneself to believe it and having it become internalized and an automatic reaction to troublesome Activating events is another thing. Clients will often not put much effort into rehearsing the EB by themselves. They can understand the importance of repeating the EB over and over again before it becomes an automatic habit. Nevertheless, they rarely will do that and will fail to discipline themselves to do it. Therapists can monitor how the client is using the EB over several sessions. After having formulated the EB and having tested its effectiveness, the client can be helped by an incentive with the following metaphor.

"Imagine that Times Square in NYC is actually in your head and that all the people walking in Times Square are your feelings, thoughts, and behaviors. Now the billboard that normally shows the news is repeating your IB all the time. So, everybody in Times Square can see your IB and takes the message home with them. If you could use all means the Government could bear to affect what people think, how could you ensure that (almost) all the people in Times Square would go home with another message, namely your EB? In thinking about it, there are a few rules that limit what you can do. You cannot force the person operating the billboard to change the text. You cannot cover the original text, your IB, with something else. Finally, you cannot demolish the billboard. In other words, the text will keep appearing on the billboard. Now what can you do to let these people go home with the new EB?"

After allowing the client some time to come up with an idea, we can provide him/her with the following solution if they have not discovered it themselves. You can place billboards in Times Square that are like the original one, but they are displaying the EB. You would need not two or three of them, but one thousand. Most people in Times Square will then get the right message. Now you could do the same thing figuratively in your head to influence what you think. How would you do that?

We can say to clients, "Don't be surprised that sometimes the Effective New Belief fails to work as effectively as you had hoped. You have to put more energy into convincing yourself than you would expect and rehearse the EB many times before it works."

Another important tool therapists can use to help the client to integrate the EB is to monitor what the client does with the EB in-between sessions. This dialogue with a client shows how.

T: Naïla, what did you do with the new belief we generated the last time?
C: Well, I printed it out and looked at it several times. Most times I could recall the belief when my children did not obey me.
T: And what happens when you say that new belief to yourself?
C: Most of the times I calm down, but sometimes I do not. Maybe it would help me if I had the sentence at hand. I keep it in my bedroom and I cannot access it at the crucial moments when my children do not do what I want them to do and I become angry about that.
T: What could you do about it?
C: As you said, I could put the printed sentence in my wallet, or in my pocket.

Monitoring clients' progress provides them with the message that it matters whether they use the new belief (EB), and that it matters if they take the change process seriously. Many clients develop psychological problems because they fail to spend the time to solve their emotional or behavioral problems. It is better for therapists to show clients that they have an ineffectual attitude toward their own psychological problems because they do not put in sufficient time, energy, and attention, and that they are better off changing that attitude.

CHOICES

Therapists make several choices in the E phase. First, therapists can choose to let clients construct an EB, or therapists can do it for the client. Which procedure is best is an empirical question. The therapist might not have the time after reviewing the A-B-C-D sequence to guide the client through this final work using Socratic questions. Therefore, the therapist faces the question of whether or not to let the client leave the session with a new EB. We think it is better if clients leave with a new EB so they can see the advantages of the A-B-C-D-E analysis. However, other clients prefer to have more time in the next session to construct a new effective rational belief.

Below is an introduction to formulating a new EB with a client, Marieke, which addresses the dilemma of limited session time.

C: Yes, I see there are many things wrong in thinking that I must have a relationship with a man and be loved by him before I am a worthwhile person. But how do I change my beliefs on that?

T: Because we're close to the end of the session, we can either do it in the next session or go over it quickly now. If we do it now you will be able to work somewhat against your irrational thinking throughout the week or if we do it next time when we have more time you can come up with the alternative thinking yourself. Which do you prefer?

C: I want to do it now, so I can try to rid myself from my inferiority thoughts and do something about not having a mate.

Formulating the EB is an important part of the REBT process. This is where cognitive change takes place. It is also the time we can see whether the suggested change can help the client, and whether s/he will use the EB to her/his benefit. Often, obstacles will hinder the client from fully profiting from the work thus far. This might give the therapist new and valuable information about the belief structure that keeps the client in the unhealthy pattern of behaving and feeling. Therefore, we recommend spending the time formulating the EB with the client and not rushing through it.

The second choice concerns the type of EB we want to offer the client. When we discuss the new belief, the therapist can leave the EB as the client formulates it, or use the EB that the therapist originally suggested to the client. In addition, the client and therapist can discuss how "thorough" they want the EB to be. Therapists sometimes prefer to construct a less powerful EB rather than a stronger one. To be careful is good, but let us realize that the whole process of therapeutic change is based on going from usual habits within one's comfort zone into less comfortable ways of reacting or acting under uneasy circumstances. Therefore, we want to give clients the opportunity to reach the most comprehensive EB they can. Clients might not be enthusiastic with a more comprehensive EB in the beginning, but when we do not try it, they may never go that far on their own.

Here is an example:

C: I have tried to use the belief that "I can accept and allow myself to not pass the exam as it will be," but that is just one step too far for me. I use "I want to pass the exam, but I do not have to."

T: Well, if that works for you, then I certainly advise you to use it. Maybe later on you can try whether the other might work, but if not, keep using this one.

To go back to a less confrontational EB can be done without damage and to go to a more comprehensive one can be done without damage so as long as the client has the say about/over it.

ALL STAGES (A, B, C, AND D) MAY HAVE TO BE REPEATED

When we are working on the E, we can expect each of the letters A, B, and C to undergo changes, because of the effect of formulating the EB. When we have found a new B, we have to redo the D as well.

Box 12.1

Do not be surprised if you discover new parts of the IB or even new IBs popping up during the formulation of the EB. We sometimes see clients contradicting self-downing statements in the EB stage that they did not mention before. Our clinical experience suggests that clients find it difficult to admit to thoughts of being inferior or to acknowledge that they think poorly of themselves. Therefore, that might come up at the end of the process when they feel confident enough to share it with us.

The C (the emotional and behavioral Consequences) could be changed because of discovering, as we saw above, denigrating statements about the self or others. A new C could be a feeling of depression because of self-downing, while an other-downing statement in the B will likely lead to anger with others. Sometimes the newfound C may even be stronger than the original one. We may come across a whole new and sometimes more essential aspect of the client's problem. The fact that one can find new As, Bs, and Cs during the E phase might surprise novice therapists, but uncovering the A-B-C-D-Es is an ongoing process even when discussing the same problem.

13

Evocative, Imaginal, and Behavior Change Strategies

Cognitive disputations are not the only techniques that REBT uses to foster change. REBT has long advocated the use of imagery to help change clients' irrational beliefs. In addition, changing irrational beliefs is irrelevant if the client does not change his/her behaviors and emotions. Direct behavior-change strategies are an important ingredient of this therapy. Emotive/evocative strategies have also been part of the therapy. In fact, Ellis's (1958) early writing described REBT as an integrative form of psychotherapy.

EVOCATIVE, EMOTIVE TECHNIQUES

Albert Ellis (1994; 2002) and other REBT authors often purport that REBT uses cognitive, behavioral, imaginative, and emotive techniques. So, what do they mean by emotive techniques? If emotions are the target for change, how do we change them without going through cognitions, behaviors, or images? In reviewing Ellis's writings and reminiscing on our experiences with him, we tried to define what he meant by an emotive therapeutic technique. Emotive techniques involve some activities that arouse the targeted disturbed emotion or the new alternative adaptive emotion. Ellis (1955) originally called his therapy RT, for rational therapy. He quickly changed the name to RET with the publication of *Reason and Emotion in Psychotherapy* (Ellis, 1962) to emphasize the emotive aspects of the therapy. Thus, arousing emotions and stressing the connections between beliefs and emotions experientially has always been part of this system. By arousing their clients' disturbed negative emotions, the therapists are more likely to have the clients experience the beliefs that are actually associated with the emotions. By challenging an IB or rehearsing an EB even though the client is experiencing a disturbed emotion, the client practices the problem they will face in the real world. That is, clients are changing beliefs while they are upset. The dispassionate, logical disputation of the clients' IBs might be philosophically correct but would ignore the human side of persuasion. Unemotional discussion of the viability or veracity of the client's irrational beliefs might be a good place to start the disputation process. However, clients eventually will have to challenge or replace a belief when they are facing a troublesome activating event and feeling a disturbed emotion. Frank and Frank (1991), in their classic book pointed out that therapy is persuasion. To persuade clients to give up their IBs and adopt EBs and to engage in new behaviors, it is best for the therapist to use techniques that are attention getting, evocative, and arousing.

In this section, we discuss some techniques that are evocatively persuasive and emotionally arousing. Robb and Backx (1999) defined emotional interventions as challenging the IBs or rehearsing the EBs "with force behind what you are saying." REBT therapists use forceful disputes in several ways. They sometimes vary the intonation of their voices, sometimes use obscenity, and they sometimes encourage the client to practice and rehearse forceful disputing in role-playing.

Intonation. If you have ever listened to a recording of Albert Ellis doing therapy, one of the first distinctive features that comes across is the change in his intonation as he identifies, disputes, or says irrational and rational beliefs. Whenever he pronounced one of the words that signify irrational concepts (e.g., "awful," "terrible," "should," or "need"), his voice emphasized the affect that was associated with the IBs, and he raised his volume and pitch of his voice, and extended and elongated the syllables in the word representing irrational concepts. These paralinguistic features were associated with a shaking hand gesture.

Why MMMMUSSSSTTTT you be loved?
Why is it AAWWWFFULLLL that you did not get what you wanted?

Later, when he changed the "awful" to "unfortunate," or a "need" to a "want," Ellis again pronounced the words, now reflecting rational concepts, in a distinct way. He spoke the key word slowly, enunciated very clearly, and raised the pitch of his voice as well as the volume. Thus, different auditory stimuli were associated with different concepts, making them more salient and easier to remember. When he offered, repeated, or suggested a rational alternative belief, his voice changed. He lowered his pitch and volume to a more relaxed comforting sound that reflected the emotional goal of the client. Folded hands and lower muscle tension throughout his body accompanied these paralinguistic features.

These paralinguistic and somatic visual cues associate the different beliefs with their different emotional states (Ellis, 2002). They helped teach the B to C connection, and allowed the client to perceive the changes in affect that accompanied cognitive change. Ellis was using a multi-sensory technique to teach and persuade his client to change. Although we do not recommend that you mimic Albert Ellis or other prominent REBT supervisors, we do recommend that you use the same multisensory technique to highlight the difference between irrational and rational beliefs and their consequences on human emotion. Find paralinguistic and non-verbal gestures that fit your authentic self and serve the same purpose.

Getting the client's attention is crucial when the therapist is about to make an important point. Monitor your typical style. If you are speaking rapidly and loudly and you want to make an important point, dramatically lower your voice and slow down. If your style is typically soft-spoken, on the other hand, you will attract the client's attention by raising your volume and speed. In other words, know yourself and be prepared to adjust your inflection when it is appropriate.

A second strategy is to signal an important concept by the content of your speech and the use of gestures. As in assertiveness training, leaning forward, touching the client on the arm, and making good eye contact are effective nonverbal cues.

Use of Obscenity. Another aspect of style that rational emotive behavior therapists are flexible about is the "sprightly use of obscenity," to use Ellis's phrase. Many therapists model their style closely after Ellis in this regard. We have observed that beginning therapists can be distinguished from more advanced students by a liberal use of four-letter words. In REBT terms, it is common to refer to the patient's self-denigration or his or her "shithood"; the therapist might ask, for example, how the patient's bad behavior makes him a "shit." Obviously, other terms will work as well, such as "worm," "no-goodnik," and "louse." You will want to use your own judgment as to which term best suits the client's manner of speaking.

Ellis was known for using obscenity but often has commented publicly on his positive reasons for doing so. He hypothesized that people typically awfulize in four-letter expletives, even if they rarely use these terms in their conversations. Sometimes even very subdued and conservative clients find that when they are describing serious life problems, four-letter words are the most appropriate and evocative descriptors. These words can help loosen people up and have a strong emotive, as well as motivating, quality.

A second reason for using obscene language is that it builds rapport. It might sound strange that clients would like a therapist who curses, but remember that most people use obscene language only within their closest circle of peers. One uses more informal language with those with whom one can be relaxed and be off guard. Thus, a common observation of therapists is that if they provide a model and thereby give permission to the client to use obscenity, the client feels at ease.

Box 13.1

Reflect on your own subvocal monologue the next time you are late for work and rush from the house, only to discover that you have a flat tire.

To prove that obscene language can build rapport, monitor your own four-letter words and note in whose presence they are comfortably used.

We do not recommend using obscenities indiscriminately. Their "sprightly use" is optimally directed at clients' irrational beliefs and self-denigration. A third use is to underscore significant points ("Isn't the goal of life to get out there and have a f—ball?"). Realize, however, we never direct obscenity toward the clients themselves and that it is not necessary to curse at all, because the same points can be made using other words. Before you use obscenity, know your client. Some clients will be offended by obscenity and other will love it and connect with you.

Role reversal. Another in-session strategy is the use of role-playing and rational role reversal. In role-playing, under the tutelage of the therapist, the client rehearses a new behavior that is more consistent with a rational philosophy. Rational role reversal consists of asking the client to play the "voice of reason" when the therapist models the client's irrational beliefs, and is similar to what Burns (1980) called "externalization of voices." This strategy can strengthen the client's conviction in a rational philosophy. This strategy also allows the therapist to check if the client is able to generate disputes and/or whether the client still holds onto the irrational belief.

We have found when doing rational role reversals that clients will often generate appropriate disputes and rational alternatives; however, they do so with a lack of conviction and with little force. It is important to point out to clients that their irrational voice is much more convincing and forceful because of rehearsal. Remind clients that they are persuading themselves to relinquish a self-defeating way of thinking and replace it with a more flexible attitude. As such, we recommend that clients practice the "voice of reason" with as much strength and conviction in order to foster a lasting change. Here is an example of what you can say to a client: "To consolidate our disputing work today, what if I play your irrational voice and see if you can play the voice of reason. Consider how you would handle the criticisms that I have heard you say about yourself in these sessions. Anytime you are stuck and cannot respond to the criticism, let us trade places and see if I can handle it. Then I will give it back to you and we will see what you can do with it. This will be a way of practicing more rational thinking."

Consider a demonstration session with RD and an REBT student, Jan. His irrational belief is that he *must* perform well in peer counseling in our primary training program. After identifying and verbally disputing the student's IB, RD played the role of personifying the irrational voice and the student took the role of personifying the rational beliefs.

RD: (Anxious and with many nonverbal gestures in a loud and forceful tone): There is our client. In addition, they are all watching us do therapy. We **HAVE** to do it well, now. We **MUST** do well, and **CANNOT** make any mistakes; otherwise, we will be **COMPLETELY WORTHLESS**!

ST: (In a very mellow, barely audible, and not forceful voice): What do you mean by worthless? Are we not allowed to make mistakes?

RD: (Forcefully again) What do you mean by we can make mistakes! We have been practicing this REBT for several months already. We're not rookies any more. *WE SHOULD GET IT RIGHT* by now.

ST: Did we ever make mistakes before when we learned new things?

RD: (Stops the role-playing): Jan, do you find it difficult to go against your irrational voice? You are so polite to me, the irrational voice, and you do not interrupt or stop me from saying all these irrational things. Let me be your rational voice and Jan, you be the irrational one and try to act and sound the way the voices do in your head when you are anxious. OK?

ST: We HAVE TO DO IT WELL; otherwise, we are NO GOOD AND THAT IS
     AWFUL.

RD: Now, *STOP CATASTROPHIZING* and let us just focus on what we have to
     do. We might make mistakes (increases volume) and that is OK. So, we will
     be fallible humans like everyone else.

ST: We would be worth....

RD: Stop. Don't continue to think this way. It is not helpful. Let's calm down and
     concentrate on what we are doing. If we make mistakes, we will learn from
     them.

RD: (Stops the role-playing): Jan, what did I do differently from you as the ratio-
     nal voice?

ST: You were more forceful and you interrupted me in the role of my irrational
     beliefs.

RD: Yes, Jan, and what do you think will happen when you will do this
     yourself?

Box 13.2

A "rational" therapist might use a "behavioral" strategy but will examine its impact
by inquiring of the client, "Now, how do you think differently about that situation?" For example, "You've now been on the elevator six times; has your thinking
about elevators changed?" or "Has your thinking about your anxiety changed?"

   Cognitions, emotions, and behaviors are all dependent variables in measuring
change. Whether change comes about by taking a pill, riding an elevator, or sitting
in the therapist's office debating whether it would be horrible to feel anxious—or
even sitting in an armchair practicing some of the symptoms of anxiety and adapt-
ing to them—the therapist always comes back to examining the client's thinking.
Until the thinking changes, the fact that the client has been on an elevator six
times might not have any relevance to future behavior. Because the B-C interface
is the heart of REBT, the client's cognitions are ultimately our primary focus.

Dealing with the "Head-Gut" Problem

As you help your client think more rationally, he/she might say something like,
"I understand that you think my rational belief will help me be less upset, but I
don't really feel different yet." or "I believe it intellectually but not emotionally."
or "I believe it in my head but don't feel it in my gut." REBT theorists have called
this the Head-Gut problem or the intellectual versus emotional insight distinction. Clients might have learned that there are arguments against their IBs and
they know that there are new EBs. However, they have not given up the IBs, and
although they know what the EB is, they do not yet believe it. Therefore, their
emotions and behaviors have not changed. There is a difference between knowing
something and believing it, or knowing it is true. At this point in therapy we want
to help clients realize that they know the EB but they are not yet convinced of its

truth; or that they hold the two beliefs, the IB and the EB, and they believe the IB more intensely.

What we usually call emotional insight has several important characteristics (Ellis, 2002).

1. Clients have some degree of intellectual insight and admit that they are disturbed and that their behavior is irrational or self-defeating.
2. Clients usually realize that their present behavior has some antecedent causes and does not magically spring from nowhere.
3. Clients assume some kind of responsibility for the dysfunctional or self-defeating behavior and realize that they have something to do with originating it and carrying it on.
4. Clients realize that even if they were helped to have learned certain IBs and to create self-defeating emotions with these Beliefs, they keep rehearsing these Beliefs right now.
5. Clients clearly and strongly "see" or "acknowledge" that they can now do something *to change* their IBs.
6. Clients are determined to work at (yes, *work* at) changing their IBs. Working at changing Beliefs includes the clients' (a) forcefully and repetitively disputing and challenging them; (b) forcing themselves to go through the pain and trouble of steadily contradicting these ideas; (c) practicing feeling differently about them or their results; and (d) directly and vigorously acting against the IBs or against the actions to which they self-defeatingly lead.
7. Clients actually do this rehearsal and work and do it often and vigorously.
8. Clients realize that their emotional disturbances are usually under their own control and that they can continue to think and act their way out of them whenever they recur. This means continual determination and action.
9. Clients keep admitting that there might be no better way to become and to remain undisturbed except by continually working and practicing against whatever disturbances they create.

To accomplish these insights, therapy can focus on convincing the client of the EB and making their commitment to the EB deeper or stronger. Indeed, you might wish to ask your clients if they have both emotional and intellectual insights, or whether they have just intellectual insight. This can be a prelude to discussing with your clients how they are going to deepen their conviction in their rational belief and weaken their conviction in their irrational one. You might ask, for example, "What do you think you will have to do to get your new rational belief into your gut?" Encourage your clients to commit themselves to a process of therapeutic change that requires them to question their irrational beliefs repeatedly and forcefully and to practice thinking rationally in relevant life contexts.

To help your client to understand why a weak conviction in rational beliefs, although important, is insufficient to promote change, briefly discuss the REBT view of therapeutic change. Using Socratic questioning and brief didactic explanations, help your client to see that she will strengthen her conviction in her RBs by questioning her IBs and replacing them with their rational alternatives within and between therapy sessions. Also, help your client to understand that this process will require her to *act* against her irrational beliefs as well as to question them cognitively. Establishing this point now will help you later, when you encourage your client to put this new learning into practice through homework assignments and as you facilitate the working-through process.

Robb, Backx, and Thomas (1999) surveyed REBT therapists concerning the interventions they used when they confronted the Head-Gut problem. These authors reported that in such situations cognitive interventions were the most common in-session interventions. They were used alone 40% of the time. Emotive interventions were used alone less than 4% of the time. Cognitive interventions were also the most frequently used homework assignments. Although no data exists that tell us which intervention works best when clients present the Head-Gut problem, Robb et al. (1999) believe that emotive and imaginal interventions would work best because the cognitive disputes have provided the knowledge. Emotive and imaginal techniques provide new experiences that are more convincing.

Rorer (1999) suggested that when the therapist confronts the Head-Gut problem it is time to step back, take a broader view, and examine the context in which the irrational belief is held. When clients say that they understand something intellectually (e.g., that there is no reason that the world should be fair, or that someone else should [or shouldn't] do something), but that they cannot accept it emotionally, the therapist might ask the client what it would mean to accept the RB. How would they try to help somebody else to acquire emotional insight?

Rorer (1999) suggested an alternative reason why clients may get stuck with the Head-Gut problem. That is that the new EBs, the new behavioral and emotional responses, are in conflict with some other major philosophy or value or schema by which they lead their life, but that they are unaware of this conflict. Thus the IB that is being discussed in therapy is embedded in a broader worldview that would have to be abandoned if they change and which would bring the person substantial trouble.

Rorer (1999) suggested that the way to discover such a conflict is to ask the client what would happen if they adopted the new RB and changed. People do not hold any belief in a vacuum; beliefs are interrelated. People might not be able to change without modifying or giving up other related beliefs that could be important to them because they involve a person's self-image, worldview, or our deepest fears. Rorer (1999) referred to this resistance as the cost of giving up the IB. Sometimes the "cost" actually becomes a gain if the person changes these conflicted beliefs in a way that creates an EB that relieves guilt or increases self-acceptance. Therapists can explore the possibility of such conflicted broad-view beliefs through imagery. The therapist can ask the client to close her eyes and imagine that she has accepted and adopted the new RB and made the corresponding changes in emotions and behaviors. Then the therapist asks the client to imagine how she would feel and behave with this new change. Sometimes a client will identify a new negative feeling and a new IB. This reflects the new conflict that the change has created.

Consider the case of Derek, a man in his midforties who came to treatment for alcohol abuse. Derek condemned himself for his alcohol abuse. Such condemnation led to depression and more drinking to alleviate the depression. Our sessions focused on having Derek accept himself and forgive himself for all the bad things he had done while drinking. Derek frequently said he understood self-acceptance intellectually, but that he just did not feel any differently and believe it. When his therapist asked him to do the imagery mentioned above, Derek started to cry. He reported that if he did not condemn himself, he clearly would leave his marriage. He had married his wife without loving her and the couple had two children, whom Derek loved. Only his strict religious belief against divorce kept him in the marriage. If he adopted self-acceptance, he had no reason to stay in the marriage. Once Derek and his therapist identified the conflict and the new problem, they focused the session on his condemnation of himself about his thoughts of leaving his marriage and the pros and cons of doing so. Derek eventually recognized that he could accept himself if he left the marriage, but decided to stay and work at being a better mate for the good of his children. He also recognized that he could leave if this no longer helped his children.

Another way to help clients overcome the Head-Gut problem is to use the diagram below in Figure 13.1. It shows the thinking, feeling, and behaving processes in interaction in the form of a triangle. The green triangle depicts the healthy functional and rational part, and the red one depicts the unhealthy dysfunctional, irrational part. When we change any one of the three components in the triangle, the other two will follow in the change. Therefore, when we change in the green triangle the belief, the feeling, and the behavior will change. Now what we aim at in the change process is to get the red triangle to

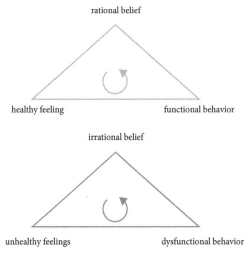

Figure 13.1 The Head-Gut Problem.

change into the green one. There are three components we can change from the red triangle into the green one: the behavior, the feeling, and the belief. When we change one, the others tend to follow. In the case of a client who says: "I know the rational belief (the EB), but I cannot feel it," we can explain, with the help of the diagram, what is going on. The client thinks the green rational belief but unfortunately experiences the unhealthy feeling in the red triangle. That means that he or she might also experience the healthy feeling in green but much lighter. When the unhealthy feeling is stronger than the healthy one, the theory states that the irrational thinking is also much stronger than the rational thinking.

IMAGINAL CHANGE STRATEGIES

Imagination is the ability to form mental images, sensations, and concepts when they are not sensed or perceived through vision, hearing, smell, taste, touch, or kinesthesia. Imagination is the work of the brain. The cognitive psychological processes and brain areas that conjure up images are the same ones that are involved in our creation of our perceptions of reality. Imagination helps provide meaning to experience, and understanding to knowledge. Imagery is a fundamental human faculty through which people make sense of the world, and it plays a key role in the learning and memory processes. Imagination helps us construct narratives to explain life events and provide the stories that give life meaning.

Developmental psychologists (see Sutton-Smith, 1988) consider daydreaming the naturally occurring form of imagery. Although daydreaming is often considered an activity for children, it plays an important function in human affairs; and most of us have spent countless hours in our daydreams. Daydreaming allows us to explore, practice, and evaluate new roles, emotions, and behaviors without having to leave the confines of our heads. Many of the great philosophers such as Hobbs and Leibniz perceived imagination, imagery, or daydreaming as an important part of the process of learning.

Imagery can be seen as a conscious attempt to construct focused daydreams to master specific tasks at hand (Byrne, 2005). All forms of psychotherapy appear to own imagery and purport that they harness the power of imagery as part of their procedures. Although each form of psychotherapy uses imagery in a different way, it has been a crucial part of many strategies to help humans in the process of self-discovery and the development of more adaptive behaviors. A complete review of these topics is beyond the scope of this chapter. We recommend Singer (2006) for a complete review of all of these topics.

A variation on cognitive disputing strategies involves the use of imagery. In one such procedure, after a verbal disputation, the therapist might ask clients to imagine themselves again in the troublesome situation; this could allow the therapist to see whether the emotion has changed. If it has, the therapist might ask clients what they are now telling themselves as a way to rehearse thinking that is more rational. If the emotion has not changed, there could be additional IBs present, and the imagery exercise allows them to emerge. If necessary, a new A-B-C-D analysis might be conducted and the results reexamined by a repeat of the imagery exercise. As an alternative, the therapist might wish to shift to one of the following imagery techniques, known as rational emotive imagery (REI) (Maultsby 1975; Maultsby and Ellis, 1974).

In negative rational emotive imagery, clients close their eyes, imagine themselves in the problem situation (A), and try to experience their usual emotional response (C). Wait until clients report experiencing C and then ask them to focus on the internal sentences that trigger these emotional consequences. Then instruct clients to change the feeling from a disturbed emotion to a more constructive negative emotion (e.g., from anxiety to concern). Assure clients that they can do this, even if it is only for a fraction of a second. Instruct clients that as soon as they have accomplished this task, they are to open their eyes. At this signal from the clients, you might simply ask, "How were you able to do that?" Almost invariably, the answer will reveal a cognitive shift; usually clients respond that they have stopped catastrophizing; for example, "I asked out this woman and she turned me down. It's not the end of the world and I can tolerate being rejected." Here is another example:

T: Now, I want you to close your eyes and imagine yourself back in the situation in which you felt so anxious yesterday. Can you do that?
   [Wait until clients indicate they have the image.]
C: Yes.
T: Now, I want you to make yourself feel anxious right now, as you did yesterday. Signal me when you are feeling anxious.
   [Wait for the client's signal.]
C: (nods)
T: OK, now tell me what thoughts are going through your head to make you feel anxious.
   [Wait for the client's response, which will be some form of IB.]
C: I'm saying, "My God, what if I get rejected?"
T: Now, I want you to change that feeling of anxiety to one of concern. Signal me when you are less anxious and now feel merely concerned.
   [Pause until the client's signal.]
T: Now, what are you telling yourself so that you feel concerned and not anxious?
C: Well, if I got rejected, it is not the end of the world, and if she thinks I'm a loser, that's too bad. I can't please everyone!

In positive rational emotive imagery (Maultsby, 1975; Maultsby and Ellis, 1974), clients imagine themselves in a problematic situation but picture themselves behaving and feeling differently. For example, clients anxious about speaking in public imagine themselves speaking up in class or at a meeting and feeling relatively relaxed while doing so. As soon as clients report experiencing that image, the therapist asks, "And what were you saying to yourself in order to do that?" This technique is useful because it allows clients to practice a positive plan and develop a set of coping skills. For example:

T: OK, Mary, now I know you have been having trouble when you think about giving that speech to the Board of Directors this week. I know you have been feeling very anxious about that.

C: Yes, I am scared.

T: What I would like you to do now is to close your eyes and picture yourself up there at the podium addressing the Board. But I want you to picture yourself doing that and feeling relatively calm while you are doing it. You are speaking slowly and clearly, and feeling not too anxious. You give your presentation in a nice loud voice, glancing up frequently to look at members of the Board. Tell me when you get that picture clear in your head.
   [Pause and wait for feedback from the client.]

C: (nods)

T: Now, what would you have to say to yourself in order to do what you pictured?

C: Well, I have my ideas down on PowerPoint. I know what I want to say. The Board is there to hear my ideas, not to judge me. I cannot really expect them all to like all of my ideas, and if some of them disagree with me, that is OK. It will make for a lively discussion. Anyway, they would probably be nervous up at the podium, too, so I am sure they will not mind if my hands shake a little. I will not think about that; I will just concentrate on getting my point across.

Tosi and his colleagues (Tosi and Murphy, 1994; Tosi and Reardon, 1976) developed a procedure that combines inducing deep relaxation or hypnosis and guided imagery that progresses the client through an A-B-C-D-E sequence; for example, the client imagines approaching a feared A, making rational statements, and then experiencing an appropriate C. Such procedures have been effective for ulcers (Tosi, Judah, and Murphy, 1989), and asthma (Silverglade, Tosi, Wise, and D'Costa, 1994). Such a procedure employs a "mastery" image that can be appropriate for children but less helpful to adults than a "coping" image (Meichenbaum, 1985). In coping imagery, clients imagine approaching an A and thinking the irrational messages they usually employ; they then imagine themselves disputing and replacing the IB statements and rehearsing rational statements. These could include, "This really isn't true... be calm... I can cope with this anxiety... things are not as terrible as I think they are"; and finally, they imagine a reduction in emotion. This approach could be more helpful than one employing a mastery image because clients are often anxious the first few times they actually approach a feared A, and they want a tool to cope with this very concrete anxiety. Thus clients can imagine the A, IB, and dysfunctional C, then imagine challenging their IBs, rehearse the new EBs, and imagine themselves experiencing the new functional emotion and performing the new adaptive behavior. This procedure requires some preliminary sessions where the A-B-C-D-and-E are identified. The therapist then teaches the client relaxation. Next the therapist and the client create the guided image with all the steps from A through E. The therapist can then read the guided instructions as the client relaxes. Eventually, the client can read the instruction into a recorder and listen at home to his own voice guide him through the imagery. Numerous sessions of such practice will help the client overlearn these responses. Eventually the client can rehearse the image in his mind without the verbal instruction. We recommend to clients that they rehearse such images when they know they will be approaching the identified **As**. In addition, we recommend that people practice this rational emotive imagery whenever they catch themselves practicing irrational emotive imagery. People frequently think of approaching or experiencing an activating event and immediately start imagining experiencing their IBs and dysfunctional emotions. At this point, they can stop their irrational imagery and activate the rational emotive imagery that they have rehearsed.

Box 13.3

An advantage of positive and negative rational emotive imagery techniques is that they encourage clients to be active in the session and allow the therapist to check whether clients are changing their dysfunctional affects by rehearsing appropriate rational cognitions. Be careful. Sometimes clients will surprise you, and you will discover that they feel better, but for the wrong reasons. For example, Fred was very anxious about approaching women at a singles event for fear that they would reject him. When he rehearsed this experience in imagery, he was indeed able to lower his anxiety, but this is how he did it: "Who cares? Who the hell does she think she is?" The therapist pointed out that this kind of thinking was not rational imagery, but hostile imagery!

A related imagery technique employed by cognitive therapists is the "blow-up" procedure, in which the client imagines future unwanted events and then blows them out of proportion, beyond what might realistically happen. For example, a client with a compulsive ritual of checking whether the gas jets were turned off imagined not only that the kitchen and his house were set afire but that his neighborhood, the city, the country, and finally the whole globe went up in flames! By the use of exaggeration, the client might learn to see the humor in his or her fears, so that the humor diffuses the fear.

Some therapists prefer to use imagery techniques after initially doing relaxation training or hypnosis to induce a state of greater suggestibility, particularly if the client is unusually anxious. We refer the therapist who wishes to learn such techniques to *Clinical Behavior Therapy* (Goldfried, Davison, and Wachtel, 1994) or to *The New Hypnosis* (Araoz, 1985).

Box 13.4

Imagery can challenge beliefs in creative ways that utilize a client's special talents. For example, Herb, an artist, brought in a picture he had sketched of himself with his father, the latter drawn in enlarged scale, and looking quite menacing. After exploring some of the thoughts and feelings that emerged from the picture, he was asked to draw in session, a picture of himself and his father, both of the same size. When completed, the therapist asked Herb, "What is the 'you' in this picture believing that is different from the 'you' in the first picture?"

Notice that the therapist is using a unique modality—one that fits the client's needs, but also clearly follows the REBT model.

BEHAVIORAL CHANGE STRATEGIES

The third basic form of dispute is behavioral, in which the client challenges his or her IBs by behaving in a way that opposes them. In fact, the REBT practitioner is not confident that the client has internalized a new philosophy until such a belief is reflected in behavioral change. Because behavioral disputes are usually performed outside of the therapist's office, they are assigned as homework assignments. We discuss this topic in more detail in Chapter 16.

As a general principle, REBT recommends and uses flooding or implosive (Levis, 2009) procedures in exposing clients to their fears. Flooding involves prolonged exposure to stimuli that evoke relatively high levels of inappropriate or excessive anxiety or fear. This procedure differs from other exposure-based procedures in that flooding begins with exposure to highly fear-evoking stimuli whereas other techniques employ graduated exposure, progressing from less to more anxiety-provoking stimuli. Flooding exposure can be conducted in vivo, or in imagery, termed imaginal exposure. The basics of exposure-based procedures include engagement with the fear-arousing stimulus, systematic prolonged and repeated exposure to this stimuli, and learning of corrective information regarding its lack of dangerousness until the anxiety and fear associated have been greatly reduced (Zoellner, Abramowitz, Moore, and Slagle, 2009). Flooding and implosion try to maximize a single therapeutic change mechanism, direct Pavlovian extinction. This principle states that the repeated presentation of an emotionally conditioned stimulus (CS) in the absence of a biological unconditioned stimulus (UCS) leads to the extinction of the conditioned response (CR; the symptom). This principle can be found to be operating in most psychotherapy techniques, and a controversy exists in CBT on whether cognitive change comes first or cognitive restructuring occurs after the emotion-arousing stimuli that maintain maladaptive behavior are extinguished (Levis, 2009).

Clients in therapy sessions usually engage in verbal learning, and it is important to assure that their behavior in the real world matches their verbal behavior in-session. Behavioral disputes provide clients with experiences that run counter to their present irrational belief system; clients act against their IBs and dysfunctional emotions. Such behavioral interventions are common in psychotherapy and are called "opposite action." They have been popularized by Linehan's Dialectical Behavior Therapy (Linehan, 1993). Numerous examples of opposite action appear on the Internet. However, one distinction exists between opposite action in REBT and DBT. In REBT, we would recommend that the behavioral assignments challenge not just the emotion but the thoughts and philosophies behind them and that the behaviors are consistent with the new rational alternative philosophy.

For example, if clients believe that they cannot stand waiting for events, you can ask them to practice postponing gratifications. If they believe that they cannot stand rejection, they are encouraged to go out and meet people until they experience rejection. They might also do Ellis's famous shame attacking exercises, where people do silly things in public to court rejection until they are experience it. If they believe that they *need* something, the therapist asks them to do without it. If they are depressed and just want to stay in bed, we would recommend various behavioral activation assignments to get up and do things. If they believe their worth is based on doing well, we ask them to purposely do poorly; or to announce to others when they make a mistake. The principle here involves having the client face or become exposed to their fears. Most therapists use a graduated approach to exposure, which involves having clients rate the degree of anxiety they experience to various anxiety eliciting stimuli; and then starting exposure with the least anxiety arousing stimuli and proceeding to more forceful anxiety arousing stimuli.

From Ellis's perspective the use of graduated exposure (Head and Gross, 2009) colluded with clients' beliefs that the feared stimuli was dangerous and with the clients' frustration intolerance beliefs that they could not stand the emotions experienced when confronting the feared stimuli. Thus it is important to know that the therapist might have to spend some time challenging the client's frustration intolerance beliefs before the client actually does the behavioral assignment.

However, you can do some behavioral disputes in-session; good examples of that are many of the anxiety challenges. An experience of anxiety or, worse, panic, seems overwhelming to the client, and usually results in a secondary fear of the onset of the panic experience. In session, the therapist and client can plan and engage in behaviors that elicit some of the very sensations the client ordinarily tries to avoid. For example, the client might be urged to hyperventilate or do some vigorous movements that stimulate rapid, shallow breathing, sweating, lightheadedness, or tingling of the extremities, and can then work with the therapist to challenge cognitions such as "I can't tolerate these sensations." or "Something terrible is going to happen." (Beck and Emery, 1985).

One of us (KD) uses a particular behavioral dispute in session with her eating disorder clients who binge and purge. She asks her clients to bring in food that would typically lead to purging behavior once eaten. Coping statements for frustration intolerance are generated in advance. The client eats the food in session and then sits with the anxiety while rehearsing the coping statements. This demonstrates that although very uncomfortable, she can in fact tolerate the feelings and does not have to purge to cope. This exposure and response prevention exercise is very useful as such clients often do not allow themselves to tolerate discomfort by engaging in purging, thereby reinforcing frustration intolerance beliefs. Clients are asked to repeat this exercise for homework to further their conviction in the rational alternative.

14

Problems and Solutions in Challenging Irrational Beliefs

TROUBLE-SHOOTING DISPUTATIONAL PROBLEMS

Having outlined some disputational strategies, we realize that you might run into some snags in getting your points across. This section anticipates some common problems that new therapists encounter in disputation and offers suggestions to deal with them. Most of these problems have to do with clients who either do not understand or do not believe disputational arguments. Thus, after you have disputed an irrational belief, check to see whether your client understood the process.

Ask yourself, "Is the client just saying the right words but not really believing them? Is the client placating me to get my approval?" How can you determine whether the client is merely parroting? We suggest four strategies.

1. If clients come to the session in obvious emotional distress, or if you can create some emotional reaction by reenacting troublesome situations with rational barbs or imagery exercises, you can validate their understanding by looking for signs of tension reduction. Examine whether or not the clients can calm themselves down in the session.

2. Sometimes you will not be able to determine the client's understanding in a particular session; instead, the proof will emerge over time. What you are looking for is *consistency* in the client's thoughts, feelings, and behavior across sessions. For example, if a male client claims that he "knows" that being rejected for a date is not terrible, but he continues to avoid approaching women, the therapist will want to eventually confront this discrepancy directly by pointing out the difference between "knowing" and "believing." One might know about the theory of Marxism or Catholic dogma and yet not believe in or choose to live by them.

3. Another strategy is to invite significant others from the client's life into the session; obviously this is done only after securing the client's agreement and making sure that he or she understands the reason for

this strategy. At such a meeting, the therapist can ask questions such as, "Do you see any changes in X's behavior?" or "How is X really acting?" Inconsistencies between reports from others and the client's self-report might enable the therapist to explore the reason for the inconsistencies: "Jack, it looks like your family does not think you have changed much. Is that because they are hard to please or because you have not changed much? We had better figure that out so you can either change more or figure out how to deal with their demands on you." In general we would advise to ask the client whether he or she agrees with inviting a significant other into the session after a few (three or four) sessions to help find blind spots that may develop between the therapist and the client.

4. Some clients remain relatively passive in therapy (often because their therapists are too active), and the therapist will want to look for indicators that they can approximate a disputation by themselves. One good technique to check on clients' understanding is to have them fill out self-help forms as homework between sessions. If they cannot accurately work through a self-help form, they probably have not understood. Time can profitably be spent in the next session going over and correcting any errors on the form. A second technique to validate the understanding of this type of patient is rational role reversal, in which clients are asked to change roles with the therapist and thus demonstrate how they would help someone with a problem like their own. In this way, the therapist can estimate how much of the disputation the clients understand and their commitment to giving up their irrational, disturbing ideas.

Clients' misunderstandings might not always be obvious. One way to check this out is to listen very carefully to their choice of words and their intonation. For example, listen for "I am..." sentences, such as "I am incompetent." Clients might not be aware of it, but when they say, "I am..." they imply unity and identity between the subject and predicate of their sentence. Help clients to rephrase these statements more accurately (e.g., "I acted incompetently."). The feedback that clients get from the way they use language could continue to propagate their irrational thinking unless the therapist corrects their statements.

Listen also to the client's tone of voice, specifically for the level of emotion. The client might say something like, "I don't have much to offer men." Said in a flat tone of voice, such a statement can be easily missed by client and therapist, and the important irrational concept behind it left undisputed. If the client is interrupted and asked to repeat the statement with more emotion, the therapist might help the client confront and deal with the IB behind his or her words.

Box 14.1

You might miss the subtle residuals of the client's IBs if your active *listening skills* are not developed. One of the impediments to new therapists' listening skills is the tendency to monitor their own performance too closely: "Was the last intervention I made good?" or "Now, what clever thing am I going to say next?" and so forth.

Here is a training exercise to check on your active listening skills. Take a recent therapy recording and stop it approximately every two minutes, asking yourself, "What did the client just say?" Check to see if you have accurately recorded all the fine points in the client's conversation. Remember, do not focus primarily on your behavior in the session but on accurately hearing the client's statements.

Frequently clients do *not fully* express entire thoughts; they use syntactic shorthand that can hide irrational beliefs. For example, a therapist asked a male client to speak spontaneously in front of a large group at work and discuss a topic. When the therapist asked what he was thinking while he was being introduced, the client replied, "I thought, 'Oh my God, what will I say?'" Do you hear the beginnings of an IB here? People do not usually beseech deities unless some kind of awfulizing is going on in their thinking. The very question, "What will I say?" implies that the client is worried and *does not* know what to say. The "Oh my God" is an additional indicator of his anxiety and the belief that he must do what has been asked of him; that he's trapped in and victimized by the situation. Thus, a great deal of hidden information is contained in a very simple sentence.

How do you get the client to state these unspoken concepts? Help the client in the translation of the assignment step-by-step; for example, guide the client into rephrasing the question, "What will I say?" to "I don't know what to say." At this point, you are in a better position to ask, "How do you feel about that?" Thus, until the premise is stated, the client cannot really explore how he or she is reacting to it. Once the client identifies that "I feel anxious," you have an A and a C. To get at the missing belief, the one-word interjection "because" can be very helpful:

T: You're anxious about not knowing what to say *because*...?
C: I might make a fool of myself.

Box 14.2

Even if you are not using a formal A-B-C format in speaking with your client, we strongly advise you to use it in your *listening* style. Go over a recent therapy recording and, as you hear the client's story unfold, write down the A, B, and C as they emerge, also noting unusual key words in the margin. After you think you have uncovered the hidden Bs, plan your next disputational strategy.

T: And if you act foolishly....
C: That would be awful!

When we first began doing REBT, we were surprised and chagrined when, following what we viewed as an exemplary dispute, clients returned the following week reiterating their irrational concepts. It took us a while to learn that REBT is not a magic therapy; although one-trial learning might occasionally occur, it is not the rule. Most clients have a long reinforcement history for their IBs, and they are not going to give them up or change them easily. Success might come only after repeating the same disputes, filling out numerous homework sheets, and engaging in many challenges to the IB. A mistake that the new therapist makes is trying an REBT strategy for two or three sessions, becoming discouraged when success is not immediate, and turning to another theoretical orientation for the "magic answer." We acknowledge that REBT might not be the necessary and sufficient therapy for each case, but we recommend that the therapist give it a fair chance. If several years of psychoanalysis are required before change is to be expected, more than a few sessions of disputation appears reasonable. The therapist might have to spend months on the same concept before the client "sees the light." Do not be afraid of repetition, therefore; repetition might be important in all communication but is essential in psychotherapy. One of us (WB) had a client who remarked after seven sessions: "You know, it is so strange, you have said these words exactly the same way five times in the past five sessions and now suddenly I understand what you say!"

As you progress through sessions with your clients, it is important to stress not only rational beliefs but also the *process* of disputing. After you have spent one or two sessions challenging clients' irrational beliefs, it is easy to get into the habit of just providing them with rational alternatives. Disputing, however, is a process of *asking questions* about their irrational beliefs, not merely mechanically replacing IBs with rational statements.

Box 14.3

When clients hold core, tacit assumptions about themselves, they are unlikely to be able to disprove such thoughts easily. Core issues about self-image, for example, are difficult and might rarely have reached consciousness. Be respectful of the task. The client deserves a lot of credit for broaching these issues and you, the therapist, deserve credit if you can create an atmosphere in which the client feels comfortable doing it.

One helpful strategy is to put off disputation until a good deal of the self-deprecatory material is brought out into awareness so that they can examine it in detail. For example, one client referred to herself as "manipulative"; another avowed that she "couldn't trust herself." These concepts were central to their self-image, and the clients had been amassing data to support their negative beliefs for most of a lifetime.

Collect the stories, examples, and images that the client believes support these core IBs. Then be prepared to slowly and methodically refute, reframe, and de-awfulize this mass of material. Remember, these are subtle, painful perceptions the client is facing. Your patience and persistence, as well as your enthusiasm for alternative points of view, will pay off in the end!

The key element here is teaching scientific thinking, the search for evidence to support a hypothesis; merely substituting a rational belief omits this important step. Until clients have learned the skill of questioning themselves, they might not be able to generalize beyond their immediate problem.

Another inappropriate style that develops among new REBT therapists is what we will call the "knee-jerk disputer." Every time they hear a "need," "should," "must," or "terrible," these therapists are quick to ask, "Where's the evidence?" This reaction frequently misses the target. Remember that these words are harmful because of the concepts for which they stand, not because of their face value. People use such words frequently in everyday language as figures of speech. For example, "That was a *terrible* steak!" or "You *have* to see the new ballet." or "I *need* a cup of coffee." Thus, the automatic disputer might be shooting down pseudo-problems; although people can be irrational about their need for coffee or the awfulness of their steak, these might not be clinically significant beliefs related to their pathology. So, make sure that you have identified the relevant IBs before moving on to D, lest you merely establish silly new taboo words. Does it make sense for the word "shit" to be OK, but "should" to be taboo?

Box 14.4

What to do when you are stuck in a disputation: as with any problem, first do an assessment so that you can reach a differential diagnosis. Perhaps you are not working skillfully. Perhaps the client does not want to give up the emotion, which often happens in anger. Perhaps the client wants you to do all the work. Perhaps the client wants the activating event to change. Perhaps the client does not really understand what disputation means. Perhaps the client has some personal, idio-syncratic, intrapsychic reason for not changing. And so on.

If you feel as though you are arguing with or lecturing a reluctant client, then you are not collaborating. *Collaboration is the hallmark of therapy.*

CLIENT BEHAVIORS THAT BLOCK CHANGE

Some clients pose special problems for the new therapist. Let us go over a few such types.

The argumentative client. Are you picking up antagonism in your clients? Do their voices have an edge? Do you feel you are fighting rather than disputing? Are you fatigued by your interaction? How can you handle such clients? First, stop fighting. If you sense that the two of you are tugging at opposite ends of a rope, let go of your end. Try to go through an entire session without trying to convince the client of anything, and see what happens. Alternatively, play devil's advocate and agree with such clients (e.g., "You're right, Bill, you really are incompetent."). Imposing your ideas on such clients might only serve to intensify their resistance to you. Focus instead on the strength of the client by intervening primarily with questions (e.g., "What do you think you could do to get over your problem, Bill?").

The "yes-but" client. Clients who counter your suggestions with a "yes-but" response are demonstrating another form of argumentative resistance. A yes-but is equivalent to a "no." Such clients are playing helpless and often render the therapist helpless. Consider whether their resistance is attributable to your behavior. Have you focused the discussion on any irrelevant issues? If not, perhaps these clients are simply unwilling to listen to you because they attribute qualities to you that they have generalized from other troublesome people in their lives. For example, they might have difficulty accepting suggestions from anyone whom they view as an authority figure. In this case, you might consider bringing in a credible significant other from their lives to whom they might be more willing to listen—such as a spouse, sibling, or close friend—and using them as disputational models. If the message comes from them, or at least is reinforced by them outside the session, you might increase the chance that these clients will accept the message.

Another possible explanation for clients' yes-but behavior is that they simply do not want to change. In this situation, a useful question to ask yourself is, "What's the payoff for the client?" In other words, what positive or negative consequences might be operating to maintain the dysfunctional beliefs or behaviors? One client of ours, for example, continually ranted and raged, and blamed her friends for not calling her as often as she liked; every disputation was met with a yes-but reply. It occurred to us that she was stuck on blaming others because it functionally served to avoid self-blame and self-examination. One technique to uncover such motivations is to ask clients repeatedly to fill in the following sentence: "The good thing about (blaming others, in this case) is...."

The intellectualizing client. REBT might be difficult to accomplish with intelligent clients whose defense against self-examination is to intellectualize. They combat the therapist with reasonable arguments, can beat the therapist at deductive logic, and even sound quite rational. Why, then, do they continue to come to therapy? Because they do not clearly recognize or verbalize that they have emotional problems. The therapist would be wise to keep the focus on emotions and, instead of relying on didactic approaches, bring in other procedures such as experiential exercises or imagery techniques. Such clients are very likely to object to these methods, however, and might refuse to do something they define as "silly." Proceed slowly.

The intellectually limited client. Disputation toward the elegant solution might not be appropriate for all clients. Among the exceptions are very young children, clients with limited intellectual ability, clients with severe brain damage, clients with severe psychosis whose pathological thought processes interfere with logical thought, and highly anxious clients, whose level of arousal is too intense to enable them to think clearly. The therapist will be more effective with such clients by simply *drilling* them in rational coping statements such as those recommended by Meichenbaum (1985), and by using opérant principles to encourage the client to exercise these rational replacements between therapy sessions.

The "it's-not-working" client. The statement that "It's not working" is common among clients who are beginning to learn REBT and are impatient to experience change. Here are four sample therapist-client interactions that illustrate this problem and provide some suggestions for dealing with it:

C: I say to myself, "I don't *have* to, I want to," but it does not make me any calmer.

T: Well, Jim, that just indicates that you have not really given up the *must.*

C: How do I do that?

T: By looking for your irrational beliefs and disputing them. Ask yourself, "Where's the evidence?" Be a scientist. We do not merely accept the fact that the world is round because it sounds good, but because of the data. Where is the evidence that you *must* do well in school?

C: I know it *intellectually,* but I don't feel any different.

T: When you say you know it "intellectually," what you really mean is that you know it *some* of the time *weakly.* But most of the time you believe your irrational belief *strongly.* Do you dispute with yourself *convincingly?*

C: I guess I could work harder at it.

T: Right, and you won't believe it strongly until you begin to *live* it, to *act* on it. Now, what could you *do* this week to prove to yourself that you do not need Mary's love?

C: I know that the rational beliefs make sense, but I cannot feel it when I am actually in the situation.

T: Well, you cannot feel more relaxed unless you rehearse a lot *before* you get into the situation. Let's practice how you will handle your anxiety right now, to set a model for you.

C: I understand this disputation stuff, but I don't know how to do it when I am not with you. I still get anxious and then I start obsessing.

T: Well, Maria, the trick is to use your symptoms as a cue to start the chain: use your anxiety as a cue to think things through! "I'm obsessing. Why am I obsessing? Am I trying to avoid anxiety? What am I anxious about? Some beliefs I am holding. What are my irrational beliefs? Now I'll start to dispute them." So, you see how your symptoms are tied together. Your obsessions are partly an avoidance behavior to distract you from your anxiety. Instead of distracting yourself, use them as a signal to face your anxiety and uproot it. Now you repeat that to me so I can see if you have it.

The point of the examples above is that clients frequently hold to a false dichotomy, that there are intellectual versus emotional insights. The idea of an emotional insight runs counter to the most basic principle of REBT, which is that thinking largely *causes* emotion. In addition, an "emotional insight" is a non sequitur; people do not achieve insight viscerally. When the client claims he or she has intellectual but not emotional insight, the therapist reinterprets this claim as either a problem of "knowing" but not "believing" the rational ideas or of inconsistency of beliefs across time. The solution in either case is clarification and harder work for the therapeutic dyad.

Now that we have covered the basics of the disputational process, you have a blueprint that will help you to build a more elaborate structure. The work of the

REBT therapist does not end with disputation, however. The product in disputation is not necessarily to get rid of the distressing Activating event, but to help the client to accept it if it cannot be changed or to calmly and methodically try to change it if this is possible. Thus, more work might be needed in and out of session. In the next chapter, we will focus on some of this in-session work.

CAUTIONS

If your clients have achieved some control over their emotional distress, you can warn them to avoid holding perfectionistic standards in this new skill. Thus, if one client says that she thinks she can now control her anger, ask, "How long do you think it will be before you get angry again?" This question not only poses a gentle warning but also can help the client prepare for this probability. If you omit this step, the client might become discouraged the next time she does become angry, and consequently devalue the gains made in therapy and no longer dispute when she is in troublesome situations. You will recall that a major tenet in rational emotive behavioral theory is that all people think both rationally *and* irrationally. With hard work, we can increase the proportion of time spent in rational thinking, but we can never expect to think completely rationally at all times.

In addition, there are often advantages to be attained by displays of strong emotion, and even if clients can think rationally, they need not give up these benefits. When clients discover the insights of REBT, they sometimes make absolutist demands of their new rational beliefs and decide, for example, that they must never behave angrily again. A tenet of assertiveness training, however, is to escalate assertive behaviors until one gets what one wants.

Ellis described a personal incident as an example in which assertive behaviors were not effective, whereas threatening, acerbic remarks were instrumental in getting others to comply with his requests. When he changed offices, new slipcovers were ordered, and were scheduled to be delivered six weeks later. This date came and went, but no slipcovers appeared. One assertive phone call later, he was promised delivery. The next week the scene was repeated, but another assertive phone call failed to change the laxity of the firm's service. Weeks later, when the man on the phone insisted that Ellis had to pick up the slipcovers himself now that they were, at long last, ready, he forcefully and deliberately suggested that he would be happy to remove the gentleman's "fornicating gonads" if the slipcovers did not arrive within the hour. The slipcovers arrived. The point of the story is that Ellis *acted angrily,* but claims he did not actually feel angry. He knew that a *show* of anger would probably promptly get him what he wanted; so he feigned it. Clients who fail to discriminate between feelings and actions might frequently not get what they want, since strong language can be an important tool when dealing with "difficult customers" such as credit agencies, the phone company, government bureaucracies, and the like.

Another distortion occasionally encountered occurs when a client uses the concept of personal responsibility for one's emotional reactions as a justification for obnoxious social behavior. In one case of marital counseling, for example, the husband refused to deal with relationship issues, would not compromise on requests for behavior change, and continued to annoy his wife. He rationalized his behavior by claiming that she was responsible for her reactions and her problems; if she was upset, she was doing it to herself. The wife, on the other hand, was evaluating his behavior quite rationally and (in the opinion of the therapist) was appropriately annoyed. Although the husband correctly understood the basic principle of REBT, he did not understand that rational thinkers could have negative feelings and want to change the A. Although the husband was not causing his wife's C, he was nevertheless a component of A and had responsibility for the marriage. REBT distinguishes between not *causing* but still *contributing* to a C by being obnoxious to someone at A. In reality, this man was demanding that his wife have no objections to his behavior and was misusing rational emotive behavioral theory to justify his position. The therapeutic response to this misinterpretation of REBT involved teaching him that marriage is a social contract, and although it is not necessary to behave ethically and responsibly, it is clearly *advantageous* to do so. The advisability of living within social contracts is a key element in rational emotive behavioral philosophy.

Although the client in the above example was misusing REBT principles, rational emotive behavioral theory holds that we are not *totally* responsible for other people's emotions. The client might clearly have the responsibility for being an activating event for another person but does not bear full responsibility for the other's emotional distress. Our behavior might not please others, but it is their own self-statements that cause their misery. If the client already understands that others do not cause his or her personal misery, this understanding might provide the most direct route to challenging any subsequent statements that indicate the converse supposition that the client directly produced misery in others. For example:

C: I feel guilty because he is so upset.
T: Now, wait a minute, Gail. You can't have it both ways. If you are responsible for your bad feelings, then so is he for his. He might not like what you did. However, if he is upset, how are you responsible for his upset?

The notion of *total responsibility* is crucial and you can teach the client as in this therapeutic segment below. "Are you making yourself totally responsible for someone else's problems? If it's a young child, you are somewhat responsible; but, for example, when your nineteen-year-old gets into drugs, your attitude had better be, "Well, I don't like that he's into drugs and I'll do what I can to influence him, but in the final analysis I can't control his behavior, and he will have to take the consequences." When the situation involves two adults, the nutty idea might take the form, "If I do this, then he'll be happy; if I don't, he'll be miserable. I therefore have to act the way he wants to prevent his misery." What's wrong with such a notion?

Again, mini-experiments might help to get the point across. The following example deals with a young widow who wanted to take her small daughter on holiday to visit a sailor she had met. Her idea met with great displeasure from her mother-in-law, who carried on in the following way: "What a bad person you are! Your husband is not cold in his grave yet. How dare you take the child to strangers at a holiday time?" The daughter-in-law was suffused with guilt, concluding that her idea of the trip had led directly to the older woman's upset and that she was therefore a rotten person. The challenge went as follows:

T: Let's do the experiment. Tell *me* you are going on a trip and see how I respond.
C: (complies)
T: That is great! (pause) So, your going on a trip cannot produce upset in others. It is your mother-in-law's irrational beliefs that make her upset. You cannot be totally responsible for the fact that she is upset.

Notice that the young woman's dilemma can be construed in terms of the ethical principles discussed earlier in rational emotive behavioral philosophy. The optimal choice is both pro-self and pro-social, and would mean pleasing both herself and her mother-in-law. There are times, however, when such choices are simply not available, as in this case. What is the client to do? She can either stay at home and please the mother-in-law or go to Italy and please herself. If she takes total responsibility for the mother-in-law's feelings, she will probably stay home, but if she realizes that her mother-in-law is creating her own unhappiness, this understanding might put a different light on the client's decision and help her to make a choice that is both ethical and rational.

We are *not* advocating that clients act in callous disregard of the feelings of other people. However, to make life decisions based only on how others feel and to take total responsibility for their feelings is both unrealistic and personally unsatisfying. The goal in REBT is to live compatibly with others and yet not be subservient to them.

Analogies might also be useful. The therapist could ask the client to contemplate going up to one hundred different people and telling each one, "My, you're ugly!" Does the client imagine that each of the one hundred people would feel miserable? Probably not. A variety of reactions, in fact, is more likely to ensue, including depression, pity, even mirth.

Box 14.5

As an exercise, list the cognitions that might lead to these three emotional consequences. Then see if you can expand the list further.

Depression
Pity
Mirth

CONCLUSION

We conclude our three-chapter discussion of disputation by providing a detailed transcript of a therapy session with a thirty-seven-year-old woman. In this meeting, therapist and client establish the A-B-Cs of a problem emotion, and the therapist helps the client to dispute her irrational demands.

T: Let's check up on things. We were talking last time about your mother. What is the progress report?

C: Well, the exact day after I sat here and talked to you about not letting my mom bully me—in the sense of just trying to ignore it and not reacting—the next morning was like a major explosion. You know, I don't even know if it pays to go into all this, the details of it, but it ended up with my mother physically attacking me, my brother coming between us, and my mother pretending to faint right on the floor, kicking her feet and banging her hands on her head and pulling out her hair!

T: A temper tantrum?

C: Right. For two days she ignored me and then pretended that it didn't happen and—OK, so that's a given—I'm living with my mother, who is really neurotic, who is going to be picking on me until I leave and there's no way out of that, really. I mean, that's given. I have tried to channel, you know, my upsets about that and many other things into my studying. I mean, just in the sense of the harder I work, the faster I will get out, and the quicker I will have money. I see it as just alleviating so many difficulties, though not all, but many of them, so if I just sit here and study and study and study I will work my way out of this situation.

T: Let me ask you a question. Are you saying that in a helpful or nonhelpful way? You see, if you are still allowing yourself to get overly upset about your mother's behavior and are still viewing your situation as horrible, then you might be working frantically. You might be saying, "I have to work faster, I have to work faster—the horror is still too close!" Is that true for you? Are you doing good work when you sit down to study?

C: Well...

T: Or are you working frantically?

C: I'm doing that. I go, "I've got to hurry up and get out of here." I really am. The nit-picking is what gets to me. It is as if she cannot come out and say, "Gee, I really don't like you and I wish that you weren't here." Although she says that, too, when she gets mad, at the times she is not saying it, she is showing it in other ways.

T: It is not pleasant to be living with somebody who does not want you around. Remember, we talked about this last time—about the three different categories of things that she does. Sometimes she says, "I don't like you, I wish you would get out of the house." Some comments are innuendos, and others perhaps no one else would react to, but you do because you are sensitized to react to them.

C: I try to sort them out. I mean, I have been hanging around you long enough to know at least to try to be rational about my problems, but it does not really stop the initial flow of rage and hurt. The feeling comes, and I start saying, "Well, even if she doesn't like me, even if she's showing obvious preference to my brother," things like that…

T: Then what? Finish the end of the sentence.

C: That it does not mean that I am not a good person.

T: Her opinion is just her opinion.

C: But at the same time, the anger is still there, and when I'm alone and when I'm riding the train and thoughts are just flowing through my mind, the anger comes over me to the point where I…I really have very vicious fantasies about her.

T: OK, let me stop you for a minute. It sounds as if you are doing one very good thing. It sounds like when she starts her routine and you find yourself reacting to it, you do a good thing—which is using your emotional reaction as a signal. You say, "Oops, I'm overreacting."

C: I do that. I did that after the fight. But the next morning (proceeds to tell another story of an encounter with her mother)—and then she came flying at me. "Get out of my house. I hate you!" And then it escalated into a big fight. Therefore, I lost my temper and in that case, I was human. Because I was angry. It was building up for a week.

T: OK, so you are not perfect.

C: No.

T: But let me get back to what I think one of the problems is. As I listen to you, it seems that sometimes you are quite good at this rational self-talk and other times it is not working. Let's problem solve and see when it is not working and *why*. Now, you said that at the time your mother was acting crazy with you, you were able to say to yourself, "Well, her opinion is her opinion. If she thinks I'm a shit, that doesn't make me a shit." Those kinds of self-statements are very useful for counteracting a specific kind of emotion. Can you figure out what emotion that would be?

*The therapist is helping the client to discriminate the **B**s and **C**s for two separate emotional problems.*

C: Well, I guess feeling hurt—or putting myself down because someone else is criticizing me.

T: Exactly. Self put-down is depression. But those cognitions, those very helpful thoughts are not going to help in *anger* because there is a different set of irrational thoughts that are going on—different from depression. So, it is like taking the wrong medicine.

C: Do you think that it fits into this kind of therapy—the idea that suppressed anger becomes depression? Because I have heard that said.

T: I have heard it said, too. Let's put it this way: I don't think that anger *expressed* is any more useful than anger *repressed*. The key to success is not whether you say it or do not say it, have your temper tantrum, or do not have your temper tantrum, but to uproot the anger itself from its antecedents. You uproot it from its causes, just as you did with your depression. You get to the head talk. You have some good coping techniques for depression; now let's develop some coping techniques for the anger, OK?

C: OK.

T: First, let's do an A-B-C analysis of the situation. A, mother does something, and C, you feel anger, not depression. What are some of the **B**s you can imagine?

C: When I feel angry?

T: Anger. Not depression.

C: OK.

T: Look for a "must" again.

C: Well, I must not be in this situation where someone is being so unjust to me.

T: OK, that is a good thought to be in touch with. Now, is that an anger-provoking thought? It sounds like a poor-me thought.

C: Yeah.

T: Poor-me's don't get you angry.

C: Well, my mother must be understanding.

T: That is usually where it falls. Anger is directed outward, not at yourself, but outward. It's mother "should." "Mother shouldn't yell at me; she shouldn't say nasty things." Any others you can think of?

C: (tells another brief story of an incident at home)

T: OK, stop there. What is the irrational belief?

C: All right. Even though they are treating me that way—they *are* treating me that way. The reality is that my brother is definitely preferred.

T: And what is the irrational belief?

C: That it doesn't mean that I am the way they see me.

T: No, what is the irrational idea that you are saying? Do you know?

C: Somehow, because I allow myself to be treated that way, it really turns me into that kind of a person. And if I really had pride, self-respect, or common sense, I could turn it around so that it wouldn't be that way.

T: That is your depression, your saying to yourself "poor-me" and "bad-me" thoughts. Let's leave those aside for the moment. What is the anger belief? Not only should she not yell at you and say nasty things to you, but also how "must" she treat you?

C: Well, she should treat me as an equal member of the family.

T: She *should* treat you fairly and squarely. These are some of your shoulds. We know from rational emotive behavioral theory that shoulds and musts are where the trouble is; your belief is that your mother *should* not do those things, that she *should* treat you fairly.

C: I also have those shoulds for myself. I should not yell at my mother. I should not express any temper or dissatisfaction in ways that are going to make people uncomfortable. When inwardly, I really want to go in there and let her have it and say, "What is this crap, I mean, here he's been lying in bed all year and you've been telling me the reason is that he's paying you money, and then you're telling him that you're giving it all back to him."

T: That would be good to say if you were not in a rage but were merely determined to try to change what could be changed. If you did those things assertively, you could do them better, more efficiently. But let's go back—we have an A, a B, and a C.

C: OK.

T: We have the anger and the anger cognitions, which are all those *musts*. Now let's do a D. What are some questions you want to ask yourself about this?

C: Why can't I tell her what to think? This is a big question to me. The fact that I have so much anger and that I just absolutely cannot find words to begin to say, "This is a raw deal." I do not know how to go about it, whether I approach my brother or my mother.

T: Wait. That is another issue. That's the "you" issue. We want the "them" issue. Those people out there who are treating you unfairly and your anger about that. First, do you agree that you would like to give up your anger? Not your determination, but your anger.

C: OK. At this point, I feel that it would really be sick not to resent it or to feel anger. It is justified at this point.

T: If you are asking, "Are you trying to get me to feel nothing or to just joyfully accept this horse shit?" I would say, "No, that's crazy." You would be crazy to be happy about it. But I don't see that getting *angry* about it is doing you any good. For that reason, I think it would be best to get rid of the rage and bring it down to where you can say, "I don't like this and I'm going to do what I can about it. I'm going to try to change the situation." After all, what does anger do for you? It gets your stomach churning and it is not good for your system, physiologically.

C: No, for a week I have been walking around definitely feeling all those physical things. And I try to hold it in so I just get really quiet and I don't want to talk to anybody, and then they get on my case that I'm depressed.

T: OK, so let's work on the anger. It has been a while since we have done an A-B-C-D formally, so let's sort of review. When you do D, you go back to the nutty ideas one by one, and you ask yourself questions.

C: Why *should* my mother be fair to me?

T: Right! Where is the evidence that your mother should act nicely to you?

C: I don't know. Going to school, I see so many people at home living well. They are running around with the family charge card and they are doing whatever they want to do, and everybody is kissing their ass and they think it is the greatest thing.

T: I absolutely agree that that would be nice. But why *should* your mother do that?

C: Why *should* she? (pause) I think she *should*! She *should* be fair.

T: Why?

C: Just because I want her to. (laughs)

The therapist has allowed the client to repeatedly struggle with the question rather than answering it for her.

T: That is right. "She *must* do what I want her to do." Where is that going to get you?

C: Hmmmmm.

T: Now I am agreeing 100% that it would be nice if your mother treated you fairly. It would be pleasant, it would make your life simpler, and it would be advantageous to you. Your life would be much easier if you had rich, loving parents who treated you fairly. We could prove that. We could do the experiment and prove that advantage. Could we do an experiment to prove why your mother *should* do that? Why does she *have to* do that?

The therapist never disputes the client's claim that it would be advantageous to have what she wants, merely the demand that it be so.

C: It's possible at some level—she is not that stupid—that if she realizes it, it can't make *her* feel good. I mean, how can a mother feel good about being unfair?

T: Right. So maybe it would even be nicer for *her* if she treated you fairly.

C: Right, it might be.

T: But why *must* she? Even though it would be good for you and maybe good for her, why does she *have* to do what would be nice for you?

The therapist repeats the same disputation.

C: OK, so she doesn't have to.

T: I do not think you believe that.

C: One thing that helps me is to think, "Well, it's not my fault, the fact is that she's doing that." And the fact is that she doesn't have to be fair, and it is not really my job to make her fair, and I don't exist in this time and place to straighten my mother out and make her realize how important it is to be fair.

T: That is right. But if you don't really work hard at giving up the belief that "she's *got* to," you are going to be, first of all, continually disappointed in her, trying to control her....

C: Once in despair, I was talking about this with my father. And she has been very domineering toward him all his life and picked on him unfairly, and he told me frankly, "I've found that the best way to deal with her is to submit. That's how I cope." And, it's true. Any observer in my home for three days would look at this man and say, "He is a slave and servant, and demeans himself rather than confront her."

T: OK, let me ask you a question. Does he upset himself? Is he quiet but seething inside, or is he philosophic about it?

C: For years, I think he walked around exactly as I did; nursing a lot of inner hurts but not expressing them.

T: Now?

C: Now he seems to have accepted her behavior and decided that this is the easiest way to behave back. My way of dealing is...I find obsequiousness very bad. If she acts in a very domineering way, it does mean that I must act in a very obsequious way. That is unpleasant.

T: I hear you saying, "It's good that my father isn't upsetting himself about her nuttiness any longer. He lays back and it rolls off him." He is not trying to train her or shape her up by confronting her.

C: Right.

T: First, that tells me there is a good reason for her not to change at all. She has had years of training and reinforcement.

C: Right! Having everyone in the family submit to her.

T: So, if you decide to challenge the system, it is going to be a tough job at best. You are going to try to retrain this woman who has had sixty-some years of reinforcement for her behavior. You are going to have a tough job. That knowledge might help you make your decision about whether or not to stand up to her—is it worth it?

C: Right.

T: Another thing I hear, however, is your choice of words to describe your father's behavior—obsequious, slavish. That he is a schlemiel; people walk all over him. That is *your* perception you are talking about.

C: Right. This has played a very big part in determining the kind of men I have been attracted to. I could never stand a guy who would do whatever I said. I watched my father do that for so many years and I did get that impression of him.

T: Right. However, that is a perception. Now, what I am suggesting is, if you were to try to *objectively* describe your father's behavior, without using words like obsequious that are rather negative or pejorative, how would you very objectively describe what he does?

C: Hmmmm. Objectively. When my mother attacks my father without any just cause, he does not defend himself and he does not attack back.

T: What *does* he do?

C: He either remains quiet or says a very gentle "now-now, dear," but then proceeds to do what she tells him to do.

T: And then the issue blows over?

C: It blows over but it is a constant thing. Not just once a day, but from the second you enter to the second you leave her presence. It is a barrage. Nothing but orders.

T: So your father lets her do that, he goes along with her requests, but he also does not *upset* himself. He is not stewing. So he has made his own kind of adaptation.

C: Right.

T: There are two components to adaptation. First, what he does internally, his emotional turmoil; and second, what he does on the outside, how he responds behaviorally.
The therapist is helping the client to empathically understand her father's behavior.

C: OK.

T: What I hear you saying is, maybe the emotional reaction is OK. His apparent ability to not upset himself about his crazy wife is something you would like to acquire. Be philosophical and let her be her nutty self.

C: Right. But not follow the same behavior patterns.

T: Right.

C: Because I find that image of myself is unpleasant. I have found that often I do just give tit for tat. When she starts digging at me, I dig back.

T: Let me suggest that maybe we could look at the behaviors as a separate issue—as a series of *strategies*. Step one, however, is still the same. You want to get over the rage. Once you accomplish that, you can probably problem-solve the situation better. "Let's see, I can try experiments. I can try retorting and see how that works. I can try reinforcing better behavior and see how that works. I can try doing what my father does and shutting up and doing whatever she asks, and see what that does. I can try being very assertive and confronting her. I could try giving her lectures. I could try giving her books to read." You might try strategies. If a strategy does not work after a reasonable effort, you end the experiment and say, "Well, that didn't affect her behavior, I'll try something else." All of these are strategies—they are just behaviors.

C: They're good, though, because they make me feel empowered. I could try this or that.

T: Yes, like a scientist. But a scientist is never going to be a good scientist if she is demanding that the data come out the way she wants!

The therapist is pointing out why an inelegant solution would not be appropriate.

C: Yeah.

T: As long as you are *demanding* that your mother change her behavior, you are going to be angry with her.

C: Yeah.

T: Step one is to give up the demand, give up the anger, and then try strategies and experiments. So the best thing to do is to give up the *shoulds*. If you can really believe what you said, that she does not have to change...that she might never change....

C: You're right. She is definitely not going to change!

T: She might or she might not. You can try strategies. But if you can give up the *shoulds*, the *demand* that she change, and absorb some of your father's philo-sophical ideas—"That's the way she is for now; she doesn't seem to want to change and she's not motivated to change, and me sitting back demanding that she change..."

The therapist is using the father as a rational model.

C: When you say it, I really see it! I feel what you are saying.

T: So you can imagine that if you can just remember this stuff and say it to yourself between sessions, you will be OK. There is a great book, *Overcoming Frustration and Anger,* by Paul Hauck. Another useful book is *How to Live With—and Without—Anger,* by Albert Ellis. If you could read either of these, it would reinforce what we did today.

C: I really feel better. I really do. I mean, it just went from this huge horrible thing to—well, she is just herself, and that is the way she is—tough noodles!

T: Bravo! That is fantastic! That is emotional proof that you can make disputing work.

C: Yeah.

T: What you had better do is work hard at remembering to do it between our meetings.

C: OK.

T: That is why a good book is a handy thing to have.

15

Therapeutic Styles: the How not the What in Disputing Beliefs Using an Active Directive Style

As a group, REBT therapists can be distinguished from therapists of most other schools by their active, directive style. Because REBT therapists work with a model of identifying, challenging, and replacing self-defeating thought patterns, they likely ask more closed-ended questions rather than open-ended questions. Key words, phrases, intonations, and nonverbal aspects of the client's behavior often trigger hypotheses in the therapist concerning what the client might be thinking or feeling. Although the therapist might open the questioning to such cues with open-ended questions, they will follow up with more focused, closed-ended questions that are designed to test the therapist's hypotheses. We envision the therapist as engaging in a Socratic dialogue to focus the client in certain directions, or as a kind of herd dog who guides the client through an open field full of distractions, keeping the client on course.

Active Directive therapy works as a dual-edged sword. On the one hand it renders therapy more effective and efficient; on the other hand it allows for the opportunity to make many more errors. Nondirectively reflecting the client's feelings and watching for important information to emerge from a few well-placed open-ended questions might be inefficient, but the therapist has fewer opportunities to say something offensive that will disrupt the therapeutic alliance. Therapists can ask too many questions too rapidly, without allowing the client sufficient time to reflect on the answer they just gave. They can stack their questions; asking several in a sequence before the client has had time to answer the first one. They can talk too much. They can engage in long monologues, as if they were a late-night talk show host. They can lecture, without getting feedback as to whether the client understands what they are teaching. They can give too much practical advice and collude with the client in avoiding the elegant, philosophical solution to the problem. New therapists often take the active directive style recommendations of REBT as a license. When we listen to recordings of such therapists drone on, we often break into a rendition of the Joe Jones 1961 rock 'n' roll song, "You Talk Too

Much." This chapter focuses on the appropriate or effective styles of doing active directive REBT, and how to avoid the errors that frequently come from practicing such a style.

Practical Advice. It is easy for active therapists to fall into the "advice trap," in which they either give clients practical solutions to their problems or recommend a particular solution. Recall from previous chapters that we distinguish between the practical and the emotional solutions to clients' problems. Practical solutions change the As, and emotional solutions change Cs. REBT is not opposed to helping clients use practical solutions to change the noxious As in their lives. Sometimes we will recommend the practical solution first and other times we will recommend that the therapist engage in practical solutions *after* they work on the emotional solution. Even when we help clients with practical solutions, we try to teach social problem solving skills rather than give clients the specific thing to do. It is important to help clients see that they have choices, and to teach them that brainstorming and problem solving are skills that they can learn, particularly when they understand how not to upset themselves. This concept of problem-solving as a skill is consistent with the goal of ultimately encouraging independence from the therapist and will be discussed more fully in Chapter 17. Active directive psychotherapy does not mean advice giving.

Didactic Assessment of the Bs. In Chapter 9, we discussed strategies to assess clients' IBs. Overly active and directive therapists often become impatient with this process, because the clients' irrational belief is not so clear to them. Therapists will want to avoid "planting" the irrational statements in the client's conversation that REBT theory suggests will be present. Telling clients what they are thinking is not active-directive therapy; it is a poor technique, and likely to result in a rupture in the therapeutic alliance. If therapists do make such suggestions to the client, they will want to speak tentatively and test that the client endorses and experiences these ideas. Thus, the therapist might say, "It sounds like you're saying you *must* do X; have I heard you correctly?"

It is preferable to draw out the irrational beliefs by phrasing questions in a guided manner. For example:

NOT: Why did you get angry?

BUT: What did you tell yourself to make yourself angry?

OR: Did you get angry because you were telling yourself something about the way you were treated?

NOT: What is related to your problems with power struggles?

BUT: What do you tell yourself to upset yourself when you find you are in a power struggle?

OR: Are you upsetting yourself because you're telling yourself something about the importance of winning when you're in a power struggle?

NOT: So you believe that he must love you?

BUT: What do you think about his not loving you?

OR: How do you evaluate him not loving you? Could you be awfulizing?

Thus, instead of suggesting ideas to clients (e.g., "You are demanding."), try to lead them to discover the ideas by themselves by questions such as, "What were you telling yourself?" Questions, rather than answers, put the responsibility for therapy properly on the client.

NOT: That's not true!
BUT: How do you know that's true?
OR: What evidence do you have that that's true?
OR: What could possibly convince you that it's *not* true?

DIDACTIC LECTURE VERSUS SOCRATIC DIALOGUE

In Chapter 10, we presented two different modes of presenting REBT principles: a lecture format and Socratic dialogue. Because REBT is a psycho-educational philosophy and therapy, many people are helped by learning REBT principles from lectures, workshops, books, blogs, and other types of presentations. Ellis helped literally thousands of people overcome their emotional disturbance through such formats. The lecturer directly imparts information to clients about how people cause their own disturbances, and uses explanatory devices such as parables, analogies, and metaphors to make the point. The lecture also teaches why some ideas are irrational and others are more rational. REBT has long advocated that clients learn the principles through any and all of these formats in the initial stages of therapy. In fact, this strategy of presenting people with psycho-education before individual or group therapy is common in all forms of CBT and is referred to as *Low Intensity Interventions* (Bennett-Levy et al., 2010). Such interventions make sense from a public health delivery perspective. Some people will be helped by such inexpensive psycho-educational procedures. By providing them first, we reserve the more expensive psychotherapy for those who fail to benefit from the psycho-education. We strongly encourage our readers to create such low intensity REBT programs. The same argument can be made concerning advocating psycho-education procedures in psychotherapy. Psychotherapy is more of a participatory and relational activity, and clients might have expectations about how they are treated in therapy. It is advisable that some didactic presentation take place in therapy, because it is an efficient way to transmit information. Didactic presentations are more appropriate in early sessions to familiarize clients with the basic principles of REBT. They might be helpful with clients of certain cultural backgrounds who expect professionals to intervene actively, or with clients with lower intellectual ability or neurological impairment who tend to require more structure. Didactic presentations can be appropriate when the client's problem results from ignorance about a particular topic.

The use of didactic presentations requires caution. If you give a lecture, even an excellent one, what is your client doing with the information? Probably what most students do: putting it in a (mental) notebook and filing it away for the next test—in this case, the next therapy session. Be aware of this tendency and return to ideas you discussed earlier and ask questions about the ideas to ensure that the client is "with you." Do not proceed to the next point until you are certain that the client has understood the previous one. Also, give behavioral homework assignments to ensure that the client actively utilizes the lecture material (see Chapter 16).

Therefore, psychotherapy will use less intense psycho-educational activities than other formats and has the advantage of having them be followed up with more exploratory questioning to help the client change. The therapist using Socratic dialogue relies on evocative questions to guide the client to an insight or an appropriate conclusion. Socratic dialogue, therefore, is a slower and more methodical procedure. Socratic dialogue results in clients discovering the ideas for themselves, and they are thereby more willing to own them and will have less resistance to the new RBs. Both techniques have value as educational devices, but the knowledgeable practitioners recognize their limitations.

Socratic dialogue has many advantages as an aid to learning and recall. Psychological research on the relative effectiveness of recall versus recognition memory suggests that getting the client to *generate* appropriate cognitions via Socratic dialogue will produce superior retention in comparison to lecturing, which merely allows the client to *recognize* appropriate cognitions. Whereas the didactic format consists of unequally weighted sequential monologues, in Socratic dialogue, the client expresses the therapeutic material in his or her own words and will recall it in this same modality, thus encouraging retention. This might be a good time to review the discussion of Socratic questioning in Chapter 10.

Contrast the following two presentations:

Didactic Presentation

"Well, Shonda, you seem upset and anxious about your mother not approving of you. Let me spend a little time explaining to you what causes people to feel anxious. Most people believe that they are made anxious by the things that happen to them. You believe that your anxiety is caused by your mother's disapproval. Actually, we don't think that is true. People usually get upset about things because of what they think about them. For example, if one hundred people were experiencing the same disapproval from their mothers, they would not all feel the same way. Some would feel happy or relieved that their mother did not care for them and left them alone. Others would feel terribly upset and suicidal. And, still others would feel indifferent. There could be a whole range of reactions. So the activating event, and what your mother is doing to you, does not cause all these different reactions. It is what you think—your beliefs. Now, different kinds of beliefs cause different kinds of emotions. Illogical or irrational beliefs that exaggerate things cause disturbed emotions, and rational, logical beliefs cause more healthy, nondisturbed emotions."

Box 15.1

Examine your own behavior when you attend a lecture. What are you doing? Not much, right? You are sitting silently, perhaps nodding your head in agreement and occasionally taking notes. These are quite passive behaviors and illustrate the advisability of not limiting your therapeutic interventions only to lecturing.

Listen to a therapy session in which you have done some didactic presentation. Try to ascertain whether the client understood your major points. What could you have done to assess the client's understanding?

Socratic Dialogue

T: OK, Shonda, I understand you feel anxious when your mother picks on you or when you think about your mother picking on you. Now, where do you think that anxiety comes from?

C: Well, from my mother, of course. If she would stop picking on me then I wouldn't feel anxious!

T: Well, it does seem that way, but there are some people who do not feel anxious when their mothers criticize them. Now, why don't those other people feel anxious when they experience the same event?

C: Because they do not have to live with their mothers!

T: Well, let's assume they do. Let's assume that there is a group of people with hostile picky mothers whom they have to live with and they do not feel anxious or upset about it. Now, what would be the difference with them?

C: Well, maybe their mothers do not do as many mean things to them as my mother does to me.

T: That could be. The word "mean" is very important, isn't it? Because it is the meaning we put on situations, in this case your mother's behavior that leads to our emotions. What meaning do you think you are putting on your mother's behavior?

C: (pause) That's a hard question.

T: But you're obviously not thinking, "Oh, it is fine that she acts that way. I'm really pleased." Are you?

C: Oh, no!

T: What are you saying?

C: It's not nice at all! It's terrible that she's acting that way! She has to like me. I mean, you need a mother's love.

T: That's right! You're saying it's awful or horrible that she's acting that way. Now we call that "awfulizing" and it's an example of an irrational idea. And irrational ideas lead to upsetting, dysfunctional emotions.

If you speak primarily in declarative sentences (as in a lecture format) rather than ask questions (as in Socratic dialogue), you run two major risks. First, you could slip into the role of "expert," who, for example, could be viewed as responsible for holding the client's marriage together. Thus, the declarative style could oversell to clients so that they unthinkingly accept the therapist's judgment or rely on the therapist to solve their problems. Another disadvantage is that you might set up ideas that clients will perversely deny or debate, even if they are quite correct. Questions are usually the better way to elicit material from clients and to help them learn to help themselves. In order to do Socratic dialogue, however, it is necessary to learn how to ask good questions.

We have found that people who come to REBT after practicing Psychodynamic, Rogerian, or Existential psychotherapies are often too nondirective. They have rehearsed nondirective techniques, and they overestimate the negative impact more activity on their part will have on the client. For them we advocate collecting the data. What happens when you increase your degree of directiveness? Therapists who come to practice REBT as graduate students or new professionals usually are too directive and we need to slow them down a bit in supervision.

As therapy progresses across sessions, you will likely use fewer didactic presentations and more Socratic questions. This allows the clients to generate the answers to their questions. In the real world, when they face an A, they will only cope if they can generate the challenges to their IBs or think their new RBs. Socratic questioning helps them practice this generating process. You might return to using more didactic presentations in later sessions if a client brings up a new problem. However, you will soon reduce the number of them and increase the Socratic questions.

Box 15.2

Listen to some of your recent therapy recordings, paying attention to who did most of the talking. Was it you or the client? Are you lecturing too much? Or are you talking too little? What is your purpose in doing either?

Now, pick two clients and decide on one therapeutic style for the first client and another for the second client, either Socratic dialogue or didactic presentation. Use that style to present a point that you want the client to understand in the next session. Then record the sessions. Later, review them to determine whether you met your objectives in each session. Which worked best in communicating your point?

FORM OF THE QUESTIONS

The form in which therapists pose questions is important, and a common error made by therapists new to REBT is to begin too many questions with the word "why." "Why" questions are difficult to answer; the responses are often redundant, simply reiterating why the client came to therapy. Why questions involve asking about motives. They draw out the purpose the person had for behaving or the ultimate or proximate causes of the behavior. "Why" questions will generate client reports about the As that preceded their unhealthy disturbed emotions, or the ultimate cause of their disturbance, such as the way their parents treated them. REBT usually wants to understand the process of what happened at A and what the client thought and felt. Here are some examples of changing WHY questions into WHAT or HOW questions.

NOT: Why are you anxious?
BUT: What do you think triggers your anxiety?

OR: Are you aware that you are in control of your anxiety?

OR: How do you think you got yourself anxious?

As a handy substitute for "why," the therapist can reach for a "how" question.

Proposing hypothetical scenarios might also be a useful device. For a client who fears certain life events, the therapist might say, for example, "What would you do if tomorrow morning you woke up and were married (or lost your job, etc.)?" These examinations of hypothetical events could aid not only in obtaining cognitive samples but also in directly reducing the client's avoidance of the feared situation. Another example, from a depressed client who suffered from headaches:

"Suppose you went to a neurologist today, and he gave you a new miracle drug that took away your headaches. Tomorrow you would wake up and have no headaches. How would that change your life? How would you cope?"

Such questions also serve as mini-extinction procedures, resembling low items on a desensitization hierarchy. That is, clients might be avoiding a specific issue or undertaking in their lives, and confronting it on a verbal level is less fear-provoking than engaging in more direct behaviors.

MAINTAINING THE FOCUS ON THE PROBLEM

A primary and often difficult task for the therapist is to keep the client focused on the problem. Many therapists assume that digressions are a sign of pathological resistance or of avoidance of upsetting topics. Although this could sometimes be the case, it is more likely that your clients are simply displaying normal social behavior. To illustrate this point to yourself, monitor some social conversations with a friend or colleague, and note how many different topics are discussed within a twenty-minute period. The conversation most likely rambles to whatever comes to the person's mind. Therapy sessions have goals and as such the conversations need to focus on the information that will lead to the goals. Some clients need to be socialized to this aspect of therapy.

Some clients like to talk a lot and report a great deal of tangential information that focuses the therapy away from the tasks at hand and the goals of the session. To stop clients' tangential monologues or to hold back an avalanche of unnecessary information, a useful strategy is to pace questions carefully. Ask the next question as soon as the client answers the last one, even if this means interrupting the client's speech. It is difficult to guide the dialogue unless the therapist is willing to be assertive.

When you ask a question, listen carefully as to whether the client answered what you asked. See that your client answers your questions. If not consider repeating the questions. Some other reasons clients might not answer questions are:

They have not paid attention.

They have misunderstood the question.

If they have not understood a question, they might be too nonassertive to
   request clarification.
They might be avoiding a painful topic.
They might be unskilled at social conversation.
They might have poor thinking habits and think illogically or tangentially.

Repeating a question is therapeutic; it models assertiveness skills and helps
clients to learn to focus their attention or to confront anxiety-provoking situations. To ignore a non sequitur encourages the pathology. If clients repeatedly
fail to answer questions, a useful strategy is to stop their tangential thoughts and
Socratically ask how the answer relates to the question. This will give you some
information about whether the problem is an attentional deficit, an avoidance
issue, or a lack of social skills. If you have a hypothesis about why the client is
avoiding the question, offer it to the client.

Many new therapists feel uncomfortable with stopping the client's digressions
and repeating unanswered questions. They object that it is rude to redirect the client and worry that the client will be offended or even harmed. In our experience,
most clients do not object to redirection. However, if they are offended, you can
explain the rationale for the procedure in detail. The point is that therapy is not a
social engagement; with approximately forty-five minutes to work on problems,
there is limited time to accomplish the goals of the session.

Listening to recordings of therapy sessions with such clients will sharpen your
skills in detecting tangential conversations. Clients could be encouraged to do the
same, so that they learn to identify the problem behavior.

Another instance in which rephrasing or repeating your questions is helpful is when you do not understand the client's response. In such situations you
could say, "I'm not sure I follow you there; could you explain that again?" If
you do not understand the client, your silence could communicate that you do.
The client could become annoyed later, when it becomes apparent that you did
not understand a point to which they are referring. You also waste valuable and
expensive time by allowing the client to go on when you are unclear about the
message. Once again, our experience suggests that most clients are not offended
by the repetition of questions for clarification, but instead perceive the therapist more positively for behaving honestly. Both parties benefit from effective
communication.

You can increase the client's ability to stay focused by not dealing with too many
A-B-Cs in one session. It is better to take one problem area and focus on it until
you devise a new alternative rational belief and some homework, or until some
closure has been reached before moving on.

Structure the conversation tightly, limiting the discussion to just a few topics.
Use retraining procedures, including rewards for staying on the topic and penal-
ties for digressions. For example, you might say to the client, "My, you have outlined your problem well! That is good, the way you stayed on the topic; it is helpful
to us." On the other hand, you might point out, "You know, you got off the track,
and I don't understand how that follows. Explain it to me again!" As in behavioral
training, we recommend putting the emphasis on the positive reinforcers.

Keeping the client focused on the problem has additional benefits. If the client has a tendency to engage in tangential thinking, the therapist can provide important feedback and help the client avoid this behavior. Confront the client genuinely and empathically; for example:

> "Jane, I'm confused. You started out talking about topic X and now you've moved to Y. What's the relationship between them [or which do you want to talk about]?" Or "Will talking about "Y" help me understand "X"; or do you want to change the problem we are discussing from "X" to "Y."

Being able to contribute to a conversation and being able to stay with the same topic for a period are prerequisite skills for effective psychotherapy. If these skills are weak or missing, the therapist might have to begin by doing attention training, which is similar to working with a hyperkinetic child; nothing will get accomplished until you train the child to attend to a task.

Suppose, however, that the client comes in obviously intending to take over the session with a topic that you believe is a deflection from a more important unresolved issue. What should you do? First, you can give yourself permission to redirect the session by assuming that you know best about therapy. How can you redirect the session? One technique is to remind the client of the goals for the session and to make use of the Premack principle; for example:

> "Jim, I'm going to let you talk about your root canal work at the end of the session; we'll save time for that. But first, I have some very important issues that I want to discuss about your marriage."

Another approach that at least sets some limits to the client's diversions is:

> "Jim, your root canal seems to be important to you. Let's give the first five minutes to discussing your problems with your teeth and then spend the last forty minutes on the issue of your marriage."

You might also, at this point, ask clients how they feel about the redirection. If they're angry, it might be useful to ask if they experience anger in similar situations—an issue that could be relevant to the main therapeutic problem.

If you sense that the client's new issue is a distraction maneuver, you might confront the client as follows:

> "I get the sense that you're avoiding something."
> More directly, you might ask the client how this topic fits in with the avoided one:
> "Jim, how does your root canal relate with the problems in your marriage that we have discussed in our other sessions?"

Ultimately, you might want to share an interpretation of the client's behavior:

> "Jim, it seems week after week you come in with an agenda that seems to get us off the track of the original problem—your marriage! It appears to me

you might be trying to avoid that problem. What do you think you could be frightened of?"

Implementing the above procedures is difficult and requires self-monitoring and self-discipline by the therapist.

Some clients are notorious for their inability to stay focused on one problem. We have several in mind who have remained in therapy for years and have worked with two or three different trainees over a couple of years. These clients' inability to focus prevents any discussion of their irrational beliefs, any new alternative beliefs, or any new behaviors they might adapt. These clients also believe that therapy involves sharing the events of their week with the therapist. With clients who have such persistent tendency to go off the topic in response to the therapist's intervention, strong measures are needed. You might bring the problem to the client's attention by saying something like, "Lin, I have your agreement to interrupt you if you're giving me far too much information?" Thus, with the client's collaboration, you can confront the problem forcefully each time by simply saying, "Wait a minute!" to the client. A "halt" hand gesture could also be useful communication. With particularly difficult clients, the therapist might temporarily have to resort to questions that allow only yes or no answers. If you become aware that the focus has already been lost and the conversation has drifted, stop and ask yourself two basic questions:

In a few sentences, what is the client's main problem? What are the most prominent irrational beliefs?

Another useful tactic for keeping clients focused is to keep asking for specific examples of their main problem.

Some of these clients avoid focus because they view therapy as the purchase of friendship. You, their therapist, could be their only social contact. You could be the only person they see all week who listens to them. Such clients may be ill served by us providing them this social contact. It is better for us to do some practical problem solving and help them find social groups they can join, or help them make new friends. Social Skills training could be the best course of action.

REPETITION

Therapy, like teaching, often requires a certain amount of repetition. It will be important for you to repeat REBT concepts with clients, even though you might feel that you sound boring. REBT philosophy contains subtle points that many clients find difficult to understand; rehearsal is therefore very important.

Remember that you are modeling REBT skills for clients, such as learning to attend to key phrases and to examine one's internal dialogue, and these skills require repetition with most clients. Particularly in the disputation phase, you could find yourself not wanting to say the same things again and again. It is interesting to contemplate how Dr. Ellis himself managed to teach the same message to so many clients over his long career. Listening to recordings of Ellis doing therapy provides a clue; rather dramatic variation in emphasis and vocal tone serve to keep up the excitement and interest of the therapist as well as the client. In disputation (as was seen in Chapters 10, 11, and 12), you can vary your style of phrasing greatly, although you are basically training the client to ask the same questions; for example, "Where is the evidence?" or "Why is it awful?" or "Who says you must … ?"

As we pointed out in Chapter 1, change rarely comes from insight. The philosopher Spinoza was the first to advocate that rehearsal of the challenges and the new RBs in response to the As is most likely the mechanism of change in therapy (Damasio, 2003). So, it is OK to be redundant. This will provide you opportunities to think of creative ways to say the same thing.

LANGUAGE STYLE

Adjustments in language style are often made because clients vary in their level of education, acculturation, and interests.

Take the hypothetical case of a young woman, a college sophomore who is concerned about getting into a sorority. She complains of her shyness, for example, explaining that she is afraid to go up to the older, more stylishly dressed girls and initiate a conversation. It sounds to you as if she has catalogued and ranked people, and declared herself to fall below some arbitrary cutoff point. Her philosophy seems to be "some people are better than others," which is expressed in her beliefs as, "I have to be as good as they are! If they don't accept me, it proves that I'm not one of them, and that would be awful!" With this client, it might not be profitable to begin by discussing "irrational beliefs" or "philosophical tenets." You might be more direct and helpful if you took a more casual approach. The first query, therefore, might be something like, "What do you think the others would *do* if you went over to them?"

INTONATION

A significant aspect of the therapist's verbal behavior to which the REBT novice will want to attend is vocal intonation. A great deal of information about attitudes can be unwittingly communicated in this modality. Therapists want to avoid expressing horror or other value judgments when clients reveal personal information. For example, suppose the client is a young man who is discussing his feelings of guilt about not visiting his parents as often as they would like. The incautious therapist might say, "You only go once a *week?*" or "You hardly go *at all?*" Inflections of the therapist's voice could make a big difference in how the client responds to such questions.

Inflection can also be used in helping clients discriminate between rational and irrational beliefs. When you listen to one of Ellis's recorded demonstrations of REBT, notice that he used his voice as an instrument for clarification. Whenever he pronounced one of the words that signify irrational concepts (e.g., "self-downing," "awful," "terrible," "should," or "need"), he dropped his voice several notes, stretched out the word, and increased his volume, producing a dreary, dramatic sound. For example, "... and it's AWWWWWFULL that he doesn't like me!" Later, when he changed the "awful" to "unfortunate," or a "need" to a "want," Ellis again pronounced the words reflecting rational concepts, in a distinct way. He spoke the key word slowly, enunciated very clearly, and raised the pitch of his voice and the volume. Thus, different auditory stimuli become associated with different concepts, making them more salient and easier to remember. Howard Kassinove of Hofstra University has made the point of encouraging trainees in REBT to model Ellis's vocal style. He points out that variety in style is important in every therapeutic encounter; a significant shift in tone and volume increases the probability that the client will attend to and learn from the therapist.

Refocusing the client's attention is crucial when the therapist is about to make an important point. We recommend that you monitor your typical style. If you are speaking rapidly and loudly when you want to make an important point, dramatically lower your voice and slow down. If your style is typically soft-spoken, on the other hand, you will attract the client's attention by raising your volume and speed. In other words, know yourself and be prepared to adjust your inflection when it is appropriate to highlight the concepts you want to emphasize.

A second strategy is to signal an important concept by the content of your speech and the use of gestures. As in assertiveness training, leaning forward and making good eye contact are effective nonverbal cues. You can also prepare the client for a confrontation with a verbal introduction, such as, "I want to suggest something that might be new to you." If clients habitually interrupt, ask them to agree not to talk for five minutes, and hold them to this.

Ellis (2002) also thought that therapists would succeed in changing clients' IBs if their disputing was forceful. He advocated strong forceful, intense challenges to IBs and the same for communicating the RBs. Ellis did not actually define what he meant by "forceful disputing"; however, in watching recordings of his therapy sessions one can hear an increase in the volume and tension in his voice at times when he challenged IBs. No studies have tested Ellis's hypotheses by having forceful and not forceful REBT with real clients. However, some research in communications studies of attitude change support his idea. Hamilton, Hunter, and Burgoon (1990) found that intensity enhanced persuasiveness for a high credibility speaker and inhibited persuasiveness for a low credibility source. Intensity had its effect on persuasion by increasing message clarity. Thus, intensity might make the communicator speak with greater clarity, or result in the receiver perceiving more clarity in the message.

SILENCES

Silence communicates. Your silent behavior might be construed as agreement with the client. As an analogy, an Old English law states that if someone signed another's name to bills, and this went on for a period of time without the first person's objection, the wife or husband could be entitled to continue to do so, because the spouse's silence was considered consent. A similar phenomenon often occurs in conversations. For example, if the client loses focus on the problem and verbally meanders, your silence could inaccurately convey to the client that s/he is making sense or doing constructive work.

Similarly, *inconsistent* silences by the therapist might provide intermittent reinforcement for irrational beliefs, thereby prolonging their existence in the cognitive system. For example, consider a client who is depressed and makes statements such as, "I'm never going to get better." A better plan of action would be to comment on or dispute such remarks, or to paraphrase them reflectively with rational statements, such as, "It sounds like you're saying that it would be hard for you to change."

The point we want to stress is that silence is a form of communication; however, we do not always know *what* we have communicated. Clients might interpret our silences as disapproval, indifference, or agreement. It is wise, therefore, to check on your client's understanding of your silences and correct any misperceptions that you uncover. Be careful about the client statements to which you do not respond.

FLEXIBILITY

The previous sections have discussed a variety of stylistic variations in doing REBT, and it is preferable that you become comfortable with all of them, and utilize these different stylistic variations when your clinical judgment suggests their effectiveness. Try not to behave rigidly—always talking fast or slowly, always using the same intonation, always being funny or glib, or never allowing any silent periods. Rigidly adhering to one mode of behavior is not productive for your client and can be boring for you.

The injunction to be flexible is consistent with REBT philosophy in that there seems to be no absolutes and thus no absolute prescriptions in psychotherapy. (Even the belief that there are no absolutes, which is *not* an REBT dictum, is dogmatic and absolutist.) Consider some of the following absolutes from areas of clinical practice:

There can *never* be secrets in marital therapy.
In family therapy, *all* family members *must* be present at *every* session.
In sexual counseling, a complete sexual history is *always* taken, and sensate focus is useful in *every* case.
Transference *must always* be analyzed.

Or from REBT practice:

Always target the meta-emotion first.
Always dispute the irrational belief before offering an alternative rational belief.

Although certain therapeutic strategies will most often foster a client's progress, we would echo Ellis's contention (1962) that there are no absolute prerequisites for personality change—even rational thinking. Always consider the context of the situation and decide whether the guideline that you are thinking of applies in this case at this time. Psychotherapy is an ideographic art and it is best applied uniquely to the individual in front of you.

SCHEDULING

The practice of psychotherapy usually assumes a forty-five- to fifty-minute hour; however, there is nothing sacred about the length of the session. Psychotherapists have long followed the tradition of a fifty-minute hour since the time of Freud, but he was known to not be limited by this restriction (Ellis, 2002). Ellis usually scheduled sessions in half-hour blocks. Sometimes clients booked two consecutive sessions for a full hour. Some clients might require a longer session of ninety minutes to two hours. Perhaps they have many pressing issues to discuss, or they find it very disruptive to leave the session before they completely understand a disputation.

There has been a dearth of research focusing on the length of the psychotherapy session, although more research has focused on the frequency and number of sessions. Turner et al. (1996) studied the effect of thirty- versus fifty-minute sessions of brief therapy with college students and found no difference on treatment outcome or client satisfaction between the two treatment groups. Students reported greater adjustment after therapy independent of session length. A survey of practicing psychotherapists by Wolff (2005) found that those surveyed preferred longer sessions of up to two hours. The reasons for the preferred longer length of sessions included: more access to the clients' emotions, integration of experience before leaving the session, deepening of the transference, overcoming the clients' defenses, more revelation of clients' traumatic experiences, and improving the likelihood of "breakthrough experiences." We suspect that clients may be less likely to take advantage of longer psychotherapy sessions because of the increased financial costs. It could be advantageous for you to alter the session length and use an individualistic approach.

Younger clients, those with attention deficit disorder, neurological impairment, or those who are defensive might not focus for the entire session. Is the session length designed for the therapist's bill practices or the needs of the client? Our experience with shorter sessions indicates that the amount of time spent discussing the crucial issues remains the same, and the amount of time spent avoiding topics or discussing unimportant issues is reduced. Not only is the client more keenly aware of time limitations and therefore the importance of getting to the point, but so is the therapist. With the shorter session, we have found that we are more directive, active, and confrontative, and a lot less distracted.

Box 15.3

Experiment with sessions of varying lengths to determine what is most benefi-cial for you and for your clients. Some clients (and therapists) could have limited attention spans and be unable to keep their attention span on one topic for more than thirty minutes. Recognizing the limitations of your client can only benefit both of you. Time spent in therapy when the client cannot attend to the discussion can be wasteful and train the client in off task behaviors.

Many mental health professionals allow more time for the first session because they wish to collect all the diagnostic information or they know that clients have a story to tell and want to feel understood. On the other hand, some clients are unable to sit through a fifty-minute discussion. Therapy could be the first time in their lives that they have undertaken such an endeavor. For these clients, it might be desirable to gradually increase the length of the session to fifty minutes. If you do schedule fixed-length sessions, you might wish to spend only part of the time in focused endeavors, and the remainder in relaxation training or less taxing exer-cises, such as walking outside together.

Psychotherapy sessions usually occur once per week. Again Ellis displayed great flexibility in allowing his clients to schedule sessions more frequently or less frequently. Some clients who are in crisis may require more sessions in the initial phases of therapy. As clients improve, they may require less frequent ses-sions. Even when clients had completed therapy, Ellis often had clients schedule booster sessions to maintain the improvement they had made and to apply what they learned to new problems.

RIGIDITY IN THERAPIST BEHAVIORS

A key to avoiding inflexibility is to monitor your therapeutic behaviors and their effectiveness. To help you become a better therapist keep questioning what you do. Here are some questions you might want to ask yourself periodically:

Does the client understand what I have said?
Am I communicating clearly?
Am I doing too much of the work?
Does the client understand and believe what I just said?
How can I get the client to think the rational beliefs more strongly?
Am I giving enough homework assignments and are they working?

ISSUES OF TRANSFERENCE AND COUNTERTRANSFERENCE

Transference refers to whether clients react (and more important, overreact) to the therapist as they do to other significant people in their lives. As you know, the analysis of the transference has always been a key component and the primary mechanism of change in psychodynamic forms of psychotherapy. Although REBT does not believe that analysis of the transference is a necessary or sufficient component of psychotherapeutic changes and we do not advocate its use in every case, transference issues can arise in this type of therapy. Transference is another word for the behavioral learning principle of generalization. It is reasonable that clients will generalize their behavior with other people to their behavior with the therapist. REBT therapists can find it useful to explore transference reactions with clients. The first task is to identify the emotional tone of the interaction and the beliefs behind the emotion. Once these are specified, you can ask clients whether they relate to others in their lives in the same way as they relate to you. For example, "You know Bernie, every time we talk about work, I notice changes in your voice, and you become distant and avoidant and avoid eye contact with me. I wonder if that is how you react with other people who discuss your responsibilities with you." Offering such a question can provide you with a way to pinpoint and discuss problem areas.

Attitudes toward the therapist can provide a good indication of attitudes in other interpersonal encounters. For example, suppose you had given your female client a homework assignment. She comes back having successfully done it but also exclaiming, "Oh, Doctor, I thought of you, and I knew how you'd react if I *didn't* do it!" The client is really telling you one of her irrational beliefs: if she failed to do her homework, you (and perhaps other authority figures) might think she was worthless, and then she *would* be worthless. At this point you have an opportunity to point out that the client was doing good things but for all the wrong reasons; and who else's instructions does she comply with for these reasons? Essentially, the client is saying that she herself is not worth doing things for, but that you are. Such a client's task in therapy is to learn that she does not have to please the therapist. By knowing who else she has to please, you can help make that insight and the new rational belief will transfer to the people in her life whom she is trying to please.

If clients do not bring up transference issues, you might choose to do so. Suppose that each time you suggest a homework assignment to a client, he sulks and accepts the assignment with resignation in his voice. At this point, you might inquire, "You know, John, each time I suggest a homework assignment, I hear some resentment in your voice. How are you feeling toward me right now?" Once these feelings are acknowledged, you can proceed to identify the irrational beliefs that cause his feelings, inquire whether he has similar beliefs and feelings about other people, and identify the beliefs that led to the inhibition of direct expression of these feelings. Thus, transference issues are not explored for directly curative reasons but to help the therapist and client recognize relevant As, Cs, and, most important, Bs that interfere with their daily effective living.

The therapists' attitudes and emotional responses toward the client are called countertransference, and again the exploration of countertransference reactions originated in psychodynamic psychotherapy. Becoming aware of your emotional reactions to a client enables you to use yourself as a measuring device. Ask yourself how you feel when you know the client is coming to see you. Do you look forward to the visit or dread it? For what reasons? What are your feelings about the client during the session? What are his or her major interaction styles? Because the client is probably behaving toward you as s/he behaves toward other people, you are in a good position to give feedback that others might not be willing to disclose; that is, how his or her behavior influences you. Try to be as specific as possible and to describe to the client the behaviors that can be monitored later (e.g., a whining tone of voice, unhappy facial expression, poor eye contact, delayed response time).

Therapists' reactions to their clients sometimes are a result of the therapists' emotional problems and not an indication of the clients' problems. Sometimes clients' personalities, appearances, voices, or presenting problems trigger strong emotional reactions in us that interfere with our objectivity and ability to help that client. REBT and other active directive forms of CBT could be more susceptible to interference through countertransference than nondirective therapies. In these therapies, the therapist can be easily undone in their role of challenging a client's beliefs when s/he strongly endorses the thoughts that are linked with the client's unhealthy, disturbed emotions. We have noticed in supervision that when a therapist avoids challenging an obvious IB, or does so tentatively, or ambiguously, s/he will admit to holding the same IB. With a nondirective approach to therapy that does not require this proscribed behavior, it could be easier to remain unaware of how your own emotions and convictions can interfere with therapy. When you discover that you agree with the client's IBs, we recommend that you think through the situation and remain true to the theory and therapy. Force yourself to follow the steps of REBT. The therapist can challenge such IBs and recommend alternative RBs, perhaps with less intensity or persuasiveness. Sticking to the course of therapy will result in your doing better as sessions go on, and will help the client. We have found that persistently following REBT in cases where we have endorsed the client's IBs has resulted in our own personal growth.

From the very beginning of training in REBT, Ellis recognized that a therapist's own emotions and IBs could interfere with effective therapy. He long recommended, but did not require, that therapists engage in therapy to help them become aware of their emotional problems and challenge their own IBs. Awareness of your own emotions and emotional reactions is an important first step in preventing these reactions from interfering with your clients' therapy.

As clients get to know us and form a bond, they think of us as people or friends. They will normally have thoughts about what type of person we are and want to know things about our personal lives. Clients will come out and ask such personal questions about your age, your interests, your intimate relationships, your children, etc. What should you do, and how will your response affect the therapeutic relationship? Ellis always recommended just answering the question directly and factually, and providing only the amount of detail for which the client asks; then he would get back to the questions about the client's emotions or beliefs.

Perhaps you are surprised that we recommend the therapist respond immediately to clients' questions. One rationale is that with such a reply, the therapist is modeling good communication in an open, spontaneous relationship. This position, of course, is quite different from that of more psychodynamic therapists, who usually respond to such a client inquiry with, "Why do you want to know if I'm attracted to you?" Such a response seems like a dodge and distancing maneuver to the client. Clients tell us a lot of personal information and they know little about us. A solid, trusting relationship is not developed with "clinical" questions such as, "Why is that important? Why do you want to know?" In REBT, the relationship rests on sincerity. It is usually preferable, therefore, to answer clients' questions fairly and honestly, and then to deal with the individual's subsequent thoughts and feelings.

Box 15.4

Let us put some interchanges into different environments and examine them. Suppose you are sitting with a person you have recently met whose company you enjoy over a cup of coffee and the person asks, "Are you married?" An answer that dodges the issue would probably make the other person think, "Hey, she's not really my friend. She won't even answer my question!"

Or suppose that you, as a therapist, go to your supervisor and ask, "How am I doing?" What might you suspect if your supervisor says, "Why do you want to know?" Wouldn't it cross your mind that the answer is not positive?

Are there any limits to the therapist's self-disclosure? Probably there are; the REBT therapist knows that nothing is inherently shameful; however, there is information that you keep from other people as well. If you feel the question is too personal, it is quite reasonable to say that you do not feel comfortable sharing the information. On the other hand, a barrage of questions might be distracting. After answering them directly, you might ask clients how they feel about this new information, how they feel about you, and what their reasons were for asking. For example, perhaps the client looks at you as a mystical deity and then rejects you after learning that you are merely mortal. This pattern might very well reflect what the client does in everyday relationships, so that you would then be able to dispute the irrational beliefs associated with this problem.

Clients could develop a dependency on authority figures in such a way that they cannot take orders except from people who are better than they are. This type of dependency often also results in self-depreciation. It might be profitable to ask such clients if they think they are as good a person as you are. If they respond, "Oh no, why you're a doctor and I'm just a lowly slob," you can guess that they are doing the same thing with other people in their lives, such as their boss, the president of their company, or the provost of their university. It will benefit these clients if you can demystify the rest of their Gods in addition to yourself.

CONCLUDING A THERAPY SESSION

We offer several suggestions to keep in mind as the therapy session is ending. First, try to end each session, whether group or individual, by negotiating a *homework* assignment with clients or having them design one for themselves. Assignments might be in the form of thinking, reading, and writing, or trying new activities (see Chapter 16). Whatever their form, the purpose is to strengthen or extend the skills learned in the session and to bridge the gap between sessions.

Summarize the main points of the session, or ask the client to do so. This will help you realize what the client thinks s/he got from the session. You can ask whether it matched the points you thought were important. If there is no match, then you can explore what you need to know about the client. If the client can talk about the ideas you discussed but communicates that s/he does not yet understand or believe the ideas, you have a topic to begin the next session.

As *feedback*, you might ask, "Was there anything I did or said in the session that bothered you in any way?" and "Was there anything I did or said today that seemed particularly useful to you?" and most important, "What did you learn from today's session?" Questions such as these enable you to adapt your style to your client, provide information to be taken up in the next session, give an opportunity for a brief rehearsal by the client, and help identify other **B**s to be taken up later.

SUMMARY: TEN COMMON ERRORS TO AVOID

Failure to listen. Among other problems, you could misdiagnose the client's problem if you fail to listen critically. Clients might say they are "angry"; be sure to inquire carefully what they mean by "anger," because they might be mislabeling their emotional state and therapy will take off in the wrong direction. Similarly, carefully attune yourself to key words, such as clients' idiosyncratic phrases, which indicate their irrational beliefs.

Failure to develop goals. Ask, rather than assume, what the client's goals are. You will also want to determine the client's expectations of therapy. It is important to know these ideas so that you can clarify and correct them, or if agreement cannot be reached, refer the client elsewhere.

Errors in information gathering. As a new therapist, you might find yourself spending too many sessions gathering data before planning an intervention, or failing to obtain sufficient information and jumping too quickly into disputation. In either case, you run a risk of alienating or losing the client, or at least of doing inefficient therapy.

Errors in assertiveness. Again, therapists can make errors in either direction, by allowing clients to ramble or cutting them off too abruptly. What is happening when you are not sufficiently directive and too often allow the client to lead? Perhaps you have forgotten your game plan and are caught up in a client's stories. Perhaps you are afraid of offending clients if you interrupt and do not want to appear rude. Clients will often let you know your error, by criticizing your behavior, asking what you think at a subsequent session, or complaining that you interrupt too much. You might keep in mind, however, that each therapy session is not a win-or-lose game; there's always a next time.

Errors in questioning. Avoid the following mistakes:

Asking irrelevant or overgeneralized questions (e.g., "How've you been?") instead of directly relevant ones.

Overusing rhetorical questions (e.g., "Where does your getting upset get you?").

Using too many "why" questions, which generally lead only to "because" excuses. Instead, use "how," "where," or "what's the evidence" questions, or ask, "What are you telling yourself?" or "When you do this, what are you thinking?"

Overusing questions with a "yes" or "no" answer; queries that require a fuller response are preferred.

Bombarding clients with numerous questions and not allowing them to answer any of them.

Answering questions for the clients instead of letting them deal with them on their own or helping them to break the questions down into simpler components.

Failing to note whether the client has, in fact, answered your question or simply digressed. If the question is unanswered, refocus the client on the task.

Tendency to lecture. Avoid lengthy lectures, particularly when you have failed to check and see whether the client is following you. Educators tell us that the best way to learn something is to teach it; the best way for the client to acquire REBT principles, therefore, is not to listen to a long didactic lecture, but to practice interactively, in session.

Failure to check understanding. Request frequent feedback from clients to ensure that they understand you. Listen to recordings of what you think are your good sessions; make sure that clients weren't "Um-hmmm-ing" you into thinking they understood. It is useful periodically to ask clients to restate what you have just said or to ask, "What's your understanding of what I've just said?" or "What is your feeling about what we've been discussing?"

Having all the answers. Avoid trying to be a "Wise Person." If you have a wise thing to say, it might be wiser not to say it. It is generally preferable to lead clients, by Socratic questioning, to their own insights.

Attitudinal errors. You will want to avoid the following:

Blaming and condemning remarks (e.g., "You know how to challenge those ideas.").

Scare tactics (e.g., "You have a big problem; it's going to take a long time to work this out.").

Being unrealistic and offering false hopes (e.g., "Oh, we can fix you up in no time.").

Judgmental remarks (e.g., "Why do you need the approval of a *creep* like him?").

Box 15.5

Listen to a recent therapy recording and check your performance in each of the categories in the text. You won't be able to listen for all of these errors at one time; monitor each one separately.

Overgeneralizations (e.g., "You *are* smart.").
Argumentative power struggles in which you try to force the client to accept
   your views (e.g., "I'm the therapist here; I'll tell you what's wrong with you.").

Errors in the use of humor. Use humor frequently, but don't direct it at your client. Try not to be giggly. See that your humor is therapeutic and not used for entertainment.

PART FIVE

The Therapeutic Whole

16

Homework Assignments

Rational emotive behavior therapy follows a cognitive-learning model of change. A major tenet of REBT is that clients practice their new philosophical thoughts in order for the effects to be meaningful or durable. This does seem to be a contradiction. REBT theory and the practice of challenging IBs and persuading clients of their new RBs suggests that there be some understanding, insight, or conviction in the new rational philosophy. However, as the Philosopher Spinoza (Spinoza, 1677/1994; see Damasio, 2003) pointed out, rehearsing new ideas is a necessary strategy to overcome many things that people believe and wish to change. So rehearsal is equally if not more important than understanding and insight.

One of the principal therapy techniques of REBT and all forms of CBT is to rehearse the cognitive changes taught in therapy and to behave differently between sessions. This provides the client an opportunity to generalize the work of therapy beyond the confines of the therapist's office. Homework assignments are a routine and significant element of REBT. Given the often negative association clients (and therapists) have to the word "homework," some therapists prefer to use more neutral terms, such as self-help work, practice exercises, experiments, rehearsal, or field-work.

The rationale for homework assignments is simple—therapy outcomes are enhanced when clients do homework. Kazantzis, Whittington, and Datillio (2010) completed a meta-analytic review of controlled studies that compared the same form of therapy with and without homework. Their results supported the conclusion that homework assignments enhance therapy outcomes (Morgan and Jorm, 2008). Therapy with homework is more effective than therapy without it. Although most varieties of CBT recommend homework, few books on the topic exist. One good exception and a fine resource consistent with REBT is Kazantzis, Deane, Ronan, and L'Abate's (2005), *Using Homework Assignments In Cognitive Behavior Therapy*.

The specific goals of the homework assignment could be to change a dysfunctional behavior or establish a new adaptive behavior, replace irrational cognitions with more helpful ones, or determine how well the client has understood the basic principles of REBT. Accordingly, homework may be cognitive, behavioral, or emotive in nature.

As we suggested above, we ultimately place the major emphasis on behavioral assignments. If that is so, you may ask, why does REBT use the other types? Different categories of assignments can accomplish different goals, but the therapist can use various types of homework aimed at the same goal. REBT is based on an educational model, which includes the use of multiple modalities and learning trials to maximize learning. After all, how much can the client learn in one forty-five-minute session per week? Even if they learn a lot, they have the rest of the week to live with their IBs, so practice is important. In college courses, students attend lectures, but also do field or laboratory exercises, writing assignments, and reading. The more actively the student is engaged in learning activities the better the outcome. The REBT practitioner can do the same. The question the therapist asks himself or herself in each meeting with the client is, "What can my client do this week to practice what we have discussed during this session?" It is important to know your client when generating a homework assignment. For example, some clients have difficulty with reading assignments and require more action-based or auditory-based assignments. Others enjoy reading and consume books but are less inclined to action.

Before we discuss specific homework suggestions, let us examine the five important characteristics shared by effective homework assignments.

Negotiate. Although you may have great ideas for homework assignments for your clients, they do not have to do them. Therapists do not really assign homework; they suggest and negotiate with clients on what they are willing to do between the sessions.

Consistency. The assignment is consistent with and follows from the work done in the session. Try to devise and negotiate an assignment that follows naturally from the main theme of the session.

Specificity. Discuss the assignment in sufficient detail and with clear instructions. For example, if you ask the client to generate possible solutions to a dilemma, do not vaguely say, "Think of as many as you can." but rather "Think of at least five possible solutions." In this way, the client has specific instructions and is more likely to stretch his or her creative faculties. Specify the assignments as fully as possible. Negotiate when, where, and how the client will do each step. The more specific the details that are provided in the assignment, the more committed s/he may be to completing the task.

Systematic follow-through. Each week, try to be systematic about negotiating a homework assignment and checking on the assignment from the last session. Most of us probably would have stopped doing our homework in the fifth grade if our teacher stopped checking for it. The same applies to our clients. Checking on their completion of homework conveys the message that homework is an important component of therapy. We suggest you do so early in the session. Do not assume that the completion of one homework assignment in a problem area will be sufficient. It is best to repeat the assignment (or variations of it) systematically for a number of weeks.

We recommend that you ask the client about the homework at the beginning of the session before you sent an agenda for the session. When the client reports that s/he successfully completed the assignment, you can then discuss what s/he learned from the assignment and then discuss a new assignment that continues the theme or process of the successful assignment. If the client failed to complete the assignment, you can ask probing questions to understand what stopped the client from completing the assignment. If they experienced a disturbed, negative emotion that blocked doing the assignment, you can explore the IBs related to the emotion. Next, you can suggest placing the issue on the agenda for the session, in order to work on it before the client proceeds to repeat the assignment. If the client thought the homework was too hard, you can explore the frustration intolerance beliefs. Because the homework assignments reflect the goals of therapy, by working on the problems that interfere with the homework, you can work on the issues that relate to accomplishing the therapeutic goals. Resolving the IBs and emotions that block the homework gets you a step closer to accomplishing the goals.

Efficiency. Behavioral exposure assignments in REBT usually follow a flooding model rather than one of a gradual exposure model. The therapist encourages the client to take large steps rather than small ones; for example, to "Ask women out for a date until you get four women to reject you." rather than "Try to speak to a woman this week." The client's fear of rejection is the problem. Exposing the client to repeated rejection is facing the fear. The rationale for this maneuver is that it is usually more efficient in producing change. Feedback from the client's weekly homework assignments will help the therapist to determine the size of the next step.

When helping the client to design homework, try to ask Socratic questions first to get them to think about what they are willing and able to do. If the client suggests some vague ideas, ask questions that will help them be more specific. If the Socratic style does not work, make some suggestions and then seek feedback from the client about how they feel doing your suggested assignment. Discuss the assignment carefully, including the rationale for selecting it; understanding will help increase your client's compliance. Remember, agreement on the tasks of therapy is an important part of the therapeutic alliance. Clients cannot consent or follow through if they do not understand the rationale for the task. It is helpful to help the client anticipate obstacles to completing the homework. You could ask the client, "What would prevent you from completing the assignment this week?" or "What emotions would interfere with your doing this?" Here you are assessing whether any emotional barriers exist (e.g., the assignment is too overwhelming for the client, in which case you may break it down into more manageable steps), or any practical barriers exist (e.g., the assignment of your client being assertive with her sister can't happen because her sister is out of the country). By identifying and addressing any barriers before the client leaves the session, you increase the likelihood of completion *and* success.

Once the assignment is agreed upon, a useful question to ask is, "How will you remember to do the assignment?" One technique to help the client remember the assignment is for the therapist to write it down in the manner of a medical prescription. Some therapists that have worked at the Albert Ellis Institute have prescription pads of paper printed with the inscription, "Behavioral Prescription from the Desk of [John Jones, Ph.D.]" for this purpose. Formalizing the assignment procedure in this way aids the client's memory and underscores the significance of the homework. We recommend that you also include the homework assigned in any session or progress note that you keep on clients. This will facilitate the therapists' memory and increase the probability you will discuss the client's experiences with the homework in the next session.

Because homework is so integral to the therapy, you might want to prepare a statement for your clients about the importance of doing self-help work between sessions. In addition, Dryden (1990) suggested that the therapist:

- Negotiate assignments with the client rather than unilaterally choosing the assignments.
- Negotiate assignments that are relevant to the client's stated goals.
- Select assignments that are not too time-consuming for the client.
- Choose assignments that are challenging but not overwhelming to the client.
- Elicit a firm commitment from the client to do the assignment.
- Identify and prepare to overcome potential obstacles that may block the client from doing the assignment.

The next issue is the type of homework that might be helpful. Homework assignments can target the steps of therapy that mirror the chapters of this book. The homework could target the following:

- Monitor and identify the crucial **As** that lead to emotional upset.
- Monitor the most dysfunctional of the client's emotional **Cs**.
- Monitor the behavioral **Cs** to understand how frequently they occur and what stimuli elicit them and what events reinforce them.
- Monitor the occurrence of IBs that correspond to troublesome emotions and behaviors.
- Learn the principles of REBT, such as the B-to-C connection and the nature of IBs.
- Rehearse challenging the IBs.
- Rehearse the new RBs.
- Rehearse images of confronting the **A**, changing the **B**s and **C**s, and performing the new adaptive behavior.
- Rehearse the new adaptive behaviors.

Early in therapy it may be best to focus on self-monitoring assignments that will help clients identify the **A**s, **B**s, emotional **C**s, and behavioral **C**s that are leading to their symptoms. Bibliotherapy, workshops, or other psycho-educational activities that teach the principles of REBT are assigned in the early stages of therapy. Next, we would move on to rehearsing the challenges to the IBs and practicing the RBs. Then we might use imagery; and finally direct in vivo behavioral assignments.

When the client brings in the results of the self-help work, be sure to determine what s/he learned or did not learn from carrying out the assignment. Identify and correct any errors that the client made in carrying out the assignment. Most important, reinforce success at doing the assignment, or if necessary, the attempt to do the assignment. In other words, do not forget the importance of reinforcement contingencies.

Improvement across sessions is directly related to the client's willingness to do self-help exercises. Clients' thoughts about doing the assignments are also important. When we ask them to act, we are asking them to be asymptomatic and the thoughts that interfere with the homework are usually related to the persistence of their symptoms. Assess these cognitions directly by asking the client, "How helpful do you think this assignment will be?" and "How willing are you to try this assignment?"

The following dialogue illustrates how the therapist can elicit from the client commitment to doing the homework.

T: Marvin, we've discussed the importance of the homework, and now I want to find out when you will do the assignment this week. Can you make a commitment to a particular day?

C: Well, I'm going to try to do it on Wednesday.

T: Ah, my trained clinical ears hear something important. I asked you when you would do it, and you told me when you would try to do it. Can you see the difference between these two things: doing and trying to do?

C: I think so.

T: Well, let's do a little experiment: I want you to try to lift your right arm, but don't do it. Try, but don't do. What happens?

C: I don't lift my arm. Nothing happens.

T: Exactly. Can you see how that's relevant to the homework assignment?

C: Sure. Let me try that again: I'm going to do the assignment on Wednesday. I will make that commitment.

EXAMPLES OF COGNITIVE HOMEWORK ASSIGNMENTS

Bibliotherapy. Ellis was a firm believer in bibliotherapy. His first self-help book, *A Guide to Rational Living*, appeared in 1967 with Bob Harper. It is now in its third edition. Ellis wrote numerous self-books, almost one for each topic.

Reading self-help books teaches clients about the B-to-C connection and the ways they can empower themselves by taking control over their emotions. They can also learn about the irrational beliefs that people with their problem are likely to have. Reading self-help books makes it easier for individuals to recognize their own irrational thinking. They also learn how to challenge their beliefs and what alternative rational beliefs they could adopt instead. Exposure to REBT self-help books makes therapy easier and quicker. Rather than teaching skills for the first time, you can focus on how the client can apply what they have learned to him/herself.

Today, self-help books are widely available to the lay public. Jacobs (2009) reported estimates of more than two thousand such books reaching the market in the United States each year. There is, however, substantial variability in the quality of these materials. It is a good idea to discuss what other self-help books your clients are reading and whether they are helpful and align with the therapy or whether they give inconsistent messages to what you think is helpful to your client. The Association of Behavioral and Cognitive Therapies (www.abct. org) maintains a website of self-help books that we believe are responsible, have documented scientific support for the methods presented, are consistent with empirically based best therapy practices, and which do not offer any advice that is contradictory to scientific evidence. You and your client can access this website at URL: http://www.abct.org/Professionals/?m=mPro&fa=shBooksPro.

Self-help forms. Completing REBT Self-Help forms helps clients examine a specific emotional event. The form contains boxes for the client to write in the Activating event, the unhealthy emotional and maladaptive behavioral Consequences, the Irrational Beliefs, Disputations, the Effective new philosophy, as well as the healthy, negative emotion(s) and adaptive behavior(s). Self-help forms allow the therapist to determine whether the client really understands the A-B-Cs of REBT. Clients could have trouble identifying their relevant rational and irrational beliefs. They could quickly identify their unhealthy negative emotions and the rational alternative beliefs, but struggle with disputation. They could write, "I feel" when they really mean, "I believe." Linguistic confusions and misunderstandings of the theory become clear in such an assignment and offer the therapist a chance to do some invaluable teaching when you discuss the assignment during the next therapy session. Several versions of such forms have been created over the years. Appendix 5 presents the most recent version we use at the Albert Ellis Institute.

Box 16.1

A client has filled out a homework form and given it to you, the therapist. A portion of the form is reproduced below. What would your response be? What corrections, if any, would you make?

Activating event— I went for a job interview.
Rational belief—I was turned down.
Irrational belief—It is horrible that I didn't get the job.
Emotional consequence—I felt depressed.
Disputing— I don't care that I didn't get the job.
Answers are given in the footnote at the end of the chapter.

Disputing Irrational Beliefs. Persuasion is an important part of REBT. Therapists actively persuade clients to relinquish their irrational beliefs and replace them with rational ones. Disputing is not an easy task for many new REBT therapists and clients. Therefore, clients will benefit from out-of-session practice in disputing their IBs. Examples of how you can use disputing in assignments include

- Asking the client to dispute his/her demandingness whenever it comes up during the week, using at least three different disputes.
- Asking the client to practice the empirical dispute when she recognizes she is thinking irrationally.
- Asking the client to dispute *others'* IBs when he becomes aware of them.
- Asking the client to convince another person that his irrational beliefs are irrational and that the alternative rational beliefs are more correct.

Dispute and Rehearse Rational Beliefs. Disputing and rehearsing the rational belief will strengthen the conviction clients have in this new way of thinking. When clients challenge their RBs, just as they do the IBs, they see that the RBs are consistent with reality, flexible, logical, and most important, do not block them from achieving their goals. Consistent practicing of the RBs is integral to the change process. Keep in mind that clients have been rehearsing the IBs for quite some time, and with some force. Clients should be reminded they need to apply that same force and diligence to the RBs. We have also asked clients to compose and write out the RBs and keep them in places where the client is likely to see them. Often clients have placed the new RB in moving text on their screen saver. Others have written them on index cards that they keep on the sun visor of their cars or in a desk drawer. The point is to place the written version of the RB in a place where the client is likely to see it and can read it in places where the activating events are likely to occur.

Referenting. Referenting is a cost benefit analysis of a particular behavior. Clients can make a box with four cells. At the top, list positive and negative consequences. On the side, divide the box into Short-term and Long-term consequences. Clients think about their behavior and write in the consequences in the appropriate cell. See Table 16.1 for an example of a referenting assignment with a client, Jacque, who sought therapy for temper outbursts.

We usually find that like Jacque, clients fail to find any long-term positive benefits for their symptomatic behavior. They are likely stuck in the short-term positive payoffs.

Table 16.1. AN EXAMPLE OF A REFERENTING ASSIGNMENT WITH A CLIENT WHO HAS CONTINUING TEMPER OUTBURSTS.

	Positive consequences	Negative consequences
Short-term consequences	People listen to me and do what I want right away.	My wife and kids leave the room and do not want to talk to me.
Long-term consequences	Nothing noted by the client.	My wife and kids are afraid of me and do not share things with me and do not want to be with me. My family dislikes me and will not share things with me I spend a lot of time alone.

Clients who want to change a habit or addictive behavior such as smoking, overeating, procrastinating, and drinking often benefit from this homework assignment. When assigning referenting, ask the client to focus on both the short-term *and* long-term advantages and disadvantages of the behavior. Clients often pass over the long-term consequences and focus on the short-term positive consequences. Once the analysis is completed, ask the clients to review it daily or to complete a form like the one in Table 16.1 each time they do the target behavior. DiGiuseppe and Tafrate (2007) report that such exercises make the consequences more salient in the clients' minds and increase motivation to work on other therapeutic tasks.

Stop and Monitor. Clients are often not aware of their IBs. We can ask clients to stop and record their thoughts at random times of the day. This assignment is especially helpful for those clients who have difficulty identifying their cognitions. We recommend that you have them keep a Post-it' on their computer at work; whenever they look up and see the Post-it', they are to write down what it is they are thinking at that moment. Although many of the thoughts will be neutral, the therapist and client will want to focus on the negative irrational thoughts.

Distraction. When clients have not successfully reduced their disturbed unhealthy emotions and must confront the stimuli that elicit them, they have two choices. Either they can experience the emotion or they can attempt to distract themselves. If they are very successful at distraction, they might keep it as their coping mechanism to avoid the emotion. The old saying to count to ten before getting angry is an example of a distracting technique. Clients can approach a difficult situation more effectively if they distract themselves from their emotionally upsetting thoughts rather than try to dispute their IBs. When disturbed emotions are running very high, clients "cannot think straight." Some strategies that have been helpful with these clients include counting details in the environment (e. g., the number of pieces of molding in the room, the number of parallel lines in a paneled wall, or how many people are wearing a red object), or reciting, either mentally or aloud (e.g., the multiplication tables, a song, or a slogan).

Distraction is not an "elegant" strategy in the classical REBT sense. Clients who rely on distraction do not develop new philosophies or rational alternative beliefs. Therefore, we would not recommend distraction unless a client had failed to master or benefit from the "elegant" or "inelegant" cognitive solutions. The use of distraction in treating anxiety has been controversial in behavior therapy (Parrish, Radomsky, and Dugas, 2008; Rodriguez and Craske, 1993). Recall that people use distraction when they must confront a stimulus. Theoretically, exposing oneself to the fear-provoking stimulus is called exposure treatment and should eventually result in a decrease of the anxiety. People are more likely to benefit from exposure treatments if they really feel anxious during the exposure. Some behavior therapists are suspicious of distraction as a therapeutic technique. The idea against its use is that distraction blocks the person from focusing on the emotion eliciting stimuli during exposure. This results in less emotional arousal and interferes with the process of deconditioning. Many studies show that distraction has the potential to hinder exposure treatment and to promote the return of fear. However, other research has provided strong evidence that some forms of distraction during exposure can facilitate both short- and long-term reductions in fear and anxiety. Research results in this area have been contradictory.

Parrish, Radomsky, and Dugas (2008) reviewed the research on distraction and anxiety treatments and reached several conclusions. They concluded that it is not the distraction per se that interferes with fear reduction, but the degree to which the distracting task consumes one's attention and leaves less available mental energy or resources for cognitive processing during exposure. When clients must confront feared stimuli, distracting strategies are less likely to become counterproductive and can be productive under several conditions. First, the distraction promotes an increase in the client's self-efficacy (via relaxation, positive affect, belief change, or some other means). Second, the distraction does not demand excessive concentration or attentional resources. Third, the distraction allows the client greater approach behavior that can allow corrective information via "disconfirmatory experiences" (e.g., "This situation is not dangerous or awful."). Fourth, the distraction does not promote incorrect attributions concerning the client's safety. That is, the client does not believe that the distraction creates safety. Therapists should encourage clients to stop utilizing distraction strategies that foster complete cognitive avoidance of feared stimuli and result in avoidance strategies that prevent emotional processing of the experience of facing the feared stimuli. Thus, the use of distraction appears complex and we recommend that you encourage such techniques with caution and with the recommendations mentioned above.

The Dialectical Behavior Therapy (DBT) literature uses the acronym ACCEPTS to teach distraction skills (Linehan, 1993).

Activities: Engage in a positive activity that you enjoy.

Contribute: Help out others or your community.

Comparisons: Compare yourself to people who are less fortunate than yourself or to how you were when you were in a worse state.

Emotions (other): Cause yourself to feel something different by provoking your sense of humor or happiness with a positive activity.

Push away: Put your situation out of your mind for some time. Think of something else temporarily first in your mind.

Thoughts (other): Force yourself to think about something else.

Sensations (other): Do something that will result in an intense feeling other than what you are feeling now, such as a cold shower.

Distraction has been demonstrated to work for depression (Morgan and Jorm, 2008), pain (Stinson 2008), and sexual dysfunction (Rodriguez and Craske, 1993). We started this section by referring to the old "count to ten rule" before you get angry. Significant research supports the idea that distraction is a better strategy than rumination (or the focus on the Activating Event) to reduce anger (Bond, Ruaro, and Wingrove, 2006; Bushman, 2002; Rusting and Nolen-Hoeksema, 1998).

Listening. You may recall our earlier suggestion to record therapy sessions after getting the client's permission. Ellis had clients record and listen to their therapy tapes since the 1970s, and said that this was one of his favorite techniques (Rosenthal, 2011). We encourage clients to record their sessions for their own use. Recordings made during office sessions can be used between sessions at home for relaxation training, systematic desensitization, covert sensitization, and, occasionally, for high intensity stimulation (flooding) (Denholtz, 1970). Hearing one's own complaining or demanding can greatly influence a client. However, it is in persuading clients to change their irrational thinking that we think listening to recordings will have its biggest benefit. We have had many a client tell us that they have cringed when they heard their excessive emotions or irrational beliefs.

Macaskill (1996) suggests that recorded therapy sessions can play a significant role with socially or geographically isolated clients who are unsupported in their living environments. Listening to the recordings increases the likelihood of their initiating therapeutic tasks such as graded activity assignments and disputing cognitive distortions and dysfunctional beliefs in vivo. Recording of therapy sessions has such a major benefit we suggest its routine use in REBT practice.

Shepherd, Salkovskis, and Morris (2009) surveyed approximately seventy clients who recorded their CBT sessions. Ninety percent of the clients reported listening to the recordings between therapy sessions to some extent. Most said they discussed the recordings with their therapist. Most clients and therapists endorsed positive attitudes toward the use of recordings. They listed the advantage of improving memory for sessions. Conclusion: The use of audio recording of sessions as an adjunct to therapy (where clients listen to recordings between sessions) and for therapist supervision is rated as both highly acceptable and useful by both therapists and clients. However, it should be noted that clients who are experiencing acute depression and prone to rumination may not benefit from listening to recorded sessions.

EXAMPLES OF BEHAVIORAL HOMEWORK ASSIGNMENTS

REBT believes that IBs mediate the relationship between the situation and the disturbed, unhealthy emotion and dysfunctional behavior. Changing one's beliefs is not an end in itself. It is a means of changing client emotions and behaviors. If a client says, "It wouldn't really be awful to be turned down for a date; it is only unfortunate," yet continues to avoid calling prospective dates, the therapist would doubt the conviction of the client's new beliefs. Thus, REBT is more than a "talk therapy"; it stresses that meaningful cognitive change is meaningless unless the client behaves differently. In addition, cognitive change is more likely to occur if clients make some initial attempts at behavior change. Following a cognitive-dissonance model of attitude change (Festinger, 1957; Harmon-Jones and Mills, 1999), behaving differently often leads to thinking and feeling differently. Cognitive dissonance is a psychological discomfort that results from holding contradictory beliefs at the same time. Cognitive dissonance leads people to have a motive or drive to reduce dissonance. They do this by changing their attitudes, beliefs, and actions. If you can convince a person to act in a way that is inconsistent with their IBs they will experience some cognitive dissonance and will be motivated to change their IB to be consistent with the way they acted. So changing behaviors will lead to a change in beliefs.

Risk-taking and shame-attacking exercises. These are two of the most widely assigned homework activities in REBT. Although these exercises can be considered as interchangeable, they can be distinguished based on the client's underlying fear. Risk-taking encourages clients to reevaluate their definition of the consequences of certain behaviors as terrible or dangerous, when in fact they are not. In such assignments, clients might try to be more assertive or to push themselves to take risks, particularly social risks that they may have been avoiding. A unique aspect of risk-taking assignments is that often the exercises are designed to have clients experience failure or face the feared consequences they have been avoiding. This is especially true in cases of perfectionism or fear of failure. As we mentioned earlier, people learn by experience: if they have never experienced failure, they will be unlikely to change their IBs about it and their avoidance of it. Thus, it is difficult to work on the fear of an aversive event unless the client actually experiences it. Clients who avoid taking risks because they believe it would be *too uncomfortable* or because they *need* others' approval benefit from risk-taking exercises. For the perfectionistic client who needs approval, you might recommend she e-mail someone she looks up to, stop midsentence and hit the send button. The client is not permitted to explain the e-mail or follow-up with another e-mail. This gives the client the opportunity to tolerate the discomfort, while at the same time, practice being a fallible human being.

Consider the case of a young man with dating anxiety who, after some social skills training, is instructed to make three social contacts in the next week. If he is successful and makes three contacts out of three trials, he will miss an important lesson. He will not become immunized against the stress of failure and may continue to be vulnerable to it. The therapist could instead suggest that the client keep making contacts until he collects three rejections in the next week. Note the win-win nature of this assignment, because the client will succeed even as he fails. If his social overtures are accepted, he has made progress toward his goal, and if they are rejected, he has succeeded in doing his homework and can bring in these incidents for analysis in therapy. Thus, the therapist may prescribe failure experiences for two reasons: they are instructive, and they allow for desensitization, because if the client is afraid to fail, he will probably not try in the first place. Such assignments also challenge the client's thinking at two levels. First, our experience is that clients overestimate the probability of negative consequences. By doing such an assignment, they learn that they overestimate the bad outcomes. By persisting in the assignment until they do confront failure or the feared stimulus, they learn that even if a bad outcome occurs they can survive it and it is not awful. Thus, risk-taking assignments often have a paradoxical quality. By encouraging clients to do what they view as a bad behavior, and simultaneously to work at not catastrophizing or putting themselves down, they realize they can succeed at the behavior and yet do not have to succeed. The insomniac may be instructed to try to stay awake all night, the obsessive to obsess one hundred times per day, the impotent male to not get an erection (Fay, 1978). Being given the assignment to do the very thing that troubles them often removes the "horror" of the behavior.

Consider the case of a certified public accountant who dreaded making errors. He had a serious case of perfectionism. His assignment was to deliberately make mistakes and to practice accepting himself nonetheless. Although the client insisted that he made mistakes routinely and did not have to try, when he came back the following week he reported that, in fact, he had made no mistakes. As the therapist predicted, he was extremely fearful of what was in reality a low-probability event. In the ensuing weeks the assignment was continued, and the client forced himself to make an occasional error. He reported experiencing a revelation: an error was not a catastrophe, and he was not a failure for making one.

Shame results from self-downing, and shame-attacking exercises (Ellis 1973b; 1977b) are designed to teach clients that if they actually perform a silly or foolish act, even in public, their world will not end and they need not denigrate themselves. The central tenet is to teach clients to discriminate between their behavior and their worth as a human being. Clients thereby learn to rate their behavior, not themselves.

Shame-attacking assignments challenge our dire need for approval, conformity, and conventionality. We often exchange conformity for approval, which is a strong social control device but which can also be unnecessarily stifling if we punish ourselves with anxiety and shame. What might happen if we challenge conformity? People might think poorly of us: people might frown. However, people's thoughts and facial expressions need not hurt us; often, however, we believe they can. Shame-attacking exercises help clients to challenge this belief. In addition, these exercises are fun and can help clients to take social disapproval less seriously. A variation on this assignment is to share your mistakes with others. Speak about them and stop covering them up.

Here are some examples of shame-attacking exercises often used in REBT:

Go up to a stranger and greet him or her warmly. Ask about his or her health. Be effusive.

Stand on a busy street corner. Stretch out your arms and say, five times, "Your messiah has come. Follow me."

In a restaurant, go up to another person's table and inquire if the meal is satisfactory and if you can get him or her anything.

Go to three nearby shopping centers and try to sell someone a copy of yesterday's newspaper.

Go into a large department store and announce the time, five times, by saying, "Ladies and gentlemen, the time is now 1:15 ... 1:16 ... 1:17 ...," etc.

Tie a long piece of string around a banana and "walk" it down a busy street.

Ride a crowded elevator standing backward (facing the rear).

Yell out five successive stops in the subway or on the bus.

Go to the local library and, in a strong voice, ask the librarian to see two books that you want to read: Dr. Seuss' *The Cat in the Hat*, and the children's classic, *The Little Engine that Could*.

Find a restaurant that offers, "Two eggs any style." Ask your waiter for one fried and one scrambled.

Go to a deli where there is a salad and fruit bar and buy two grapes.

You can assign shame-attacking exercises to all the members of a therapy group and you can have them do the assignments individually or together as a group. For example, you could ask a group of socially anxious clients to sing a song, do a dance, or perform a "spotlight" act. The group activity is a successive approximation of the ultimate assignment, which is for them to each do it alone.

Clients can adopt one of these stock assignments or, preferably with the help of the therapist, design one that is more personally relevant. For example, one client claimed that she could not be assertive with her mother for fear of harming her mother's health, which would in turn lead others to conclude that she was a bad daughter. Her homework assignment was to tell her friends, "My mother must have had her nervous breakdown because of my bad behavior"; she was to watch their reactions and practice accepting herself nonetheless.

There are some caveats to consider when discussing shame attacks with clients. The shame attack is supposed to be an exercise for the client, not for those around him/her. If the client acts in a way that draws attention and social censure to her/ his peers, and the peers are not in REBT, the exercise could result in loss of friendships. It is better not to do a shame attack that is an inconvenience or creates problems for others. Again, it is the client's assignment and store clerks and bystanders have not signed on to be bothered by the client's growth exercises. Avoid shameful activities that could result in the loss of a job, expulsion from school, or arrest. If the consequences of his or her behavior could be disadvantageous, the assignment will be harmful, not helpful.

Thus, shame-attacking assignments accomplish two goals. The first is to help clients behaviorally dispute their sense of shame. To achieve this goal, it is necessary to do the exercises as prescribed. Preparing for the activity often involves the cognitive rehearsal and an A-B-C-D analysis may prepare clients to perform them properly.

The second goal is to help clients evaluate the accuracy of their predictions of how the world will react to them. Most of us overestimate the extent to which others care about or even notice our behavior. For example, Ellis told of one of his clients who, for weeks, tried to find the courage to call out the stops in a New York subway. Finally, he succeeded in calling out one stop and saw that nothing disastrous happened. The next week he gave himself the assignment of calling out each of the seven stops between his home and his work. What happened? No one on the subway said anything to him—except one person inquired, "What stop is Lexington Avenue?"

Act against the IB—Opposite Action. Whatever the client's symptom it is important for the client to learn to act against his/her irrational beliefs and disturbed emotion. DBT has used the simple phrase "opposite action" to describe the plan to behave against one's disturbance (Linehan, 1993). If you are avoiding socializing because you think it would be awful to be rejected, go toward people and interact with them. If you have a fear of speaking out in class because you would be worthless if you were wrong, speak up. If you feel angry and want to say something nasty, find a kind word or compliment for the target of your anger.

Relaxation. Relaxation training is a common behavioral assignment that works for many psychological symptoms. It could be the aspirin of psychotherapy. Researchers and therapists have found relaxation techniques to be successful for a wide range of problems, including anger, anxiety attacks, cardiac issues, depression, headaches, high blood pressure, immune system support, insomnia, pain management, stress management, and addictions. Relaxation techniques also enhance general well-being. Most relaxation methods are performed alone, while sitting or lying quietly, with minimal movement. Methods include autogenic training, biofeedback, deep breathing, meditation, Zen-yoga, progressive muscle relaxation, pranayama, visualization, *yoga nidra*, and self-hypnosis. Some of these (e.g., yoga) usually require the help of a trained professional. Some relaxation techniques involve movement, such as exercise, walking, gardening, or t'ai chi. In these activities, the mind is relaxed even though there is movement (see Ferguson and Sgambati, 2009 for a review).

Research shows that all relaxation techniques are equally effective and have the same mechanism of change. Many therapists teach clients relaxation by having them listen to a prepared recording of instructions. Soon, however, clients can do the exercises without external cues. In fact, as their skill at relaxation increases, they may find that they can best practice it at their own pace. They may not need to work on isolated muscle groups (e.g., the right hand) but can combine them into larger units (e.g., both arms).

Professionally recorded relaxation scripts can be recommended. Recommended scripts can be found in *Clinical Behavior Therapy* (Goldfried and Davison, 1994). Alternatively, therapists can record their own relaxation instructions, or simply record a session of teaching relaxation techniques to the client. This last procedure could increase the effectiveness of the training for some clients, because the therapist's voice becomes associated with the procedure and can aid in generalizing the effects of relaxation from the therapist's office to the client's home. The client could be instructed to play the relaxation recording each night, perhaps just before bedtime. At the next therapy session, the client can bring in the recording and practice using it in the therapist's presence. In this way, the therapist can periodically stop the recording and assess the client's degree of relaxation. Teaching relaxation techniques can become a tedious chore for the therapist and use up valuable session time, but having the client do much of the work as a homework assignment can minimize both of these problems.

One aspect of achieving success with relaxation homework assignments is ensuring that clients have structured both their time and their environment to maximize the probability of doing exercises. Ideally, they will find a quiet room away from distractions where they can recline. Family members can cooperate by not disturbing clients and by taking phone messages while they do their homework.

Writing. Writing assignments are often used in REBT. For example, clients could write a debate on the logic, veracity, and utility of one or more of their irrational ideas. They can be told to pretend that they are on a debating team and their job is to argue the opposite side, whether they believe it or not. The therapist is thus employing cognitive dissonance with clients who claim that they can write the debate but would not believe it. Attitude-change research suggests, and clinical experience verifies, that performing such a debate often convinces debaters of their own arguments. Thus, at the end of a therapy session, the therapist can write out the statement to be challenged at the top of a sheet of blank paper (using a separate sheet for each debate); the client fills in the debate below. In this way, disputations that are unfinished in the session can be continued at home, or the work of a completed disputation can be consolidated. Here is a debate written by a female client:

> Statement: If my children make mistakes in their lives, it proves that I am a bad mother.
> Challenge: Everyone makes mistakes, whether they had good or bad parents. It is a human characteristic.

My children need to learn by trial and error. Mistakes that I have experienced had a positive growth aspect. I learned to try not to repeat the mistake. Pain helps develop aversion to the pain. Also, having experienced mistakes has made me able to be more compassionate and insightful with others. I feel more sharing with people and enjoy more maturity. The same may be so for my children.

I am not the only influence on my kids. They have had input from many formative sources besides me. The difference between my two children shows that I couldn't have fully created their personalities or they'd have to be more alike. They continue to have even greater input from other people and experiences, and from themselves. As they meet each new life situation, they respond and make subtle adjustments called for by the moment. So I am not totally responsible for their problems. My kids have even indicated to me that I'm not a bad mother because they make mistakes—"that's silly!" they said.

I might as well take some credit for their good qualities, too, if I were to insist on responsibility for their negative qualities. I know I've done much good for my kids.

If I concentrated on my finished mistakes as a mother, I would trap/freeze myself in the past. I would deny recognition of time elapsed, growth, and change taken place. That would be living the life of another (albeit someone I know most intimately). And continued guilt amounts to self-pity. That's bor-ring!

In a related assignment, the client can be asked to reverse a "should" and defend it. This is especially effective with clients who are lawyers. They are asked to bring into session their opening remarks for the therapist who is serving as the jury. The client comes in the next session and presents his argument, standing up facing the jury. Clients who have difficulties with ratings of worth are asked to defend the position that all humans have equal worth; clients who believe that they *must* succeed at everything they do are asked to defend why mistakes can be helpful, etc. When the client is presenting his/her argument, be mindful of the client's tone of voice, nonverbal mannerisms, and the force with which his or her voice projects. If clients present with a soft, unsure voice, ask them to start over and present their opening to the jury as if their "client" is facing the death penalty.

Another form of written assignment used in REBT would be a logbook to keep track of evidence in support of or against specific negative automatic thoughts. Although this is an inelegant solution, we often use this strategy in REBT. The client identifies a recurring negative automatic thought, and then keeps track of specific events and evaluates whether his or her prediction in the automatic thoughts was accurate. The client could complain, "Every time I call upon a new client to make a sale, I get turned down!" What are the data? How many potential customers did he actually call, who were they, and how many refusals did he get? Similarly, the depressed patient who claims to be depressed "all the time" may discover useful information by keeping track of happy moments or times in the day when the despairing mood lifts (Freeman and Davis, 1990). Obese clients can keep a log of the amount and kind of foods eaten, time, and place of eating, and so forth. Accurate data records may serve to correct the client's distorted perception of A and attributions for why things occur, and to identify the appropriate antecedents and consequences of a troublesome behavior.

A very successful form of homework is expressive writing. Expressive writing involves a person composing narrative prose about upsetting experiences (Pennebaker, 1997; 2004; 2011). Research supports that this procedure benefits people for a wide range of physical health, medical utilization, and psychological problems, as well as improvements in their well-being. The revelation and exposure to upsetting past events by the retelling of personal thoughts and feelings is a component of all psychotherapies. All psychotherapies assume that the effectiveness of psychotherapy is mediated by how the therapist responds to the client's disclosures. Different theories of therapy have different conceptions of what responses the therapists should provide to their clients. Despite these differences, almost all therapies are effective. The expressive writing intervention is effective in the absence of a therapist or any other audience or any other activities. This suggests that disclosure to oneself in writing is therapeutic either on paper or in electronic forms. This is the least costly technique clients can perform (see Baddeley, and Pennebaker, 2009). The research supporting expressive writing is very extensive. A search in *PsychLit* for the term expressive writing in the title of articles revealed more than 185 manuscripts at the time of this writing (October, 2011).

Pennebaker (2011) provides the following instructions for expressive writing assignments:

- Find a time and place where you will not be disturbed. Ideally, pick a time at the end of your workday or before you go to bed.

- Promise yourself that you will write for a minimum of 15 minutes a day for at least three or four consecutive days.
- Once you begin writing, write continuously. Do not worry about spelling or grammar. If you run out of things to write about, just repeat what you have already written.
- You can write longhand or you can type on a computer.
- If you are unable to write, you can also talk into a tape recorder.
- You can write about the same thing on all three or four days of writing or you can write about something different each day. It is entirely up to you.

Having clients write stories about their conflicts, past difficulties, failures, or traumas between sessions will help get them on the road to improvement.

Box 16.2

To persuade the reluctant client to do a shame-attacking assignment, the therapist may set an example. For example, the therapist might go out on the street with the client and model unusual behaviors to show the client that people are more tolerant of our behavior than we think. Could you do this?

We suggest that new rational emotive behavior therapists follow the training example at the Albert Ellis Institute and give themselves the task of doing a series of shame-attacking or risk-taking assignments. Pick from the list in the text or design your own, and do an exercise this week yourself. In fact, it is a good idea to schedule a shame-attacking exercise for yourself at periodic intervals to keep up your skills.

EXAMPLES OF EMOTIVE HOMEWORK ASSIGNMENTS

Rational Emotive Imagery (REI). As we have previously discussed, REI involves having the client imagine a situation in which s/he experiences an unhealthy, negative emotion. The client is asked to change the unhealthy emotion to a healthy, functional negative emotion, and indicate to the therapist when s/he has done so. The therapist asks the client how s/he changed the emotion, and if the client understands and agrees with the B-to-C connection, the response will be that s/he changed the thought. Clients can be assigned to do REI several times a week for homework.

Rehearse Rational Self-Statements with Strong Emotion. This assignment is a combination of cognitive and emotive (and probably behavioral given the rehearsal aspect). Clients have spent years of their lives reindoctrinating themselves with their IBs, and with some force we might add! It is very important to stress to clients that in order for them to not only *feel* better, but also more importantly *get* better, they are going to have to *forcefully* rehearse the healthier cognition. In other words, we are looking for strong, persuasive emotion when they engage in the rehearsal. Merely stating the RBs in a monotonous, soft voice will hardly do the trick of buying into the healthier belief.

Watch movies and television programs. For clients who have difficulty identifying and labeling their emotions, consider assigning them homework to come up with several movies or TV characters who manifest a particular emotion that has been the discussion in therapy. In session, the client is asked to discuss why they determined the character was experiencing the emotion, what it might have felt like physically, what the character looked like, what was happening (the A), and what the character might have been thinking. This is an opportunity to teach the ABCs of REBT.

Emotion Logs. Have clients keep a log where they record the time of day, what was happening, the emotion they experienced, and the intensity of the emotion. This can be valuable to the therapist to detect any common triggers or themes for the client.

HAPPINESS ASSIGNMENTS

One additional bit of homework, not often mentioned in the formal REBT literature, but which we find very important, are assignments that focus on pleasure, happiness, and joy. To shift from a purely problematic focus to a more positive one, it may be useful to have clients write down a list of things that they enjoy during the day—focusing on the small sensual pleasures of everyday experience, such as the smell of coffee or a good sandwich. This assignment can remind clients of the pleasant practical realities of life. Some of these pleasant moments will be interpersonal: Who smiled at me today? Who did I enjoy seeing? What positive moment did I share with my spouse?

Encourage fantasies about upcoming positive activities and past positive events. Mental activity can be playful as well as aimed at disputing negative or dysfunctional thinking habits. Developing the habit of playful thinking can also be equally salient to feeling better. Our job, as therapists, can be viewed as not merely working to dispel misery, but actively working to promote happiness.

Another route to happiness is to develop the habit of doing nice things for other people. In depression, for example, the patient's focus is narcissistic and negatively self-focused. Reminding oneself to focus outward, and especially to do something for another person that has no immediate payback to oneself, may redirect and energize the client.

TROUBLE-SHOOTING HOMEWORK PROBLEMS

When your clients return to therapy each week, be sure to check their homework assignments first. Unless clients bring up a new issue that is clearly of greater importance or they are in obvious emotional distress, following up on assignments provides you with a systematic way to integrate therapy visits.

Clients may expect their homework assignments to change each week, as they do in a classroom or in a physician's office when medication or dosage level is adjusted. In fact, however, the client may work at a behavioral assignment for a number of weeks before cognitive or emotional change occurs. Be sensitive to your client's expectations; if uncorrected, they may lead to depressive cognitions (e.g., "Uuggh, I'm not making progress."), which can increase the client's distress.

What do you do if clients have failed to do their homework assignments? You investigate; such failures often provide valuable diagnostic information about clients' belief systems. The uncompleted assignment may be treated as a new activating event that may have resulted in additional emotional stress to the client. Thus, the therapist may ask the following useful series of questions.

T: How do you feel about not doing the assignment?
C: Terrible.
T: Terrible? In what way?
C: I feel guilty. I should've done my homework.
T: You believe you should have done it? Well, why did you have to?
C: Because I feel so terrible about not doing it.
T: Do you think you'd feel differently if you didn't say should've? Try it now: "It would have been nice if I did it, but I didn't. Too bad. I'll do it next week."
C: I didn't do it. Too bad. I'll try it again next week.
T: Do you think you'd feel better if you just stuck to that belief?
C: Yes; it would be better if I thought about it that way.
T: Well, can you remind yourself to think that way?
C: How?
T: What would you do if you wanted to be sure to remember to buy milk at the store?
C: I'd write it down! I'm going to do that now. Now, what was it we just said? ...

Depressive cognitions may follow the failure to do a homework assignment, as in the example above, or may be the cause of the failure. Thus, the client may have been stopped by the cognition, "It's hopeless—why try?" Typically, the client will not have answered this question, and the therapist may then help the client to challenge the notion of helplessness and to review the reasons why the situation is not hopeless.

Box 16.3

How do you feel when your client fails to do a homework assignment? Do you find yourself getting angry? If so, it would be wise to examine your own musts and dispute them. Or do you feel somewhat anxious or depressed? Look for cognitions such as, "If I were a good therapist, he'd have done his assignment," and challenge them. Homework assignments can indeed be diagnostic tools.

Don't be afraid to confront your client and ask why the assignment was not completed. Why was it so difficult to accomplish? One hypothesis is that the client defined the required step as *too* large. As we stated earlier, rational emotive behavior therapists tend to follow a flooding model, urging clients to take large rather than small steps. Although the theoretical model is clear, the practical reality is that it is often desirable to go down the hierarchy of difficulty a step or two in order to find a task that the client is willing to confront. Remember that the goal is to get clients to carry out their behavioral challenges, and a little patience and creativity in breaking down difficult assignments into smaller steps may be important in accomplishing this goal. Thus, if the client is a dependent adult who has always phoned her mother every day and wants to loosen this attachment, she may be unwilling to refrain from calling her mother for a week but agree to a two-day hiatus at first. Success at an easier task makes it more likely that she will attempt more difficult tasks later.

Similarly, the therapist will want to investigate the response cost of the assignment. Perhaps the client is more likely to listen to a CD than to read a book. Perhaps an adolescent is more willing to read a smaller book than a larger one. Perhaps a woman will practice relaxation exercises twice a week but "cannot find the time" to do them nightly. While the therapist will want to continue to urge the client to work steadily and with increasing effort, it is wise to praise the client for any accomplishments at first; learning is, after all, a gradual procedure. The therapist may still confront clients with the reality that the less they do, the more slowly they will improve. Clients always have a choice, but the therapist can be sure that they understand the consequences.

A common problem encountered among clients who do not do their homework is the "mañana contingency" (Ellis and Knaus, 1977). The client continually makes excuses for not beginning the assignment and ardently vows to begin it tomorrow; when tomorrow comes, the cycle is repeated. For example, "Today is too hectic—I'll relax tomorrow." or "I'm too anxious to study today—I'll really buckle down tomorrow." Frustration intolerance is common with clients who do not complete homework assignments. Beliefs such as "It's *too* difficult to do this homework." or "It's too uncomfortable to take a risk." often impede clients.

A related problem is the double-bind contingency (Ellis and Knaus, 1977). Here are some examples. An anorexic client complains that she has no friends. Although her stated goal is to cultivate a friendship, the therapist finds out that she has turned down two invitations from a fellow bridge player to visit her home after the bridge game. Why? Food might be served at the other woman's house and, being anorexic, the client believes that she is overweight and needs to lose ten pounds. A more common illustration is the smoker who wants to give up cigarettes and also lose some weight. Neither goal is accomplished because he fears that if he gives up cigarettes, he will eat more; and if he diets, he will smoke more.

Problems such as those just described illustrate a philosophy of Frustration Intolerance and are best treated by direct confrontation, a determined course of action, and perhaps a program of external contingencies. It might be pointed out to the smoker, for example, that he has three choices for change: he could stop smoking and not worry about his weight for the first few difficult weeks of withdrawal; he could work very hard at losing ten pounds and then begin his smoking cessation program; or he could do both at the same time, which is merely harder. Thus, the client is confronted with the fact that the two problems can be treated independently. Once a goal is selected, a strategy can be outlined.

Doing the homework is critical for the therapeutic process to be effective. It is particularly important that clients understand this fact. Whenever possible, rewarding contingencies can be established for the successful completion of homework. This does not mean that clients have to succeed in the homework by getting what they want, but rather "succeed" in the sense of doing what they have been assigned. It is even desirable when clients repeatedly avoid doing their homework for reasons of frustration intolerance, to make the next appointment contingent upon the client's completion of the homework assignment. Of course, the use of clinical judgment is necessary here; certainly this strategy would be contraindicated with a depressed client or others whose problems require regular attention.

PHASING OUT THE THERAPIST'S DEVELOPMENT OF HOMEWORK ASSIGNMENTS

A goal prior to terminating therapy is to have clients function independently and to acquire the cognitive and behavioral skills necessary to be their own therapist. To achieve this goal, the therapist can gradually fade out his or her role as the active agent in assigning homework projects and encourage clients to develop their own assignments. Thus, when clients report on their previous week's progress, the therapist can ask, "What could you do next week to follow up on that?" By gradual shaping and fading out directiveness, clients will acquire the ability to design their own self-help work.

As an REBT therapist, we recommend that you develop a Homework Policy that you share with your client in the first session. Given the research that supports homework's effects on treatment outcome, it behooves therapists to incorporate it into our practice. There are 168 hours in a week, one of which is spent in the therapy office. Ask your clients how much change they think they will make, and how fast they will make it, if they rely solely on that one hour a week. A copy of the Albert Ellis Institute's Homework Policy appears in Appendix 6 on page 354.

Note
Answers to Box 16.1:

Activating event- I went for a job interview and was turned down.

Rational belief- It's unfortunate that I didn't get the job.

Irrational belief- It's Horrible that I didn't get the job.

Emotional consequence- I felt depressed.

Disputing- How does it help me achieve my goal by telling myself that it is horrible that I did not get the job? Is it really the end of the world that I did not get the job? Could it be no worse?

17

Comprehensive Rational Emotive Behavior Therapy

The early writings of Ellis focused almost exclusively on the "elegant" or philosophical solution to emotional problems and a logical, persuasive model of therapy. In fact, this focus on philosophical content best had distinguished REBT from other psychotherapies. You will recall that an elegant solution hypothesizes that the A–(inference) could be true ("assume the worst") and encourages clients to change their IB–(imperative/demands) ideas that the worst must not occur and their IB–(derivatives) about the given reality. Ellis (1973a, 1977b, 1979b) subsequently noted that therapy often requires both elegant and inelegant procedures to maximize therapeutic effectiveness. Inelegant solutions are attempts to help clients change their misperceptions of A and, if feasible, to change the A. Ellis also noted that REBT would utilize other behavioral interventions to help clients change the behavioral C.

After reviewing the CBT literature, we noticed that cognitive-learning therapies fall into at least twelve different categories. These include:

- Classical REBT, which with its emphasis on philosophical solutions is the major focus of this text.
- Self-instructional training or Stress-inoculation training (SIT) programs that teach the use of language to rehearse self-statements or to guide clients' behavior (Meichenbaum, 1993; 2009).
- Challenging the accuracy of clients' perceptions and inferences about reality to develop more realistic thoughts about themselves, others, and the world (Beck, 2005; Dobson and Hamilton, 2009).
- Constructivist approaches that help people to understand the reasons things happen and to develop more accurate and helpful attributions, schema, or constructs of the self, others, and the world (Laird and Metalsky, 2009).
- Problem-solving skills training that helps clients more effectively change their world (Nezu, Maguth-Nezu, and McMurran, 2009).
- Modeling and rehearsal procedures that teach new adaptive responses, such as social skills (Segrin, 2009) or assertiveness (Duckworth, 2009).

- Relaxation training that teaches an alternative physiological response to disturbed negative emotions (Ferguson and Sgambati, 2009).
- Exposure procedures to learn new responses to stimuli that elicit unhealthy disturbed emotions (Hazlett-Stevens and Craske, 2009).
- Reinforcement procedures that arrange positive outcomes for adaptive behaviors.
- Behavioral activation procedures that encourage clients to do things they have enjoyed in the past and that will be reinforcing (Dimidjian et al., 2011).
- Diffusion techniques that encourage clients to act to accomplish their goals despite distressing feelings and thoughts (Hayes, Villatte, Levin, and Hildebrandt, 2011).
- Values clarification exercises that help clients decide how they want to live their lives and what goals to pursue (Hayes, Villatte, Levin, and Hildebrandt, 2011).

REBT integrates all these modalities of cognitive-learning therapies. This chapter briefly describes some of these therapies and how we mix them with classical REBT.

DIRECTLY CHANGING THE BEHAVIORAL C

Behavior therapy has long maintained that a successful strategy to decrease an undesirable response is to engage in a behavior that is incompatible with the behavior you wish to change. Several interventions use this strategy to engage clients to do things that are opposite to their symptoms. This instructs clients to act in ways that one would expect if they were symptom-free. These behavioral interventions encourage clients to change the ***behavioral C*** in our A-B-C model. REBT has always been a form of behavioral therapy and these interventions are consistent with the classical REBT. Therapists can use these interventions before, concurrently, or after challenging IBs. Linehan (1993) has termed the intervention opposite action, because clients behave in direct opposition to their symptoms.

Relaxation Training. Relaxation training has been called the aspirin of CBT. It improves almost any mental health problem. Teaching a person to relax is incompatible with their disturbed, unhealthy negative emotions. It facilitates attention to the task at hand. It slows the person down to process the surrounding information accurately. Therapists have integrated REBT with relaxation training by teaching it at either the beginning of therapy, after the elegant solution is accomplished, or when the client is having difficulty learning the classical REBT. It has almost no negative side effects or counterindications. There are many different relaxation techniques. They all have the same effect on the body, emotions, and behavior. Therefore, you are free to use the one that works best for your client (Ferguson and Sgambati, 2009). Goldfreid and Davison (1994) provide a detailed discussion of several relaxation techniques.

Box 17.1

Relaxation training, like any other behavioral skill, is taught with the emphasis on changing thinking. In addition to mitigating unhealthy, disturbed negative emotions directly, it can change cognitions that lead to the distressed emotions that result in anxiety.

When teaching relaxation, emphasize its use as a coping skill rather than a mastery skill. Its use will not preclude episodes of disturbed negative emotions, but can help to manage them. In the relaxation instructions, stress self-efficacy. For example, "Notice the sensation of relaxation that *you are bringing* forth... notice what *you can evoke* in yourself."

Imagery can add to the experience. Before inducing relaxation, you might ask clients to think of an image or scene in which they feel totally relaxed and safe. Almost all clients will be able to provide an image that has a great deal of personal meaning for them. Ask the client to use all sensory modalities in describing the scene in detail—the colors, sounds, smells, and so on.

Other procedures that might deepen the state of relaxation include the following:

Ask the client to say the word "relax," perhaps fifty to one hundred times in a row (without actually counting), as the client exhales, which establishes a rhythm. This strategy helps to make the word "relax" a discriminative stimulus for the state of relaxation.

Have a client with good imagery skills imagine the word "relax" in the form of a neon sign, blinking on and off rhythmically.

Remind the client to focus on the breathing, making sure it is slow and deliberate.

Toward the end of the process of inducing relaxation, say, "Soon, I'm going to count to ten. Even though you are now relaxed, when I get to ten, you will be profoundly relaxed." Then count slowly to ten, intermittently directing the client to notice and deepen the state of relaxation.

Exposure interventions. Regardless of how forcefully one gives up the irrational beliefs that elicit anxiety, clients have not benefited from therapy until they have faced their fears. Exposure interventions have a long history in psychotherapy and are the treatment of choice for anxiety disorders (Hazlett-Stevens and Craske, 2009). We strongly recommend that all clients be encouraged to confront their fears. Exposure to feared stimuli can be accomplished through imagery or by directly approaching the feared stimuli. All therapists need to be aware of the literature of exposure interventions; exposure has been a crucial component of REBT as long as we have been involved with it. Facing one's fears is the opposite action of feeling anxious.

Behavioral activation. Behavioral theories of depression have maintained that depression results from a lack of reinforcers in one's environment (see Dimidjian et al., 2011 for a review). People stop doing the things that bring them pleasure, mastery, or satisfaction. Behavioral activation encourages people to do the things that they used to enjoy before they were depressed or to try new things that might be enjoyable. This is considered a first-line intervention for depression and we recommend using such interventions concurrently in all cases of depression. Doing enjoyable things is the opposite action of feeling depressed.

Values Clarification and Committed Action. One of the core components of Acceptance and Commitment Therapy (ACT) is helping clients become aware of their values and discovering what is most important to one's true self (Hayes, Villatte, Levin, and Hildebrandt, 2011). Once clients discover this awareness, they "ACT" on their values and do the things that will provide them a meaningful life. Committed action involves setting goals according to one's values and carrying them out responsibly. When clients arrive at therapy, instead of committed action, they are likely to stew in their negative thoughts and emotions and not behave in a way that will bring them a meaningful and enjoyable life. Because Ellis was greatly influenced by the Existential philosophers such as Sartre (1948/1977) and psychotherapists (Frankl, 1946/2006; Yalom, 1980), REBT has always encouraged clients to seek happiness by engaging in positive behaviors that are larger than themselves. REBT has conceptualized the pursuit of happiness as a problem for the latter part of therapy, or as an endeavor for those not in therapy (Bernard, Froh, DiGiuseppe, Joyce, and Dryden, 2010). ACT has refocused this pursuit of positive behaviors as a main part of therapy. This can be a most important addition to classical REBT.

DEVELOPING A NEW COGNITIVE RESPONSE TO THE A

Self-Instructional Training or Stress-Inoculation Training

Meichenbaum (1977) developed a method of using the clients' internal speech to guide adaptive behavior; he called it self-instructional or stress-inoculation training (SIT). Meichenbaum based his treatment on the work of the Soviet psychologists Vygotsky (1975; Diaz and Berk, 1999). Vygotsky explored the interaction of thought and language and discovered that the dominant brain cortex influenced people's language and sequential processing. Because most complex adaptive behaviors require the performance of a series of behaviors emitted in the right order, Vygotsky believed that adaptive behavior required the linguistic encoding of a sequence of behaviors, the rehearsal of the sequence, and the decoding of the instructions to guide behavior upon the occurrence of appropriate cues. These behavior-guiding subroutines become overlearned, occur quickly, and will fail to reach consciousness when well-rehearsed.

Meichenbaum discovered that some people failed to follow this process at all and others had encoded behavior patterns in some situations but not others (Meichenbaum, 1977; 1993; 2009; Meichenbaum and Cameron, 1973; 1974). By training in this skill, people learn to talk to themselves and guide more adaptive behavior. SIT has been used across all ages and applied to a wide variety of problems ranging from impulsive classroom behavior, aggression, anxiety, and depression, to pain management (see Meichenbaum, 2009).

SIT could be the treatment of choice for children younger than eight years (DiGiuseppe, 2006), or for any clients who are intellectually limited, overwhelmed by anxiety and thus unable to think clearly, have a psychotic thought disorder, or have a neurological injury that interferes with reasoning. Sometimes disputing IBs fails with clients with impulsive behaviors, such as reactive aggressive, addictions, or fleeing in panic. In these cases, clients need to stop the impulsive act before they have the time to dispute. SIT helps clients rehearse adaptive behaviors directly, or rational statements that counter their disturbed unhealthy emotions and behaviors. SIT can be used in the following situations:

- *Confronting and handling a Stressor.* The self-statements focus the client on the task rather than on the emotion. The principle is that task-relevant cognitions are incompatible with anxiety-producing ones.
- *Coping with the feeling of being overwhelmed.* These self-statements focus the client on understanding anxiety and reinterpreting it. The message is that anxiety itself is not awful.
- *Reinforcing self-statements.* These statements are an important component when others might not be able to reward the client for small increments of control.

SIT does not provide clients with a philosophic understanding of their problems, but does provide instructions for adaptive behaviors or rational thoughts that are incompatible with the unhealthy negative emotion. SIT is derived from a behavioral model and treats covert stimuli (thoughts), responses, and reinforcers in the same manner as external stimuli, motor responses, and externally applied reinforcers. Meichenbaum's procedures place less emphasis on logical analysis than REBT and as a result change could be less likely to generalize across problems.

Consider the use of SIT in the case of Helene an overweight thirty-five-year-old woman who avoided all contact with men. Helene had a traumatic upbringing with an alcoholic father and was raped by a stranger at the age of fourteen. She experienced guilt, depression, and severe anxiety. Initial attempts at the philosophical solution helped Helene feel sad instead of depressed, and she surrendered her guilt about the rape experience. However, her fear of men persisted unabated. She and the therapist constructed a fear hierarchy. The first item was walking alone on a beach and seeing a man about 200 yards away. Across items, the man was imagined to come closer and closer. The highest item was sitting in the college cafeteria, talking to a man. After relaxation training, each item was imagined and paired with rational self-statements: "I do not have to let these thoughts control my life; I accept feeling anxious and act." "I am tense, but I can stand it." "I have had these feelings before and I know they pass." "What could I say to introduce myself?" After five sessions, Helene could have lunch with men in the school cafeteria with minimal anxiety.

Box 17.2

You might try to suggest some coping statements, utilizing Meichenbaum's three categories, for clients with the following types of problems:

A married individual afraid of dealing with an argumentative spouse

A child afraid of sleeping alone in the dark

A man afraid he will not be able to satisfy his sex partner

An employee who is afraid to disagree with her supervisor

The problem of a client you are presently treating.

The "rational barb techniques" (Kimmel, 1976; Tafrate and Kassinove, 1998) use SIT in anger provoking situations. The therapist deliberately re-creates specific activating events that confront many clients who are teased, mocked, insulted, or taunted by others. Consider the case of a Sam who becomes upset when his wife taunts and insults him. The therapist asked Sam to share the names that the wife called him. Then Sam and therapists devise a set of self-statements that would counteract the client's disturbed emotions and guide adaptive behavior. These included, "I don't have to get upset. Stay calm and take a deep breath. Just tell her we can discuss this topic later when we both are calm." Sam then said the insults to the therapist who then models both coping self-statements and the absence of emotional and behavioral disturbance. Next, the client agrees that the therapist would call the client the insults (i.e., give her a "barb") so that the client can practice the same responses.

TESTING THE ACCURACY OF THE A–(INFERENCE)

As mentioned in earlier chapters, directly challenging the truth of A–(inferences) is not a typical strategy in REBT. However, this intervention may be the treatment of choice in two situations. First, Ellis recognized that not all clients understand or accept the philosophical intervention of classical REBT. After repeated failure to get them to adopt RBs, another intervention could be tried. Challenging the truth of the A–(inference) could be tried if in fact the A–(inference) is very unlikely to be true. When using this intervention we might return to challenging the IBs after changing the A–(inference).

Some clients have understood and profited from challenging their "musts," yet they continue to inaccurately perceive one or more unpleasant activating events; in such cases therapy might not be optimal. Clients could feel sad (rather than depressed), annoyed (rather than angry), and apprehensive (rather than anxious), and could have these feelings a substantially higher portion of the time than necessary if they are rational yet hold inaccurate perceptions and inferences about reality. In such cases, aspects of the clients' lives remain unpleasant and this is worthy of psychological intervention. Clients could make poor life decisions based on such cognitive distortions and nondisturbed negative emotions. In such situations, the therapist could examine the accuracy of the clients A–(inferences). Although, inaccurate perceptions occur less often when clients surrender their irrational demands.

Consider the case of Maurice who entered therapy with the A–(perceived) that his wife was spending less time with him, and who erroneously drew the A–(inference)—"My spouse does not love me." He also had the IB–(imperative/ demand) "I must be loved by my spouse." and the IB–(derivative/self-evaluation), "I am worthless because my spouse does not love me." Classical REBT succeeded. Maurice changed his IB–(imperative/demand) and his IB–(derivative/evaluation) to more adaptive ones. However, his A–(perception), "She is spending less time with me" and his A–(inference), "My spouse does not love me." remained. This negative distortion of reality could change once Maurice surrendered his IB–(imperative/ demand). However, as Allport's (1937) notion of *functional autonomy* indicates, some psychological constructs persist although the factors that caused them are eliminated. Maurice was no longer disturbed by his IB (imperative/demand) about A–(perception) and A–(inference), but he felt very sad about the perceived loss of his wife's affection. Maurice decided he would leave her based on his A (inference) that his wife did no love him. If the A–(inference) was wrong Maurice could leave a marriage based on erroneous conclusions. In such cases, the best intervention is to examine the accuracy of the A–(inferences).

The best example of a therapy that challenges A–(inferences) is Aaron Beck's (1976; 2005; Dobson and Hamilton, 2009) Cognitive Therapy (CT). CT advocates a stance of collaborative empiricisms to help the client observe and report his or her observations objectively and accurately. Following this model, we asked Maurice for data to support his hypothesis that his wife did not love him. To start, we had to agree on what the terms mean and what data to collect. So the therapist asked, "How do you know if someone loves you?" "How would they behave if they did or did not love you?" Maurice responded to these questions with a list of behaviors that are important and the frequency with which his wife did them.

CT posits two primary ways in which clients distort data: selective abstraction and magnification or minimization. Selective abstraction "consists of focusing on a detail taken out of context, ignoring other more salient features of the situation and conceptualizing the whole experience on the basis of this element" (Beck et al., 1979, p. 7). Magnification/minimization "is reflected in errors in evaluation that are so gross as to constitute a distortion" (p. 8). In both types of cognitive errors, clients ignore features of the world around them, and gather biased data. In selective abstraction, clients focus on one category of data and ignore others; in magnification/minimization, clients ignore information within a category.

For example, Maurice selectively attended only to some features of his wife's behavior, such as her working late; he ignored her smiles when she came home, and her eagerness to share the activities of her day with him. He might have inaccurately discounted these data as being irrelevant to his hypothesis. In addition, Maurice might minimize the importance of her desire to talk to him.

The therapist and the client agree on what data are relevant to the hypothesis, thus avoiding selective abstraction (e.g., eye contact, greetings, minutes spent in conversation, relaxed intonations in speech). Then Maurice made frequency counts in a logbook of the desired behaviors to keep accurate records and avoid the problem of magnification/minimization.

Maurice returned to therapy with more accurate data, he reported that on four days his wife came home and kissed him, shared her day, brought him some food, and asked about his day. With such specific data, Maurice started to abandon his hypothesis that she did not love him. However, if he still believed it, he could be making logical errors in drawing conclusions from his data.

Beck has outlined three errors in inductive logic commonly made in drawing conclusions from data, which are all examples of improper inductive reasoning. Induction is difficult because to make an accurate judgment, it is necessary to examine every instance of a particular phenomenon from which the conclusion is being made. For example, if you hypothesize that all little red hens have high IQs, it is logically necessary to examine the IQ of each little red hen. Because such a task is impossible, conclusions drawn inductively are usually based on a sampling procedure, subjected to inferential statistics, and accepted within probability limits, and therefore are always tentative. Clients, however, rarely follow these canons of science.

The cognitive errors or faulty inferences to which Beck refers are as follows:

Arbitrary inference—drawing a conclusion in the absence of supporting evidence or in the face of contrary evidence.
Overgeneralization—drawing a general conclusion based on a single incident.
Personalization—relating external events to oneself when there is no basis for making such a connection.

In summary, two major procedures are to train the client to (a) objectively collect and accurately label data outside the therapy session, and (b) question his or her automatic conclusions from these data. Consider the following hypothetical examples.

Consider another example where we challenged the A–(inference) after successfully challenging the elegant solution. Georgina reported that she experienced disturbed guilt over her A–(inference) that she acted selfishly. She had the IB–(imperative/demand) that, "I must not act selfishly," and the IB–(derivative/self-downing), "I am worthless for acting selfishly."

After the therapy helped Georgia change her demanding and self-downing, she no longer experienced disturbed guilt; but she remained concerned. She thought, "I can be selfish sometimes, and I am not worthless when I act this way; however, being selfish might not be the best way to act. It can interfere with my success at work, keeping friends, and finding a romantic partner. So, I will avoid being selfish." Was Georgia accurate that she acted selfishly? First, the therapist and Georgia defined selfish acts and how to distinguish them from self-interest. Then they examined what Georgia actually did. This discussion led to the conclusion that Georgia did not act selfishly but often failed to act in her best interest and put others before herself. This inelegant intervention led to the discussion of a new problem—Why did Georgia usually put others first to her own disadvantage? Could she act in her self-interest if it inconvenienced others?

Also consider the client Chaim, who often became angry when other people insulted him. Chaim experienced the A–(inference)—"People are insulting me." He thought the IB (imperative/demand)—"They must treat me with respect." He also had the IB–(derivative/other condemnation)—"People who insult me are despicable and deserve being attacked." The therapist chose the elegant solution and targeted Chaim's demand that others must respect him and his condemnation of them when they did not. This greatly reduced Chaim's anger at work and resulted in increased productivity. However, he remained aloof from his peers and failed to work effectively on teams projects. This was not surprising because he believed that his coworkers were disrespecting him. Although he reacted with only displeasure and annoyance it was not pleasant being annoyed each day. Perhaps Chaim overreacted to his coworkers' comments. An examination of Chaim's A–(inference) resulted in a discussion of what the people actually said to him and how they said it. This revealed that when someone criticized him or made a suggestion, Chaim thought they were insulting him.

Wendell Johnson, in his 1946 work on semantic therapy, pointed out that two important questions for the therapist are "What do you mean? and "How do you know?" These questions are embedded in the following transcript, in which Chaim's annoyance at his colleagues insults is discussed.

T: He made a suggestion concerning the best way to do that task. Does that mean that he is insulting you?

C: Well...no.

T: Is it possible that you know every way and the best way to do all projects at work?

C: I can expect him not to think less of me if he does have a better idea!

T: OK, but if you are going to believe that people are thinking less of you every time someone has a better idea than you, what's going to happen to you?

C: I will be insulted a lot.

T: Yes, you will constantly be on guard, won't you?

C: Yes, I guess so.

T: And it is possible that someone will have a better idea than you. How is that an insult to you?

C: Well, if they didn't have better ideas once in a while I would have to do all the work and thinking.

T: Does offering an idea on how to do a project really mean you are being insulted?

C: No, I guess it just means they are doing their jobs.

Some therapists new to REBT engage in procedures such as those outlined above. We hope that this description will make clear what they are doing, and inform the new therapist how to challenge A–(inferences) more efficiently. Although REBT sometimes recommends challenging the A–(inference), this is preferably done after an attempt to execute the classical and philosophical solution. Even if the philosophical solution is successful, the therapist might explore the inaccuracy of the A–(inference) if continuing to hold the belief could lead to extended and needless negative emotions or ineffectual decision making.

EXPLANATIONS ABOUT THE A–(CONFIRMABLE)

Many psychologists believe that humans function as scientists in our attempts to understand the world around us (Laird and Metalsky, 2009; Mahoney, 1977; 1991). Scientists try to classify, understand, predict, and control the environment. To accomplish these goals, they develop theories or explanations of events. Understanding an event increases the chance that one can predict and control the event. All humans do this in their personal lives. Humans want to understand why their lovers leave them, why they did not get the promotion at work, why a fiend ignored them, or why someone insulted them. These explanations are referred to as personal constructs (Kelly, 1955; Mahoney, 1991), attributions (Seligman, 1975; Weiner, 1989), or schema (Piaget, 1954: Young, Klosko, and Weishaar, 2003).

Kelly (1955) noted that people develop a system of constructs to make the world predictable. An individual's construct system influences his or her expectations about and perceptions of the world. Some constructs are more important than others. A person's construct system is her or his truth as she or he understands and experiences it. A person's system of construct need not be internally consistent. Psychotherapy often involves assessing and understanding clients' constructs, and then helping them evaluate whether their constructs help them maneuver in the world effectively.

Kelly's theory lead to the development of interventions on scientific reasoning as a model of human adjustment and a correction for maladjustment (Mahoney, 1979; 1991) and to the constructivist methods that conceptualize therapy as a task of understanding a person's epistemology or philosophy of understanding the world (Mahoney, 1991; Mahoney and Lyddon, 1988; Neimeyer, 1993). Seligman (1975; Alloy, Peterson, Abramson, and Seligman, 1984) proposed that a person's attributions or explanatory style present the key to understanding why people respond differently to adverse events. Although people may experience similar negative events, each person's interpretations explaining the event will affect the likelihood of acquiring learned helplessness and depression (Abraham, Seligman and Teasdale, 1978). People with pessimistic explanatory style see negative events as permanent ("It will never change."), personal ("It's my fault."), and pervasive ("I can't do anything correctly.") and are most likely to suffer from learned helplessness and depression.

Weiner (1979; 1985), a cognitive psychologist, developed a similar attribution theory based on research from children's academic achievement motivation. Weiner proposed that people attribute a cause or explanation to an unpleasant event. Attribution theory includes the dimensions of globality/specificity, stability/instability, and internality/externality (Weiner, 1985). A global attribution occurs when the individual believes that the cause of negative events is consistent across different contexts. A specific attribution occurs when the individual believes that the cause of a negative event is unique to a particular situation. A stable attribution occurs when the individual believes the cause to be consistent across time. Unstable attribution occurs when the individual thinks that the cause is specific to one point in time. An external attribution assigns causality to situational or external factors, while an internal attribution assigns causality to factors within the person (Abraham et al., 1978).

Sometimes clients' IBs are psychologically deduced from their constructs designed to explain important life events. Changing the IB is difficult until the client has an explanation for the life event that is consistent with an RB that will support a healthy, adaptive negative emotion. Consider the following case study.

Paul entered therapy after verbally threatening his girlfriend Katia and throwing phones, keys, or whatever was at hand at her. The couple had dated for more than five years, and were about to be engaged when Katia announced that she was leaving Paul. Paul was enraged. He screamed and threatened Katia, and he texted and e-mailed her constantly demanding and begging that she return. These temper tantrums were punctuated with periods of depression. Paul had several IBs. His IB–(imperative/demand) was that he needed Katia. Paul also held two IB–(derivative global evaluations). She was totally bad and he was as well. After he and the therapist changed this demanding belief, Paul said he needed to understand why Katia left him. Paul had several theories. His IB–(derivatives) was closely related to his explanation for their breakup. First, he proposed that all women were crazy and impossible to please. This global condemnation of women led to more anger and to verbal attacks on other women whom he had never dated. Next, he thought that Katia was a selfish, disturbed person who had purposely used him. This also increased his anger. Sometimes, Paul thought that Katia must have left him because he was inadequate. He was not good enough and just did not understand women. This global self-condemnation led to depression. Paul was stuck in a trap. All of these explanatory constructors involved condemnation of individuals or groups that led to either anger or depression. One can understand his reason for wanting an explanation for the breakup so he could pick a better partner the next time and avoid the pain of unrequited love.

After challenging the global denigration theories, the therapist asked Paul to review why other couples he had known had separated. Many it seemed were poorly matched to begin with, others had grown apart. Through such discussion, the therapist Socratically led Paul to a new explanation. People separate because they are not compatible. This happens without malice or intention or evil or psychopathology. Noticing that one was not compatible with a person one had fallen in lust with did not mean that a person was condemnable. With this explanation Paul could give up his global condemnation of all women. Women were just as impaired in picking long-term mates as were men. He could give up his global condemnation for Katia and surrender his anger. He could give up his global condemnation of himself and surrender his depression. Paul adopted the RB that people are fallible and make bad choices, and they are not evil, only human for doing so. He also committed to understanding himself and the women he dated better so he could make better choices, which was the purpose of the explanatory construct in the first place. We think that global condemnation beliefs can often serve such explanatory functions. Developing schema that can coexist with rational beliefs can be a major part of successful therapy.

CHANGING THE A

Once we have helped clients cope with the world not being as they want it, they can learn to more effectively make the world more compatible with their desires. Thus, a client might discover that although some people in his office like him, the percentage is lower than he would like. A psychological intervention is then appropriate. Helping the client change those As that can be changed is a legitimate and important endeavor for the rational emotive behavior therapist. This concept comes from Ellis, who in his therapy groups spent a significant portion of time helping clients develop social survival skills. Attempts to change the A can fall into two basic categories: (1) attempts to change the environment in which the client operates, and (2) attempts to change personal aspects of the client.

Changing the World

Clients frequently experience real-life adversities that can be changed. As we discussed in Chapter 1, once the classical REBT approach to changing clients' IBs has led to functional, adaptive, negative emotions, clients can still work to change the A to make life better. There might be severe financial, legal, in-law, medical, educational, career-related, and marital or family problems. In dealing with these issues, the therapist can fill two basic roles: giving information where appropriate and, more important, teaching problem-solving skills.

Social Problem Solving. One cognitive-learning therapy involves teaching Social Problem Solving (SPS) (Nezu, Maguth-Nezu, and McMurran, 2009). Spivack and Shure (1974) first developed a curriculum to prevent adjustment problems in inner-city poor children. They demonstrated that focusing on kindergarten and first-grade children could prevent the development of problems; and the success of this program led to the use of these methods as a therapy and their application to other problems and patient groups. Working independently D'Zurilla and Goldfried (1971) developed a similar approach within behavior therapy. SPS involves a process that defines and formulates the problem, generates a variety of response alternatives for resolving problems, considers the possible consequences for the alternatives, and chooses the most likely successful plan of action. Training in problem solving can be considered a self-control skill for the individual to learn how to solve problems and discover the most effective way of responding.

SPS methods represent one of the most researched areas in CBT, and are a good first-line intervention for most problems. An extensive research literature supports the efficacy and effectiveness of SPS with age groups with many different problems and disorders (Nezu, Nezu, and D'Zurilla 2006; Nezu, Maguth-Nezu, and McMurran, 2009). Training materials are available for clients of many ages and with numerous presenting problems.

Many theories of psychotherapy focus only on factors that influence disturbed emotions that inhibit or interfere with appropriate functioning and assume that clients know or can produce more appropriate and adaptive responses once the disturbed emotions are removed. The work of SPS researchers points out, however, that learning problem-solving skills might be necessary to add appropriate, adaptive behaviors to the client's repertoire. This model suggests that dysfunctional behavior can be caused by deficits in determining a functional response. A therapy that combines both approaches could lead to the optimal outcome for the client.

Ellis often combined classical REBT with SPS. He often conducted a workshop called "Creative Contacts for Singles," one of the most popular ones given at the Albert Ellis Institute. In this workshop, he first helped people identify and challenge IBs that lead to their inhibitions and then taught them to practice the social skills needed in making contact with potential dates. When teaching problem-solving skills, however, REBT would advocate going one step further and teaching the client how to cope with failure. On many occasions, clients will find that they have only a choice of very imperfect alternatives, that each solution has a probability of producing undesirable consequences, or that the problem is simply unsolvable. Cold reality sometimes thwarts the best problem solvers. When this is the case, finding the elegant solution (e.g., anti-awfulizing) is an indispensable tool.

Assertiveness and Social Skills training. The rationale for using assertiveness training and social skills training with REBT is the same as we mentioned above of SPS. Clients may have replaced their IBs with RBs, but despite the fact that they have adaptive, healthy negative emotions, they do not know how to implement adaptive behaviors to improve the quality of their lives. Both social skills training (Segrin 2009) and assertiveness training (Duckworth, 2009) use a combination of Modeling, rehearsal, and feedback to teach the behaviors. Deficiencies in these areas might result from lack of verbal and nonverbal repertoires, or from cognitive factors that impede the expression of these behaviors, or both. In addition, deficiencies in assertiveness and social skills could be situation-specific. Thus, a client might be quite assertive or socially skilled with employees at work, yet timid with family members at home. A client might be quite adept at expressing negative feelings, but tongue-tied when it comes to expressing tender, gentle, or loving thoughts. Changing these aspects of the client's behavior could help to change the client's **A**s, as long as two antiabsolutist notions are kept in mind. Behaving assertively or developing social skills are not guarantees that clients will get what is wanted, although it might increase the probability of a favorable outcome. Also, if clients know how to behave assertively, that does not mean that they must behave this way all the time. In some instances, discretion might be the better part of assertion. In other words, the skill of consequential thinking is relevant.

The first step in teaching the client such skills is outlined below using the example of assertiveness. First, we teach clients the differences between assertive, nonassertive, and aggressive behavior. Assertive behavior is characterized as a statement of a preference or a request for change from another person, which is communicated directly, but without hostility or defensiveness. One is open/receptive to the rejection of the request. Nonassertive behavior is characterized by indirect communication, inhibition, and anxiety, and perhaps by not attempting to get what one wants at all. One avoids the rejection of the request. Aggressive behavior typically communicates demands rather than preferences, is righteous or hostile, and has the intent of punishing the other person. One tries to enforce the request with aggressivity. Both in aggressive behavior and nonassertive behavior, one is not open/receptive to rejection of the request.

A second task in assertiveness training would be to correct the client's irrational self-statements: notions that lead to unassertive, hostile, or aggressive responses; or ideas with which the client punishes himself or herself for inept assertive responses, for assertions that do not prove immediately successful, or for failures to respond at all.

An eye-opening step for clients is to perceive their right to be assertive. What are their rights as human beings? What are their rights in specific social roles—as spouse or as parent? Such questions often provide a provocative homework assignment. The following suggestions might help clients get started: "I have the right to have feelings and express them, including complaints and criticisms. I have the right to set my own priorities. I have the right to say no without feeling guilty."

Assertiveness training also entails assessing the clients' strengths and weaknesses in assertive communication and developing training procedures to bridge the gaps in their skills. The following checklist is adapted from one prepared by Janet Wolfe's Guidelines for Behaving Assertively.

- When refusing, express a decisive "no"; explain why you are refusing, but do not be unduly apologetic. When applicable, offer the other person an alternative course of action.
- Give as prompt and brief a reply as you can, without interruption.
- Request an explanation when asked to do something unreasonable.
- Look directly at the person to whom you are speaking.
- Check your body language for postures that might convey indirectness or lack of self-assurance (e.g., hand over mouth, shuffling feet).
- Watch your vocal inflection, making sure that you speak neither too loudly nor too softly.
- When expressing annoyance or criticism, remember to comment only on the behavior; avoid a personal attack.
- When commenting on another person's behavior, try to use "I" statements. For example, instead of saying, "You rat—you made me so mad!" try, "I feel annoyed when you cancel out on social arrangements at the last minute; it's

inconvenient." Whenever possible, offer an alternative behavior: "I think we'd better sit down and try to figure out how we can make plans together and cut down on this kind of inconveniencing."

- Keep a log of your assertive responses. Review them and talk them over with a friend. Observe role models. Remember that you do not unlearn bad habits or learn new skills overnight.
- Reward yourself in some way each time you have pushed yourself to make an assertive response, whether or not you get the desired results from the other person.
- Do not berate yourself when you behave nonassertively or aggressively; rather, try to figure out where you went astray and how to improve your handling of the situation next time.

A useful model for constructing an assertive communication that is found in the self-help literature is DESC, a four-step communication package:

> *Describe*—the client is trained to briefly and objectively describe the troublesome A, without editorializing, personalizing, or elaborating.
> *Emotion*—this is simply stated, using "I" language.
> *Specify* what you want—the client makes a request (not a demand), and does so with clarity, concreteness, and specificity.
> *Consequence*—the communicator spells out to the listener the positive consequences that might accrue if the request is met.

An example will probably make this model clearer. Recall our client Maurice who was upset that his wife did not spend as much time with him as he would like. After the Classical REBT and the examination of his A–(inferences), he learned assertiveness training to ask his wife to do things together.

> D—You make plans to work on weekends and holidays without discussing it with me…
> E—I feel disappointed. I miss you when you work on weekends and holidays and I do not get to see you.
> S—I would be willing to rearrange my schedule if you would let me know when you had to work so we could spend some time together on a different day.
> C—This way we could spend more time together.

Box 17.3

As a training exercise, try to compose two DESC communications, one for a positive emotion or request and another for a negative emotion or request. Perhaps the positive DESC could include a request for a change in a sexual behavior with one's sex partner or an increase in social activity.

The preceding list and model provide only a synopsis; they do not provide sufficient guidance if assertiveness training is new to you. Remember, assertiveness
training is one technique that you can use in helping clients to change their **As**.

The same model can be provided for social skills training; however, the range
of behaviors and responses is wider and provides responses in situations such as
conversations.

Providing Practical Advice to Help Clients Change the A

Suppose you, as a therapist, think that the client could make some changes in physical appearance to improve his or her chances of reaching certain goals. Would you
feel comfortable giving your client honest feedback or initiating such discussions?

For example, suppose your client is an older woman who is looking for a mate
yet has allowed herself to become a bit dumpy and dresses in a dowdy fashion.
Wouldn't you be irresponsible if you withheld practical advice that might be relevant? How could you tactfully suggest changes that might enhance her chances
of reaching her goal? You might say something like, "You know, Mary, it's been my
experience that a woman has a better chance of getting into a relationship if she
loses some weight, gets a new hairstyle, and learns what she can about putting her
best foot forward. Does that sound like anything that would appeal to you?" or
"Is that something you'd be interested in?" In other words, without being critical,
you can make suggestions in the third person, not directly aimed at the client. The
suggestion implies, "You can do what you wish, but this might be helpful," and
allows the client to make the decision to change.

If the client accepts the suggestion, be sure to reinforce any positive changes
that you observe from week to week. For example, "Mary, what an attractive dress
you're wearing!" or "I like the way you've done your hair; it's very flattering." The
changes made might also begin pleasing the client herself.

Box 17.4

How would you feel about confronting and openly discussing any of the following
topics with a client?

Obesity
Body odor
Breaches of etiquette
Psychotic speech

Do you give yourself the freedom to tell your clients that some aspect of their
behavior or appearance is socially unacceptable or goal defeating? Be alert to
whether you are avoiding such topics because they are uncomfortable for you.
Are you afraid of your client's reactions? If so, is your hesitance based on rational
reasons or on an irrational need for your client's approval, or belief that your client
would be harmed by such feedback?

In other cases, feedback might be more direct. More seriously, disturbed clients might be grossly unaware of the effects of their appearance or behavior on others, and your confrontation therefore will be more forceful and persistent. Remember that few people, if any, in the client's life have been brave enough to provide such feedback; your timidity in the guise of "unconditional acceptance" is counterproductive.

In a recent example, a young anorexic woman's emaciated appearance immediately struck the therapist. Her presenting problem was her lack of friends, about which she was puzzled and depressed. One symptom of anorexia is a distorted body image; the skinnier such clients get, the more acceptable they appear in their own eyes, even when their physical state has deteriorated so much that hospitalization is required. The therapist in this case example shared with the client his own reaction to her appearance: discomfort of the same sort he might feel upon visiting someone with a terminal disease—hardly the sort of reaction a young woman in search of friends would desire. At first, the patient vehemently denied that her appearance played any role in her social difficulties, but with repeated and vigorous challenges by her therapist, she finally recalled a recent interaction with a coworker. The other woman had timorously inquired whether the client was suffering from leukemia. In the ensuing weeks, with continuing persistent confrontations by the therapist, the client began clearly to realize the impact of her appearance on others, and although she preferred her cachectic state, she became determined to make some changes in her diet and choice of clothing.

ACCEPTING THE A–(INFERENCE) THOUGHTS, IRRATIONAL BELIEFS, AND UNHEALTHY C

Acceptance and mindfulness interventions (Hayes, Villatte, Levin, and Hildebrandt, 2011) have become popular in recent years as adjuncts or alternatives to cognitive interventions. In these interventions, the client learns to become aware of thoughts and emotions that interfere with their functioning and to hold a nonjudgmental attitude toward these experiences and behave despite the presence of these distracting thoughts and emotions. Mindfulness and diffusion interventions do not try to change the thoughts or emotions that the client experiences, but attempt to break the connection between these internal stimuli and the disturbed behaviors they usually elicit. The person is taught to have a more flexible reaction to the presence of the distracting and uncomfortable thoughts and emotions. This comes close to REBT's concept of secondary level or meta-emotions and cognitions.

Let us return to our client Maurice whom we discussed above. Maurice could use acceptance intervention in several ways. When Maurice experienced his A–(inference) "My spouse does not love me," and his IB–(imperative demand) "She must love me," instead of trying to challenge the truth of these ideas, he would engage in cognitive diffusion (Hayes, Villatte, Levin, and Hildebrandt, 2011), which would propose that he not engage in an evaluation of the truth of this thought. Similarly, when he experienced his C–(unhealthy, disturbed emotion) of fear, he would notice that he experienced the emotion, not try to change it, and continue to act as he had planned.

In summary, in addition to the classical disputations and philosophical restructuring used by REBT, many other skills and techniques can be incorporated into therapy to help clients. In touching upon these varied techniques drawn from the wide range of existing cognitive-learning therapies, we have not been able to do them justice, but we do want the reader to understand how REBT incorporates all of these techniques. We tried to discuss those that we thought would be hardest to conceptualize integrating with REBT. We suggest that readers familiarize themselves more thoroughly with these other techniques.

18

The Course of Therapy and Beyond

Let us review what we have learned so far. The therapist has identified a problem situation (A), an unhealthy disturbed emotion and/or maladaptive behavior (C), and the irrational belief (IB) held by the client, and the therapist has attempted to dispute these irrational notions. Of course, clients typically have more than one A or C on which to work. If you have seen video or live demonstrations of REBT, you might have an oversimplified impression of the process of therapy, for these demonstrations purposely focus on only one or two problems in one session. In ongoing therapy, it is appropriate to focus on one problem at a time, but clients typically have multiple problems. An error that novice therapists often make is to try to condense the client's problems into one. Instead, we recommend that you work on each problem separately and develop a treatment plan to ensure that you do not neglect any problems or become mired in the client's complaints.

Treatment plans are frequently used at mental health clinics and psychiatric hospitals; they can be required by many third-party payment systems and are the inevitable consequence of professional peer review systems. Treatment plans are best developed from a problem-oriented record system such as the one outlined below. Realize that not every therapist constructs treatment plans, nor will it be necessary to do so for each of your clients. We offer this model to help you understand the ongoing therapeutic process and as a guide for satisfying formal requirements to document treatment.

To begin a treatment plan, list each of the client's dysfunctional, unhealthy emotions or dysfunctional behaviors; these are the emotional and behavioral aspects of the C. Look for relationships among these components and their accompanying cognitions.

A SAMPLE TREATMENT PLAN

Table 18.1 provides a problem list that was developed over the first several sessions with a client. The next step is to arrange these problems in order of priority. This

Table 18.1. SAMPLE PROBLEM LIST

Problems	Cognitions	Emotions	Behaviors
1. Relationship with boss	He must not criticize me. It is terrible if the boss doesn't like me.	Anger, anxiety	Talking angrily to boss. Inefficiency at work due to time spent catastroph-izing. Lack of assertiveness.
2. Problems dating	I must have a lover in my life. It is awful to get rejected.	Anxiety	Avoidance of social contact. Lack of social skills.
3. Relationship with mother	I must visit my mother more often. I am worthless for being a bad son.	Guilt	Undesired daily phone calls with mother. Undesired Saturday night dinners at mother's house.
4. Obesity	I must have what I want (FI). It is hopeless. I will never control my eating and that makes me worthless.	Agitation when not eating, depres-sion after eating	Overeating.

would be done in consultation with the client. For each problem identified, plan behavioral and cognitive strategies to ameliorate the problem. In addition, we recommend that you plan ahead for your next three sessions with the client, organizing how you will utilize the sessions in blocks of time. Keep your plan flexible, so that you remain sensitive to your client's immediate concerns; yet be alert to and guard against unnecessary distractions. If your client introduces a new problem every week, you could lose sight of your original goals. Another purpose of a treatment plan, therefore, is to help the therapist and client remain on track.

The following treatment plan was constructed after four sessions with the client whose problem list appears in Table 18.1. You might find this plan useful as a general model.

Session 5
Problem 1
Check on homework assignment(s) from previous week.
If the client was successful, reinforce him; if unsuccessful, trouble-shoot.
What thoughts and emotions got in the way?
Continue disputing the irrational demands creating anger at client's boss.
Dispute IB–(imperative/demand) about the boss.
Teach and role-play some assertive responses for client to use at work.

Generate homework assignment: (a) read *Your Perfect Right* (Alberti and Emmons, 2008); (b) implement the behavior rehearsed in session with the boss; (c) monitor work efficiency and when off-task, use as a cue to do A-B-C-D homework sheet on catastrophizing.
Problem 2
If time permits, begin inquiry into client's anxiety in social situations.

Session 6
Problem 1
Check on homework assignments from previous session; reinforce or trouble-shoot.
Review disputation of IBs leading to client's anger or anxiety in work situation.
Role-play assertive responses in different hypothetical work situations to increase generalization.
Give homework assignment: (a) continue to read *Your Perfect Right* and begin *Overcoming Frustration and Anger* (Hauck, 1974); and (b) do homework sheets on anger and anxiety when work efficiency drops.
Problem 2
Dispute awfulizing about rejection.
Give homework assignment: do A-B-C-D homework sheet disputing fears of rejection.
Summarize major points in session and review homework assignments for coming week.

Session 7
Problem 1
Review homework assignment; reinforce or trouble-shoot.
Briefly review disputation of anger-producing beliefs.
Homework assignments: (a) continue monitoring work performance and do homework sheets as needed; and (b) continue trying to implement new assertive responses as needed.
Problem 2
Check homework sheet disputing fears of rejection. Reinforce or trouble-shoot.
Do rational emotive imagery in dating situations to uncover anxiety, and do in-session disputing.
Begin social skills training: role-play asking a woman for a date.
Homework assignment for risk taking: attempt to elicit three rejections this week; if distressed, do homework sheet(s).

Session 8
Problems 1 and 2
Review and check on progress. Put problems 1 and 2 on working agenda for the session if needed.
Assign relevant homework.

Problem 3

Dispute beliefs about self-worth that cause guilt.

If client appears to understand the disputation, check veracity of perception of the A.

Summarize major points of session and review homework assignments for coming week.

After reading this treatment plan, you might find it overwhelming. Is therapy so tightly organized? Do therapists accomplish that much in every session? And do clients really move that quickly? The sample was designed to make three major points:

1. It is important to work *consistently* on each of the problems outlined by the client. Notice that the therapist continues to work on the first problem across several sessions. Although the percentage of time spent on this problem can be reduced over sessions, therapeutic follow-up is built into the plan. The therapist's attention to this problem is faded slowly, principally by assignment and review of homework tasks, as the client improves.
2. New problems are introduced systematically into treatment as the more significant problems show improvement. Note also the multiplicity of treatment strategies implemented. (Some of these strategies will be discussed below.)
3. Although all of these steps could be taken in therapy, the number of steps per problem, the number of problems per session, and the number of sessions required to accomplish each goal vary widely from client to client and for the same client at different points in therapy.

Note that each session begins with a review of homework (in this case a written disputation by the client) and a review of a previous disputation in session. In both instances the therapist is checking to see whether the client has understood the D and the EB. If the client has not comprehended the D or the EB, or fails to do the homework sheet, trouble-shooting is called for.

New therapists frequently experience impatience or even anger at clients who make mistakes. Monitor your reactions in this situation. If you are impatient, look for your own irrational beliefs—specifically, that the client *should* have felt better, or at least have performed better. Avoid rating yourself based on your client's behavior. Disputation involves subtle and sophisticated philosophical points and taps skills that clients ordinarily do not use. Allow yourself and your client permission to be beginners.

If your client has successfully worked out a homework sheet and has experienced a reduction in emotional stress during an in-session dispute, you might recognize one of two possible outcomes at this point:

The client could continue to experience the same unhealthy, disturbed C regularly and will use this as a cue to utilize his or her REBT skills as modeled in therapy. Disputation thus serves as a coping technique.

A new C could emerge. If the client has been able to replace the old IBs with more rational philosophies, the original As will automatically be followed by more appropriate emotional reactions. When well-practiced, the new RBs become as automatic to the client as the original IBs were.

EXPANDING THE FOCUS OF THERAPY

When a person starts to change, it is important to recognize that the change might have implications—provide activating events—for other family members. They could be happy to see the change, or become distressed about it. The change could be threatening to the family, and they could even attempt to sabotage it. Therapists want to assess any ripple effects of the impact of the psychotherapy on the family.

Thus far, we have written about REBT as if it were only conducted in the context of individual therapy. We would like to suggest at this point that REBT and all therapies might appropriately be used for couples, families, or groups. As your skills in managing the REBT model grow, we recommend that you invite family members into the sessions. In this way, you can independently assess the changes in your client and how this change affects others, perhaps thereby forestalling negative reactions from the family. You could teach family members what you and the client are working on; and with your client's agreement, it could be helpful to conduct some therapy in the presence of family members or the client's spouse, as long as the "other" can remain a largely silent observer and be supportive of the client's change.

Box 18.1

Can you imagine how it could help therapy for the wife of a man with erectile problems to attend some sessions and to share the process as an observer? What benefits might accrue as she watched the therapist work with her husband? List three.

Would the issues be different if the husband were watching the therapist work with his wife on her emotions about him?

One can do individual REBT within a family context, by having other family members present as participant-observers, and with the therapist actively coaching helpful responses and modeling therapeutic interactions. Also, once the therapist has learned the perspective of the other family members, the therapist can have individual sessions and think of the client's problems from the perspective of the family. Often, other issues will come up in a family meeting that expand the individual's psychotherapeutic work. Comprehensive family therapy within an REBT context is beyond the scope of this book; however, other texts do provide such material (Ellis, 1986; 1993; Huber, 1997; Huber and Baruth, 1989).

Box 18.2

If family members are not available for sessions, some therapists make use of an "empty chair" strategy: as an issue is being discussed, the therapist might say, "What do you think your husband would say to this if he were sitting right over there?"

CONTINUING THERAPY

When clients' presenting problems have been resolved, they might wish to continue to schedule appointments or continue therapy. Very often the behavioral changes made in therapy will provide clients with new social opportunities that they might not have the skills to handle. For example, the formerly obese man might now find himself confronted with new dating issues or find that colleagues at work have higher expectations of output from him. A formerly nonassertive, reclusive housewife might encounter new problems as she secures a job and adjusts to the working world. In other words, although there might no longer be evidence of the psychopathology that brought the client to therapy, the client might profit from continued therapeutic work.

In other instances, clients could bring up new problems when they experience some relief from the original ones. This pattern might be viewed as a *figure-ground* effect; as the primary problem (figure) gets resolved, it recedes and minor problems (background) come into the forefront. Such cases do not necessarily provide an example of symptom substitution, a term that implies that curing one problem leads to an increase in or the development of other problems. Rather, the client could now have the time and energy to focus on less pressing issues. With low socioeconomic status clients, who seem to live by "crisis management," a new "figure" might be presented to the therapist each week.

When clients present new problems they could become discouraged, making predictions of a gloomy future filled with problems for which they must continue to get professional help. At such times, it is useful to have clients recollect their earlier problems, now in the background; point these out to them and reinforce your clients lavishly for the progress they have already achieved. An analogy such as the following one could also be helpful: "If you go to your physician with fourteen splinters in your hand, even after five are out, your hand might still hurt because nine more remain. It just takes more work." Remember that your client's confidence in allowing you to go on removing "psychological splinters" might waver unless you point out that five have already been removed. Pointing out the figure-ground analogy discussed above might also be useful. If you have a minor cut on your finger, sore feet, and a pounding headache and then receive a punch in the nose, you probably won't notice the first three troubles until the pain of the last one recedes.

Box 18.3

Is REBT a short-term therapy? This question is asked by clients (e.g., "How long will I have to be in treatment?") as well as by insurance companies.

The cognitive-behavioral therapies in general and REBT in particular claim to be fast-acting, and we have seen clients catapulted into positive changes in mood and behavior in just a few sessions. However, it would be foolhardy to conclude that all clients will respond so quickly.

Under what conditions do clients remain in therapy for longer periods of time? The following list, although not complete, provides some answers to this question.

Protracted As, such as a difficult divorce

Chronic, albeit intermittent conditions, such as physical disability, or certain affective illnesses

Axis I conditions compounded by an Axis II diagnosis

Behaviorally indefinable goals; for example, existential dilemmas or self-actualization issues

Clients' narcissistic entertainment in hearing themselves talk, and enjoying the therapy hour for this reason alone

Client not completing homework assignments consistently

Periodic progress reviews are recommended as a routine part of therapy. Clients come to therapy because they feel pain, and as soon as it is alleviated they tend not to think about it or how the relief was accomplished. We all forget the stone that was in our shoe yesterday. If clients become aware of how they accomplished the pain reduction, they could be more likely to use the same techniques in the future. If you think that clients have made gains that are not clear to them, point these out and discuss with them how they were accomplished.

Also, ask your clients for periodic feedback on the therapy experience. They can usually recall what preceded an "Aha!" reaction, and this feedback might be a rich source of information for you. In addition, their comments might reinforce your therapeutic interventions. Ask the following kinds of questions: "How did I help you?" or "How could I have helped you more?" and "Was there anything I did that interfered with my helping you?" Some therapists ask these questions at the end of every therapy hour, not only for personal feedback but also to identify any lingering irrational beliefs or to correct misperceptions.

Box 18.4

Beginning therapists often get assigned clients who are chronically disturbed, characterologically disordered, and minimally motivated; that is, those clients least likely to participate actively in therapy and profit greatly from it. The novice therapist might erroneously end up concluding, "REBT really doesn't work" or "I'm no good as a therapist." As the therapist gains experience, he or she learns to set realistic, yet limited goals for such clients and to be pleased with small changes.

The periodic review could also help prepare for the client's termination. Terminating is often uncomfortable for clients; for example, they might feel that they need an excuse to terminate, or that they will be unable to function independently after therapy has ended. When it is time for a review, therefore, you might also ask, "How are we doing in getting you closer to your goals? How much longer do you want to work together? When shall we schedule our next review?"

TERMINATION OF THERAPY

In a sense, therapy provides ongoing preparation for termination. REBT in particular follows an educational model and attempts to teach the client rational self-analysis skills, which we hope can generalize to new problem situations. As the client improves, the therapist can do less of the disputing in the session and leave more of it to the client. We recommend that as sessions progress, you remain active but shift the content of your speech.

In early sessions, you will talk more about the IBs and why they are irrational. Toward the final sessions, you will comment more about how well your clients are disputing their own IBs. Thus, by the end of therapy, most clients have acquired some basic understanding of the theory of emotional disturbance and have learned some skills to combat it, so that you can merely guide them through the application of REBT to specific problems.

When clients announce that they feel ready for termination and you agree that the goals outlined at the beginning of therapy have been met, you might wish to inquire whether they have any new goals or issues that they wish to discuss. Such an invitation might be helpful to clients who feel inhibited about bringing up what they view as minor or unrelated problems. Occasionally, you might believe that clients are terminating before they are ready; the original goals might have been met, but the clients have a number of other significant issues that you can help. By all means, bring these to their attention; however, if clients do not contract to work on them, you could be making an ethical error by insisting that they remain in therapy.

Therapists could have to deal with their own perfectionist standards. Do you have an absolute "should" about how clients will perform at the end of therapy? Clients will not always arrive at the end points you'd prefer, and little will be achieved by pestering them or worrying whether they've gotten their money's worth. It is possible and acceptable for therapy to terminate before all goals are accomplished. In fact, some clients report that major gains occurred after therapy was terminated; there might be a significant lag time between learning the principles and deciding to implement them wholeheartedly. Of course, you might suggest to clients that you perceive them to be selling themselves short, and the merits of working on further problems can be discussed. Ultimately, however, it will be the client's choice.

When Is Therapy Completed?

The question of when therapy is completed is frequently asked of us when we do supervision training. Poignantly, it is asked also by clients in the process of therapy. Clearly, there are no hard-and-fast rules to answer this question, and sometimes the end of therapy occurs for practical or financial reasons that are extraneous to the process. Nonetheless, there are some general criteria to offer the student or client in making the decision to terminate therapy.

Among these criteria, we have found ourselves discriminating between necessary and sufficient criteria; that is, some outcomes seem to be important for termination, but perhaps are not sufficient for us to feel comfortable that the client's gains can be maintained. One such criterion is insight. In the process of therapy, it is hoped that clients will understand the principles of REBT. Either in the form of an "Aha!" or by gradually discovering a new idea that makes sense, we expect the client to understand the B-C connection that links thoughts to moods. If our goal is for clients eventually to function as their own therapist, they will need to be able to analyze their problems, catch their self-talk, and recognize their own variations of common irrational beliefs. Insight might be necessary, but typically is not sufficient for successful termination.

Box 18.5

When is therapy done? Below are some questions to ask your clients in answering this question.

Have you acquired some new behaviors? Are they permanent habits?
Are your emotional responses more adaptive?
Can you laugh at yourself and not take yourself so seriously?
Can you tolerate frustrations better?
Can you cope by doing, instead of by avoiding?
Can you manage your own A-B-C analysis of a problem?
Can you productively challenge your distressing cognitions?
Have you stopped blaming others and taken responsibility for your own problems?
Do you have fewer problems to work on?
Are you coming to session and chatting about the week rather than working on a goal?
Do you feel better, or have you genuinely gotten better?

The box on this page contains a list of possible criteria for termination, stated as questions, that you could ask your clients when they express confusion about how they will know when it is time to end therapy.

New Habits

In one sense, therapy is never done. We might stop going to visit our therapist, but the process of managing our moods and behaviors is ongoing. We easily understand that we cannot make ourselves thin this year and then coast through the rest of life, eating whatever we want. We accept that we cannot get in shape with an exercise program and maintain our fitness without continued effort. In a similar way, cognitive therapy or rational emotive living skills require maintenance.

Therapy is a prevention program for the rest of our lives. As Ellis (1975) pointed out, we have a natural tendency to think irrationally. In REBT, clients acquire new philosophies, and new philosophies, like other new habits, require maintenance work. As REBT therapists, we get to practice these philosophies almost every day in our work with clients. Therefore, we might be the least likely to backslide—and yet we do! It is difficult to live rationally, and none of us are likely to be perfect at it. Even if the skills acquired in therapy have been neglected, however, we probably will not slide back to zero; with a little practice our unused skills will come back again fairly readily. We believe REBT helps clients to bounce back faster rather than break when they do backslide.

As we suggested above, insight is a necessary precursor to ending therapy, but not sufficient without behavior change. If one continues to behave in self-defeating ways, understanding why and articulating how one gives oneself permission to go on doing so is mere sophistry. Ideally, we want our clients' changes in behavior to be stable across various situations, and so automatic that they can be called habits. Even habits are fragile at first, however, and if not practiced will often be lost. If therapy ends before behavior change is stabilized, the outcome might be less than desirable, although not terrible. Clients can always return to therapy for booster shots and further practice if needed.

Emotive Reduction

When therapy gets bogged down, it is often because the client is not bringing in emotionally loaded material. In fact, some of the more prolonged courses of therapy have been with clients who were raised in families in which feelings were considered unseemly, uncomfortable, or at best, unnecessary. Often the first step in therapy with these clients is to help them to acknowledge their intense feelings and to share them in the safety of the therapeutic relationship (Marzillier, 2010).

The successful completion of therapy, therefore, does not mean that the client is devoid of feelings, but rather that unhealthy disturbed emotions have become the trigger for practicing REBT. In some instances, clients report that the As that formerly set off distress are so well worked through that the clients' responses are now emotionally neutral or they experience a healthy, negative emotion. More typically, however, the emotions are modulated in frequency, intensity (for both negative and positive feelings), and duration.

Laughing at Oneself

Various schools of therapy seem to hold divergent views on what might be called the "essence of man." Carl Rogers, for example, teaches that man is inherently loveable and deserves unconditional positive regard. Freud seemed to stress our evil nature and the necessity of developing adequate superego and ego strength to keep the "lid on the id." The broad position of CBT might be stated as follows: humans are not, in essence, any one thing; in other words, we are far too complex to be viewed simplistically. The REBT position is basically in agreement, but adds that humans are merely fallible and full of imperfections—about which we would do well to hang onto our sense of humor!

Part of ending therapy is the recognition that we're more like other people than unlike other people. REBT does not promote the idea that we are special because of our uniqueness as individuals. Rather, our kinship renders none of us special. The awareness of our kinship with others has a number of benefits, including reduction of personal perfectionism and the lessening of humiliation (e.g., "So, I goofed. We all do, from time to time."). It might also bolster our frustration tolerance ("It's not only hard for me; it's hard for everybody.") and tolerance of others ("You won't believe what he did!" "Oh yes I would; we all do foolish things!"). Every human, by definition, is vulnerable to feeling, thinking, and behaving in a foolish or self-defeating manner.

Finally, from an aerial, if not existential, perspective we find it helpful to remind ourselves to look at the relative significance of life events. If you were observed from an airplane, you'd be only a speck on the map, and as the airplane passed by, your speck would be there for only an instant. The significance of our goofs and our accomplishments begins to recede, so that a more rational, lighthearted, and hedonic focus is possible. That is an elegant stance from which to consider termination of therapy!

Higher Frustration Tolerance

The client who is preparing to end therapy will no longer be surprised by frustrations, but will come to expect them. For example, one client concluded that if he didn't have at least ten frustrations in a day, it was because he probably hadn't yet gotten out of bed!

When something unfortunate happens, we could always say, "Oh, rats!" (or some more colorful expletive). When we have really learned our REBT lessons, what happens next is where we really see the difference. We no longer get swept away by an emotional tide, but instead bring our skills into play.

Some of us can do even better than that. One colleague had a sibling and then a son diagnosed with diabetes. Over the years, he gradually turned his research and clinical interests to the topic of coping with diabetes. When congratulated on how elegantly he made "lemons into lemonade" he demurred, "It's funny. I don't even think of it as "lemons"; it's just what is..." He had gone beyond frustration tolerance to a more advanced stage: acceptance.

Coping by Doing

By writing out A-B-Cs, by talking them through, by going to therapy, the client is problem solving and actively trying to make changes. "Doing," in a behavioral paradigm, means actively searching for reinforcers, rather than settling for the avoidance of pain.

We have two choices in dealing with problems: we can either do nothing or do something. We can function as fighters or flee-ers, and REBT tends to turn us into fighters. Why? When we remain anxious or depressed, we feel like powerless victims. Even when we function like "survivors," we are hunkering down; "standing it." The REBT stance, by contrast, is exemplified by the person who says, "I can stand any problem until I solve it and work out a better plan." REBT does not recommend mere stoicism, rationalizing, or passivity.

A passive stance doesn't teach us anything useful that we can generalize from one problem to the next. The passive person flees down a narrow path that leads to denial or dissociation. By contrast, the mental set of a do-er is more of an open field: "I won't necessarily do the same thing every time I have a problem, but I will change the conditions so that something else can happen." If we make errors, they are ones of commission, not omission; in that way, we see the problem as a challenge that will at least bring about a new set of conditions.

Premature Termination

Some clients come in after just a few sessions announcing complete success. In these instances of "flight into health," it is extremely important to ask the clients how they account for the change. Have they improved because they've applied REBT principles? Have they changed for the wrong reasons (e.g., to please the therapist)? Have they improved because the obnoxious As in their lives are less frequent? The therapist will want to remind him/herself of the content of the previous session. Perhaps there was a discussion of an activating event or emotional reaction that overwhelmed the client. As a check on clients' improvement, you might ask them to think of examples of problems that they once upset themselves over but now do not, and to explain why. The last part of this question highlights cognitive change and enables the therapist to evaluate whether clients are in fact thinking more helpfully.

If a client terminates abruptly, without notification, what is the appropriate course of action? Many clinics send the client a letter noting the failure to keep an appointment and offering further treatment if desired. A phone call by the therapist is acceptable in most cases; although more intrusive, it might also be more informative to the therapist and helpful to the client. If you do not know the client well, however, a phone call might not be desirable. For example, some clients might have kept their foray into therapy a secret from family members; leaving a message might prove awkward, and even if the client is at home, he or she might not feel able to talk openly. In any case, it is recommended that you contact no client more than once, since doing otherwise might legally be viewed as harassment.

In many instances, because of external factors, clients terminate therapy before either they or you feel they are ready. It would be helpful for you to stop and ask yourself, "This might be my last session to work with the client. How can I structure the session so that it will be of maximal value to him/her?" Here are some suggestions:

Ask the client what he or she wants to accomplish in the final session(s).

Try to elicit a recapitulation of the therapy: why the client originally came to treatment, what has been learned, and what the client still wants to change. You might then compare your own ideas on these three questions and share them with the client.

Suggest a continuation of behavioral assignments to fill the gap after therapy ends. Assignments might also serve as a reminder of the concepts you have taught the client.

If clients are terminating therapy because of a geographical move, you can discuss whether they plan to resume therapy in the new location. It might be possible for you to make a referral to another REBT professional or to suggest how clients can go about locating a new therapist. The Albert Ellis Institute has a referral list of REBT therapists in the United States and abroad. This can be accessed at www. albertellis.org.

It is also helpful to point out to clients that the move itself might be a life stressor. In this way, clients might be prepared for backsliding, if it occurs, and be given a non-self-blaming attribution for it. Otherwise, they might view any new emotional distress as evidence that they are never going to get better, which might induce further panic and depression, or a decision to stop working at therapy. Understanding and accepting their backsliding might help clients to move forward in their future work with therapy. At termination, some clients might not readily discuss their reactions to this change but instead act in a depressed manner. In this instance, you would respond to body language and voice inflection cues and comment on this behavior. Later in the session, you might wish to add, "You know, if you hadn't been my client, I have a feeling we could have been good friends. I feel badly about not seeing you in the future. How do you feel about our terminating?" If you avoid such a confrontation, clients might never receive this message or have the opportunity to discuss what might have been a very significant relationship in their lives.

ENHANCING TREATMENT BENEFITS AFTER TERMINATION

It is helpful to send clients off with some final recommendations for how to continue to profit from therapy after regular therapy sessions have ended. The task is to maximize generalization from therapy to real life, and thus extend the results of treatment over time and new life issues. The following list of suggestions, adapted from the work of Norma Campbell, might be prepared as a handout for clients. Go over it carefully with them, and urge your clients to refer to it often.

How Can I Enhance the Benefits of Therapy?

Read—Keep your texts handy, read new REBT books and articles, reread helpful passages.

Think—Rehearse your REBT skills; try keeping a "healthy self-talk" journal; use pencil and paper to dispute when you feel yourself getting upset.

Practice—Every day, practice increasing your frustration tolerance. Do something hard. Scary. Boring. With no immediate payoff. This exercise will build your frustration tolerance, help you control your temper, and lead to honestly earned self-respect and pride.

Build—Empathy and tolerance can be built by trying daily to do something kind: pay a compliment, listen to the other side, and give a gift of time or interest— with no payoffs.

Prevent—To avert a return of perfectionism and grandiosity, every day do one of these: yield gracefully, apologize and admit your mistake, laugh at yourself when you goof, make a mistake on purpose; ask yourself, "So what if I goofed? How terrible is that?"

Promote—Happiness. Every day, do something fun. When you have a good time, remember it and tell someone else about it.

Ellis (1984, p. 3) adds two more good points. Try to keep in touch with several other people who know something about REBT and who can help go over some of its aspects with you. Tell them about problems that you have difficulty coping with and let them know how you are using REBT to overcome these problems. See if they agree with your solutions and can suggest additional and better kinds of REBT disputing that you can use to work against your irrational beliefs.

Practice using REBT with some friends, relatives, and associates who are willing to let you try to help them with it. The more often you use it with others, and are able to see what their IBs are and to try to talk them out of these self-defeating ideas, the more you will be able to understand the main principles of REBT and to use them with yourself. When you see other people act irrationally and in a disturbed manner, try to figure out—with or without talking to them about it—what their main irrational beliefs probably are and how these could be actively and vigorously disputed.

Booster Sessions

After your clients have terminated therapy, they might occasionally find reasons to call for an appointment, or to resume therapy for a brief period. Before terminating, therefore, be sure they understand that there is no stigma to coming back for further work, which you might suggest is analogous to getting immunization booster shots. The future probably holds new challenges that they might want to discuss with you, and it would be incorrect to assume that no further problems will emerge or that clients who have successfully learned REBT principles will henceforth be absolutely rational.

Many therapists find that a particularly satisfying aspect of their work is serving as the family psychologist. Therapists who trained with Dr. Ellis soon realized that he often had a multigenerational portrait of a given client because he recalled working with the client's mother or other relative. Communicate that it is not only OK for the client or his or her family members to return for help as needed, but would be welcomed by you.

SUPERVISION

There are a variety of ways to obtain supervisory feedback, including self-supervision, peer supervision, finding a certified local REBT supervisor, mailing in recordings to an REBT supervisor, or enrolling in a training program in your geographic area or at the Institute in New York City.

No matter what form of supervision you choose, prepare yourself by doing your homework (see below, "Self-Checking Supervision"). More important, get your ego off the line; accept this as a learning experience, accept yourself as an REBT beginner (although you might otherwise be an experienced clinician), and accept that a modicum of concern or tension is normal in a training situation. If your anxiety level begins to soar before sessions or your mood plummets afterward, be sure to capture that mood and the attendant cognitions as grist for your own therapy mill. Conquering your supervision anxieties is a great way to practice and master REBT.

Self-Checking Supervision

Actively begin supervising yourself. One way to monitor your progress in learning to do REBT is to evaluate your sessions on a regular basis and to have your client do the same. Checklists are useful as standards against which to compare your work. Here are some suggested items:

Was the session actively structured?
Were you able to specifically elicit the client's thoughts and feelings?
Could you identify any major irrational beliefs? Automatic thoughts?
  Underlying assumptions?
Were these IBs, automatic thoughts, and underlying assumptions
  challenged?
What were the results of the challenge?
Were homework assignments given?
Did you help the client to stay on task?

How do you feel about the therapist-client relationship?
Who was leading the session, you or the client?
Did you feel you were offering advice? Was it appropriate?
Did you do any problem-solving? Was it effective?
Was there closure at the end of the session?

Appendix 1: A-B-C-D-E Learning Worksheet

Appendix 2: A-B-C-D-E Session Notes

Appendix 3: Biographical Information Form

Appendix 4: Training in REBT: Practicing Disputation Strategies

Appendix 5: REBT Self-Help Form

Appendix 6: Statement of Homework Policy

Appendix 7: Session Note Form for Comprehensive REBT

APPENDIX 1

A-B-C-D-E Learning Worksheet

Complete these worksheets while listening to others conducting live counseling sessions or while listening to a recording of a session. These worksheets help focus your attention and assist you in learning the A-B-C-D-E model and providing feedback to your colleagues.

Case 1

A Activating Event(s)	**B** Beliefs	**C** Consequences	**D** Disputes/ Interventions	**E** Effective Emotional Responses

Homework:

Case 2

A Activating Event(s)	**B** Beliefs	**C** Consequences	**D** Disputes/ Interventions	**E** Effective Emotional Responses

Homework:

APPENDIX 2

A-B-C-D-E Session Notes

Client Name: _____ Date: _____

Session Number: _____ Therapist's Signature: _____

A Activating Event(s)	B Beliefs	C Consequences	D Disputes/Interventions	E New Effective Responses

___1. Assessed the presence of dysfunctional emotions or behaviors.

___2. Explored the adaptability of the client's emotions and behaviors.

___3. Assessed the presence and type of dysfunctional cognitions.

___4. Explored the adaptability of the client's belief system.

___5. Clarified the activating events.

___6. Offered the client a hypothesis about what irrational belief the client is holding.

___7. Taught the B→C connection.

___8. Taught the difference between irrational and rational beliefs.

___9. Offered alternative rational beliefs to replace the client's irrational beliefs.

_____ 10. Used Elegant/Philosophical disputing of IBs.

_____ 11. Used Rational Emotive imagery.

_____ 12. Generated and rehearsed new RB or EB.

_____ 13. Negotiated homework.

_____ 14. Assessed the client's emotions, thoughts, and behaviors when the client attempted to implement the homework.

_____ 15. Empirical dispute of the A– (Inference).

_____ 16. Provided instruction for rehearsal of self-statements.

_____ 17. Helped the client generate alternative solutions to practical problems.

_____ 18. Helped the client evaluate the effectiveness of alternative solutions.

_____ 19. Rehearsal of new solutions to practical problems (e.g., assertive or social skills training.)

_____ 20. Rehearsed relaxation training or relaxing imagery.

New Homework:

Homework:

Rate the client's attempts to complete homework from the last session.

1	2	3	4	5
Made no attempt at homework	Made a partial attempt at homework	Completed some homework	Completed most homework	Completed all homework

Comments:

Biographical Information Form

Instructions: To assist us in helping you, please fill out this form as frankly as you can. You will save much time and effort by giving us full information. You can be sure that, like everything you say at the Institute, the facts on this form will be held in the strictest confidence and no outsider will be permitted to see your case record without your written permission. PLEASE PRINT YOUR ANSWERS.

Name: _____
                (last)   (first)   (middle)

1. Date of birth: _____ Age: _____ Sex: M __ F __ Ethnicity: _____
            mo.   day   yr.

2. Address: _____
              street   city   state   zip code

3. Home phone: _____ Business phone: _____

4. Permanent address (if different from above): _____
_____

5. Who referred you to the Institute? _____ (1) Self _____ (2) Family doctor _____
(3) Psychologist or psychiatrist (4) _____ Web/Internet_____ (5) Social agency _____
(6) Hospital or clinic _____ (7) School or teacher _____ (8) Friend _____
(9) Relative _____ (10) Other (explain) _____
Has this party been here? _____ Yes _____ No

6. Relationship status:
_____
Number of years in current relationship _____
Number of Children: _____ Ages: _____

7. Years of formal education completed (Circle no. of years):
  1 2 3 4 5 6 7 8 9 10 11 12 13 14 15 16 17 18 19 20 more than 20

8. How religious are you? (Circle number on scale that best approximates your degree of religiosity):
    very   average   atheist
     1   2   3   4   5   6   7   8   9

9. How religious is/was each of your parent/caretaker?
    very   average   atheist
     1   2   3   4   5   6   7   8   9
    very   average   atheist
     1   2   3   4   5   6   7   8   9

10. Mother's age: _____   If deceased, how old were you when she died? _____

11. Father's age: _____   If deceased, how old were you when he died? _____

12. If your mother and father separated, how old were you at the time? _____

13. If your mother and father divorced, how old were you at the time? _____

14. Total number of times mother divorced _____ Number of times father divorced _____

15. Ages of living brothers _____ Ages of living sisters _____

16. I was child number _____ in a family of _____ children.

17. Significant medical history: _____
_____
_____

18. Were you adopted? _____ Yes _____ No

19. Have you ever had any individual psychotherapy, group or couples counseling?
_____ Yes _____ No
(Summarize approximate dates and length of treatment): _____

20. Have you ever been hospitalized for emotional problems? _____ Yes _____ No

21. Are you undergoing treatment anywhere else now? _____ Yes _____ No

22. Have you ever taken medication for emotional problems? _____ Yes _____ No
If yes, specify the medications(s) and indicate whether you are currently taking it or
when you *last* took it and who prescribed it:
_____

23. Type of psychotherapy you have had (briefly describe method of treatment—e.g.,
psychodynamic / free association, behavior therapy, cognitive therapy, other): _____
_____

24. Have you ever attempted suicide?
_____

25. Are you currently having suicidal thoughts?
_____

26. Briefly list your main complaints, symptoms, and problems: _____
_____
_____
_____

27. Briefly list any additional **past** complaints, symptoms, and problems: _____
_____
_____

28. Under what conditions are your problems worse? _____
_____
_____

29. Under what conditions are they improved? _____
_____
_____

30. List the activities you like to do most, the kinds of activities and persons that give you
pleasure:_____
_____
_____

31. List your main strengths: _____
_____
_____

32. List your main weaknesses: _____
_____
_____
_____

33. List your main **social** difficulties: _____
_____
_____

34. List your main **love and sex** difficulties: _____
_____
_____

35. List your main **school or work** difficulties: _____
_____
_____

36. List your main life goals: _____
_____
_____

37. List the behaviors and emotions about yourself you would most like to change: _____
_____
_____

38. For what occupation(s) does your training mainly prepare you? _____

39. Are you currently employed? Full Time: _____ Part Time: _____

40. Mother's occupation: _____ Father's occupation: _____

41. If your mother and father did not raise you when you were young, who
did? _____

42. Describe how each of your parents/caretakers treated you when you were a child and
the relationship you have with them now: _____
_____
_____
_____

43. If there were any unusually disturbing features in your relationship to any of your
siblings briefly describe them: _____
_____
_____

44. In your childhood did you experience any?

Emotional abuse	_____ Yes	_____ No
Physical abuse	_____ Yes	_____ No
Sexual abuse	_____ Yes	_____ No
Drug abuse	_____ Yes	_____ No
Household mental illness	_____ Yes	_____ No
Household drug abuse	_____ Yes	_____ No

45. In your childhood did you experience?

Parental separation or divorce?	_____ Yes	_____ No
Incarcerated household member?	_____ Yes	_____ No
Emotional neglect?	_____ Yes	_____ No
Physical neglect?	_____ Yes	_____ No
Mother treated violently?	_____ Yes	_____ No

44. Close relatives that have been seriously emotionally disturbed
    (specify): _____
    Close relatives that have been hospitalized for emotional problems or attempted
    suicide (specify): _____

45. Please add any additional information that you think might be helpful: _____
    _____
    _____

Originally devised by Albert Ellis and Janet Wolfe. Revised 10/ 2012 by K. Doyle, R. DiGiuseppe, and the staff of the Albert Ellis Institute.

APPENDIX 4

Training in REBT: Disputational Strategies

Irrational Belief to Dispute: _____

DISPUTING STRATEGY

DISPUTING STYLES	Logical	Empirical	Functional	Rational alternative
Didactic				
Socratic				
Metaphor				
Humor				

Reprinted from Springer: *Journal of Rational-Emotive and Cognitive Behavior Therapy* 14 (1996): 215–29, Disputing Clients' Irrational Beliefs, Beal, D., Kopec, A.M., DiGiuseppe, R., *Training in REBT: Disputational Strategies*, with kind permission from Springer Science and Business Media.

Creating Effective Rational New Beliefs Form (Developed W. Backx, R. DiGiuseppe, and K. Doyle, June 2012)

IRRATIONAL BELIEF	Imperative cognition: *Demand or must*	EFFECTIVE RATIONAL NEW BELIEF			
		Derivative cognition: *Self-downing*	Derivative cognition: *Other-downing*	Derivative cognition: *Awfulizing*	Derivative cognition: *Frustration Intolerance*

REBT Self-help Form

A (Activating Events or Adversities)

Briefly Summarize the Situation as Objectively as Possible: _____

Critical A (What I Was Most Disturbed About): _____

Examples:
- A can be internal or external, real or imagined
- A can be an event in the past, present, or future

- Situation: "My wife and I disagreed about something"
- Critical A: "She criticized me badly"

Bs (Beliefs): Irrational (Unhelpful/Dysfunctional) Beliefs

To Identify Irrational Beliefs, Look For:

1) **Demands** (musts/absolute shoulds/oughts)
2) **Awfulizing/Catastrophizing** (It's awful, terrible, horrible!)
3) **Frustration Intolerance** (I can't stand it!)
4) **Self-Downing, Other-Downing, or Life-Downing** (I'm bad or worthless, He/she is bad or worthless, or Life is not worthwhile)

© Windy Dryden and Jane Walker, 1992.
Revised by Albert Ellis, 1996. Revised by Windy Dryden and Daniel David, 2009.

Ds (Disputation): Debate Your Irrational (Unhelpful/Dysfunctional) Beliefs

To Change Irrational Beliefs, Ask Yourself:

- Where is holding this belief getting me? **Is it helpful** or getting me into trouble?
- **Where is the evidence** to support my irrational belief?
    - Is it really awful (as bad as it could be)?
    - Can I really not stand it?
    - Am I really a totally bad person?
- **Is it logical?** Does it follow from my preferences?
- **Use metaphorical disputation** (e.g. metaphors, stories, humor)

C (Consequences)

Major Dysfunctional/Unhealthy Negative Emotion (Feeling): _____

Maladaptive/Unhelpful Behaviors (and/or Action Tendencies): _____

Dysfunctional Negative Emotions include:
- Anxiety/fear
- Shame/embarrassment
- Rage/anger
- Guilt
- Depression (depressed mood)
- Problematic jealousy
- Problematic envy
- Hurt

Maladaptive Behaviors include:
- Social avoidance
- Not taking care of yourself (e.g. not exercising, not resting)
- Being aggressive

Es (Effective): Rational (Helpful/Functional) Beliefs

To Think More Rationally, Strive For:

1) **Flexible Preferences** (e.g. I want to do well, but I don't have to do so.)
2) **Anti-Awfulizing** (e.g. It may be bad or unfortunate, but it is not awful, and I can still enjoy some things.)
3) **High Frustration Tolerance** (e.g. I don't like it, but I can stand it, and I can still enjoy many things.)
4) **Self-Acceptance, Other-Acceptance, Life-Acceptance** (e.g. I can accept myself as a fallible human being.)

GOALS

Es (Functional): Major Functional/Healthy Emotion and Adaptive/Helpful Behaviors

(Goal): New Functional/Healthy Negative Emotion:

(Goals): New Adaptive/Helpful Behaviors:

Functional/Healthy Negative Emotions include:
- Concern
- Disappointment
- Healthy anger/annoyance
- Remorse/regret
- Sadness
- Healthy concern for relationship
- Healthy envy
- Sorrow

Adaptive/Helpful Behaviors include:
- Meeting friends or seeking support
- Exercising
- Assertive behaviors

Statement of Homework Policy

Our experience and research has shown that an important key to making rapid and optimal progress in psychotherapy is to work on your problems at home as well as in the therapy office. In Rational Emotive Behavior Therapy, every client is given homework assignments at each session to be done between sessions. The purpose is to help maximize your progress toward achieving therapy goals. We take this homework policy seriously and hope you will also. If you have questions about this homework policy or any other aspects of therapy, please discuss it with your therapist.

Session Note Form for Comprehensive REBT

Session No.: _____ Date: _____

Name of Client: _____

Problem Worked on: _____

___1. Assessed the presence of dysfunctional emotions or behaviors.

___2. Explored the adaptability of the client's emotions and behaviors.

___3. Assessed the presence and type of dysfunctional cognitions.

___4. Explored the adaptability of the client's belief system.

___5. Clarified the activating events.

___6. Offered the client a hypothesis about what irrational belief the client is holding.

___7. Taught the B→C connection.

___8. Taught the difference between irrational and rational beliefs.

___9. Offered alternative rational beliefs to replace the client's irrational beliefs.

___10. Philosophical disputing.

___11. Rational emotive imagery.

___12. Exposure Imagery.

___12. Generated and rehearsed new RB or EB.

___13. Negotiated homework.

___14. Assessed the client's emotions, thoughts, and behaviors when the client tried to implement a homework assignment.

___15. Disputed A–(inferences)

___16. Rehearsed self-statements.

___17. Helped the client generate alternative solutions to practical problems.

___18. Helped the client evaluate the effectiveness of alternative solutions.

___19. Rehearsed new solutions to practical problems. (e.g., assertive or social skills training)

___20. Rehearsed relaxation training or relaxing imagery.

___21. Other _____

Rate the client's attempts to complete homework from the last session.

1	2	3	4	5
No attempt at homework	Partial attempt at homework l	Completed some homework	Completed most homework	Completed all homework

Comments: _____

_____

_____

Homework Assigned: _____

_____

_____

Supervision Recommendation: _____

_____

_____

(R. DiGiuseppe July/2012)   Signature_____

REFERENCES

Abramson, L. Y., Seligman, M. E., & Teasdale, J. D. (1978). Learned helplessness in humans: Critique and reformulation. *Journal of Abnormal Psychology, 87*(1):49–74.

Alloy, L. B., Peterson, C., Abramson, L. Y., & Seligman, M. E. (1984). Attributional style and the generality of learned helplessness. *Journal of Personality and Social Psychology, 46*(3), 681–687. doi: 10.1037/0022-3514.46.3.681

Allport, G. W. (1937). The functional autonomy of motives. *The American Journal of Psychology, 50,* 141–156. doi: 10.2307/1416626

Amsel, A. (1990). Arousal, suppression, and persistence: Frustration theory, attention, and its disorders. *Cognition and Emotion, 4,* 239–268.

Anderson, N. (1990). Schemas in person cognition. In N. Anderson (Ed.), *Contributions to information integration theory, Vol. 1: Cognition; Vol. 2: Social; Vol. 3: Developmental* (pp. 57–103). Hillsdale, NJ England: Lawrence Erlbaum Associates, Inc.

Araoz, D. (1985). *The New Hypnosis.* New York: Plenum.

Ard, B. (1990). Living without guilt and/or blame: conscience, superego, and psychotherapy. *Volume 19 of American University studies: Psychology American University Studies.* State College, PA: P Lang.

Areeda, P. (1996). The Socratic method. *Harvard Law Review, 109,* 911–930.

Backx, W. (2012). The distinction between quantitative and qualitative dimensions of emotions: Clinical implications. *Journal of Rational Emotive and Cognitive Behavior Therapy, 30,* 25–37. doi: 10.1007/s10942-010-0122-0

Baddeley, J. L., & Pennebaker, J. W. (2009). Expressive Writing pp. 295–299. In W. T. O'Donohue, & J. E. Fisher (Eds.) *General principles and empirically supported techniques of cognitive behavior therapy.* Hoboken, NJ: John Wiley & Sons.

Bartley, W. W. (1987). In defense of self applied critical rationalism. In G. Radnitzky & W. W. Bartley (Eds.), *Evolutionary epistemology, Theory of rationality and sociology of knowledge* (pp. 279–312). LaSalle, IL: Open Court.

Baumeister, R. F., Campbell, J. D., Krueger, J. I., & Vohs, K. D. (2005). Exploding the Self-Esteem Myth. *Scientific American* (January 2005), *292,* 84–91. doi: 10.1038/scientificamerican0105-84.

Baumeister, R. F., Heatherton, T. F., & Tice, D. M. (1994). *Losing control: How and why people fail at self-control.* San Diego: Academic Press.

Baumeister, R. F., Smart, L., & Boden, J. M. (1996). Relation of threatened egotism to violence and aggression: The dark side of high self-esteem. *Psychological Review, 103*(1), 5–33.

Beal, D., & DiGiuseppe, R. (1998). Training supervisors in rational emotive behavior therapy. *Journal of Cognitive Psychotherapy, 12,* 127–138.

Beal, D., Kopec, A. M., & DiGiuseppe, R. (1996). Disputing clients' irrational beliefs. *Journal of Rational-Emotive & Cognitive Behavior Therapy, 14*(4), 215–229.

Beck, A. T. (1976). *Cognitive therapy and the emotional disorders.* New York: International Universities Press.

Beck, A. T. (1999). *Prisoners of hate: The cognitive basis of anger, hostility and violence.* New York: Harper Collins.

Beck, A. T. (2005). The current state of cognitive therapy: A 40-year retrospective. *Archives of General Psychiatry, 62*(9), 953–959.

Beck, A. T., & Emery, G. (1985). *Anxiety Disorders and Phobias.* New York: Basic Books.

Beck, A. T., Rush, A. J., Shaw, B. F., & Emery, G. (1979). *Cognitive therapy of depression: A treatment manual.* New York: Guilford.

Beck, A. T., Steer, R. A., & Brown, G. K. (1996). *Manual for the beck depression inventory-II.* San Antonio, TX: Psychological Corporation.

Beck, J. S. (1995). *Cognitive therapy: Basic and beyond.* New York: Guilford Press.

Bennett-Levy, J., Richards, D., Farrand, P., Christensen, H., Griffiths, K., Kavanagh, D., Klein, B., Lau, M., Proudfoot, J., Ritterband, L., Williams, C., & White, J. (2010). *Oxford guide to low intensity CBT interventions.* London: Oxford University Press.

Bernard, M. E. (1990). *Validation of general attitude and belief scale.* Presented at the World Congress on Mental Health Counseling. Keystone, Colorado.

Bernard, M. E., & DiGiuseppe, R. (1989). *Inside rational-emotive therapy: A critical appraisal of the theory and therapy of Albert Ellis.* New York: Academic Press.

Bernard, M. E., Froh, J. J., DiGiuseppe, R., Joyce, M. R., Dryden, W. (2010). Albert Ellis: Unsung hero of positive psychology. *The Journal of Positive Psychology, 5*(4), 302–310.

Bohart, A. C., Elliott, R., Greenberg, L. S & Watson, J. C. (2002). Empathy. In J. C. Norcross (Ed.), *Psychotherapy relationships that work: Therapist contributions and responsiveness to patients* (pp. 89–108). New York, NY: Oxford University Press.

Bond, A. J., Ruaro, L., & Wingrove, J. (2006). Reducing anger induced by ego threat: Use of vulnerability expression and influence of trait characteristics. *Personality and Individual Differences, 40*(6), 1087–1097.

Brainerd, C. J., (2003). Jean Piaget, learning research, and American education. In B. Zimmerman, & D. Schunk, (Eds.). *Educational Psychology: A century of contributions* (pp.251–287). Mahwah, NJ: Lawrence Erlbaum Associates.

Breuer, J., & Freud, S. (1955). *Studies on hysteria* (Standard Edition Vol. II). London: Hogarth Press (First German edition, 1895).

Burgess, P. M. (1990). Toward resolution of conceptual issues in the assessment of belief systems in rational-emotive therapy. *Journal of Cognitive Psychotherapy, 4*(2), 171–184.

Burns, D. (1980). *Feeling good.* New York: William Morrow.

Bushman, B. J. (2002). Does venting anger feed or extinguish the flame? Catharsis, rumination, distraction, anger and aggressive responding. *Personality and Social Psychology Bulletin, 28*(6), 724–731.

Byrne, R. M. J. (2005). *The rational imagination: How people create alternatives to reality.* Cambridge, MA: MIT Press.

Cabaniss, D. L., Cherry, S., Douglas, C. J., & Schwartz, A. R. (2011). *Psychodynamic psychotherapy: A clinical manual*. New Jersey: John Wiles & Sons Ltd.

Campbell, I. M. (1985). The psychology of homosexuality. In A. Ellis & M. E. Bernard (Eds.). *Clinical applications of rational-emotive therapy* (pp. 153–180). New York: Plenum.

Carkhuff, R. (1969). *Helping and human relations: A primer for lay and professional helpers*. New York: Holt, Rinehart and Winston.

Chessick, R. (1982). Socrates: First psychotherapist. *American Journal of Psychoanalysis, 42,* 71–83.

Ciarrochi, J., Robb, H., & Godsell, C. (2005). Letting a little nonverbal air into the room. Insights for Acceptance and Commitment Therapy. Part 1: Philosophical and theoretical underpinnings. *Journal of Rational-Emotive and Cognitive-Behavior Therapy, 23.*

Cook, J. M., Biyanova, T., & Coyne, J. C.(2009). Influential psychotherapy figures, authors, and books: An Internet survey of over 2,000 psychotherapists. *Psychotherapy: Theory, Research, Practice, Training, 46,* 42–51.

Corsini, R. J. (Ed.). (1994). *Encyclopedia of psychology, 2nd ed.* New York: Wiley.

Damasio, A. (2003). *Looking for Spinoza: Joy, sorrow, and the feeling brain*. Orlando, FL: Harcourt Inc.

Darwin, C. (1872). *The expression of the emotions in man and animals*. London: John Murray.

David, D., David, A., Cristina, G., Macavei, B., & Kallay, E. (2006). A Search for the 'Hot' cognitions in a clinical and a non-clinical context: appraisal, attributions, core relation theme, irrational beliefs, and their relation to emotion. In A. Columbus (Ed.), *Advances in psychology research (Vol 40)* (pp. 1–37). Hauppauge, NY: Nova Science Publishers.

David, D., Freeman, A., & DiGiuseppe, R. (2009). Rational and irrational beliefs: Implication for clinical conceptualization and practice in psychotherapy. In D. David, S. J. Lynn, &A. Ellis (Eds.). *Rational and irrational beliefs in human functioning and disturbances; Implication for research, theory, and practice*. New York: Oxford University Press.

David, D., Lynn, S. J., & Ellis, A (2010). *Rational and irrational beliefs: Research, theory, and clinical practice*. New York: Oxford University Press.

David, D., Schnur, J., & Belloiu, A. (2002). Another search for the "hot" cognitions; Appraisal, irrational beliefs, attributions, and their relation to emotions. *Journal of Rational-Emotive and Cognitive-Behavior Therapy, 20,* 94–131.

Davison, G. C., & Neale, J. M. (1990). *Abnormal psychology*, 5th ed. New York: Wiley.

de N. Abrantes-Pais, F., Friedman, J. K., Lovallo, W. R., & Ross, E. D. (2007). Psychological or physiological: Why are tetraplegic patients content. *Neurology, 69*(3), 261–267. doi: 10.1212/01.wnl.0000262763.66023

Delucia-Waack, J. L., & Gellman, R. A. (2007). The efficacy of using music in children of divorce groups: Impact on anxiety, depression, and irrational beliefs about divorce. *Group Dynamics: Theory, Research, and Practice, 11*(4), Special issue: Groups in educational settings. pp. 272–282.

Denholtz, M. (1970). The use of tape recordings between therapy sessions. *Journal of Behavior Therapy and Experimental Psychiatry, 1*(2), 139–143.

Diaz, R. M., & Berk, L. E. (1999). A Vygotskian critique of self-instructional training. In P. Lloyd, & C. Fernyhough (Eds.), *Lev Vygotsky: critical assessments: Future directions,* Vol. IV (pp. 221–252). Florence, KY: Taylor & Frances/Routledge.

DiGiuseppe, R. (1986). The implications of the philosophy of science for rational emotive theory and therapy. *Psychotherapy: Theory, Research, Practice, 23*(4), 634–639.

DiGiuseppe, R. (1991). *Maximizing the moment: How to have more fun and happiness in life. Cassette recording.* New York: Institute for Rational Emotive Therapy.

DiGiuseppe, R. (1996). The nature of irrational beliefs: Progress in rational emotive behavior therapy. *Journal of Rational Emotive & Cognitive Behavior Therapy, 14*(1), 5–28.

DiGiuseppe, R. (2006). Rational assessment and treatment with children. In A. Ellis & M. E. Bernard (Eds.). *Rational emotive behavioral approaches to childhood disorders: Theory, practice, and research.* New York: Springer.

DiGiuseppe, R. A., & Froh, J. J. (2002). What cognitions predict state anger? *Journal of Rational-Emotive and Cognitive-Behavior Therapy 20*(2), 133–150.

DiGiuseppe, R., & Jilton, R. (1996). Developing the therapeutic alliance in child-adolescent psychotherapy. *Applied and Preventive Psychology, 5*(2), 85–100.

DiGiuseppe, R., Leaf, R., Exner, T., & Robin, M. (1988). The development of a measure of irrational/rational thinking. Poster session presented at the World Congress of Behavior Therapy, Edinburgh, Scotland, September 6.

DiGiuseppe, R., & Muran, J. C. (1992). The use of metaphor in rational-emotive psychotherapy. *Psychotherapy in Private Practice, 10*(1–2), 151–165.

DiGiuseppe, R., Robin, M., & Dryden, W. (1991). On the compatibility of rational-emotive therapy and Judeo-Christian philosophy: A focus on clinical strategies. *Journal of Cognitive Psychotherapy: An International Quarterly, 4*(4), 355–368.

DiGiuseppe, R., & Tafrate, R. (2004). *The anger disorder scale: Manual.* Toronto, Ontario, Canada: MultiHealth Systems.

DiGiuseppe, R., & Tafrate, R. (2007). *Understanding anger disorders.* New York: Oxford University Press.

DiLorenzo, T. A., David, D., & Montgomery, G. H. (2007). The interrelations between irrational cognitive processes and distress in stressful academic settings. *Personality and Individual Differences, 42*(4), 765–776. doi: 10.1016/j.paid.2006.08.022

Dimidjian, S., Barrera, M., Martell, C., Ricardo F., Muñoz, R.F., & Lewinsohn, P.M. (2011). The origins and current status of behavioral activation treatments for depression. *Annual Review of Clinical Psychology, 7*, 1–38

Dobson, K. S., & Hamilton, K. E. (2009). Cognitive restructuring: behavioral tests of negative cognitions. In W.T. O'Donohue, & J.E. Fisher (Eds.). *General principles and empirically supported techniques of cognitive behavior therapy.* Hoboken, NJ: John Wiley.

Dollard, J., & Miller, N. E. (1950). Personality and psychotherapy. New York: McGraw-Hill.

Dryden, W., DiGiuseppe, R., & Neenan, M. (2010). *A primer on rational emotive behavioral therapy, Third Edition.* Champaign, Illinois: Research Press.

Dryden, W. (2008). *Rational emotive behaviour therapy: Distinctive features.* Hove, East Sussex: Routledge.

Dryden, W., DiGiuseppe, R., & Neenan, M. (2003). *A primer on rational emotive behavioral therapy, Second edition.* Champaign, IL: Research Press.

Dryden, W., DiGiuseppe, R., & Neenan, M. (2010). *A primer on rational emotive behavioral therapy, Third edition.* Champaign, IL: Research Press.

Dryden, W., Ferguson, J., & McTeague, S. (1989). Beliefs and inferences: A test of a rational-emotive hypothesis. 2: On the prospect of seeing a spider. *Psychological Reports, 64*, 115–123.

Duckworth, M. P. (2009). Assertiveness skills and the management of related factors. In W.T. O'Donohue, & J.E. Fisher (Eds.). *General principles and empirically supported techniques of cognitive behavior therapy.* Hoboken, NJ: John Wiley.

D'Zurilla, T., & Goldfried, M. R. (1971). Problem-solving and behavior modification. *Journal of Abnormal Psychology, 78,* 107–126.

Edwards, R. R., Haythornthwaite, J. A., Smith, M. T., Klick, B., & Katz, J. N. (2009). Catastrophizing and depressive symptoms as prospective predictors of outcomes following total knee replacement. *Pain Research & Management, 14*(4), 307–311.

Efran, J., Lukens, M., & Lukens, R. (1990). *Language, structure, and change: Frameworks of meaning in psychotherapy.* New York: Norton.

Eisenberger, R. (1992). Learned industriousness. *Psychological Review, 99,* 248–267.

Ellis, A. (1933). *Youth against the world: A novel.* Unpublished manuscript.

Ellis, A. (1955). New approaches to psychotherapy techniques. *Journal of Clinical Psychology, 11,* 207–260.

Ellis, A. (1957a). Rational psychotherapy and individual psychology. *Journal of Individual Psychology 13,* 38–44.

Ellis, A. (1957b). Outcome of employing three techniques of psychotherapy. *Journal of Clinical Psychology 13,* 344–350.

Ellis, A. (1958). Rational psychotherapy. *Journal of General Psychology, 59,* 35–49.

Ellis, A. (1962). *Reason and emotion in psychotherapy.* Secaucus, NJ: Lyle Stuart.

Ellis, A. (1971). *Growth through reason.* North Hollywood, CA: Wilshire Books.

Ellis, A. (1973a). *Humanistic psychotherapy.* New York: McGraw-Hill.

Ellis, A. (1973b). *How to stubbornly refuse to be ashamed of anything (cassette recording).* New York: Institute for Rational-Emotive Therapy.

Ellis, A. (1976a). The biological basis of human irrationality. *Journal of Individual Psychology, 32,* 145–168.

Ellis, A. (1979a). Discomfort anxiety: A new cognitive behavioral construct. *Rational Living, 14,* 3–8. Also in A. Ellis & W. Dryden (Eds.), *The Essential Albert Ellis.* New York: Springer Publishing, 1990.

Ellis, A. (1979b). *The intelligent woman's guide to dating and mating.* Secaucus, NJ: Lyle Stuart.

Ellis, A. (1979c). Rational-emotive therapy. In R. J. Corsini (ed.), *Current psycho-therapies, 2nd ed.* Itasca, IL: Peacock.

Ellis, A. (1987a).The impossibility of achieving consistently good mental health. *American Psychologist, 42,* 364–375.

Ellis, A. (1991). The philosophical basis of rational-emotive therapy (RET). *Psychotherapy in Private Practice, 8*(4), 97–106.

Ellis, A. (1992). Alfred Korzybski memorial lecture 1991: General Semantics and Rational-Emotive Therapy. *General Semantics Bulletin, 56,* 12–49.

Ellis, A. (1993). The Rational-Emotive Therapy (RET) approach to marriage and family therapy. *The Family Journal, 1*(4), 292–307. doi: 10.1177/1066480793014002

Ellis, A. (1994). *Reason and emotional in psychotherapy: A comprehensive method of treating human disturbance.* Revised and updated. New York: Birch Lane Press.

Ellis, A. (1996). *Better, deeper, and more enduring brief therapy: The rational emotive behavior therapy approach.* Philadelphia, PA: Brunner/Mazel.

Ellis, A. (2001). *Feeling better, getting better, staying better: Profound self-help therapy for your emotions.* Atascadero, CA: Impact Publishers.

Ellis, A. (2002). *Overcoming resistance: Rational-emotive therapy with difficult patients, 2nd edition.* New York: Springer Publishing.

Ellis, A. (2002). *Overcoming Resistance.* New York: Springer Publishing Company, LLC.

Ellis, A. (2003a). Discomfort anxiety: A new cognitive-behavioral construct (Part I). *Journal of Rational-Emotive & Cognitive Behavior Therapy, 21*(3–4), 183–191. doi: 10.1023/A:1025881810501

Ellis, A. (2003b). Discomfort anxiety: A new cognitive-behavioral construct (Part II). *Journal of Rational-Emotive & Cognitive Behavior Therapy, 21*(3–4), 193–202. doi: 10.1023/A:1025833927340

Ellis, A. (2003c). *The myth of self-esteem: How rational emotive behavior therapy can change your life forever.* Amherst, NY: Prometheus Books.

Ellis, A., & Abrahms, E. (1978). *Brief psychotherapy in medical and health practice.* New York: Springer Publishing.

Ellis, A., & Bernard, M. (1986). What is rational-emotive therapy (RET)? In A. Ellis & R. M. Grieger (eds.), *Handbook of rational-emotive therapy* (vol. 2). New York: Springer Publishing.

Ellis, A., & DiGiuseppe, R. (1993). Are inappropriate or dysfunctional feelings in rational-emotive therapy qualitative or quantitative? *Cognitive Therapy and Research, 17*(5), 471–477.

Ellis, A., & Harper, R. (1967/1975). *A new guide to rational living.* Englewood Cliffs, NJ: Prentice-Hall.

Ellis, A., & Knaus, W. (1977). *Overcoming procrastination.* New York: Institute for Rational Living.

Ellis, A., McInerney, J. F., DiGiuseppe, R., Yeager, R. J., & Mahadevan, K. (1990). A rational-emotive theory of addictions: Rational-emotive therapy with alcoholics and substance abusers. *Journal of Cognitive Psychotherapy, 4*(4), 397–398.

Ellis, A, & MacLaren, C. (2005). *Rational emotive behavior therapy: A Clinician's guide.* San Luis Obispo, CA: Impact Publishers.

Ellis, A., & Tafrate, R. C. (1997). *Control your anger before it controls you.* New York: Kensington Books.

Eysenck, H. J. (1952). The effects of psychotherapy: an evaluation. *Journal of Consulting Psychology 16*(5):319–324.

Fadyl, J., & McPherson, K. (2008). Return to work after injury: A review of evidence regarding expectations and injury perceptions, and their influence on outcome. *Journal of Occupational Rehabilitation, 18*(4), 362–374. doi: 10.1007/s10926-008-9153-0.

Fay, A. (1978). *Making things better by making them worse.* New York: Hayworth Press.

Ferguson, Kyle E., & Sgambati, R. E. (2009). Relaxation. In O'Donohue, W. T. (Ed.), & Fisher, J. E. (Ed.) *General principles and empirically supported techniques of cognitive behavior therapy* (pp. 532–542). Hoboken, NJ: John Wiley & Sons.

Festinger, L. (1957). *A theory of cognitive dissonance.* Palo alto, CA: Stanford University Press.

Finn, T., DiGiuseppe, R., & Culver, C. (1991). The effectiveness of rational-emotive therapy in the reduction of muscle contraction headaches. *Journal of Cognitive Psychotherapy, 5*(2), 93–103.

Fodor, I. G. (1987). Moving beyond cognitive-behavior therapy: Integrating Gestalt therapy to facilitate personal and interpersonal awareness. In N. S. Jacobson (Ed.) *Psychotherapists in clinical practice: Cognitive and behavioral perspectives* (pp. 190–231). New York: The Guilford Press.

Folkman, S., & Lazarus, R. S. (1991). Coping and emotion. In A. Monat & R. S. Lazarus (Eds.), *Stress and coping: An anthology* (3rd ed.) (pp. 207–227). New York: Columbia University Press.

Frank, J., & Frank, J. B. (1991). *Persuasion and healing: A comparative study of psychotherapy* (3rd ed.). Baltimore, MD: Johns Hopkins University Press.

Frankl, V. (1946/2006). *Man's search for meaning*, Boston, MA: Beacon Press.

Freeman, A., & Davis, D. D. (1990). Cognitive therapy of depression. In A. S. Bellack, M. Hersen, & A. E. Kazdin (Eds.), *International handbook of behavior modification and therapy* (2nd ed.) (pp. 333–352). New York: Plenum Press.

Freud, S. (1965). *New introductory lectures on psychoanalysis*, ed. and trans. by J. Strachey. New York: Norton.

Frijda, N. H. (1986). *The emotions: Studies in emotion and social interaction*. New York: Press Syndicate of the University of Cambridge.

Gambrill, E. (1993). What critical thinking offers to clinicians and clients. *Behavior Therapist, 16*, 141–147.

Goldfried, M. R., Davison, G. C., & Wachtel, P. L. (1994). Clinical behavior therapy (exp. ed.). *Wiley series in clinical psychology and personality*. Oxford, England: John Wiley & Sons.

Goldstein, A. J., & Chambless, D. L. (1978). A re-analysis of agoraphobia. *Behavior Therapy, 9*, 47–59.

Hamilton, M. A., Hunter, J. E., & Burgoon, M. (1990). An empirical test of an axiomatic model of the relationship between language intensity and persuasion *Journal of Language and Social Psychology, 9*(4), 235–255.

Harmon-Jones, E. (Ed); Mills, J. (Ed). (1999). *Cognitive dissonance: Progress on a pivotal theory in social psychology. Science conference series*. Washington, DC: American Psychological Association.

Harrington, N. (2005a). The Frustration Discomfort Scale: Development and Psychometric Properties *Clinical Psychology and Psychotherapy, 12*, 374–387.

Harrington, N. (2005b). Dimensions of frustration intolerance and their relationship to self-control problems. *Journal of Rational-Emotive & Cognitive-Behavior Therapy, 23*(1), 1–20. doi: 10.1007/s10942-005-0001-2

Harrington, N. (2006). Frustration intolerance beliefs: Their relationship with depression, anxiety, and anger, in a clinical population. *Cognitive Therapy and Research, 30*, 699–709. doi: 10.1007/s10608-006-9061-6

Harrington, N. (2011a). Frustration and discomfort intolerance: Introduction to the special issue. *Journal of Rational-Emotive and Cognitive-Behavior Therapy, 29*, 1–3. doi: 10.1007/s10942-011-0125-5002E

Harrington, N. (2011b). Frustration Intolerance: Therapy issues and strategies. *Journal of Rational-Emotive and Cognitive-Behavior Therapy, 29*, 16. doi: 10.1007/s10942-011-0126-4.

Hauck, P. (1985). Religion and RET: Friends or foes? In A. Ellis & M. Bernard (eds.), *Clinical applications of rational-emotive therapy*. New York: Plenum.

Hayakawa, S. I. (1962). *The use and misuse of language*. Greenwich, CT: Fawcett.

Hayes, S. C., Strosahl, K. D., & Wilson, K. G. (1999). *Acceptance and commitment therapy: An experiential approach to behavior change*. New York: Guildford Press.

Hayes S. C., Villatte, M., Levin, M., & Hildebrandt, M. (2011). Open, aware, and active: Contextual approaches as an emerging trend in the behavioral and cognitive therapies.

Annual Review of Clinical Psychology, 7, 141–168. doi: 10.1146/annurev-clinpsy-032210-104449.

Hayes, S. C., Wilson, K. G., Gifford, E. V., Follette, V. M., & Strosahl, K. (1996). Experiential Avoidance and Behavioral Disorders: A Functional Dimensional Approach to Diagnosis and Treatment. *Journal of Consulting and Clinical Psychology. 64*(6), 1152–1168.

Hazlett-Stevens, H. & Craske, M. G. (2009). Live *(in vivo)* exposure. In W. T. O'Donohue & J. E. Fisher (Eds.). *General principles and empirically supported techniques of cognitive behavior therapy.* Hoboken, NJ: John Wiley.

Head, L. S., Gross, A. M., (2009). In W. T. O'Donohue & J. E. Fisher (Eds.). *General principles and empirically supported techniques of cognitive behavior therapy* (pp. 640–647). Hoboken, NJ: John Wiley

Hollon, S. D., & DiGiuseppe, R. (2010). Cognitive psychotherapies. In J. C. Norcross, & G. VandenBos (Eds.) *History of psychotherapy: Continuity and change (2nd ed.).* Washington, DC: American Psychological Association.

Horney, K. (1945). *Our inner conflicts.* New York: Norton.

Huber, C. & Baruth, L. (1989). *Rational-emotive family therapy.* New York: Springer Publishing.

Huber, C. H. (1997). Rational-emotive family therapy. In J. Yankura, W. Dryden, J. Yankura, W. Dryden (Eds.). *Special applications of REBT: A therapist's casebook* (pp. 101–129). New York, NY: Springer Publishing Co.

Hurley, M., Dennett, D., & Adams, R. (2011). *Inside jokes: Using humor to reverse-engineer the mind.* Cambridge, MA: MIT Press.

Jacobs, N. N. (2009). Bibliotherapy utilizing CBT. In W. T. O'Donohue. & J. E. Fisher, & E. Jane (Eds.) *General principles and empirically supported techniques of cognitive behavior therapy* (pp. 158–165). Hoboken, NJ: John Wiley & Sons.

Johnson, S. (2006). The congruence of the philosophy of rational emotive behavior therapy within the philosophy of mainstream Christianity. *Journal of Cognitive & Behavioral Psychotherapies, 6*(1), 45–56.

Johnson, W. (1946). *People in quandaries.* New York: Harper & Bros.

Johnson, W. B., DiGiuseppe, R., & Ulven, J. (1999). Albert Ellis as mentor: National survey results. *Psychotherapy: Theory, Research, Practice, Training, 36*(3), 305–312.

Kazantzis, N., Deane, F. P., Ronan, K. R., L'Abate, L. (Eds.). (2005). *Using homework assignments in cognitive behavior therapy.* New York: Routledge/Taylor & Francis Group.

Kazantzis, N., Whittington, C, & Datillio, F. (2010). Meta-analysis of homework effects in cognitive and behavioral therapy: A replication and extension. *Clinical Psychology: Science and Practice, 17*(2), 144–156.

Kelly, G. (1955). *The psychology of personal constructs.* New York: Norton.

Kimmel, J. (1976). The rational barb in the treatment of social rejection. *Rational Living, 11*, 23–25.

Kohlberg, L. (1976). Moral stages and moralization: The cognitive developmental approach. In T. Leckona (ed.), *Moral development and behavior: Theory, research, and social issues.* New York: Holt, Rinehart & Winston.

Kopec, AM., Beal, D., & DiGiuseppe, R. (1994). Training in RET: Disputational strategies. *Journal of Rational-Emotive & Cognitive-Behavior Therapy, 12*(1), 47–48.

Korzybski, A . (1933) *Science and sanity: An introduction to non Aristotelian systems and general semantics.* Lakeville, CT: The International Non-Aristotelian Library Publishing Co. (now part of the I.G.S., Englewood, NJ). 4th edition, 1958.

Kübler-Ross, E. (1969). *On death and dying.* New York: Macmillan.

Kuhn, T. (1996). *The structure of scientific revolutions,* 3rd ed. Chicago: University of Chicago Press.

Kuhn, T. H. (1977). *The essential tension.* Chicago: University of Chicago Press.

Lageman, A. (1989). Socrates and psychotherapy. *Journal of Religion and Health, 28,* 219–223.

Laird, R. & Metalsky,G. (2009). Attribution Change pp. In W.T. O'Donohue, & J.E. Fisher (Eds.). *General principles and empirically supported techniques of cognitive behavior therapy.* Hoboken, NJ: John Wiley.

Lambert, M. J., Burlingame, G. M., Umphress, V., Hansen, N. B., Vermeersch, D.A., Clouse, G. C., & Yanchar, S. C. (1996). The reliability and validity of the outcome questionnaire. *Clinical Psychology & Psychotherapy, 3*(4), 249–258. doi: 10.1002/(SICI)1099-0879(199612)3:4<249::AID-CPP106>3.0.CO;2-S.

Lane, R. D.,Ahern, G. L.;Schwartz, G. E., & Kaszniak, A. W. (1997). Is alexithymia the emotional equivalent of blindsight? *Biological Psychiatry, 42*(9), 834–844. doi: 10.1016/S0006-3223(97)00050-4.

Lazarus, A. A. (1972). *Behavior therapy and beyond.* New York: McGraw-Hill.

Lazarus, A. A. (2009). Multimodal behavior therapy. In W. T. O'Donohue & J. E. Fisher (Eds.). *General principles and empirically supported techniques of cognitive behavior therapy* (pp. 440–444). Hoboken, NJ: John Wiley & Sons.

Lazarus, R. S. (1991). *Emotion and adaptation.* London: Oxford University Press.

LeDoux, J. E. (2000). Emotion circuits in the brain. *Annual Review of Neuroscience, 23,* 155–184. doi: 10.1146/annurev.neuro.23.1.155

Levis, D. J. (2009). The prolonged CS exposure techniques of implosive (flooding) therapy. In W.T. O'Donohue, & J.E. Fisher, J. E. (Eds.), *General principles and empirically supported techniques of cognitive behavior therapy* (pp. 370–380). Hoboken, NJ: John Wiley.

Linehan, M. (1993). *Cognitive behavioral treatment of borderline personality disorder.* New York: Guilford.

Linton, S. J., Nicholas, M. K., MacDonald, S., Boersma, K., Bergbom, S., Maher, C., & Refshauge, K. (2011). The role of depression and catastrophizing in musculoskeletal pain. *European Journal of Pain, 15*(4), 416–422. doi: 10.1016/j.ejpain.2010.08.009

Livneh, H., & Cook, D. (2005). Psychosocial impact of disability. In R. M. Parker, E. Szymanski, & J. Patterson (Eds.), *Rehabilitation counseling: Basics and beyond* (4th ed.) (pp. 187–224). Austin, TX: PRO-ED.

Livneh, H., Martz, E., & Bodner, T. (2006). Psychosocial adaptation to chronic illness and disability: a preliminary study of its factorial structure. *Journal of Clinical Psychology in Medical Settings, 13*(3), 251–261. doi: 10.1007/s10880-006-9028-5

Luria, A. (1969). Speech and formation of mental processes. In M. Cole & I. Maltzman (eds.), *A handbook of contemporary soviet psychology.* New York: Basic Books.

Lu, Q., & Stanton, A. L. (2010). How benefits of expressive writing vary as a function of writing instructions, ethnicity and ambivalence over emotional expression. *Psychology and Health, 25,*(6),669–684.

Macaskill, N. D. (1996). Improving clinical outcomes in REBT/CBT: The therapeutic uses of tape-recording. *Journal of Rational-Emotive & Cognitive Behavior Therapy, 14*(3), 199–207.

Machiavelli, N. (1532/1998). *The prince (second edition).* Chicago: The University of Chicago Press.

Mahoney, M. (1977). Personal science: A cognitive learning therapy. In A. Ellis & R. Grieger (eds.), *A handbook of rational-emotive therapy*. New York: Springer Publishing.

Mahoney, M. (1991). *Human change processes*. New York: Basic Books.

Mahoney, M. J. (1974). *Cognition and behavior modification*. Cambridge, MA: Ballinger.

Mahoney, M. J. (1979). *Self-change: Strategies for solving personal problems*. Oxford, England: W. W. Norton.

Mahoney, M. J., & Lyddon, W. J. (1988). Recent developments in cognitive approaches to counseling and psychotherapy. *Counseling Psychologist, 16*(2), 190–234.

Marks, J., Boulougouris, J., & Marset, P. (1971). Flooding vs. desensitization in the treatment of phobic patients. *British Journal of Psychiatry, 119*, 353–375.

Marzillier, J. (2010). *The Gossamer thread: My life as a psychotherapist*. London: Karnac Book Publishers.

Maultsby, M. (1975). *Help yourself to happiness*. New York: Institute for Rational Living.

Maultsby, M., & Ellis, E. (1974). *Techniques for using rational-emotive imagery*. New York: Institute for Rational Living.

Meichenbaum, D. (1977). *Cognitive behavior modification: An integrative approach*. New York: Plenum.

Meichenbaum, D. (1985). *Stress inoculation training*. New York: Pergamon.

Meichenbaum, D. (1993). Changing conceptions of cognitive behavior modification: Retrospect and prospect. *Journal of Consulting and Clinical Psychology, 61*, 202–204.

Meichenbaum, D. (2009). Stress inoculation training. In W. T. O'Donohue & J. E. Fisher (Eds.). *General principles and empirically supported techniques of cognitive behavior therapy*. Hoboken, NJ: John Wiley.

Meichenbaum, D., & Cameron, R. (1974). The clinical potential of modifying what clients say to themselves. *Psychotherapy: Theory, Research & Practice, 11*(2), 103–117. doi: 10.1037/h0086326

Metcalfe, C., Winter, D., & Viney, L. (2007). The effectiveness of personal construct psychotherapy in clinical practice: A systematic review and meta-analysis. *Psychotherapy Research, 17*(4).

Miller, N. E., Mowrer, O. H., Doob, L. W., Dollard, J., & Sears, R. R. (1958). Frustration-aggression hypothesis. In C. L. Stacey, M. DeMartino (Eds.), *Understanding human motivation* (pp. 251–255). Cleveland, OH: Howard Allen Publishers.

Morgan, A. J., & Jorm, A. F., (2008). Self-help interventions for depressive disorders and depressive symptoms: A systematic review. *Annals of General Psychiatry, 7*. ArtID 13.

Moriarty, D. L. (2002). *Effects of disputation strategies in Rational Emotive Behavior Therapy (REBT) on the treatment of depression* (unpublished doctoral dissertation). Hofstra University, New York.

Muran, C., & DiGiuseppe, R. A. (1990). Towards a cognitive formulation of metaphor use in psychotherapy. *Clinical Psychology Review, 10*, 99–85.

Muran, E. M., & DiGiuseppe, R. A. (1994). Rape. In F. M. Dattilio & A. Freeman (Eds.), *Cognitive behavioral strategies in crisis intervention*. New York: Guildford Press.

Neimeyer, R. A. (1993). Constructivist psychotherapy. In K. T. Kuehlwein & H. Rosen (Eds.). *Cognitive therapies in action: Evolving innovative practice* (pp. 268–300). San Francisco, CA: Jossey-Bass.

Nezu, A. M., Maguth-Nezu, C., & McMurran, M, (2009). Problem-solving therapy. In W. T. O'Donohue, & J. E. Fisher (Eds.). *General principles and empirically supported techniques of cognitive behavior therapy*. Hoboken, NJ: John Wiley.

Nezu, A. M., Nezu, C., & D'Zurilla, T. J. (2010). Problem-solving therapy. In N. Kazantzis, M. A. Reinecke, & A. Freeman (Eds.), *Cognitive and behavioral theories in clinical practice* (pp. 76–114). New York: The Guildford Press.

Nielsen, S. L, Johnson, W. B., & Ellis, A. (2001). *Counseling and psychotherapy with religious persons: A rational emotive behavior therapy approach*. Mahwah, NJ: Lawrence Erlbaum Associates.

Norcross, J. C., & Lambert, M. J.(2011). Psychotherapy relationships that work II. *Psychotherapy, 48*(1), 4–8. doi: 10.1037/a0022180

O'Donohue, W. T., & Fisher, J. E. (Eds.) (2009). *General principles and empirically supported techniques of cognitive behavior therapy*. Hoboken, NJ: John Wiley & Sons.

O'Leary, D., & Borkovec, T. (1978). Conceptual, methodological, and ethical problems of placebo groups in psychotherapy research. *American Psychologist, 33*, 821–830.

Ortony A. (1975). Why metaphors are necessary and not just nice. *Educational Theory, 25*, 45–53.

Overholser, J. C. (1993a). The elements of the Socratic method: I. Systematic questioning. *Psychotherapy, 30*(1), 67–74.

Overholser, J. C. (1993b). The elements of the Socratic method: II. Inductive reasoning *Psychotherapy, 30*(1), 75–85.

Overholser, J. C. (1994). The elements of the Socratic method: III. Universal definitions. *Psychotherapy, 31*(2), 286–293.

Overholser, J. C. (1995). The elements of the Socratic method: IV. Disavowal of knowledge. *Psychotherapy, 33*(1), 549–559.

Overholser, J. C. (1996). Elements of the Socratic method: v. Self-improvement. *Psychotherapy, 32*(2), 283–292.

Overholser, J. C. (1999). Elements of the Socratic method: VI. Promoting virtue in everyday life. *Psychotherapy: Theory, Research, Practice, Training, 36*(2), 137–145.

Overholser, J. C. (2010). Psychotherapy according to the Socratic method: Integrating ancient philosophy with contemporary cognitive therapy. *Journal of Cognitive Psychotherapy, 24*(4), 354–363.

Paivio, A. (1986). *Mental representations: A dual coding approach*. New York: Oxford University Press.

Parrish, C. L., Radomsky, A. S., & Dugas, M. J. (2008). Anxiety–control strategies: Is there room for neutralization in successful exposure treatment? *Clinical Psychology Review, 28*(8), 1400–1412.

Pennebaker, James W. (1997). *Opening up: The healing power of expressing emotion*. NY: Guilford Press.

Pennebaker, J. L. (2011, October). Writing and Health: Some Practical Advice. URL http://homepage.psy.utexas.edu/homepage/Faculty/Pennebaker/Home2000/WritingandHealth.html

Pennebaker, J. W. (2004). *Writing to heal: A guided journal for recovering from trauma and emotional upheaval*. Oakland, CA: New Harbinger Press.

Piaget, J. (1954). *The construction of reality in the child*. New York: Basic Books.

Popper, K. (1962). *Conjecture and refutation*. New York: Harper.

Popper, K. R. (1968). *The logic of scientific discovery*. New York: Harper & Row.

Power, M. J., & Dalgleish, T. (2008). *Cognition and emotion: From order to disorder, 2nd Edition*. Hove: Psychology Press.

Prochaska, J. O. (1999). The heart and soul of change: What works in therapy. The heart and soul of change: What works in therapy. In Hubble, M. A. (Ed); Duncan, B. L. (Ed); Miller, S. D. (Ed), *The heart and soul of change: What works in therapy* (pp. 227–255). Washington, DC: American Psychological Association.

Protinsky, H., & Popp, R. (1978). Irrational philosophies in popular music. *Cognitive Therapy and Research, 2*, 71–74.

Rachman, S., Marks, I. M., & Hodgson, R. (1973). The treatment of obsessive-compulsive neurotics by modeling and flooding in vivo. *Behavior Research and Therapy, 11*, 463–471.

Raimy, V. (1975). *Misunderstandings of the self: Cognitive psychotherapy and the misconception hypothesis*. San Francisco, CA: Jossey-Bass.

Reynolds, R. E., & Schwartz, R. M. (1983). Relation of metaphoric processing to comprehension and memory. *Journal of Educational Psychology, 75*, 450–459.

Robb, H., Backx, W., & Thomas, J. (1999). The use of cognitive, emotive and behavioral interventions in Rational Emotive Behavior Therapy when clients lack "emotional" insight. *Journal of Rational-Emotive & Cognitive Behavior Therapy, 17*(3), 201–209.

Rodriguez, B. I., & Craske, M. G. (1993). The effects of distraction during exposure to phobic stimuli. *Behaviour Research and Therapy, 31*(6), 549–558.

Rogers, C. (1951). *Client-centered therapy*. Boston, MA: Houghton Mifflin.

Rorer, L. (1999). Dealing with the intellectual-insight problem in cognitive and rational emotive behavior therapy. *Journal of Rational-Emotive & Cognitive- Behavior Therapy, 17*(4), 217–236.

Rorer, L. G. (1989). Rational-emotive theory: II. Explication and evaluation. *Cognitive Therapy and Research, 13*(6), 531–548. doi: 10.1007/BF01176066

Rosenthal, H. G., (Ed). 2011). *Favorite counseling and therapy techniques* (2nd ed.). New York: Routledge/Taylor & Francis Group.

Rusting, C. L., & Nolen-Hoeksema, S. (1998). Regulating responses to anger: Effects of rumination and distraction on angry mood. *Journal of Personality and Social Psychology, 74*(3), 790–803.

Ruth, W. J., & DiGiuseppe, R. (1989). Setting and response generalization in rational-emotive therapy: A case study. *Journal of Rational-Emotive & Cognitive-Behavior Therapy, 7*(4), 237–252.

Sartre, J. P.(1948/1977). *Existentialism and humanism*. Brooklyn, NY: Haskell House.

Scherer, C R., & Sagarin, B. J (2006). Indecent influence: The positive effects of obscenity on persuasion. *Social Influence, 1*(2), 138–146.

Schwartz, R. M., & Gottman, J. M. (1976). Towards a task analysis of assertive behavior. *Journal of Consulting and Clinical Psychology, 44*, 910–20.

Segrin, C. (2009). Social skills training. In W. T. O'Donohue & J. E. Fisher (Eds.). *General principles and empirically supported techniques of cognitive behavior therapy* Hoboken, NJ: John Wiley.

Seligman, M. E. (1978). Comment and integration. *Journal of Abnormal Psychology, 87*(1), 165–179. doi: 10.1037/0021-843X.87.1.165

Seligman, M. E. P. (1975). *Helplessness: On depression, development, and death*. San Francisco: W.H. Freeman.

Seligman, M. E. P., & Maier, S. F. (1967). Failure to escape traumatic shock. *Journal of Experimental Psychology, 74,* 1–9.

Shepherd, L., Salkovskis, P. M., & Morris, M. (2009). Recording therapy sessions: An evaluation of patient and therapist reported behaviours, attitudes and preferences. *Behavioural and Cognitive Psychotherapy, 37*(2), 141–150.

Silverglade, L., Tosi, D., Wise, P. S., & D'Costa, A. (1994). Irrational beliefs and emotionality in adolescents with and without bronchial asthma. *Journal of General Psychology, 121*(3), 199–207.

Singer, J. L. (2006). *Imagery in psychotherapy.* Washington, DC: American Psychological Association.

Smith, D. (1982). Trends in counseling and psychotherapy. *American Psychologist, 37,* 802–809.

Smith, C. A., & Lazarus, R. S. (2001). Appraisal components, core relational themes, and the emotions. In W. Parrott (Ed.), *Emotions in social psychology: Essential readings* (pp. 94–114). New York, NY: Psychology Press.

Spinoza, B. (1677/1994). *A Spinoza reader: the Ethics and other works.* Princeton, NJ: Princeton University Press.

Spivack, G., Platt, J., & Shure, M. (1976). *The problem-solving approach to adjustment.* San Francisco, CA: Jossey-Bass.

Stanković, S., & Vukosavljević-Gvozden, T. (2011). The relationship of a measure of frustration intolerance with emotional dysfunction in a student sample. *Journal of Rational-Emotive & Cognitive Behavior Therapy, 29*(1), 17–34. doi: 10.1007/s10942-011-0128-2

Steel, P. (2007). The nature of procrastination: A meta-analytic and theoretical review of quintessential self-regulatory failure. *Psychological Bulletin, 133*(1), 65–94.

Sternberg, R. (1998). The dialectic as a tool for teaching psychology. *Teaching of Psychology, 25,* 177–180.

Stinson, J., Yamada, J. Dickson, A., Lamba, J., & Stevens, B. (2008). Review of systematic reviews on acute procedural pain in children in the hospital setting. *Pain Research & Management, 13*(1), 51–57.

Stott, R., Mansell, W., Salkovskis, P., Lavender, A., & Cartwright-Hatton, A. (2010). *Oxford guide to metaphors in CBT: Building cognitive bridges.* Oxford, UK: Oxford University Press.

Styron, W. (1990). *Darkness Visible: A Memoir of Madness.* New York: Random House.

Sutton-Smith, Brian. (1988). In search of the imagination. In K. Egan and D. Nadaner (Eds.), *Imagination and Education.* New York: Teachers College Press.

Szentagotai, A., Schnur, J., DiGiuseppe, R., Macavei, B., Kallay, E., & David, D. (2005). The organization and the nature of irrational beliefs: Schemas or appraisal? *Journal of Cognitive and Behavioral Psychotherapies, 5*(2), 139–158.

Tafrate, R., & Kassinove, H. (1998). Anger control in men: Barb exposure with rational, irrational, and irrelevant self-statements. *Journal of Cognitive Psychotherapy, 12*(3), 187–211.

Tice, D. M., Baumeister, R. F., Shmueli, D., & Muraven, M. (2007). Restoring the self: Positive affect helps improve self-regulation following ego depletion. *Journal of Experimental Social Psychology, 43*(3), 379–384. doi: 10.1016/j.jesp.2006.05.007

Tosi, Donald J., & Murphy, M. A. (1994). Cognitive hypnotherapy in psychosomatic illness: A cognitive experiential perspective. *Journal of Cognitive Psychotherapy, 8*(4), Special issue: Hypnotherapy, 313–329.

Tosi, D. J., Judah, S. M., & Murphy, M. A. (1989). The effects of a cognitive experiential therapy utilizing hypnosis, cognitive restructuring, and developmental staging on psychological factors associated with duodenal ulcer disease: A multivariate experimental study. *Journal of Cognitive Psychotherapy, 3*(4), 273–290.

Tosi, D. J., & Reardon, J. (1976). The treatment of guilt through rational stage-directed therapy. *Rational Living, 11,* 8–11.

Trexler, L. D. (1976). Frustration is a fact, not a feeling. *Rational Living, 11,* 19–22.

Turner, P. R., Valtierra, M., Talken, T. R., Miller, V. I., & DeAnda, J. (1996). Effect of session length on treatment outcome for college students in brief therapy. *Journal of Counseling Psychology, 43*(2), 228–232. doi: 10.1037/0022-0167.43.2.228

Twain, M. (1971/ 1972). *What is man? and other essays.* Freeport, NY: Books for Libraries Press.

Vygotsky, L. (1975). *Thought and language.* New York: Wiley.

Walen, S., DiGiuseppe, R., & Dryden, W. (1992). *The practitioner's guide to rational emotive therapy, 2nd edition.* New York: Oxford University Press.

Wampold, B. E., (2007). Psychotherapy: The humanistic (and effective). *American Psychologists, 62*(8), 857–873.

Wegner, D. M., & Smart, L. (1997). Deep cognitive activation: A new approach to the unconscious. *Journal of Consulting and Clinical Psychology, 65*(6), 984–995. doi: 10.1037/0022-006X.65.6.984

Weiner, B. (1979). A theory of motivation for some classroom experiences. *Journal of Educational Psychology, 71,* 3–25.

Weiner, B. (1985). 'Spontaneous' causal thinking. *Psychological Bulletin, 97,* 74–84.

Wolfe, J. L. (2000). *REBT Resource Book for Practitioners (2nd Edition).* New York: Albert Ellis Institute.

Wolfe, J. L., & Bernard, M. E. (2000). *The REBT resource book for practitioners.* New York: Albert Ellis Institute.

Wolff, R. P. (2005). Evaluation of effectiveness of individual therapy sessions over 60 minutes. *Dissertation Abstracts International: Section B: The Sciences and Engineering, 65*(12-B), 6680.

Wolpe, J. (1961). The prognosis in unpsychoanalysed recovery from neurosis. *American Journal of Psychiatry, 118,* 35–39.

Wolpe, J. (1990). *The practice of behavior therapy.* Needham Heights, MA: Allyn & Bacon.

Yalom, I. D., & Leszcz, M. (2005).*Theory and practice of group psychotherapy, fifth edition.* New York: Basic books.

Yerkes, R. M. & Dodson, J. D. (1908). The relation of strength of stimulus to rapidity of habit formation. *Journal of Comparative Neurology and Psychology, 18,* 459–482.

Young, J. E., Klosko, J. S., & Weishaar, M. E. (2003). *Schema therapy: A practitioner's guide.* New York: Guilford Press.

Zaza, C., & Baine, N. (2002). Cancer pain and psychosocial factors: A critical review of the literature. *Journal of Pain and Symptom Management, 24*(5), 526–542. doi: 10.1016/S0885-3924(02)00497-9.

Zimmerman, M., & Mattia, J. I., (2001). A self-report scale to help make psychiatric diagnoses: The psychiatric diagnostic screening questionnaire. *Archives of General Psychiatry, 58,* 787–794.

Zimmerman, M., & Matia, J. I. (2001). The psychiatric diagnostic screening questionnaire: development, reliability, and validity. *Comprehensive Psychiary, 42*(3), 175–189.

Zoellner, L. A., Abramowitz, J. S., Moore, S. A., & Slagle, D. M. (2009). Flooding. In W.T. O'Donohue, & J. E. Fisher, (Ed.). *General principles and empirically supported techniques of cognitive behavior therapy* (pp. 300–308). Hoboken, NJ: John Wiley.